Legacies of *Brown*

Multiracial Equity in American Education

Edited by

DORINDA J. CARTER

STELLA M. FLORES

RICHARD J. REDDICK

REPRINT SERIES NO. 40
HARVARD EDUCATIONAL REVIEW

Library of Congress Control Number 2004108775

ISBN 0-916690-43-1

Published by Harvard Educational Review,
an imprint of the Harvard Education Publishing Group

Harvard Educational Review
8 Story Street
Cambridge, MA 02138

Typesetting: Sheila Walsh
Cover Design: Anne Carter
Cover Photo: Getty Images

The typefaces used in this book are Nueva Roman and Nueva Bold
Extended for display and New Baskerville for text.

Contents

To our parents, families, and mentors,
who crossed borders and contributed to the positive
legacies of educational movements in this country.

To the current and future multiracial generations
of youth and educational activists, who will continue
to fight for equity in education.

Editors' Introduction

Brown v. Board of Education was not written for Blacks alone. . . . The theme of our school desegregation cases extends to all racial minorities treated invidiously by a State or any of its agencies.[1]

Fifty-four years ago, a seven-year-old African American girl named Linda Brown was denied admission to a White elementary school near her home in Topeka, Kansas. Her father and other plaintiffs embarked upon a four-year legal journey to end segregation in America's public schools. What is unknown to many is that six years earlier, in 1944, an eight-year-old Mexican American student named Sylvia Méndez was denied admission to a local White school in Westminster, California. The *Méndez v. Westminster School District*[2] case was the first federal school segregation decision that broke with the "separate but equal" doctrine of *Plessy v. Ferguson.*[3] Shortly after, and also before the *Brown* decision, the U.S. Supreme Court decided *Hernandez v. Texas,*[4] a juried discrimination case that extended constitutional protection to Mexican Americans and, unlike the reach of *Brown,* set the standard for when the state should ban group-based discrimination.[5]

As African Americans were fighting for educational equity in the South, Mexican Americans championed similar struggles for equity in California and Texas. Although *Méndez* never made it to the U.S. Supreme Court, the case marked the initial end to de jure segregation in California.[6] Moreover, this case involved the critical and historical collaboration of Thurgood Marshall, who was a coauthor of an *amicus curiae* brief in support of the *Méndez* case on behalf of the National Association for the Advancement of Colored People (NAACP). Had it not been for early trailblazers like the families of Sylvia Méndez and Linda Brown, as well as this early multiracial collaboration of legal counsel, educational opportunities and conditions for students of color might be more limited today.

Thus, as we celebrate the fiftieth anniversary of the *Brown* decision, there is much to be thankful for. In many schools throughout the United States, students of various races and ethnicities share common educational spaces — school buses, playgrounds, classrooms, lunchrooms, hallways, and athletic fields. The racial desegregation of public schools prompted the desegregation of other public spaces as well. One such legacy of *Brown* included the beginning of the end of the Jim Crow era in the South.[7] No longer could

1

Blacks or Mexican Americans be legally discriminated against due to the color of their skin.

In many times of celebration, however, there is frequently "rain on the parade." While U.S. Supreme Court Chief Justice Earl Warren's opinion in *Brown I* (1954) rightly stated that "separate educational facilities are inherently unequal,"[8] there were no clear provisions for how schools should actually implement desegregation. In fact, a year later, *Brown II* (1955) stated that districts should proceed "with all deliberate speed,"[9] and that "school authorities have the primary responsibility for elucidating, assessing and solving the varied local school problems which may require solution in fully implementing the governing constitutional principles."[10] The Court relied on "good faith compliance at the earliest practicable date,"[11] and evident in these words is the haphazard accountability put on states to enforce desegregation and strive for true integration. Such language guaranteed that the promise for public schooling intended in *Brown* would be applied unevenly across the nation, depending on community support, enforcement from civil agencies, and monitoring by government agencies and activist groups.

Even today, in the twenty-first century, many would argue that, in the face of segregated housing patterns, the charter and pilot school movement, Afrocentric schooling, homeschooling, and many other educational and environmental factors, America's schools are more reflective of the *Plessy* era. In some of the nation's largest cities and metropolitan areas, such as Los Angeles, New York, Chicago, and San Francisco, half or more of the public school students are students of color.[12] In fact, in 1998, 70 percent of Black students and 76 percent of Latino students attended a predominantly Black and Latino school.[13] Moreover, Gary Orfield and Chungmei Lee report that the western United States is now the first predominantly minority region in terms of public school enrollment.[14]

In the 2001–2002 school year, White students made up the majority of the American public elementary and secondary student population (61.2%), followed by Blacks (17.2%), Latinos (16.3%), Asians/Pacific Islanders (4.1%), and American Indians/Alaska Natives (1.2%).[15] Despite this diversity, racial and ethnic segregation in schools is steadily increasing. Indeed, much of the progress made to desegregate the nation's schools during previous decades was dismantled by the end of the 1990s, a decade that witnessed the greatest return to segregation for the Black community since *Brown*. Equally important, Latinos are now the most segregated of all ethnic groups in terms of race, ethnicity, and poverty.[16] In the face of celebrating *Brown*, we must ask ourselves, Where are the *equity* and *equality* in American education? How far have we really come in achieving integration — and, for that matter, desegregation?

We believe, as Sonia Nieto suggests in her essay, that equity and equality should not be used interchangeably. *Equal education* often means providing the same resources and opportunities for all students. *Equity,* however, sug-

Rally to defend affirmative action, U.S. Supreme Court, Washington, D.C., April 1, 2003.
Photo: Luis Angel Alejo

gests fairness and the real possibility of equality of outcomes.[17] Much of the research on these two measures for marginalized students indicates that students of color continue to have fewer qualified and effective teachers and less access to challenging and rigorous curricula. Their schools, by and large, get less state and local money without legislative intervention, and public education, as represented by political will and financial support, invests fewer of its hopes, expectations, and aspirations in students of color.[18] In fact, various studies have shown that all students perform at higher levels in desegregated schools, are more likely to enroll in college, and live more integrated lives as adults.[19]

This volume aims to explore some of the *legacies* of the *Brown* decision — legacies that expand conversations on educational equity beyond Black and White students. These conversations now include several Asian, Latino, and Native American groups and extend beyond racial group differences. We believe that *Brown* has improved access to equitable educational opportunities for students with various markers of difference (e.g., race, ethnicity, immigrant status, sexual orientation, religion, gender, social class, disability, etc.). We also believe that *Brown* provided a framework to analyze and attack "legacy issues" regarding many civil rights, as Martha Minow discusses in her introductory essay. Indeed, with all these viable forces alive and well in U.S.

schools, the primary aim of this book is to critically examine America's meager efforts since 1954 at the "practice of integration."

Finally, we believe, as many educational scholars do, that the terms *desegregation* and *integration* are often incorrectly used interchangeably, and it is therefore necessary to distinguish them from each other. Desegregation is best defined by Thomas Pettigrew as the coexistence of students from different racial and ethnic backgrounds in the same school.[20] In other words, desegregation represents an essential removal of legal and contextual barriers for students of color. In a desegregated setting, these students are able to attend the same educational institutions as White students. We challenge readers to recognize that this is not the same as *integration*. As David L. Kirp states in his essay,

> Integration takes a changed racial composition as the starting point for rethinking the premises of the educational system. . . . To make something of that new [educational] environment, to integrate . . . requires attention to, among other things, the attitude of teachers and students, devising situations in which people of different racial and ethnic groups confront each other as status equals, and the substance of the educational offering. . . . Integration also demands an administrative structure that can responsibly accommodate what may well be convulsive change while adhering to some coherent sense of educational purpose.

Kirp's words, written in 1976, still have not caught the attention of many policymakers and administrators of public schools. When his words are critically examined in 2004, one understands that only in pockets of America's educational settings has this type of integration been achieved. We believe true integration is a transformation of the hearts and minds of the clients and workers in schools, communities, government, and the judiciary. In the absence of this type of integration, the promise of *Brown* will never be fulfilled.

In planning this volume, we struggled to unearth essays in our journal that explicitly discuss the linked, yet exclusive, concepts of desegregation and integration. In fact, the *Harvard Educational Review* did not publish any essays related to desegregation until 1973, when Gordon Foster, in his article "Desegregating Urban Schools: A Review of Techniques," reviewed the growth of desegregation in the early years of the 1970s and evaluated the advantages and disadvantages of various techniques of desegregation. Perhaps this lapse in attention to conversations regarding (de)segregation and integration represents society's resistance, at that time, to critically examine its most obvious form of racial discrimination. However, the essays in this volume explore the complexities of enacting desegregation policy and integration practices in American education. What distinguishes this volume from other books published on *Brown* is its focus on educational equity for other racial and ethnic groups in America. Our intention is to challenge the reader to think beyond traditional notions of desegregation and integration

Students and families marching to defend affirmative action, Washington, D.C., April 1, 2004. Photo: Luis Angel Alejo.

and expand explorations of the U.S. student population that has benefited from *Brown*.

The book begins with an introductory essay by Harvard Law School professor Martha Minow. We chose this essay to open the book in order to engage the reader in an exploration of what we term *legacy issues,* which many traditionally marginalized groups have battled using the arguments of *Brown* as a gateway to enhanced civil rights for all people in education and the general society. Minow examines these "surprising legacies" of *Brown* and looks at how the "inherent inequality in separateness" mantra has been used to champion human rights.

The book is divided into two main parts, focusing first on policies resulting from the *Brown* decision, and second on the practice of integration inside schools. We wanted to provide readers with some insights into the legal battles that followed the *Brown* decision as a way to inform the thinking around the practice of integration then and now. We strongly believe that this nation has attempted to practice integration — though never truly achieving it. Furthermore, we find it important to revisit the history of educational struggles embarked upon by other racial and ethnic groups as a result of *Brown* as a way to critically analyze the failed promises of the case in to-day's multiracial and multiethnic society.

Part One provides a historical overview and examination of the effects of significant legal cases on equity in education across the K–21 sector following *Brown*. In the 1970s, many communities of color began to challenge school systems for the right to equal access to educational opportunities. Although the battle for desegregation for the entire nation was spearheaded in the South, the essays in this section illustrate similar struggles in the West and Southwest — struggles for equal education despite status as a minority or non-native English speaker. The essays in this section also challenge readers to reexamine what constitutes education and to whom education "belongs." Particularly, Catherine Prendergrast provokes readers to consider that for too long Americans have viewed literacy and the right to a high-quality education as "White property." As long as we carry this mindset, the educational playing field will never be equal for all students.

Part Two examines desegregation and the practice of integration in America's K–21 sector. While no one volume can cover the educational experiences of all students of color, we have tried to present an array of student and ethnic group experiences in the nation's schools pre- and post-*Brown*. As students of color (two of us are African American and one of us is Mexican American/Chicana), attendees of desegregated schools in the South (Georgia and Texas), participants in busing programs, and current student-scholars at an elite institution of higher education (doctoral candidates at the Harvard Graduate School of Education), we aimed to include essays in this section that detail the educational plight of Blacks and Latinos in U.S. schools. We were also dedicated to highlighting the experience of Native Americans (in this case, the Inupiat of Northern Alaska), since this group is often overlooked in conversations on desegregation and educational equity in general.

The essays in Part Two reinforce the notion that integration in schools involves more than the racial mixing of students. Integration requires a transformation of thought in several areas: 1) what constitutes knowledge, 2) whose knowledge is valued in schools, 3) whose culture is valued in schools, and 4) how to educate all students using the same standards. The authors of these essays remind us that the celebration of difference in education is a good thing — something neither to be feared nor taken lightly. Lastly, as scholars and practitioners, we wanted to ensure that student voices would be a marker in this volume. Hence, this section concludes with two essays by Imani Perry. In 1988, at the age of fifteen, *Harvard Educational Review* published an essay by Perry in which she examined her experiences attending both public and private schools in Massachusetts and the advantages and disadvantages of each educational environment. Sixteen years later, Perry reflects on her earlier work in a new essay that draws on her experiences as a law professor. In her second essay, she proposes a new theory of integration toward which we should strive.

This book is for anyone interested in wholeheartedly working to fulfill the promises of *Brown*. We hope this volume will be used in secondary and higher education classrooms throughout the country. Similarly, we hope that educational researchers will gain insight into new ways to examine segregation, desegregation and integration, and equity and equality in education. Furthermore, we hope policymakers will adhere to the lessons imparted from the selected authors' voices. Yes, separation is inherently unequal. Yet, in many areas of the country, we continue to provide America's students with separate educations.

DORINDA J. CARTER
STELLA M. FLORES
RICHARD J. REDDICK
Editors

Notes

1. In Guey Heung Lee v. Johnson, 404 U.S. 1215 (1971).
2. Méndez v. Westminster School District, 64 F. Supp 544 (S.D. Cal 1946), affirmed 161 F.2d 774 (9th Cir 1947).
3. Plessy v. Ferguson, 16 S.Ct. 1138 (1896).
4. Hernandez v. Texas, 347 US 475 (1954).
5. Lopez, I. H., "Hernandez v. Brown," *New York Times*, 22 May 2004, 17.
6. Gonzalez, G. G., *Chicano Education in the Era of Segregation* (Philadelphia: Balch Institute Press, 1990).
7. Williams, J. *Eyes on the Prize: America's Civil Rights Years 1954–1965* (New York: Penguin, 1987).
8. Brown v. Board of Education I. 347 U.S. 483 (1954).
9. Brown v. Board of Education II. 394 U.S. 294 (1955).
10. Ibid.
11. Ibid.
12. Irvine, J. J., *Educating Teachers for Diversity: Seeing with a Cultural Eye* (New York: Teachers College Press, 2003).
13. Orfield, G., "Schools More Separate: Consequences of a Decade of Re-Segregation." *Rethinking Schools, 16*, No. 1 (2001), 14–18.
14. Orfield, G., and Lee, C., Brown *at 50: King's Dream or* Plessy's *Nightmare?* (Cambridge, MA: The Civil Rights Project at Harvard University, 2004).
15. Frankenberg, E., Lee, C., and Orfield, G., *A Multiracial Society with Segregated Schools: Are We Losing the Dream?* (Cambridge, MA: The Civil Rights Project at Harvard University, 2003); Orfield and Lee, Brown *at 50*. Also, see U.S. Department of Education, National Center for Education Statistics, Common Core of Data (CCD), "State Nonfiscal Survey of Public Elementary/Secondary Education," 2001–2002. Available online at http://nces.ed.gov/pubs2003/snf_report03/#4.
16. Orfield, G., *Schools More Separate: Consequences of a Decade of Resegregation* (Cambridge, MA: The Civil Rights Project at Harvard University, 2001). Also, see Frankenberg, Lee, and Orfield, *A Multiracial Society*.

17. Nieto, S., *Affirming Diversity: The Sociopolitical Context of Multicultural Education* (4th ed., Boston: Pearson Education, 2004).
18. See Weiner, R., "10 Things Every American Needs to Know about *Brown v. Board of Education*" (2004). Available online at http://www2.edtrust.org/EdTrust/Federal+and+State+Policy/ross+10things. htm.
19. Hanushek, K., and Rivkin, S., "New Evidence about *Brown v. Board of Education:* The Complex Effects of School Racial Composition on Achievement" (NBER Working Paper No. w8741, 2002); Schofield, J. W., "Review of Research on School Desegregation's Impact on Elementary and Secondary School Students," in *Handbook of Research on Multicultural Education,* ed. James Banks and Cherry Banks (New York: Simon & Schuster Macmillan, 1995), 597-617; Boozer, M., Krueger, A., Wolkon, S. Haltiwanger, J., and Loury, G., "Race and School Quality Since *Brown v. Board of Education,*" *Brookings Papers on Economic Activity: Microeconomics* (1992): 269-338. Wells, A. S., and Crain R. L., "Perpetuation Theory and the Long-Term Effects of School Desegregation," *Review of Educational Research* 64, No. 4 (1994): 531-555. Studies also cited in Orfield and Lee, Brown *at 50.*
20. Pettigrew, T. F., *Racial Discrimination in the United States* (New York: Harper & Row, 1975).

Surprising Legacies
of *Brown v. Board*

MARTHA MINOW

hen Representative Diane Wilkerson stood at the recent Massachusetts constitutional convention, she spoke of growing up in Arkansas after the U.S. Supreme Court decision in *Brown v. Board of Education*. Fighting tears, she recalled how the public hospital refused to admit her pregnant mother to deliver her children. She said, "I know the pain of being less than equal and I cannot and will not impose that status on anyone else. . . . I was but one generation removed from an existence in slavery. I could not in good conscience ever vote to send anyone to that place from which my family fled."[1]

About what pending issue was Representative Wilkerson speaking? She was voicing her opposition to proposals to ban same-sex marriage in the Massachusetts constitution. Proposals to create a separate civil-union status would offer legal and social benefits to these couples, but excluding them from marriage would erect a "separate but equal" regime that would not grant real equality. This argument is one surprising legacy of *Brown*. The analogy to *Brown* has been ringing ever since the Massachusetts high court found the marriage law excluding same-sex couples in violation of the state constitution.[2] The court initially did not say whether civil unions would be satisfactory, or if marriage itself had to become available to meet the state constitution's equality guaranty. The debate has registered in the public imagination the fact that the struggle for gay rights is indeed the civil rights struggle of our day. A key legacy of *Brown* is that people now convinced of its rightness must ask themselves what current struggle will look similarly so right, fifty years hence.

Perhaps the most powerful legacy of *Brown* is this: Opponents in varied political battles fifty years later each claim their ties to the decision and its meaning. So although the analogy between *Brown* and same-sex marriage has divided Black clergy, each side vies to inherit the civil rights heritage.[3] President George W. Bush invoked *Brown v. Board* in opposing race-conscious college admission practices.[4] The success of *Brown* in reshaping the nation's moral landscape — the context within which race and all other markers of difference are judged and treated — has been so profound that I

fear we do not fully comprehend its legacies and may fail to attend sufficiently to continuing controversy and complexities in its wake.[5]

I was born the year of the initial *Brown* decision and grew up as the nation
fought over whether and how to implement it. Attending civil rights rallies
with my family and coming to see the centrality of education to fulfilling the
vision of equal opportunity for all, I aspired to work on school reform and
pursued first graduate study in education and then law school toward that
end. I had the good fortune to serve as a law clerk to Justice Thurgood Marshall, who argued *Brown* on behalf of the National Association for the Advancement of Colored People (NAACP). I learned from him to pick my battles — and to try to take the perspective of those who have been excluded,
politically disempowered, misunderstood, or neglected.[6] It would not surprise Justice Marshall, I think, but it might surprise others how much *Brown
v. Board* has affected how schools treat gender, disability, language differences, nationality, and sexual orientation. I will examine those surprising
legacies after first considering how to understand what the *Brown* decision
did and did not accomplish directly.

Brown and Racial Desegregation in Schools

Widely recognized as the most famous decision of the U.S. Supreme Court,
Brown v. Board of Education, stands both as the landmark emblem of social justice and the symbol of the limitations of court-led social reform.[7] The
Court's own words eliminated racial segregation as an acceptable social practice in domains governed by the Constitution's equal protection clause, but
the Court-supervised remedial process produced protracted and sometimes
violent conflicts over the succeeding decades. Since the 1980s, judicial withdrawal from school desegregation suits and patterns of residential segregation have contributed to increasing racial resegregation in public schools in
the United States. The Civil Rights Project at Harvard University concluded
a recent study by noting:

> Although American public schools are now only 60 percent White nationwide
> and nearly one fourth of U.S. students are in states with a majority of non-White
> students, most White students have little contact with minority students except
> in the South and Southwest. The vast majority of intensely segregated minority
> schools face conditions of concentrated poverty, which are powerfully related
> to unequal educational opportunity. Students in segregated minority schools
> can expect to face conditions that students in the very large number of segre-
> gated White schools seldom experience. Latinos confront very serious levels of
> segregation by race.[8]

In the 5,300 communities with fewer than 100,000 people in this country, at least 90 percent of the residents are White.[9] White families who have
options avoid racially mixed schools.[10] Large urban districts, in which 70
percent of the students are non-White and over half are poor or near poor,

face higher levels of violence, disruption, dropouts, and lower test scores than suburban schools.[11] The gap in achievement when students are compared by race persists across all age groups, even when controlled for economic class. Thus, speaking of *Brown* today means speaking both of landmark social change and obdurate racialized practices. This makes the fiftieth anniversary of the decision a complex moment for simultaneous celebration and critique.[12]

Celebration and critique: This is reminiscent of Justice Thurgood Marshall's view during the bicentennial celebrations of the U.S. Constitution.[13] He warned of complacent beliefs that such a celebration could engender.[14] He emphasized that the founding document was flawed from the start, riddled as it was with the contradiction between preserving slavery and committing to freedom and equality for "We, the People."[15] To be fair, the specific notion of an original flaw resonates less with the 1954 *Brown I* decision, which declared "separation inherently unequal,"[16] than with the "all deliberate speed" language in the Court's 1955 *Brown II* opinion about the timing for remedying intentionally segregated schools. Like the clause in the original Constitution counting slaves as three-fifths of a person for apportionment purposes and protecting the property rights of slaveholders, "all deliberate speed" was the compromise offered by a Court preoccupied with White resistance to racial equality.[17]

The dramatic moment of resistance in Little Rock — when Governor Faubus brought out the Arkansas National Guard to prevent nine Black students from enrolling in Central High School — led a reluctant President Eisenhower to send in national troops.[18] The Supreme Court affirmed this federal power to implement *Brown*, but southern resistance persisted in almost every school district.[19] Many people viewed the "all deliberate speed" language of *Brown II* as a signal that encouraged both noncompliance with, and even resistance to, desegregation. Hence, we have the continuing national failure to achieve racial justice.[20]

Martin Luther King Jr.'s leadership of a movement of civil disobedience, 300,000 people participating in the 1963 March on Washington, and President Lyndon Johnson's political skills following the assassination of President John F. Kennedy each crucially contributed to the political and social struggles producing the Civil Rights Act of 1964. For the first time, we had serious federal enforcement of *Brown*. That law not only authorized the U.S. Department of Justice to enforce *Brown* through litigation, but also to withhold federal funds from school systems that discriminated against African Americans. We will never know what would have happened if the words had instead been "full speed ahead," but the critical phrase marks a fault line between the two *Brown* opinions. The continuing failure to realize the vision of *Brown* seems persistently linked to the White resistance that fault line represents.

Justice Marshall's warning about the complacency of celebration remains relevant, though, even to the first *Brown* decision. For if it contained no internal flaw itself, it bequeathed a legacy of complexity about what precisely is equality. What is the normative vision of a just and equal society? Is separate always inherently unequal? Among the memorable ideas present in the Supreme Court's landmark *Brown* opinion, two stand out:

1. In these days, it is doubtful that any child may reasonably be expected to succeed in life if he is denied the opportunity of an education. Such an opportunity, where the state has undertaken to provide it, is a right that must be made available to all on equal terms.[21]
2. We conclude that, in the field of public education, the doctrine of "separate but equal" has no place. Separate educational facilities are inherently unequal.[22]

In the context of intentional and invidious racial segregation, these two ideas seem obviously compatible. The way to produce equal opportunity in education would be to end racial segregation; if separation is inherently unequal, then equality requires its ending. Yet even in this context, it has become unclear over time whether equal opportunity demands simply ending the official assignment of students to different schools based on their race, or also demands integration in the same school and in the same classrooms of students with different racial and ethnic identities. Denise Morgan made the point sharply: "Attending predominantly Black schools can be harmful to Black children because those schools tend to be educationally inferior, not because Black children are inferior, or because access to White children is inherently positive."[23]

Did *Brown* find racially separate education inherently unequal because it tended to be educationally inferior, or because it is always inferior unless racially integrated? Does segregation inherently convey the stamp of hierarchy? Or is its inherent limitation the deprivation of vital social interactions across group identities? Whatever the moral or empirical answer, the legal answer is clear: Racially segregated education is permitted in cases where it did not directly or recently stem from intentional governmental action.

The Supreme Court has allowed the termination of judicially supervised integration plans when the vestiges of official racial segregation seem remote — even in the face of resegregation through housing patterns. As a result, the percentage of Black students attending schools where the majority of other students are children of color has increased across the country over the past decade.[24] This reverses the trend from the prior decade, when courts monitored school assignments.[25] The resegregation does not stem from decisions by school officials, but from patterns of housing and jobs that in turn reflect a mix of private preferences and subtle discrimination. White families with financial means prefer predominantly White communities and White schools, which they associate with better opportunities for their children.[26] Families of color face not only economic barriers but also direct discrimination in the mortgage and housing markets.[27] The contemporary litigation under state constitutions and related state legislative efforts to promote "adequate" education represents serious efforts to improve instruction and student performance, with requisite investment in schooling but without seeking racial integration of the student body.[28]

Is racial integration the measure of racial justice? Richard Kallenberg recently surveyed national attitudes and asserted that there is a consensus that integrated schools seem like a good idea, but "we shouldn't do anything to promote them."[29] Justice Clarence Thomas voiced the views of many even within the African American community who are insulted by the suggestion that educational excellence cannot occur in an entirely or predominantly Black or Black and Hispanic school. According to that view, finding students of color largely in schools with other students of color is not itself a betrayal of the promise of *Brown*. Such a betrayal comes instead in low expectations and low achievement levels among such students.[30]

A legacy of *Brown* is an apparently enduring debate over racial integration. Equal opportunity is the aspiration if not the given, but does equal opportunity mean ending the symbolic and practical subordination of segregation and paying attention to race, or does it mean creating a color-blind society and halting the explicit use of race? Our national ambivalence on these issues is well captured in the Supreme Court's recent affirmative action decision. The Court extended approval for diversity rationales for racially conscious admissions to universities and colleges, but Justice Sandra Day O'Connor's opinion tethered this approval to an expectation that attention to race and ethnicity would no longer be necessary — and perhaps no longer acceptable — twenty-five years from now.[31]

Equality in Schools, but Not about Race

Let's consider the legacies of *Brown* in schools but beyond the context of race. I suggest that *Brown* enshrined equal opportunity as the aspiration if not the given for students whose primary language is not English; for students who are immigrants; for girls; for students with disabilities; for gay or lesbian or transgendered students; and for religious students. The racial-justice initiative has expanded to include all these students so that today, American public schools are preoccupied with the aspiration of equality and the language of inclusion. Fifty years after *Brown*, equality is the drone string, the underlying tone of school missions and evaluation. Yet no less pervasive is the struggle over realizing equality through integrated or separate settings, and it is to the permutations I now turn. As I will show, these ongoing debates point increasingly to educational expertise to answer a question implicit but not central to *Brown v. Board:* What kinds of instruction actually promote equal opportunities for all children?

Language

Brown — the social movement behind it and the strategy of law reform leading up to it — inspired people concerned with the exclusion and inequality in schools experienced by minority racial groups, but also by minority ethnic groups, minority nationality groups, women, and others.[32] For cloudy reasons, the 1964 Civil Rights Act itself included national origin in its scope of protection, and the U.S. Department of Health, Education, and Welfare exercised its authority under the act to issue guidelines governing bilingual education and students learning English. The U.S. Supreme Court in 1974 upheld such regulations, and found the San Francisco school district in violation because it failed to develop tailored programs for Chinese-speaking students.[33] Here, the act of including the Chinese-speaking students in the mainstream classroom with no accommodation amounted to discrimination that was forbidden on the basis of national origin to any school district receiving federal financial assistance, because the Chinese-speaking students received fewer benefits than the English-speaking majority.[34] Besides representing a key decision to use impact rather than intention as the measure of illicit discrimination, the decision exposed a new version of the tension between integration and separate treatment.[35]

Congress soon responded with the Equal Education Opportunities Act of 1974, which required recipient schools to take appropriate action "to overcome language barriers that impeded equal participation by its students in its instructional programs."[36] With the Bilingual Education Act of 1974, Congress also extended some degree of funding to schools offering bilingual education.[37] As court challenges pressed for greater bilingual education programming, some courts agreed and others deferred to local school boards.[38] One influential decision declined to require bilingual education as the means for ensuring equal educational opportunity.[39] Eliciting both strong support and strong opposition, such programs, when well run, afford real access to the curriculum for students learning English. But they also risk segregating students learning English from other students and undermining racial desegregation plans. Amid competing scholarly assessments of the effectiveness of varied kinds of bilingual programs with immersion in English-speaking classrooms,[40] the evidence strongly suggests that the quality of teachers is a more significant factor in student achievement than the choice between bilingual instruction and English immersion.[41] Does the centrality of teaching quality support continuing experiments with bilingual education on the grounds that it has never been given a fair chance? Or will separate instruction never be equal, practically or symbolically?[42]

Intense political pressures on both sides of the debate over bilingual education affect the quality and perception of evaluation efforts and the movement for legal bans on bilingual education. A California entrepreneur, Ron Unz, successfully crafted, financed, and pushed for the passage of an initiative to eliminate bilingual education first in that state and then in Arizona and Massachusetts.[43] Courts rejecting these bans on bilingual education rely on deference to educational expertise, as do courts that resist arguments for judicially imposed bilingual education.[44] No one suggests a goal other than integration, eventually, but many people still urge short-term separate instruction to promote acquisition of language, to maintain learning in other subjects while the student learns English, and to support positive experiences in school that respect the child's heritage. Because many bilingual programs have not achieved these short-term goals and because students often remain in separate classes for years, the question must consider how programs really work rather than their aspirations.

Gender

No less controversial has been the treatment of gender, which again includes both an overt commitment to equal opportunity and intense disagreement over whether to pursue that commitment through integration or separate instructional settings. Good, though not undisputed, authority suggests that "sex" made its way into the employment section of the 1964 Civil Rights Act (Title VII) only as a ploy to defeat its passage.[45] Whatever the truth, deliberate argument and advocacy overcame strong opposition and produced a commitment to gender equality in the 1972 Education Amendments that produced Title IX. Yet the analogy between race and gender has always been disputed, especially around the issue of whether separate can ever be equal.[46] Partly because the ideology surrounding gender historically accorded women — or at least privileged White women — a special place in home and family as a separate sphere, the inclusion of women in male settings has at times seemed to involve a loss of privilege or protection.[47] This has contributed to the long judicial fight over the proper method for analyzing constitutional challenges to gender-based distinctions.[48] The analogy to *Brown* has inspired women's rights advocates to challenge single-sex education, with mixed results and increasing debate among advocates about what to seek.

The Supreme Court rejected single-sex education in nursing, a traditional women's field,[49] and in military training, a field where women historically were excluded.[50] Yet, the Court has not rejected single-sex public schools where enrollment is voluntary and the equality is "substantially equal" with other schools.[51] The appellate court in the leading case, *Vorchheimer v. School District of Philadelphia*, distinguished race and gender for purposes of separate education by asserting that real differences remain by gender but not race, and by emphasizing the value in local control and family choice.[52] The same situation produced a later decision allowing girls entrance into the all-boys school, but preserving the all-girls schools through a combination of tradition, informal policy, and "success in warding off the handful of boys who express interest."[53] Compensatory rationales for separate instruction for girls may still be defensible.[54] Plausible rationales for single-sex education could include compensating for inadequate opportunities in the past, improving educational outcomes, and diversifying school choice.[55] Some teachers and experts suggest that, given societal expectations and pressures, girls perform better in all-girls schools or all-girl mathematics classes.[56]

The most recent word from the Supreme Court is Justice Ruth Bader Ginsburg's opinion rejecting exclusion of women from the Virginia Military Institute. The decision itself leaves room for single-sex instruction where justifiable as "exceedingly persuasive" in terms of an important government interest that is substantially related to that purpose.[57] Because Virginia offered a patently inferior alternative to the women excluded from the Virginia Military Institute, the Court did not need to resolve whether single-sex education could ever be equal. That general question certainly remains open for single-sex programs premised on remedial and compensatory rationales.

In this vein, sometimes to their own surprise, some feminists have defended the Young Women's Leadership School in Harlem and other single-sex educational experiments, while others challenge them in court.[58] Empirical research on student achievement presents a mixed picture, with different gender gaps running to the advantage of both boys and girls, although these gaps do not approach the divide in school performance between economically advantaged and disadvantaged students.[59] These very patterns motivated the plan for all-male schools in Detroit and Milwaukee that address the situation of urban African American boys, but under pressure and in the face of a lawsuit, the schools became co-ed.[60] Single-sex education may have seemed less justifiable for boys, given the historic status and resource differences in educational opportunities for boys and girls. But symmetrical treatment, permitting both kinds of single-sex education, may emerge. Judges may find permitting all-girls but not all-boys schools awkward or difficult to justify or put in practice. Further, recent research indicates academic vulnerability for boys.[61] Just to complicate matters, research suggests that all-male environments may actually hinder the achievement of White boys but improve the achievement of Black and Hispanic boys.[62]

Congressional efforts to support single-sex education experiments faced strong opposition in the 1990s.[63] The U.S. Department of Education signaled in May 2002 its intention to permit experiments with single-sex classrooms and schools with public monetary support, but has not yet acted on it.[64] The legacy of *Brown v. Board* hovers in debates over single-sex education — and single-sex athletic teams — but equal opportunity is asserted both by those defending and those opposing separation by sex.[65] To meet the goal of equal opportunity, single-sex education should resist perpetuating stereotypes — yet can the fact of single-sex education ever avoid implying some need for protection or some inferiority of girls? In any case, single-sex education looks most acceptable when it is available on a voluntary basis as one of many quality options; otherwise it is too redolent of historic practices of exclusion.[66]

Disability

In 1967, Judge J. Skelly Wright applied *Brown v. Board* and its companion, *Bolling v. Sharpe,* to the system of ability-level tracking used in the District of Columbia public schools, and found the resulting racial pattern across tracks violative of the Constitution.[67] Besides demonstrating how any one school can use tracking to segregate internally by race, the decision helped to inspire advocates for children identified with disabilities to pursue desegregation and other equality strategies to end de jure exclusion of, and dismal programs for, students with disabilities from schooling. Before the 1970s, only seven states provided education for more than half of their children with disabilities.[68] Those children with disabilities who did receive educational programming did so largely in classrooms or schools separate from their peers. Parents and educators pressed both for more funding and for experiments placing students with disabilities in regular educational settings.[69] Two landmark decisions produced orders requiring free public educational programs for students with disabilities. The 1972 consent decree in *Pennsylvania Association for Retarded Children v. Commonwealth*[70] specifically preferred placement of students in a regular public school classroom over a separate class for students with disabilities.[71] A summary judgment in *Mills v. Board of Education,* also in 1972, rejected the exclusion of children with disabilities from the District of Columbia schools and called for publicly supported education "suited to the [student's] needs."[72] Following the decree in the *Mills* case, the system held three hundred hearings in the first nineteen months.[73] Congress relied on these court actions when, in 1975, it adopted the Education for All Handicapped Children Act, since renamed the Individuals with Disabilities in Education Act.[74] This statute, and the Rehabilitation Act Amendments of 1973, shifted legal treatment of people with disabilities to a framework of rights, rather than support or care.[75]

From the start, the federal law recognized the value of integration — triggered by the requirement that, to the maximum extent feasible, the school system place the child with disabilities in the "least restrictive environment,"[76] known in this context as mainstreaming or inclusion. The law also requires the educational program and related services to be tailored to meet the needs of the individual child.[77] The statutory scheme promotes identification of students who could well have gone undetected in the past and protects against faulty identification, which can produce stigma and misallocation of resources.[78] The law offers participating states money in exchange for plans to ensure appropriate education and related services and administrative procedures for creating individualized education plans with parental participation and opportunities for review.[79] At once an entitlement and an equality commitment, the special education law has become a major focus of attention for schools and parents and a basis for struggles over resources, balancing the interests of individual children and groups of children, and as sessing when equal opportunity calls for integration and when it calls instead for specialized, separate instructional settings.

Before the adoption of the federal disability law, nearly 70 percent of children with disabilities who received education did so in separate classrooms or in separate schools that provided education and services.[80] With the law, advocacy, and the related changes in educational philosophy the law represents, by 1996 more than 70 percent of students with disabilities spent at least part of their day in the regular classroom with other students.[81] Nearly half — 47 percent — of students with disabilities now spend all their time in a mainstream classroom.[82] Courts initially ordered mainstreaming only if shown to be beneficial, but over time judges began to read the statutory call for mainstreaming to "the maximum extent appropriate."[83] Some of this transformation grew from the interpretation and implementation of the federal statute and from regulations by educators and the development of new instructional techniques that support inclusion of students with disabilities in regular classrooms. But the change also reflected intensive litigation efforts. Although a line of court decisions favor mainstreaming, courts, educators, parents, and scholars continue to disagree over precisely when equal opportunity calls for integration or separate instruction.[84]

In favor of inclusion are these considerations: 1) socializing with nondisabled peers offers real academic and non-academic benefits for the student with disabilities, both in the present and in preparation for navigating life in the future;[85] and 2) learning alongside students with disabilities can benefit nondisabled students by enhancing their understanding of others, their patience and appreciation of the struggles of others, and their ability to see their classmates as individuals rather than embodiments of stigmatized categories.[86] Factors competing with the integration commitment are: 1) due to resource restrictions, confusion, and misguided worries about teaching the child differently from others, a child with disabilities may not receive tailored instruction or necessary support services while mainstreamed in the regular classroom; and 2) the nondisabled classmates risk interference with their education due to disruptions or distractions caused by the students with disabilities or disproportionate teacher attention required by those students.[87] A separate line of contention, less immediately germane to the mainstreaming debate, concerns the allocation of financial and other resources, given that students with disabilities typically require more resources whether placed in regular or special classrooms.[88] Some may assume that mainstreaming will be cheaper, but when implemented with appropriate supplemental aids and supports, it may well be as costly as separate classrooms with specially trained teachers.

Courts continue in varying degrees to grant deference to the expertise of school officials over placement of students with disabilities, but they nonetheless recognize the law's dual demand for appropriate placements and placements that, to the extent feasible, permit the child with disabilities to go to school alongside nondisabled peers.[89] Yet the courts have disagreed over precisely how to combine deference to educators with the statutory preference for the least restrictive alternative, producing no single clear test for measuring state compliance with the "least restrictive environment" provision of the law.[90] No simple test could work, however, given the variety of disabling conditions, competing views about the purposes of education and the value of integration toward those purposes, and even shifting ideas about the capabilities of children with certain conditions. One commentator warns that the influence of *Brown v. Board of Education* contributes to a simplistic embrace of mainstreaming for all children.[91] An inappropriate placement in the regular classroom does not afford equal educational opportunity if the student cannot benefit from it. Thus, for some students with serous mental impairments, learning life skills such as shopping for groceries or even dressing oneself are essential, which makes the regular classroom a poor fit.[92] Yet even this warning echoes historic assumptions that students with physical disabilities could not learn, and cautions against shielding from review the assignment of a disabled student to a separate classroom or program. At the same time, segregation or exclusion seems not to trouble parents, especially those with children with learning disabilities, who view the law as a way to obtain special help.[93] This should serve as a reminder that integration is not the exclusive way to achieve equal opportunity; treating people the same who are different is not equal treatment.[94]

Brown v. Board provides the template for demanding both equal opportunity and integration for students with disabilities, and working out what that means for individual students will continue to require complex assessments that are subject to review. It will also require careful treatment of students with disabilities under emerging regimes of mandatory statewide assessments, and scrutiny of the racial and gender disparities in special education labels and placements. Including students with disabilities in mandatory statewide assessment could be at least as crucial to equalizing educational opportunities as classroom integration. Teachers and administrators are more likely to become committed to improving the educational performance of these students in comparable domains with other students when these accountability measures are extended to them.[95] Evidence of overidentification of disabling conditions by race and gender and segregation as a result that affects chiefly African American boys provides serious grounds for concern, and eerie echoes of *Hobson v. Hanson*'s finding that the District of Columbia's tracking system amounted to illegal racial segregation.[96] Racial and gender disparities are clues to patterns of underidentification of students in some categories of disability as well, a further complexity in realizing equality in this context.

And then there is the enduring problem of quality of instruction. I have been struck by the ability of truly gifted teachers to teach heterogeneous classes that include students with disabilities; the same children may seem unteachable as a whole group to another teacher, who then may turn to the special education apparatus to identify some students and remove them or obtain a classroom aide or other assistance. It is far from clear that ordering either inclusion or separate instruction will improve quality. Either strategy necessarily increases the demand for talented teachers; either strategy can fail without more direction, teacher preparation, and resources for recruiting and sustaining high-quality instruction.

Citizenship, Sexual Orientation, and Religion

Echoing *Brown*, but perhaps in surprising ways, many students, parents, schools, and communities are occupied with equality in schools' treatment of noncitizen immigrants and students who identify with or explore lesbian, gay, or transgendered orientations. Perhaps even more surprising are the uses of equality arguments on behalf of religious students and religious schools. Each of these contexts confirms the dominance of an equality framework launched by *Brown;* each recapitulates in different ways debates over integration as the sole or best way to achieve equality.

— Immigrants and Noncitizens

Noncitizen children have faced exclusion as well as segregation in schooling. Arguments for exclusion include claims that their parents have not financially supported the schools and that free education will create an undesirable incentive for people to immigrate unlawfully. Arguments for inclusion echo *Brown*'s commitment to equal opportunity and recognition of the central importance of education to success in life. Beyond the normative claim of dignity of the person, many make the practical point that many, if not most, of these children will stay in this country and will contribute more economically, socially, and politically if they have received an education.

After the U.S. Supreme Court in 1982 rejected efforts by Texas to deny a free public education to undocumented school-age children,[97] California proceeded through a citizens' initiative to exclude undocumented immigrants from the public schools and to enlist school districts in investigating the legal status of each child.[98] A district court barred implementation of the initiative on the grounds that it interfered with federal immigration law.[99] California governor Pete Wilson appealed the decision, but his successor eventually dropped the appeal and ended questions about the exclusion of noncitizen children from the schools.[100]

Meanwhile, many communities have created "newcomer schools," which are separate school facilities for recent immigrants. Intended to provide a comfortable transitional environment, these schools include bilingual and bicultural education and address issues for older students who have not attended school previously or have little schooling or literacy instruction in any language.[101] The school systems are especially worried about the probability that enrollment in regular schools will frustrate adolescent immigrant children and lead them to drop out. By design, these schools separate these immigrants from other students for at least a year and sometimes longer, but do so in order to provide tailored instruction and a supportive environment. Yet how can such programs avoid stigmatizing the students? Do they provide equal resources and instruction?

The federal No Child Left Behind Act requires states to include new immigrants in state standardized performance assessments, which could raise curricular expectations but could also lead to counterproductive experiences of failure, especially if the states fail to provide tests in the students' native languages.[102] Recently, the federal government announced that recent immigrants could be exempt from the English assessments during their first year in school in the United States, which also avoids including their scores in the overall results for each school.[103] These students would still be expected to take the exams in mathematics, with help in their native languages.[104] A deputy superintendent in Massachusetts commented on the way testing policy can be punitive: "It's a form of child abuse to require students to take this test when we know they're going to fail."[105] Many school officials remain worried about the moment when English-language learners must be counted within schoolwide English assessments for their scores, because their inclusion would distort what the schools actually are achieving both with these students and with the students who already speak English. Under the No Child Left Behind Act, costly remedial efforts — as well as stigmatizing sanctions attached to schools with low performance scores — and backlash against the law, have led states to seriously consider opting out of the funding that attaches the assessment obligations.[106]

— Gay and Lesbian Students

The New York City public school system established the Harvey Milk High School in 1985 for gay and lesbian teenagers.[107] Its goal was to create a supportive and safe place for students who faced violence or intimidation.[108] When it expanded in the fall of 2003 from two classrooms with fifty students to eight classrooms with 170 students, the school triggered protests, especially from conservative religious groups.[109] Critics include gay rights supporters who oppose segregation and warn that the separate schooling fails to equip these students for the real world and fails to dismantle discrimination.[110] One critic said, "Through long, painful years we reached a consensus that we couldn't allow segregation. This is a short-term gain and we need to look at the long-term, larger issues."[111] A Michigan editorial took up the issue and also opposed the separate school:

> Advocates say that by having their own school, gays will feel more comfortable and won't be subjected to the intimidation that many of them now face in public schools. That argument comes uncomfortably close to racial segregationists in the 1950s and 1960s who insisted that Black students did best when they were "among their own."[112]

Yet advocates indicate that, due to harassment and violence, gay teens are much more likely to drop out or attempt suicide than other students, and thus they need a special school.[113] Given evidence that calling someone "gay" remains a common insult among teens, sorting out how best to assist students today while also addressing prejudice and cruelty aimed at lesbian and gay students will undoubtedly pose challenges for some time to come.[114] A voluntary separate school along these lines may seem more acceptable in a large system like New York's, which also includes citywide special schools in science, fashion, and other areas. As a result, the Harvey Milk School includes gay and lesbian students who enroll in the larger city project of magnet schools with special themes.[115] Yet, it remains troubling to conceive as "voluntary" enrollment the student selection of a special school in order to escape harassment at the regular school. Whether separate instruction is equal seems less relevant than determining how to make integrated education safe. Meanwhile, although some people object to any public school acknowledgment of students' sexual orientation, the commitment to equal opportunity for gay and lesbian students animates most of the arguments on both sides of this issue.

— Religious Students

Perhaps advocacy of educational opportunities for religious students is the least predictable legacy of *Brown v. Board*. I admit, the influence is indirect and requires standing back from much of the explicit legal arguments to look at the broader context. Yet both in the context of public aid to religious schools and the treatment of religion in public schools, concerns about equality have reframed preoccupations with separating church and state. A principal architect of this shift is Michael McConnell, long-time law professor and now appellate court judge, whose scholarship and advocacy argued against separate public and private spheres, with religion relegated to the private, and argued for full and equal rights for religious individuals in the public sphere.[116] It is no accident that McConnell also has written extensively on the Fourteenth Amendment and racial desegregation.[117]

As counsel for students seeking state university funding for their Christian publication, McConnell successfully persuaded five justices of the U.S. Supreme Court to focus on the inequality in the denial of funding, given subsidies to other student publications.[118] Accordingly, the Court rejected as unconstitutional the exclusion of a religious student newspaper from eligibility for funding by a state university. The Court reasoned that such exclusion amounted to impermissible viewpoint discrimination under the guarantee of freedom of speech.[119] Similarly, it would be illegal viewpoint discrimination to deny access to space in the public school after the school day to a religious afterschool program.[120] This argument shrinks concerns about government establishment of religion and brings religious students and their families into the pluralist, multicultural world created by *Brown* and its advocates.

McConnell has also articulated a generous view of the constitutional duty to accommodate religious believers.[121] McConnell, as law clerk for Justice William Brennan, advanced the view that prevailed in the Supreme Court: Campus religious organizations cannot be denied the right of access to facilities that a public university grants to other organizations.[122] Offering access to the religious group would not amount to a violation of the Establishment Clause because similar access would be accorded to other groups; refusing access to a group because of its religious identity or message in turn would violate the Free Speech Clause by disfavoring one message or viewpoint.[123] Therefore, a state university regulation that prohibited student use of school facilities for religious worship or preaching violated the guarantee of freedom of speech, and an equal access policy would not violate the Establishment Clause. This is precisely how the Court summarized its decision when later interpreting the federal Equal Access Act to establish similar requirements for public secondary schools receiving federal funds.[124] The Court subsequently found a public school district in violation of the Free Speech Clause in denying a church access to school facilities after hours to show a film with a religious approach to childrearing.[125] Similarly, the Court found that a school was violating the Free Speech Clause when it denied access to a religious afterschool program, and found that such access would not violate the Establishment Clause.[126]

McConnell testified before the Senate Judiciary Committee in favor of the general idea of a religious equality amendment that would allow prayer in public schools.[127] Both equality and freedom were at a stake in his view, and he drew an analogy to racial equality in defending the need to recognize the rights of individuals to exercise their religious beliefs without fear of discrimination or denial of benefits. Thus, after a court of appeals found it within the discretion of a ninth-grade teacher to disallow a student's proposed research paper on Jesus Christ, McConnell declared that he had "little doubt that the case would have come out the other way if a racist teacher had forbidden a paper on Martin Luther King Jr., or an anticommunist teacher had forbidden a paper on the evils of capitalism."[128] Mindful of the comparison between race and religion, advocates like McConnell have successfully extended the legacy of *Brown* to religious students and schools.

Even when it comes to public financial support for parochial schools, McConnell and other lawyers have effectively shifted the legal framework from Establishment Clause and even Free Exercise claims to considerations of equality and viewpoint discrimination, contrary to the free speech guaranty. Recasting earlier concerns about public funds contributing to religious activities — and leaving behind the 1960s and 1970s jurisprudence that rather incoherently sorted acceptable and unacceptable public aid to religious schools — the Supreme Court has asked instead whether the aid comes through a general program with neutral, secular criteria that neither benefit nor disadvantage religion. Under such a test, the Court has upheld a voucher program enabling parents to select a private parochial school for their children[129] and to use public dollars to pay for books, computer software, and other secular materials for use in a private religious school.[130] In his concurring opinion, Justice Clarence Thomas compared *Brown v. Board*'s declaration of the importance of schooling to an individual's success in life with facts about the failing Cleveland schools in order to bolster the rationale for the voucher program.[131] He also stressed that minority and low-income parents express the strongest support for vouchers, which enable them to select private schools for their children, and rejected opposition as being preoccupied with formalistic concerns far from the core purposes of the Fourteenth Amendment.[132]

The Court has also warned that excluding religious schools from generally available aid could present a violation of the Free Exercise Clause.[133] Not only is there no constitutional violation in including religious schools in the eligibility criteria for public funds that are otherwise generally available; the courts could also find a constitutional defect if religious schools generally are excluded from public aid.[134] Commentators expressly describe these developments as ending second-class treatment of religious schools.[135] The traditional separation of church and state becomes unacceptably unequal in this light.

The structure of this last point looks a bit like an equality argument, but the influence of *Brown* in the context of challenges to public aid to religious schools is even more direct. In the majority opinion in *Zelman v. Simmons-Harris* — the voucher decision — the Court emphasized the explicit justification for the voucher experiment in Milwaukee as improving educational opportunities for low-income minority children.[136] In his separate concurring opinion, Justice Thomas, holding Justice Thurgood Marshall's seat on the Court, stressed that *Brown*'s promise remained distant because of the deterioration and continuing segregation of urban schools.[137] Justice Thomas embraced the irony that, although vouchers seemed a tool to provoke "White flight" at the time of *Brown*, nearly fifty years later vouchers could open quality instruction to students otherwise trapped in failing public schools.[138] He emphasized that minority and low-income parents are among the strongest supporters of voucher programs because they open up better educational opportunities for their children. But if some see the voucher case as a step toward fulfilling *Brown*'s vision of equal educational opportunities for students of color,[139] others caution that, because need may induce parents to send their children to religious schools, voucher programs using public dollars could violate the Establishment Clause or Free Exercise Clause.[140]

With advocates and courts reframing the question from aid to religious schools to equal treatment for religious students and religious ideas, *Brown v.*

Board's legacy may also reflect a broader commitment to pluralism, or perhaps the triumph of identity politics.[141] Jeffrey Rosen puts it this way:

> Americans have always been deeply religious and deeply suspicious of state-imposed uniformity. In an era when religious identity now competes with race, sex and ethnicity as a central aspect of how Americans define themselves, it seems like discrimination — the only unforgivable sin in a multicultural age — to forbid people to express their religious beliefs in an increasingly fractured public sphere. Strict separationism, during its brief reign, made the mistake of trying to forbid not only religious expression by the state, but also religious expression by citizens on public property.[142]

In practice, vouchers may produce more segregation by enabling more students to enroll in parochial schools, thereby diminishing the ability of public schools to serve as the meeting place for all students.[143] Vouchers and subsidies for private schools may well draw Protestant students into Catholic schools and continue the diversification of the urban Catholic school that has proceeded for the past several decades.[144] Greater accommodation of religious students in public schools may push in the other direction by making public schools more hospitable for them, but there are risks in introducing new forms of peer exclusion and hierarchies where religious activities and affiliations are divisive. An eerie mirror image of our paradoxes and challenges in religious accommodation rises across the ocean as France contemplates banning head scarves and other highly visible religious symbols in the public schools, for this ostensible commitment to reinforcing the inclusive features of French republican identity may not only symbolically exclude some, but may actually drive observant Muslim girls into self-segregated religious schools.[145]

Assessing the Legacies

There are other surprising legacies of *Brown*. Advocates for Romá children in Eastern Europe not only cite *Brown*, but also model their movement for educational rights after the NAACP's strategy in that case.[146] The high courts in South Africa and India have also cited *Brown*'s principles, and the comparison to separate but equal does indeed dominate the current controversy over same-sex marriage and the compromise position of civil unions. The enormous influence of *Brown* probably cannot accurately be assessed by those of us who live in its wake, but I suspect that historians will look back and see how much it spread equality as the framework for legal, political, and social arguments within the United States and beyond.

But what of integration? Outside the racial context, *Brown*'s recognition that separate is inherently unequal rightly disturbs ready tendencies to pursue separate solutions — in schools and elsewhere — for girls, gays, immigrants, and children with disabilities. Yet the gnawing sense that specialized, separate settings are sometimes valuable or necessary persists. I suggest that *Brown* crucially put to us the dual insight:

1. Educational opportunity is so crucial to any individual's realistic chances of success in life that it is a right that must be made available to all on equal terms.[147]
2. Against a history of mandated segregation, separate educational facilities are inherently unequal.[148]

Segregation, even if so-called voluntary, should therefore raise concerns and assumptions that it is better or easier and be scoured for evidence that it actually promotes equal opportunity for each individual to have real success in life.

The reasons offered for separate instruction differ, and this difference should matter in resolving doubts about its particular use. Thus, for some children with disabilities and for adolescents who have recently arrived in the United States with little or no formal schooling, separate instruction seems crucial in order to provide the content appropriate to the students' needs. The activities of the regular classroom are simply too remote from where these students are, at least for a time, in order to provide meaningful educational opportunities. For some girls — and some boys — separate instruction may reduce distractions and create an ethos of achievement that boosts learning. Perhaps this is also true for some students in majority-minority schools, although arguments about their ethos often seem to reflect the lack of realistic chances for integration. Researchers continue to find evidence of higher student achievement for students of color who attend integrated schools.[149] For some gay and lesbian teens, separate instruction seems crucial for protection from harassment, hatred, and violence. Separate instruction for them seems almost a desperate response to inhospitable and dangerous settings, but also a concession to the negative attitudes and behaviors of others that could and should be challenged and changed. It is important to consider how much changing those attitudes and behaviors depends upon tackling the assumption that separate settings are safer — and are acceptable.

In scrutinizing contemporary uses of separate instruction, we should return to *Brown*. The Supreme Court's decision fundamentally represented recognition that the entire community is affected by the treatment of any of its members. Hannah Arendt, Holocaust refugee and political theorist, initially did not understand much of this and wrote a controversial critique of President Eisenhower's use of federal troops to enforce the token desegregation of Little Rock's Central High School.[150] Reflecting her own experience with Nazism, Arendt worried in print about the loss of a private right of freedom of association, cautioned against Black demands for social equality, given the risks to more fundamental rule of law, and warned about the forced participation of children to lead social and political changes sought by adults.[151]

Ralph Ellison challenged Arendt and told her she did not understand the role of schoolchildren in the struggle for racial desegregation as initiation into a racist world — and also part of an African American tradition of self-sacrifice.[152] In reply, Arendt acknowledged that she had not fully understood the situation. The issue of sacrifice deserves more attention in today's segregative and integrative debates for the variety of students I have discussed; perhaps we have fallen too quickly into a view of children as vulnerable and neglected — underestimating not only their resilience, but also how much strength they may find in tackling social problems if they have adults on their side.

Even before her change of heart, Arendt wrote that, given the lack of a common past or homogeneous population in the United States, the very survival of the country would depend upon "its all-comprehensive, typically American form [of] equality," which "possesses an enormous power to equalize what by nature and origin is different."[153] Discerning precisely how to realize this potential remains our challenge today. Race, ethnicity, language, disability, gender, citizenship, sexual orientation, religion — none of these should interfere with an individual student's equal chance to learn. But what should this mean for us? The surprising legacies of *Brown* must make this the question for us all.

Notes

1. Frank Phillips and Raphael Lewis, "Two Marriage Amendments Fail, Lawmakers to Reconvene Today," *Boston Globe*, Feb. 12, 2004, A1, B7 (quoting Wilkerson).
2. Goodridge v. Dep't of Pub. Health, 440 Mass. 309, 798 N.E.2d 941, 2003 Mass. LEXIS 814 (2003). The Supreme Judicial Court also declined to approve the subsequent legislative inquiry about whether civil union rather than marriage could satisfy the court's demand for revamping the marriage law that had excluded same-sex couples. Opinions of the Justices to the Senate, 440 Mass. 1201, 802 N.E.2d 565, 2004 Mass. LEXIS 35 (2004).
3. Michael Paulson, "Black Clergy Rejection Stirs Gay Marriage Backers," *Boston Globe*, Feb. 10, 2004, B1.
4. Ralph Reed, "History Shows GOP on Side of Civil Rights," *Atlanta Constitution*, Dec. 19, 2002, 25A.
5. Some scholars have made careers in debating whether the Supreme Court's decision in *Brown* itself deserves credit for the civil rights revolution. See Gerald Rosenberg, Hollow Hope, and Michael Klarman responses. In the years between 1954 and the adoption of the 1964 Civil Rights Act, southern Whites used harassment, intimidation, and outright resistance to any movement toward school desegregation. I do not mean to resolve that debate here and instead take the confluence of social movement, court action, and legislative action surrounding *Brown* as a whole.
6. Martha Minow, "A Tribute to Justice Thurgood Marshall," 105 Harv. L. Rev. 66 (1991); Martha Minow, "Choices and Constraints: For Justice Thurgood Marshall," 80 Geo. L. J. 2093 (1992).

7. A LEXIS search of law review articles produced 465 such references (Brown w/2 Board w/9 landmark).

8. "*Brown* at 50: King's Dream or *Plessy*'s Nightmare?" http://www.civilrightsproject.harvard.edu/research/reseg04/resegregation04.php.

9. Id., at 37.

10. Id., at 4 (describing both selections of private schools and movement to White suburbs).

11. Jennifer Hochschild and Nathan Scovronick, *The American Dream and the Public Schools* (New York: Oxford University Press 2003), 25.

12. For example, the University of Illinois announced its plans for celebration with two sharply contrasting sentences: "On May 17, 1954, America was changed forever when the United States Supreme Court ruled unanimously to outlaw racial segregation in the nation's public schools," and "That landmark decision in favor of simple social justice set the country on a course of debate, dissent, and change that continues today" http://www.oc.uiuc.edu/*Brown*/.

13. Thurgood Marshall, "Reflections on the Bicentennial of the United States Constitution," 101 Harv. L. Rev. 1 (1987).

14. Id.

15. Id.

16. 347 U.S. 483, 495 (1954).

17. Brown v. Board of Education (II), 394 U.S. 294, 301 (1955).

18. Robert J. Cottrol, Raymond T, Diamond, and Leland B. Ware, *Brown v. Board of Education:* Caste, Culture, and the Constitution (Lawrence: University Press of Kansas 2003), 192–4.

19. Id., at 193–4.

20. Charles J. Ogletree, Jr., *All Deliberate Speed* (New York: W.W. Norton & Co., 2004), 10–11.

21. Brown v. Board of Education, 347 U.S. 483, 493 (1954).

22. Id., at 493.

23. Denise C. Morgan, "What Is Left to Argue in Desegregation Law? The Right to Minimally Adequate Education," 8 Harv. Black Letter L. J. 99, 106 (1991).

24. "*Brown* at 50: King's Dream or *Plessy*'s Nightmare?" http://www.civilrightsproject.harvard.edu/research/reseg04/resegregation04.php (table 8).

25. See Oklahoma City Bd. of Education v. Dowell, 498 U.S. 237 (1991) (New neighborhood assignment plan producing essentially single-race schools does not violate equal protection in a district previously subject to a school desegregation decree). Freeman v. Pitts, 503 U.S. 467 (1992) (Withdrawing judicial supervision of aspects of school system after finding those aspects had achieved unitary status after historical segregation).

26. Hochschild and Scovronick, at 45.

27. One detailed study of the Boston area explores the complex interaction among these factors. David J. Harris and Nancy McArdle, "More than Money: The Spacial Mismatch Between Where Homeowners of Color in Metro Boston Can Afford to Live and Where They Actually Reside" (prepared for The Civil Rights Project at Harvard University 2003), http://www.civilrightsproject.harvard.edu/research/metro/residential_choice.php#fullreport.

28. By 2002, forty-three suits challenging state school finance regimes generated nineteen decisions striking down state schemes under the relevant state constitution. See Liz Kramer, "Achieving Equitable Education through the Courts: A Comparative Analysis of Three States," 31 J.L. & Educ. 1 (2002). See also Stewart G. Pollock, "School

Finance in the Courts," 1998 Ann. Surv. Am. L. 133 (1998) (summarizing developments). For a helpful overview of recent suits, see Molly McUsic, "The Law's Role in the Distribution of Education: The Promises and Pitfalls of School Finance Litigation," in *Law and School Reform: Six Strategies for Promoting Educational Equity* (Jay B. Heubert ed., Yale University Press: New Haven 1999). See generally William E. Thro, "Judicial Analysis during the Third Wave of School Finance Litigation: The Massachusetts Decision as a Model," 35 B.C. L. Rev. 597 (1994). See also Patricia F. First and Barbara M. DeLuca, "The Meaning of Educational Adequacy: The Confusion of DeRolph," 32 J.L. & Educ. 185 (2003) (Ohio litigation). See Michael Paris, "Legal Mobilization and the Politics of Reform: Lessons from School Finance Litigation in Kentucky," 1984–1995, 26 Law & Soc. Inquiry 631 (2001); see also James E. Ryan, "Sheff, Segregation and School Finance Litigation," 74 N.Y.U. L. Rev. 529 (1999) (Connecticut).

29. Richard Kallenberg, *All Together Now: Creating Middle-Class Schools through Public School Choice* (Washington, DC: Brookings Institution Press 2001), 42.

30. See Grutter v. Bollinger, 539 U.S. 306 (2003)

31. Grutter v. Bollinger, 539 U.S., at 342.

32. See Juan F. Perea, "*Brown v. Board of Education* After Forty Years: Confronting the Promise: Ethnicity and the Constitution: Beyond the Black and White Binary Constitution," 36 Wm. and Mary L. Rev. 571 (1995).

33. Lau v. Nichols, 414 U.S. 563 (1974).

34. Id.

35. For my earlier treatment of this issue, see Martha Minow, *Making All the Difference: Inclusion, Exclusion and American Law* (1990).

36. 20 U.S.C. section 1703 (f).

37. 20 U.S.C. section 880(b).

38. William Ryan, "Note: The Unz Initiatives and the Abolition of Bilingual Education," 43 B.C. L. Rev. 487 (2002).

39. See Castañeda v. Pickard, 648 F.2d 989 (5th Cir. 1981) (directing that school districts be evaluated in terms of adoption and implementation of a pedagogically sound approach for meeting the needs of limited-English-proficient students).

40. See Lisa Elhern, "Proposition 227: The Difficulty of Ensuring English Language Learners' Rights," 33 Colum. J.L. and Soc. Prob. 1 (1999), Christina Rossell and K. Baker, "The Educational Effectiveness of Bilingual Education," 30 Research in the Teaching of English (Feb. 1996). "Comment: The Bay State Buries Bilingualism: Advocacy Lessons from Bilingual Education's Recent Defeat in Massachusetts," 24 Chicano-Latino L. Rev. 43 (2003). See also Marcelo Suárez-Orozco, Peter D. Roos, and Carola Suárez-Orozco, "Cultural, Educational, and Legal Perspectives on Immigration: Implications for School Reform," in Jay P. Heubert, ed., *Law & School Reform: Six Strategies for Promoting Educational Equity* (New Haven: Yale University Press 1999) 160, 190–191(discussing debate over whether proficiency in English requires up to six years to acquire).

41. See "Comment: Sink or Swim? The State of Bilingual Education in the Wake of California Proposition 227," 48 Cath. U.L. Rev. 843 (1999).

42. Both options may remain inadequate due to other factors — such as the economic class of the affected students and neighborhoods. See infra (discussing school finance and adequacy litigation).

43. Id.; and 24 Chicano-Latino L. Rev. 43 (2003). California still allows parents to elect either bilingual education or immersion under certain circumstances. See William Ryan, "Note: The Unz Initiative and the Abolition of Bilingual Education," 43 B.C. L. Rev. 487, 509 (2002).

44. The Casteñeda decision contrasts with the district court's view in Valeria G., 23 F. Supp. 2d, 1007 (N.D. Cal. 1998).

45. Barbara Whalen and Charles Whalen, "The Longest Debate: A Legislative History of the 1964 Civil Rights Act" 234 (1985); see 110 Cong. Rec. 2581 (1964) (statement of Congresswoman Edith Green) (suggesting that Rep. Howard W. Smith proposed to insert "sex" to prevent the passage of Title VII); but see Jo Freeman, "How "Sex" Got into Title VII: Persistent Opportunism as a Maker of Public Policy," 9 Law & Inequality 163, 165 (1991); Robert C. Bird, "More than a Congressional Joke: A Fresh Look at the Legislative History of Sex Discrimination of the 1964 Civil Rights Act," 3 Wm. & Mary J. Women & L. 137, 137 (1997).

46. For a thoughtful treatment, see Christine Littleton, "Reconstructing Sexual Equality," 75 Cal. L. Rev. 1279 (1987).

47. See Id., and A. Brown et al., "The Equal Rights Amendment: A Constitutional Basis for Equal Rights for Women," 80 Yale L.J. 871, 876 (1971); Minow, "Rights of One's Own (Book Review), 98 Harv. L. Rev. 1084 (1985) (considering Elizabeth Cady Stanton's views).

48. Compare Craig v. Boren, 429 U.S. 190 (1976) (requiring important objectives behind gender distinctions) with Rostker v. Goldberg 453 U.S. 57 (1981) (accepting differential treatment of men and women in the military context); Michael M. v. Superior Court of Sonoma County, 450 U.S. 464 (1981) (asking whether men and women are similarly situated in relation to the statutory rape law); and Mississippi University for Women v. Hogan, 458 U.S. 718 (1982) (requiring an "exceedingly persuasive justification" for sex-based distinctions); United States v. Virginia, 518 U.S. 515 (1996) (same).

49. Hogan, supra.

50. U.S. v. Virginia, supra.

51. Vorchheimer v. School District of Philadelphia, 532 F.2d 880 (3d Cir. 1976) (aff'd by an equally divided court, 430 U.S. 703 (1977).

52. Id.

53. Mary B. W. Tabor, "Planners of a New Public School for Girls Look to Two Cities," *New York Times,* July 22, 1996, B2 (quoted in Rosemary C. Salomone, *Same, Different, Equal: Rethinking Single-Sex Schooling* 127 (2003)).

54. So argues Denise Morgan, who revisited the early writings of Justice Ruth Bader Ginsburg, surely the architect of modern gender equality jurisprudence. Denise C. Morgan, "Finding a Constitutionally Permissible Path to Sex Equality: The Young Women's Leadership School of East Harlem," 14 N.Y.L. Sch. J. Hum. Rts. 95, 104 (1997) (analyzing Ruth Bader Ginsburg, "Sex Equality and the Constitution: The State of the Art," 4 Women's Rts. L. Rptr. 143, 146 (1978)).

55. See Kimberly Jenkins, "An Analytical Framework for Public Single-Sex Elementary and Secondary Schools" (draft Jan. 2004).

56. See Kay Bailey Hutchison, "The Lessons of Single-Sex Education: Both Successful and Constitutional," 50 A. U. L. Rev. 1075, 1082 n. 5 (20001) (citing R. Hawley, Kenneth Rowe, "Single Sex and Mixed Sex Classes: The Effects of Class Type on Student Achievement, Confidence and Participation in Mathematics," 32 Austl. J. Educ. 183, 195 (1988); Good Research Group, "Nat'l Coalition of Girls' Schools in the U.S., Achievement, Leadership and Success: A Report on Educational, Professional and Life Outcomes at Girls' Schools in the United States," (2000)); Kimberly M. Schuld, "Rethinking Educational Equity: Sometimes, Different Can Be an Acceptable Substitute for Equal," 1999 U. Chi. Legal Forum 461, 491 n. 108 (1999).

57. U.S. v. Virginia, 518 U.S. 515, 530 (1996).

58. Morgan, supra (supporter); Fred Kaplan, "Storm Gathers Over School in Flower," *Boston Globe,* Feb. 23, 1998, p. A1 (describing lawsuit by National Organization for Women and New York Civil Liberties Union claiming the school violates Title IX). For a thoughtful treatment of the suit and underlying issues, see Rosemary C. Salomone, *Same, Different, Equal: Rethinking Single-Sex Schooling,* 1–25, 61–3 (2003).

59. Salomone, supra, at 114–5; American Association of University Women, *Gender Gaps: How Schools Still Fail Our Children* (1998).

60. Salamone, supra., at 133–140.

61. See William S. Pollack, *Real Boys: Rescuing Our Sons From the Myths of Boyhood* (Random House: New York 1998); Christina Hoff Sommers, *The War Against Boys* (2000). Although special concerns are rightly raised about Black boys' academic risks, the data suggest problems across the color line. Cynthia Tucker, "Pushy Parents Are the Best Boost for Black Boys," *Atlanta Journal Constitution,* May 25, 2003, 10C.

62. Morgan, supra, at n. 81 (discussing studies).

63. Id., at 139–140.

64. Office of Civil Rights, U.S. Department of Education, "Nondiscrimination on the Basis of Sex in Education Programs or Activities Receiving Federal Financial Assistance: Notice of Intention to Regulate," 34 CFR Part 106 (May 8, 2002), http://www.ed.gov/policy/rights/reg/ocr/t9-noi-ss.html?exp=0

65. On athletics, some courts have entertained arguments that girls need to be protected from the risks of injury in male contact sports, see Force v. Pierce City R-VI School District, 570 F. Supp. 1020 (W.D. Mo. 1983), and federal law leaves this as a local question. 34 C.F.R. section 106.41 (b). But the courts are tending to allow girls try out for competitive, contact sports. See Barnett v. Texas Wrestling Association, 16 F. Supp. 690 (N.D. Tex. 1998); Adams v. Baker, 919 F. Supp. 1496 (D. Kan. 1996). Yet the courts also accept exclusion of boys from girls' teams in order to preserve opportunities for girls. See Clark v. Arizona Interscholastic Association, 695 F.2d 1126 (9th Cir. 1982).

66. See Jenkins, supra at 63 (discussing difficulties in ensuring truly voluntary choice where educators may press parents and students toward single-sex options).

67. Hobson v. Hanson, 269 F.Supp. 401 (D.C. Cir. 1967). The decision also criticized the segregation of class, due to the use of neighborhood school assignments.

68. Jeffrey J. Zettel and Joseph Ballard, "The Education for All Handicapped Children Act of 1975 (P.L. 94-142): Its History, Origins, and Concepts," in *Special Education in America: Its Legal and Governmental Foundations* 12 (Joseph Ballard et al., eds. 1982).

69. Robert L. Hughes and Michael A. Rebell, "Special Educational Inclusion and the Courts: A Proposal for a New Remedial Approach," 25 J.L. & Educ. 523 (1996).

70. 334 F. Supp. 1257 (E.D. Pa. 1971), 343 F. Supp. 279 (E.D. Pa. 1972).

71. 334 F. Supp., at 1260.

72. 348 F. Supp. 866, (D.D.C. 1972).

73. Patricia M. Wald, "Whose Public Interest Is It Anyway? Advice for Altruistic Young Lawyers," 47 Me. L. Rev. 311 (1995).

74. 20 U.S.C. sections 1400–1490.

75. Laura F. Rothstein, "Reflections on Disabilities Discrimination Policy — 25 Years," 22 U. Ark.Little Rock L. Rev. 147 (2000).

76. 20 U.S.C. 1412 (a)(5).

77. See Section 1412 (5); 34 C.F.R. section 104.33(b)(1)(i).

78. Millions of students are currently identified as having a disability — and a 30 percent increase in such identifications has occurred over the past ten years. National Education Association, Special Education and the Individuals with Disabilities Education Act, http://www.nea.org/specialed/

79. 20 U.S.C. sect. 1401 , 1414, 1415.
80. Hughes and Rebell, supra, at 524.
81. See also Hughes and Rebell, supra at 524 (as of 1996, 34.9 percent of disabled children were placed in regular classrooms full-time, and 36.3 percent in part-time programs; 23.5 percent in separate classrooms, 3.9 percent in separate schools, 0.9 percent in residential facilities, and 0.5 percent in hospitals or visiting programs in the students' homes).
82. In 1998, the states reported that 47 percent of these students spent at least 80 percent of the school day in regular classrooms, which is a notable increase over the 31 percent of such students who did so in 1978. National Center for Education Statistics, Inclusion of Students with Disabilities in Regular Classrooms, http://nces.ed.gov/programs/coe/2002/section4/indicator28.asp (visited Feb. 17, 2004).
83. 20 U.S.C. sec. 1412(5) (B).
84. See Harmann v. Loudoun County Board of Education, 118 F.3d 996 (4th Cir. 1997) (mainstreaming should be tried, but an autistic child placed with aids in general classroom until disruptions proved excessive and child received no benefits in the class); Oberti v. Board of Education of the Borough of Clementon School District, 995 F.2d 104 (3d Cir. 1993) (district's duty to consider inclusion in regular class before exploring alternatives); Sacramento City Unified Sch. Dist. v. Michael H., 14 F.2d 1398 (9th Cir. 1994) (affirming placement of child with moderate retardation in regular classroom with supplemental support); Greer v. Rome City School District, 950 F.2d 688 (11th Cir. 1991) (using a cost/benefit analysis, child with Down's syndrome appropriately mainstreamed); Daniel R.R. v. State Board of Education, 874 F.2d 1036 (5th Cir. 1989) (where possible, child to be mainstreamed with appropriate services), see also Martha M. McCarthy, "Inclusion of Children with Disabilities: Is It Required?," 95 Educ. L. Rep. 823 (1995) (discerning trend toward inclusion). For proposals to refine the trend toward inclusion with exceptions for students who are disruptive or not capable of benefiting academically from placement in the regular classroom, see Kathryn E. Crossley, "Note: Inclusion: A New Addition to Remedy a History of Inadequate Conditions and Terms," 4 Wash. U. J. L. & Pol'y 239 (2000).
85. Oberti, 995 F.2d 1204, 1216–17; Daniel R.R., 874 F.2d 1036, 1047–48.
86. Daniel H. Melvin II, "Comment: The Desegregation of Children with Disabilities," 44 DePaul L. Rev. 599 (1995).
87. See Marissa L. Antoinette, "Comment: Examining How the Inclusion of Disabled Students into the General Classroom May Affect Non-Disabled Classmates," 30 Fordham Urb. L.J. 2039 (2003) (proposing a "three strikes" removal policy for a student who disrupts the regular classroom); Anne Proffitt Dupre, "A Study in Double Standards: Discipline, and the Disabled Student," 75 Wash. L. Rev. 1 (2000) (examining how the treatment of disruption and discipline poses problems for students).
88. See Wald, supra, at 12.
89. Board of Education v. Rowley, 458 U.S. 176, 181 n.4 (1982) (deference to educators while recognizing Congressional preference for mainstreaming); Oberti v. Board of Education, 995 F. 2d 1204.
90. Therese Craparo, "Note: Remembering the Individuals of the Individuals with Disabilities Education Act," 6 N.Y..U.J. Legis & Pub. Pol'y 467, 503–505 (2002/3).
91. Id., at 524.
92. Id., at 523. See also Theresa Bryant, "Drowning in the Mainstream: Integration of Children with Disabilities after Oberti v. Clementon School District," 22 Ohio N.U. L. Rev. 83 (1995) (urging consideration of costs and whether the child with disabilities can benefit from the mainstream classroom and disrupts that classroom).

93. Bryant, supra, at n. 283 (citing cases).
94. See Martha Minow, *Making All the Difference* (Ithaca, NY: Cornell University Press 1990).
95. See Jane K. Babin, "Adequate Special Education: Do California Schools Meet the Test?" 37 San Diego L. Rev. 211 (2000).
96. Dan Losen, *Racial Inequity in Special Education* (Cambridge, MA: Harvard Education Press 2002); Theresa Glennon, "Race, Education, and the Construction of a Disabled Class," 1995 Wis. L. Rev. 1237 (1995). See also Patrick Linehan, "Guarding the Dumping Ground: Equal Protection, Title VII and Justifying the Use of Race in the Hiring of Special Educators," 2001 B.Y.U. Educ. & L.J. 179 (2001) (recommending hiring special educators of color to reduce the overidentification of students of color).
97. Plyler v. Doe, 457 U.S. 202 (1982).
98. Proposition 187, reprinted in Mark G. Yudof, David L. Kirp, Betsy Levin, and Rachel F. Moran, *Educational Policy and the Law* (Belmont, CA: West Publishing 2002), 691.
99. League of United Latin American Citizens v. Wilson, 908 F. Supp. 755 (C.D. Cal. 1995).
100. See McDermott, "Are Embittered by Fate of Prop. 187," *L.A. Times*, Aug. 2, 1999, A1.
101. Deirdre Fernandes, "Schools to Open Special Program: Newcomer's Academy Will Help Hispanics with Language Barrier," *Winston-Salem Journal*, April 22, 2003, A1.
102. See Robert A. Frahm, "Big Test, No Hope: No Child Left Behind Offers No Break for Language Barrier," *Hartford Current*, Oct. 19, 2003, A1.
103. Jared Stearns and Suzanne Sataline, "New Immigrants get Break on MCAS Test," *Boston Globe*, Feb. 21, 2004, B1.
104. Id.
105. Id., at B4 fol. 3 (quoting Steven Mills, deputy school superintendent in Worcester).
106. Virginia opted out; Utah House of Rep. voted to accept only adequately funded provisions, http://www.edpress.org/infoarchives/current/ncibchalleng.htm, but the state Senate let the provision die. See Connie Lynn, No Child Bill About to Be Left Behind for the Year, *Salt Lake Tribune*, Feb. 27, 2004, http://www.sltrib.com/2004/Feb/02272004/utah/142952.asp
107. It may also be a haven for students who are transgendered and others who are perceived to be gay or lesbian.
108. See Katherine Zoepf, "Protests Mar Opening of Expanded Harvey Milk School," *New York Times,* Sept. 9, 2003, B3.
109. Id.
110. See Tania Branigan, "Responding to a Need, or to Fear?: Criticism Greets School for Gay Youth," *Washington Post*, Sept. 9. 2003, A03.
111. Id. (quoting Bill Dobbs).
112. Editorial, "Gay School Not Right Solution," *Battle Creek Enquirer*, Aug. 4, 2003, 6A.
113. Branigan, supra (quoting students and advocates).
114. See James Quinn, "Voices of Students: Reactions to a 'Gay School'," Student Briefing Page, Feb. 20, 2004, http://www.newsday.com/#news/education/sbp/ny-sbp_120403,0,5281926.story?coll=ny-sbp-headlines
115. Thanks to Susan Steinway for this observation.
116. See Michael W. McConnell, "Religious Participation in Public Programs: Religious Freedom at a Crossroads," 59 U. Chi. L. Rev. 115 (1992): Michael W. McConnell, "The Problem of Singling Out Religion," 50 DePaul L. Rev. 1 (2000); Michael W. McConnell, "The Origins and Understanding of the Free Exercise of Religion," 103 Harv. L. Rev. 1410 (1990). This view should be distinguished from the conception that religion should never be treated differently from other personal views or commit-

ments. Christopher Eisgrouber and Lawrence Sager argue that equality would forbid the government from treating religion differently from any other category, even if that difference takes the form of a preference or accommodation. See Christopher L. Eisgrouber and Lawrence G. Sager, "The Vulnerability of Conscience: The Constitutional Basis for Protecting Religious Conduct," 61 Chi. L. Rev. 1245 (1994).

117. Michael McConnell, "Originalism and the Desegregation Decisions," 81 Va. L. Rev. 947 (1995). Michael W. McConnell, "The Originalist Case for *Brown v. Board of Education*," 19 Harv. J. L. & Pub. Pol'y, 457 (1996).

118. See Rosenberger v. University of Virginia, 515 U.S. 819 (1995); see also Transcript of Oral Arguments (No. 94-329), available at 1995 WL 117631.

119. Rosenberger v. University of Virginia, 515 U.S. 819 (1995).

120. Good News Club v. Milford Central School, 533 U.S. 98 (2001).

121. Michael McConnell, "Accommodation of Religion," 1985 Sup. Ct. Rev. 1; Michael McConnell, "Accommodation Under the Religion Clauses," 81 Nw.U.L. Rev. 146 (1986).

122. Widmar v. Vincent, 454 U.A. 263 (1981). See Jeffrey Rosen, "Is Nothing Secular?," *New York Times Magazine,* Jan. 30, 2000, 40, 43.

123. See Douglas Laycock, "Equal Access and Moments of Silence, The Equal Status of Religious Speech by Private Speakers," 81 Nw.U.L. Rev. 1986.

124. Board of Education of Westside Community Schools v. Mergens, 496 U.S. 226 (1990). The Equal Access Act is codified at 20 U.S.C. sections 4071–4074.

125. Lamb's Chapel v. Center Moriches Union Free School District, 508 U.S. 384 (1993).

126. Good News Club v. Milford Central School, 533 U.S. 98 (2001).

127. *Religious Freedom: Hearings before the Senate Judiciary Comm.*, 104th Cong., 1st Sess. (Sept. 29, 1995), 1995 WL 11095849.

128. Id. (referring to Brittany Kay Settle v. Dickson County School Board, 53 F3d. 152 (CA 6 1995)).

129. Zelman v. Simmons-Harris, 536 U.S. 639 (2002).

130. Mitchell v. Helms, 530 U.S. 793 (2000) (plurality opinion) (rejecting Establishment Clause challenge because the program was generally available).

131. 536 U.S., at 676 (Thomas, J., concurring).

132. Id., at 682.

133. 530 U.S. at 835 n. 19.

134. See Christopher P. Cabal, "Religious Schools after *Zelman v. Simmons-Harris,*" 83 B.U. L. Rev. 705 (2003).

135. Arnold H. Loewy, "The Positive Reality and Normative Virtues of a 'Neutral' Establishment Clause," 41 Brandeis L.J. 533, 543 (2002).

136. 536 U.S. 639, 644 (2002).

137. 536 U.S., at 676 (Thomas, J., concurring).

138. Id.

139. Frank J. Macchiarola, "Why the Decision in *Zelman* Makes So Much Sense," 59 N.Y.U. Ann. Surv. Am. Law. 459 (2003). See also Mark Tushnet, "Vouchers after *Zelman,*" 2002 Sup. Ct. Rev. 1 (2002).

140. See Ira C. Lupu and Robert Tuttle, "Sites of Redemption: A Wide-Angle Look at Government Vouchers and Sectarian Service Providers," 18 J. L. & Politics 539 (2002). I have in the past worried that vouchers will undermine the vision of the "common school" where children of different backgrounds learn together, a vision predating *Brown* but invigorated by it. See, e.g., Martha Minow, "Contemporary Challenges Facing the First Amendment's Religion Clauses," 43 N.Y.L. Sch. L. Rev. 101, 124 (1999).

141. See Rosen, supra; see Minow, "On Being a Religious Professional: The Religious Turn in Professional Ethics," 150 U. Penn. L. Rev. 661 (2001).

142. Id.

143. See Martha Minow, *Partners, Not Rivals: Privatization and the Public Good* (Boston: Beacon Press 2002), 89–93, 116–118.

144. See Anthony S. Bryk et al., *Catholic Schools and the Common Good* (1993).

145. Elaine Sciolinio, "Ban Religious Attire in School, French Panel Says," *New York Times*, Dec. 12, 2003, A1 col. 2.

146. In 2002–3, I advised Harvard Law School students in their efforts to assist legal arguments before the European Court of Justice on behalf of Romá students and using a litigation strategy inspired by the NAACP efforts. See also Bill Taylor, "50 Years after *Brown v. Board of Education*," Romá Rights website, http://www.errc.org/rr nr3-4_2002/noteb6.shtml

147. Brown v. Board of Education, 347 U.S. 483, 493 (1954).

148. Id., at 495.

149. Molly McUsic, "The Future of *Brown v. Board of Education:* Economic Integration of the Public Schools," 117 Harv. L. Rev 1334, 2004.

150. Hannah Arendt, "Reflections on Little Rock," 6 Dissent 45 (1958).

151. Id.

152. See Elizabeth Young-Bruehl, *Hannah Arendt: For Love of the World* (New Haven: Yale University Press 1982), 316.

153. Arendt, supra, at 47–48. For a thoughtful use of this insight, see James. S. Liebman, "Desegregating Politics: 'All-Out' School Desegregation Explained," 90 Columbia L. Rev. 1463, n. 507 (1990).

PART ONE
INTRODUCTION
Desegregation Policy and the Law

Today, education is perhaps the most important function of state and local governments. . . . It is the very foundation of good citizenship. Today it is a principal instrument in awakening the child to cultural values, in preparing him for later professional training, and in helping him adjust normally to his environment. In these days it is doubtful that any child may reasonably be expected to succeed in life if he is denied the opportunity of an education. Such an opportunity, where the state has undertaken to provide it, is a right which must be made available for all on equal terms.[1]

Fifty years after the above words were written into U.S. Supreme Court history, the right to an equal education for all children — regardless of cultural heritage — continues to have immeasurable meaning for the future of American democracy. Although *Brown v. Board of Education* challenged educational inequities for Black children in America's public schools, this landmark decision was a springboard for many other legal and policy decisions involving educational equity for racial and ethnic minority groups throughout the country. This watershed moment in America's history sparked educational debate around several issues involving desegregation and integration: busing, bilingual education, rights to literacy, access to higher education, among others. Indeed, these "legacy [of *Brown*] issues" expand the boundaries of a Black and White educational debate. They affect immigrant youth, several Asian groups, Latinos, and Native Americans in this country. As these essays show, what has also evolved is the demographic character of the beneficiaries of desegregation, as defined by the Supreme Court in 1954.

Although *Brown* launched a movement for desegregation and integration of Black and White students in four southern school districts, nonsouthern cities began to challenge segregation and other equity related issues before the early 1970s. By 1971, in the western city of San Francisco, desegregation policies and laws of that region involved the (de)segregation of more than one racial minority. Forty-nine years after *Brown*, in 2003, U.S. higher education inherited another equity battle from the *Brown* decision that involved the use of race as a consideration for admissions, among other factors, to selective colleges and universities. A difference between these two similar circumstances is the evolving character of the groups involved as beneficiaries of race-conscious policies. While Asian groups were considered a "have-not" group in the desegregation battles of the 1970s, in 2004 these students were not considered an underrepresented group in higher education and therefore are not direct beneficiaries of affirmative action.[2] Despite the changing definition of underrepresented groups, what remains consistent is the underrepresentation of Black Americans, Latinos, Native Americans, and, as the result of immigration, some Asian groups in high-quality educational settings. As the essays in this section illustrate, access to a quality education as the result of race, ethnicity, and/or language continues to be a contentious legal and policy issue in all educational sectors.

This section provides a chronological overview of significant court cases that evolved from the equity philosophy of the *Brown* decision, which targeted educational equity issues for both Black and non-Black minority groups. These articles span the educational and employment sector and reflect the influence of the educational arguments of the *Brown* decision, which, as Herbert Teitelbaum and Richard Hiller, and Guadalupe San Miguel Jr. and Richard Valencia demonstrate, were also influenced by lower court decisions and by collaborations from other parts of the country. In the first article, David Kirp offers a detailed political portrait of San Francisco's desegregation battles surrounding the *Johnson v. San Francisco Unified School District decision, between school board officials and various minority groups from the immediate post-Brown* era to the early busing days of the 1970s.[3] Kirp provides a detailed description of a multiracial city's failed political resolution to enforce new desegregation demands. This account captures a school board's attempt to address the growing and specific demands from various racial and ethnic communities under a superintendent who promoted a color-blind student assignment policy. This description is especially informative because it also captures the reviews of policy research and language of that time. For example, Kirp cites newly released research of his era by authors such as James Coleman and refers to various minorities as "third-world" groups, a term no longer used in today's policy forums. This article is critical to understanding the evolution of the additional beneficiaries of desegregation and integration as it focuses on the role of Asian American groups who, along with Mexican Americans, were instrumental in spurring the next stage of the desegregation movement — bilingual education.

Representing another important legacy of *Brown,* the U.S. Supreme Court upheld the right to an education designed to meet the needs of non-English-speaking students in the 1974 *Lau v. Nichols* decision.[4] Three years after this decision, Teitelbaum and Hiller offer an even more complex angle on the desegregation battles of the 1970s, which involve the increasingly prominent voices of non-Black minority groups. The authors credit *Brown* for creating the conditions that allowed passage of the bilingual education ruling and highlight the fact that Mexican Americans were not considered a nationally segregated minority until the 1973 *Keyes v. School District No. 1* decision, another significant Supreme Court desegregation ruling.[5] Teitelbaum and Hiller address concerns noted by Kirp regarding the split between the assimilationist ideals of desegregation activists and the perceived "separatist" demands of groups that call for bilingual and bicultural programming as a factor necessary to achieve educational equity. The authors conclude that the bilingual education litigation, which began before *Lau* in states such as Texas, should not be considered at odds with desegregation cases, since "proponents of bilingual education are natural allies" and the "minority groups who now support bilingual education were themselves victims of segregation."

While the early bilingual education movement provided a fertile political foundation for civil rights activism among Mexican Americans in the late 1960s and beyond, the educational plight of this group in the Southwest has been a longstanding reality for over 150 years.[6] In their essay, Guadalupe San Miguel Jr. and Richard R. Valencia cover the four major eras of Mexican American schooling in the Southwest, from the origins of schooling for Mexican children in the new "American" Southwest to the contemporary anti-affirmative action era of the mid-1990s, defined by the federal-court imposed *Hopwood* decision in 1996.[7] This vast historical portrait of what is now the largest minority group in the United States reviews court litigation and the educational policies of *Brown, Keyes, Lau, Bakke,*[8] and *Hopwood,* the latter of which has recently been struck down with the Supreme Court decision on affirmative action in *Grutter v. Bollinger.*[9] The authors conclude that the educational condition of Mexican Americans and other Latinos is worsening as their populations continue to grow at significantly more dramatic rates than other racial and ethnic groups.

Finally, in a legal analysis of three major U.S. Supreme Court decisions that utilized the concept of literacy in obtaining educational equity, Catherine Prendergast challenges the victorious outcomes of the *Brown* decision by framing literacy as a form of White property and privilege that racializes educational opportunity as the opportunity to be educated among Whites. She documents the political climates in which each of the three landmark decisions occurred: the 1950s cold war era of the *Brown* decision and the late 1970s era of the *Washington*[10] and *Bakke* decisions, a time that witnessed increased opposition to busing and an erosion of civil rights measures and enforcement at various levels of government. Prendergast also provides a detailed legal historical account of how the Harvard admissions plan became the national model for a public medical school as a result of the *Bakke* decision. Ironically, Prendergast concludes that these three court decisions have stalled rather than stimulated the civil rights movement by "perpetuating the economy of literacy as White property."

Taken as a whole, these essays invite readers on a critical exploration of policy decisions that were forged out of the legacy of *Brown*. The decisions reflected in these articles show how the educational fortunes of groups both within and beyond a Black-and-White paradigm have been shaped since *Brown*. With this series of policy and legal examinations, we encourage readers to consider to what extent educational equity for all is still an unmet goal for both "minority" and White students in this country.

Notes

1. Brown v. Board of Education of Topeka, 347 U.S. 483, at 493 (1954).
2. Orfield and Lee also find that by 2003 Asian students are the most integrated ethnic group in public schools. See Orfield, G., and Lee, C., Brown *at 50: King's Dream or* Plessy's *Nightmare?* (Cambridge, MA: The Civil Rights Project at Harvard University, 2004).
3. 399 F. Supp. 1315 (N.D. Cal. 1971), *vacated and remanded*, 500 F.2d 349 (9th Cir. 1974).
4. Lau v. Nichols, 414 U.S. 563 (1974).
5. Keyes v. School District No. 1, Denver, Colorado, 413 U.S. 189 (1973).
6. San Miguel, G., Jr., *Contested Policy: The Rise and Fall of Federal Bilingual Education in the United States, 1960–2001* (Denton: University of North Texas Press, 2004).
7. Hopwood v. Texas, 78 F. 3d 932 (5th Cir. 1996).
8. Regents of the University of California v. Bakke, 438 U.S. 265 (1978).
9. Grutter v. Bollinger, 539 U.S. 306 (2003).
10. Washington v. Davis, 426 U.S. 229 (1976).

Race, Politics, and the Courts:
School Desegregation in San Francisco

DAVID L. KIRP

School desegregation is today the most fervently debated of educational-policy issues. While that has been intermittently true for the past quarter-century, the focus of the desegregation discussion has shifted. Until recently there was broad consensus, at least within what might be called the enlightened community, that racial justice could be secured only through desegregation and that the courts were the one institution fit (or at least willing) to attempt that task. But as the effects of desegregation began to be felt in the North and West, what was previously taken as a given has now become a source of conflict.

At the center of this conflict is the widespread, judicially required use of busing to achieve desegregation. Sociologist James Coleman has cast the argument against busing in policy terms, arguing that busing has worked new mischiefs by assertedly hastening the departure of White families from center cities and consequently exacerbating divisions between city and suburb; in so doing, Coleman has lent his considerable reputation to what was earlier derided as a "know nothing" viewpoint.[1] By drafting new federal legislation which would limit the scope of permissible busing and by requesting that the Justice Department seek judicial reconsideration of the Supreme Court's standards for busing, President Ford has sought to shape the argument in legal form in order to test the judiciary's commitment to this remedy.[2] On the other side of the argument are civil-rights advocates who decry these new assaults as a reemergence of racism. They view busing as the only plausible means of bringing White and Black[3] children together and hence securing racial justice in the public schools.[4]

What is most troubling about the current debate is that it is cast wholly in global terms and for that reason represents nothing less than a war among social-policy paradigms. In this context the idiosyncrasies of particular settings go ignored, for these cannot readily be accommodated by any particular paradigm or policy recommendation. A viewpoint — a sense of policy rightness concerning desegregation — is both essential and inevitable; desegregation does not breed many agnostics. But as long as policy is perceived

Harvard Educational Review   Vol. 46 No. 4 November 1976, 572–611

to be exclusively derivable from any single grand scheme, sensible decisions may not be readily forthcoming. Satisfactory resolutions of the dilemma of desegregation may instead turn on sensitive, incremental adjustments to the demands of particular settings. This case study, which uses San Francisco's experience as a lens to focus on broader national concerns, suggests such a particularistic perspective.[5]

The San Francisco Case

The July, 1971, federal-district-court order in *Johnson v. San Francisco Unified School District*,[6] the first court-ordered desegregation of a large non-southern city, climaxed one decade-long political struggle and triggered another which remains unresolved. The pre-decision struggle centered on the meaning of racial equality in the schools. Diverse groups, each with its own ideological stance and power base, jockeyed for dominance in the political process. Recourse to the court signaled the failure of this process and decisively altered the dimensions of the issue: with *Johnson*, desegregation in San Francisco became a constitutional as well as a political problem.

The *Johnson* decision imposed a legally authoritative definition of racial equality — one stressing racial mixing, or desegregation — upon a community unable to resolve the question politically. Although the decree was appealed and its wisdom is still questioned, San Francisco has come generally to accept the court's view of equality. In this sense, the court's role was decisive.

The post-decision phase has involved giving meaning and content to the *Johnson* order through the actions of school board members, administrators, and teachers. These actions, undertaken largely outside the purview of the court, have been less than successful. While San Francisco's schools are substantially less segregated today than in 1971, some essentially one-race schools do remain and others are imbalanced. Of greater moment, the school district has made few efforts to go beyond racial mixing to achieve an integrated environment; racial heterogeneity is seen as a legal requirement, not as a potential educational resource. This narrow reading of *Johnson* — one consistent with the formal mandate but not the implicit integrationist aspirations of the case — has been damagingly consequential.

This study examines judicial decision making in the context of evolving constitutional doctrine and shifting political perceptions.[7] While it focuses chiefly on the success of the court in responding within the constraints of its role to the complexity of the school-desegregation issue, that focus is intelligible only in terms of what preceded and what has followed the decision. The critical questions may be simply put. Why did the pluralist political process, which came tantalizingly close to resolving the desegregation dilemmas, ultimately prove unfit for the task? Why has that process failed to fulfill the aspirations of *Johnson*? Could the court have intervened to bring aspiration and reality closer together?

The Symbolic Politics of Desegregation

The National Political Context

Although in the North, as earlier in the South, school desegregation has largely resulted from judicial decree, civil-rights supporters worked throughout the 1960s for a political resolution of the issue.[8] They attempted to convince school boards and superintendents that there existed a problem — the concentration of minority students in particular schools — that could be addressed through voluntary action. In response to this plea, a few cities, among them Providence, Evanston, and Berkeley, restructured school boundaries in order to desegregate. Others permitted minority students to attend predominately White schools outside their own neighborhoods.

Generally, however, the road to political resolution became a dead end. The meaning of racial justice evolved rapidly, and with that evolution the potential for irresolvable conflict grew. Initially, a symbolic recognition of the problem, coupled with modest policy change, sufficed. In rapid sequence, civil-rights advocates sought to assure first that all minority students have the opportunity to attend a desegregated school and then that all schools be desegregated.[9] Many Black leaders came to criticize anything less than racial balance as mere tokenism. The new desegregation demands put school boards in a quandary. The civil-rights pressure was appreciated, but school boards felt politically disabled from extending their modest efforts to desegregate. To press on in the face of growing resistance from Whites who opposed full-scale desegregation and busing seemed to mean political suicide, and school board members preferred moderation to martyrdom. The result, in San Francisco and elsewhere, was an effort by civil-rights groups to break this impasse by seeking vindication in the courts for a position that had proved politically unfeasible.

The San Francisco Setting: The New Minorities

San Francisco prides itself, and not without some justification, on being better than most other American cities. It perceives itself as a *rara avis,* a politically progressive and tolerant community.[10] This image conceals recent, politically consequential demographic changes. As former residents have moved to the suburbs while continuing to use the city as a workplace, the city's population has declined from 775,357 in 1950 to 679,200 in 1974.[11] Its racial and ethnic composition has changed notably: the city, 88 percent White (excluding Spanish-surnamed persons) in 1950, was approximately 63 percent White in 1974. Between 1965 (the first year for which school racial data are available) and 1975, the percentage of White students declined from 46.4 to 24.5.

Blacks currently constitute the largest single minority group, almost 15 percent of the population. Drawn to San Francisco by the promise of wartime employment in the 1940s, they found housing in Hunter's Point, the isolated southeastern corner of the city, and many have remained clustered there. Until recently, Asians, rather than Blacks, were the city's have-not group. The traditional kinship ties of the Chinese and Japanese and the out-right prejudice of San Franciscans encouraged both groups to withdraw into their own enclaves.[12] Since wartime internment, the Japanese community — about 2 percent of the population — has remained stable in size. Other Third World groups — the Chinese, Filipino, and Samoan populations — grew rapidly in number following the liberalization of immigration laws in 1965: in 1974, about 9 percent of the population was of Chinese origin; about 4 percent was Filipino. In addition, some 11 percent of the city was of Hispanic descent, primarily Mexican and Central American, and concen-trated in the center-city Mission District.

During the mid-1960s, these ethnic groups began to demand from city government generally, and the public schools particularly, better jobs, better schools, and — perhaps most important — the political recognition of their worth. The school-desegregation issue was one important focus of this new politics.

The Stirrings of the San Francisco Civil-Rights Movement: 1962–1967

From 1922 to 1972, the San Francisco Board of Education consisted of seven persons named by the mayor and ratified pro forma by the voters for four-year terms. In effect, the board was appointed, an elite group whose mem-bers saw their obligation as assuring that San Francisco maintained a reputa-tion for public school excellence.[13]

The maxims of public administration have it that a board of education sets policy while school administrators carry out that policy. Because the line be-tween the two functions is neither clear nor invariably respected, school su-perintendents have sought to prevent board "meddling" in their affairs. Har-old Spears, superintendent from 1955 to 1967, typified the philosophy that school governance lies with professionals and not with politicians or lay-people. His attitude on race and schooling reflected the classic liberal tradi-tion of racial neutrality: institutional decisions should turn on individual at-tributes, not on the irrelevancies of racial or other group characteristics. He saw the longstanding neighborhood-school policy as a splendid exemplifica-tion of that tradition. "We have all races in our schools," observed Spears. "Everyone living in a certain area, regardless of race, goes to the school in that area. . . ."[14] In 1960, Spears asserted to the United States Civil Rights Commission that, in San Francisco, racial discrimination was not a problem; the district was scrupulously color-blind in its student-assignment and per-sonnel policies.[15]

These avowals implied a denial that problems of racial injustice even ex-isted in the schools; hence, they were unacceptable to the local chapter of the Congress of Racial Equality (CORE) and to the Council for Civic Unity, an umbrella organization representing several civil-rights groups.[16] In January, 1962, leaders of the two groups urged the board to recognize that the schools were de facto segregated, to declare that segregated schools (by which they mean predominantly Black schools) were educationally undesirable, and to prepare a program for eliminating segregation. No specific alternative plans were offered; what was really being sought at this time was an expression of official awareness and concern, a willingness to acknowledge the reality of the problem.

Reacting with political prudence, the board asked the superintendent to review the matter and report back. Spears's mid-June report, entitled "The Proper Recognition of a Pupil's Racial Background," was not similarly prudent.[17] It met the de facto segregation accusation head-on and flatly rejected it; not surprisingly, it became a focus of controversy. Spears insisted that providing adequate schooling for Black children was a "highly complicated educational matter" and hence to be left to professional educators. The problem, however, stemmed not from the schools but from "disproportionate housing, indifferent parents, limited job opportunities for youth, and unresponsive pupils." Blunt words, indeed, and Spears's rejection of the taking of a racial census was even more blunt:

> We are now faced with the movement to emphasize differences in the color and races of pupils. . . . If we are preparing to ship these children to various schools, in predetermined racial allotments, then such brands would serve the purpose they have been put to in handling livestock. But until somebody comes up with an educationally sound plan for such integration, then this racial accounting serves nothing but the dangers of putting it to ill use.

The upshot of Spears's position was to uphold the status quo: "I have no educationally sound program to suggest to the Board to eliminate the schools in which children are predominantly of one race."

The superintendent's statement turned a debate over the meaning of equal educational opportunity into a battle between the school board and superintendent on the one side and the civil rights movement on the other. In September, 1962, at the most stormy meeting in the history of San Francisco's public schools, fourteen hundred citizens appeared, variously to denounce and defend Spears's position. Fifty-two speakers addressed the marathon session.[18] The civil rights groups demanded, in the words of National Association for the Advancement of Colored People (NAACP) spokesman Terry Francois, that the "racial composition of the schools become a matter of concern to the board and its administrators." They urged the board to act voluntarily, not in response to a court order. Those criticizing the civil-rights organizations' position were the established minorities — Italian, Irish, German, French — fearful of the demise of neighborhood schools and, indeed, of their own neighborhoods. Other minority groups — the Chinese, Japanese, Filipino, and Spanish-surnamed — went virtually unheard at the board meeting: at this time, desegregation was perceived solely as a Black-White problem.

Faced with a rapidly escalating issue, the board appointed an ad hoc committee of its own members to review the question. The strategy did not satisfy the civil-rights organization. CORE staged a sit-in following the meeting and threatened more protests; the NAACP filed suit against the school district, charging that San Francisco had discriminated against Black students through pupil-assignment and transfer policies, and seeking district-wide relief.[19] The board of education took the lawsuit seriously and hired former school-board commissioner and local attorney Joseph Alioto as counsel, paying him a handsome $10,000 retainer. The civil rights groups saw both the sit-in and the suit as efforts to step up political pressure. What they really hoped for was not a legal confrontation but rather a statement committing the district to work toward desegregation and the appointment of an administrator to handle individual grievances concerning discrimination.

The board's ad hoc committee provided such a resolution. Its April, 1963, report gently rebuked the superintendent.[20] It admitted that segregation, although not deliberately practiced by the school district, persisted nonetheless and recommended that promoting desegregation be one criterion for drawing attendance-zone boundaries. That declaration, the appointment of a Black community-relations officer, and the reassignment of several hundred minority students to predominately White schools could not "cure" the problem of racial segregation nor were they intended to. But they provided at least momentary satisfaction. The NAACP allowed the desegregation litigation to lapse, praising the board's endorsement of a racial criterion as a "step forward."[21] The superintendent urged unity. The chairman of the Committee for Neighborhood Schools was soon to propose limited desegregation "experiments."[22] A process of mutual accommodation seemed to be working, as demonstrations and lawsuits became new tactics in the traditional political pattern of negotiation and compromise.

The resolution would be short-lived. One year after the ad hoc committee report, the board had undertaken no desegregation policy initiatives. Civil-rights organizations regrouped into the Coordinating Council for Integrated Schools; from the roster of member groups, it appeared that everyone supported desegregation. The council demanded a racial census of the school population in order to make plain the extent of segregation. Through picketing and persuasion, its demand prevailed.

The census, released in 1965, proved anticlimactic: while it revealed the existence of some predominantly one-race schools in San Francisco, it also showed considerable desegregation.[23] There was substantially less segregation than in most other large school districts. The eight high schools had Black enrollments ranging from 8 to 34 percent, and only two of the fifteen junior high schools were more than half Black. Racial disproportion was greatest in the ninety-five elementary schools. Four schools were more than 90 percent White; seven were more than 90 percent Black.[24]

Although the census prompted no further desegregation efforts, an important symbolic shift was occurring: racial isolation in San Francisco's schools was increasingly recognized as a problem worth studying. During the last years of the Spears era, studies were the order of the day. Beginning in 1966, the NAACP Education Committee undertook the thankless task of gathering data on school expenditures in an effort to demonstrate that low expenditures in predominantly Black schools caused the low achievement-test scores of students in those schools. These data were intended to embarrass the board of education into action. The board also turned to research, contracting with the Stanford Research Institute (SRI) to conduct a preliminary study upon which a master plan for desegregation could be based. By commissioning a study, the board hoped both to buy time and to meet a desperate need for wisdom offered from the vantagepoint of detachment. At least the first objective was achieved: SRI's report was not made public until mid-1967, the waning days of Spears's administration, and the board postponed its response until Spears's successor could study and react to the document.[25]

Too Little, Too Late: 1967–1970

In July, 1967, Robert Jenkins was appointed as the new superintendent. Jenkins had survived ten years in Pasadena, California, a community which had undergone limited school desegregation. He was chosen for his talents both at innovating and at involving citizens' groups in his administration. To an increasingly desegregation-minded board, Jenkins appeared capable of leading San Francisco into the new era.

The board gave Superintendent Jenkins six months to study and respond to the SRI report, *Improving Racial Balance in the Public Schools*, before making its own recommendations. The SRI study was technically commendable and offered a dozen alternative ways for San Francisco to desegregate.[26] Yet it showed little awareness either of the diversity of San Francisco's ethnic groups and neighborhoods or of pedagogical and administrative issues involved in desegregation.

Whereas SRI's study focused specifically on desegregation, Jenkins's mid-December response emphasized "educational equality/quality," an ambiguous phrase that was to shape San Francisco's planning efforts for the next three years. The shift was more than semantic. SRI's primary concern lay with such mundane matters as restructuring school-attendance patterns and devising a transportation system to facilitate city-wide desegregation. Jenkins argued that a commitment to educational quality as well as equality required "ways to achieve a better racial and ethnic balance in the schools, ways that are consistent with the maintenance and extension of high educational standards for all studnets."[27] Desegregation, he asserted, should be coupled with ambitious (and costly) new educational ventures, so attractive that they would make racial mixing something that both White and Black parents would actively want.

Jenkins proposed a number of new educational options — among them, an "educational Park . . . a bold and dramatic approach to the pursuit of excellence for urban areas." The result would link increased desegregation (as to how great the increase would be, Jenkins was silent) with pedagogical innovation. The superintendent asked the board to treat his ideas, together with those of SRI, as suggestions for community reaction, but community forums held in response to this recommendation produced only conflict. For the first time, attention in San Francisco was focused on a key element of the SRI report, the possibility of busing children to promote desegregation. The superintendent sought to defuse the hostile reaction. He appointed a Citizens' Advisory Committee selected to include a cross section of community sentiment. The committee was charged with reviewing the "equality/quality" proposals and the ideas that had surfaced at the community forums and with drafting recommendations.

The committee report, submitted in February, 1969, was not unanimous.[28] The dissenters charged that the committee was "an effrontery to the citizens of San Francisco . . . a tool of Dr. Jenkins . . . to implement his report despite the mandate of the majority of this city as presented at the nine public forums." The majority report embraced desegregation in a markedly limited sense. It focused on the possibility of creating "School Complexes," subdistricts within the city, in two preponderantly middle-class neighborhoods, Richmond and Park South. The two neighborhoods had been carefully chosen for ease of school desegregation. Both were residentially integrated to some degree, and both had stable student populations. Black and White students living in these neighborhoods would have to be bused only short distances. Speedy implementation was urged: "Every additional day of delay will only further reduce what faith remains in the School District's willingness to move ahead."

Before approving this recommendation, the superintendent solicited the views of the parents, teachers, and administrators whose schools were to become part of the new complexes. The response was generally enthusiastic; substantial numbers of parents became intimately involved in the enterprise and put forward a cornucopia of new ideas. That reaction encouraged the board of education — a body more liberal in its views than ever before — to approve implementation of the complexes, beginning in September, 1970. Prospects for the venture seemed remarkably good. There existed substantial support for the complexes, both in the affected neighborhoods and citywide. The planning process had produced a desegregation plan that aspired to do more than mix racial groups.[29] It was tacitly understood that if the two complexes succeeded the model might eventually be adopted throughout the city. Thus, at the beginning of 1970, it seemed that a peaceful revolution was at hand.

The critical unresolved question was financial. The board's approval of the complexes was contingent on $1.2 million in outside funds being raised for the "quality" aspects of the program. Superintendent Jenkins reported in December, 1970, that he had identified "promising [funding] possibilities," but by spring it became clear that his early optimism was unfounded. Jenkins and the board then recommended implementing both complexes in reduced forms: Jenkins suggested scaling down the quality components; the board voted to reduce the number of participating schools. Representatives of the complexes, however, requested that the board reconsider its vote and implement the Richmond Complex while providing some funds to permit the Park South group to continue its planning. At its May 27 meeting, the board acceded to this position.

As so often happens, the unanticipated political crisis proved crucial. Joseph Alioto, mayor since 1967, had declined to involve himself publicly throughout the desegregation process, correctly pointing out that the board of education had exclusive responsibility for school policy.[30] Yet early in 1970, to the surprise and consternation of the civil-rights groups, he chose to become the focal point for political opposition to the complex proposal. Alioto had built his reputation in good part on his capacity to work with the Black community.[31] The mayor's seeming inconsistency on the desegregation issue was partly an act of political calculation. No one had emerged to speak forcefully for the city's ethnic backbone, the Italians, Irish, and Germans who were fearful of efforts to alter the traditional neighborhood-school system; there was political capital to be gained from the issue.

Alioto's position was also consistent with the views he had held since he represented the board in the 1962 NAACP litigation. He favored limited desegregation, including voluntary busing of students. He believed that school-attendance boundaries should be gerrymandered to reduce racial isolation. He had appointed outspoken liberals to the board of education. But at mandatory elementary-school busing, even to the limited extent necessary to desegregate schools within the complexes, he drew the line. In his view, seven- and eight-year-old children should not have to ride a bus in order to affirm a principle.[32]

Alioto's position produced political shock waves. He was promptly joined in his fight by conservative Supervisor John Barbagelata, who proposed a ballot measure to poll voters' attitudes concerning mandatory busing. Although the referendum was advisory in nature, it served further to heat up the controversy. The strongest response came from Charles Belle, president of the local NAACP chapter: "I am sick and tired and ashamed of the segregated school situation in San Francisco. We know White racists want to keep segregated White and Black schools here."[33]

In June, by nearly a three-to-one margin, voters endorsed the proposition that the board of education should not be permitted to bus or reassign elementary-school children to schools outside their neighborhoods without parental consent. The referendum did not sway the school board, which pursued its planning for the complex. Mayor Alioto recognized that he had lost this round of the political battle. He urged those who agreed with his position to file a lawsuit seeking to halt the implementation of the Richmond Complex.

Suit was duly filed in California Superior Court.[34] It was not, however, the most important case to be filed that month. Alioto's statements had persuaded NAACP President Belle that educators' concern for "quality" was irrelevant and that a suit to compel district-wide desegregation could wait no longer. As Belle told Superintendent Jenkins: "I had hoped that we might avoid this, but the mayor has turned desegregation into a political and emotional battleground. We'll get an instant solution in federal court."[35] The advent of *Johnson v. San Francisco School District* signaled the failure of political bargaining and moved the dispute into a new and very different arena. Board President Allan Nichols remarked bitterly that Alioto's "bringing politics and the judiciary into educational decisions will . . . result in damage to the tremendous progress we are making."[36] Decisions concerning desegregation policy would never again be exclusively the board's to make.

Desegregation in the Courts:
Johnson v. San Francisco Unified School District

Johnson was heard at a time when judicial doctrine concerning both the nature of the segregation outlawed in *Brown v. Board of Education*[37] and the scope of appropriate remedy was in a state of flux. Those doctrinal ambiguities shaped the course of the litigation.

In the 1954 *Brown* decision, the Supreme Court unanimously held that public-school segregation, based solely on race and permitted or required by law, denied Black children the equal protection of the laws guaranteed by the Fourteenth Amendment.[38] That decision, although formally binding, was not self-enforcing. Its implementation required the willing cooperation of school districts or, failing that, the continuing imposition of judicial will. The Supreme Court recognized this fact in *Brown II*. Rather than insisting on a uniform remedy, the Court endorsed a "practical flexibility" to meet diverse local situations. While desegregation was to occur with "all deliberate speed,"[39] *Brown II* rested primary responsibility on school authorities and left the task of policing and evaluating their efforts to lower federal courts.

For more than a decade, the expectations of *Brown* were thwarted in implementation. In measurable outcome terms, the frustration was real: in 1964, only 2.14 percent of all Black students in the Deep South attended school with Whites. By the late 1950s, the Supreme Court had become increasingly impatient with the snail's pace of "all deliberate speed." In *Green v. New Kent County School Board*,[40] the Court spoke out, overturning a plan that allowed all students free choice among public schools. During three years of the plan, no White student had chosen to attend the formerly all-Black school, while only 15 percent of the Black students had enrolled in the formerly all-White school. It was this outcome, not the existence of a continuing policy of deliberate discrimination, that offended the Court and led it to redefine the obligation of formerly dual school systems. "The burden on a school board today is to come forward with a plan that promises realistically to work, and promises realistically to work *now . . .* to [yield] a system without a 'White' school and a 'Negro' school, but just schools."[41]

Green marked a major shift in constitutional doctrine from a focus on discriminatory means — devices clearly designed to separate the races — to one on remedies that guaranteed a unitary, nondiscriminatory outcome. But *Green* raised more questions than it answered. Was the Court intimating that racial balance was necessary proof of the "cure"? Did *Green* apply to large, residentially segregated cities? In *Swann v. Charlotte-Mecklenburg Board of Education,*[42] decided while *Johnson* was pending, the Court concluded that district-wide desegregation — using extensive busing, if necessary — was an appropriate remedy in cities with previously dual school systems. Although *Swann* somewhat restricted the discretion of trial judges, whose efforts had often undermined the promise of *Brown,* the Court again refused to impose simple and uniform remedial standards.

Whether *Green* and *Swann* had relevance outside the South also remained uncertain.[43] *Brown* condemned de jure segregation, established through force of law. Because in 1954 no northern state formally mandated or permitted segregated public schools, the *Brown* mandate was initially understood to pertain only to southern and border states.[44] Yet, because neighborhoods were often racially segregated, many northern city schools were segregated in fact.

During the 1960s, civil-rights advocates challenged this pattern in the courts. This challenge assumed two forms. Segregation, it was argued, is detrimental to Black children, whatever its cause: inadvertent, or de facto, segregation works the same harm as de jure segregation. Although lower federal courts generally rejected this argument as beyond the scope of *Brown,*[45] the constitutionality of de facto segregation had not been definitely resolved at the onset of the San Francisco litigation.

The second type of challenge to northern segregation questioned whether the origins of racial isolation in the North and West were as innocent as had been presumed. Inquiries into the drawing of school boundaries, the location of new schools, the assignment of teachers, and the like often revealed school-board decisions apparently intended to preserve predominantly one-race schools. These findings prompted litigants to assert that the presumed legal difference between "racial isolation" and de facto segregation had no factual basis. The insistence upon a national standard extended to remedy as well: if substantial student reassignment was required in southern cities, it was thought equally appropriate in the North.[46]

The expansion of the legal concept of de jure segregation to encompass practices of northern and western cities had already been embraced in several lower-court decisions when the San Francisco case was filed, but the Supreme Court had not yet confronted the issue.[47] For that reason, the *Johnson* case drew upon both strands of the constitutional argument for desegregation. The Supreme Court was not to consider northern school problems until 1973, when, in *Keyes v. School District No. 1, Denver, Colorado*, it held that "intentional" segregation, whether or not imposed by statute, was unconstitutional.[48] By that time, city-wide desegregation in San Francisco had become a fact of life.

The Unprosecuted and Undefended Suit

It was in this ambiguous constitutional context that the San Francisco NAACP filed the *Johnson* suit. A lawsuit, always regarded as a vital tactic in the struggle to improve opportunities, had become the appropriate symbolic response to what was viewed as the White community's attempt to frustrate Black aspirations. More pragmatically, the constitutional meaning of de jure segregation had expanded markedly since the NAACP filed its first complaint in 1962. A favorable court ruling, if not inevitable, could reasonably be expected.

The complaint, filed on June 24, 1970, by Arthur Brunwasser, a young solo practitioner in San Francisco who assumed primary responsibility for the case, made page-one news. It asked for sweeping relief: "a preliminary and permanent injunction ordering the immediate and complete desegregation of the student bodies, faculties, and administrative personnel in the public elementary schools in San Francisco."[49] It also sought a temporary restraining order assuring that the district would proceed with plans for the Richmond Complex; the board's wavering on that issue had left Brunwasser and the NAACP uneasy. The scope of the suit was deliberately limited to the elementary schools. The NAACP leadership believed that desegregation during the early years of schooling, before children's racial attitudes hardened, was crucial. Time constraints also forced the limitation; it was felt that deliberate segregation could be more easily and quickly demonstrated with respect to elementary schools.

The complaint in *Johnson* was consciously patterned after recently concluded litigation in Pontiac, Michigan, which had stretched the meaning of de jure segregation further than any other federal-court decision.[50] To establish that San Francisco was de jure segregated, plaintiffs' case cited school-district data revealing increases in racial segregation between 1964–65 and 1969–70. The decade-long history of discussion and investigation of racial injustice in San Francisco's schools was reiterated in order to show the district's awareness of segregation; plaintiffs claimed that legal culpability should attach to its failure to rectify that segregation. Particular emphasis was placed on ten schools built during the past decade that allegedly had increased segregation. Ironically, among these were several neighborhood schools in largely Black Hunter's Point that the NAACP had earlier insisted upon as the price for its support of a school-bond issue.

Two depositions were critical in proving the district's culpability. William Cobb, the district's human-relations officer, noted that he had advised the superintendent that several contemplated construction projects would increase racial imbalance. Building had proceeded nonetheless because other factors, such as availability of land and accessibility, were treated as controlling. Board member Laurel Glass corroborated Brunwasser's assertions that a neighborhood-school policy actively "discourages the achievement of racial integration" and that little had been done to improve racial balance. Conspicuously absent from plaintiffs' case were some of the characteristic elements of de jure segregation suits, such as detailed accounts of gerrymandering school boundaries in order to maintain racial separation, busing Black children past White schools to attend predominantly Black schools, and assigning Black teachers to Black schools. Such evidence either was not available or had not been located.

The heart of plaintiffs' argument lay in the claim that segregation, whether deliberate or adventitious, was harmful to Black children. Brunwasser relied on the SRI Report, the nationally known Coleman Report, and his one witness, education professor Allen Wilson, as authoritative sources for the proposition.[51] In short, plaintiffs' case combined the two strands of prevalent legal argument: a thinly argued claim of de jure segregation and a strong emphasis on the hurtfulness of segregation.

As it turned out, plaintiffs did not have to do more in order to prevail, for the case was as weakly defended as it was argued. The board of education believed in the rightness of desegregation.[52] Its membership had become markedly liberal since the mid-1960s; a majority was closely associated with the NAACP and viewed the educational complexes as a possible prelude to more far-reaching desegregation efforts. The board had shown its political mettle in defying Mayor Alioto's attempts to wreck the Richmond-Park South plan: after the mayor had urged the board to reconsider its support of the complexes at a jammed board meeting February, 1970, each board member had stood up to reject the request.

As individuals, the board members' attitudes favored city-wide desegregation; as a body, the board lacked the political will to achieve it. This tension was reflected in its decision not to retain experienced outside counsel, as it had in the 1962 litigation, but to rely instead on the city attorney's office. For George Krueger, an inexperienced but competent trial lawyer and deputy city attorney representing the district, the *Johnson* case was a first federal-court appearance. Krueger viewed plaintiffs as legally obliged to demonstrate specific acts of de jure segregation if they were to prevail. The district's case was straightforward. Krueger argued that the district had no duty to correct racial imbalance and that "the best refutation of the de jure charge was the history of voluntary efforts to integrate." He did not seek to prove that the district had *not* acted illegally, believing that to be an impossible and time-devouring task.[53] Thus, plaintiffs and defendants found themselves relying largely on the same record; the difference lay in its interpretation. To plaintiffs, the record revealed a decade of evasion and delay; to defendants, it demonstrated the district's good will in trying to desegregate.

Plaintiffs and defendants were not the only parties or would-be parties to the litigation, and the introduction of other intense and divergent views confirmed that the desegregation issue had retained its political dimensions. A modest attempt by Blacks to use *Johnson* as a vehicle to gain power with which to run their own schools was quickly thwarted by the court. Concerned Parents, a racially integrated, Richmond-based group, sought more vigorously to oppose the NAACP's efforts. The members of the group had filed their own suit in state court, charging that the Richmond complex plan violated federal and state constitutional and statutory rights. When they found themselves upstaged by *Johnson*, a case seeking far broader relief than they were resisting, they were permitted to intervene in that case. While Concerned Parents was not opposed to "natural integration," its essential aims were to stop the Richmond Complex and to halt district efforts to uproot the neighborhood school. Neither issue was of interest to the *Johnson* court. Concerned Parents' attorneys also made a broader argument that existing segregation in San Francisco was not unconstitutional, but they were denied full opportunity to demonstrate it because the court confined their participation at the critical fact-finding state of the inquiry.

The multiplicity of positions advanced in *Johnson* could have proved troubling to a less firm judge. But Judge Stanley A. Weigel, a federal-district-court judge since 1962, was able closely to control the proceedings — all too well, in the judgment of the intervenors and some outside critics.[54]

From the very first day of the proceedings, Weigel had a clear command of both the record and the issues; his questions, particularly those addressed to the defendants, were pointed and sometimes barbed. There was no trial in the case, and little testimony was taken orally at preliminary injunction hearings. The district's own data, the depositions, and the briefs: these were the bases upon which argument proceeded.

Weigel's approach, although expeditious, had serious costs. In his desire to hasten the adjudicative process, the judge quickly cut off arguments he viewed as extraneous. As a consequence, many of plaintiffs' factual allegations concerning the causes of segregation in San Francisco were never tested by the time-honored process of cross-examination. Nor did Judge Weigel ever make clear during oral argument the constitutional standard he was applying. He posed a critical question: "Does not a school board, which for ten years has known of the existence of serious racial imbalance, have a positive duty to do everything it can to act effectively in the interest of eliminating that imbalance?" Insofar as the question suggests that, whatever its cause, segregation is unconstitutional, that position was of questionable validity in 1970.

Throughout the hearings, Judge Weigel hoped for a settlement: "I still very much prefer . . . to have the Board . . . come up with a specific plan for the provision of equal educational opportunity, including meaningful correction of the racial imbalance. . . . " On September 22, 1970, he postponed decision in the case until the Supreme Court decided *Swann v. Charlotte-Mecklenburg Board of Education*,[55] a suit that was expected to define the duties of school authorities and the powers of federal courts concerning desegregation. The September 22 order was also expressly cast as an invitation to the district to plan for eventual desegregation:

> Defendants should prepare themselves to be ready promptly to meet whatever requirements may be delineated by the Supreme Court. . . . . *If, for example, the Board of Education works out details for maximum changes based upon the assumption that the Supreme Court will require them, the Board will then be able to act effectively, in case of need, without causing confusion and with a minimum of unnecessary dislocation.*[56]

In one respect, Weigel's request was wholly reasonable: he was simply asking the district to undertake contingency planning. Yet if Weigel wanted the *Swann* decision in hand before issuing an opinion, did not San Francisco also need that decision to determine what, if anything, it would be obliged to do?

The fact-finding stage of the litigation had been quickly concluded — perhaps too quickly. Conflicting viewpoints had been aired but not fully explored. The merits of the charge that San Francisco had deliberately segregated its schools consequently went unargued, undefended, and to some extent unjudged.

Respite from the Court: September 1970–April 1971

Every year during the past decade has witnessed a "crisis" in American education. For San Francisco, the 1970–1971 school term was worse than most. The district found itself faced with a bewildering assortment of problems, few of them directly linked with desegregation. The year included, among other events, a protracted teachers' strike; a report that sixty-two schools were vulnerable to earthquake damage and would imminently have to be reconstructed or closed; student strikes over asserted administrative recalcitrance and demonstrably wretched conditions; a busing protest in the Richmond Complex; suits filed by the Chinese and Mexican American communities alleging that their children's educational needs had been ignored; a demand that a $500,000 Black Studies program be created in an inner-city high school; approval of a student-drafted "bill of rights"; and the district's first financial "crisis" in recent history — a reported $6.7 million deficit.[57] In that strained atmosphere, every district activity was converted into a maiginal enterprise, struggling within the organization for survival. Small wonder, then, that planning for desegregation was not a high-priority issue.

Administrative leadership was also in turmoil.[58] Superintendent Jenkins resigned suddenly in June 1970, leaving the board little time to search for a successor. Thomas Shaheen, previously superintendent in Rockford, Illinois, although not the board's first choice, appeared strong, articulate, and a man of principle. He convinced board members that he was totally committed to desegregated education and that he saw no need to incorporate "quality" components to make the concept practicable. Shaheen's reputed aggressiveness was perceived as essential in coping with the prevailing, politically charged climate. The superintendent, however, did not live up to his billings.

Shaheen "communicated" endlessly with top administrative staff, teachers, and political groups, bringing to all of them a vaguely messianic message of change. But communicating is not the same thing as administering, and very little of the latter was done under Shaheen. Instructional programs, the heart of Superintendent Spears's concerns, were left to the discretion of site administrators and staff, as the central administration simply ignored the schools' educational mission. With respect to a host of activities — community-based educational ventures in the residentially integrated Oceanside-Merced-Inglewood section of the city and in the predominantly Black Hunter's Point neighborhood; an emerging demand for bilingual education; more mundane problems of building maintenance, class-size reduction, and the like — there existed no consensus concerning the district's obligations and little money for institutional expansion.

In addition to problems caused by his weak administering, Shaheen became personally identified with an effort to demote 125 White administrators in order to increase efficiency and to expand the proportion of non-White administrators. Those scheduled for demotion successfully challenged the action in court as discrimination in reverse.[59] The demotion fiasco further eroded Shaheen's authority with his staff and made it harder to him to convince hostile San Franciscans to embrace city-wide desegregation.

The Richmond complex, San Francisco's attempt to wed "quality" with desegregation, was also afflicted by this failure of leadership. The experiment was beset with struggles for autonomy and for internal control. The complex did demonstrate that desegregation within a relatively homogeneous extended neighborhood could work and permitted teachers to try out new instructional styles and materials. Neither was a trivial achievement. But the complex did not meet the expectations of its creators. Like numerous other district programs, it could be described as an organizational prodigy, deserving of support. The district's inability to establish priorities made special attention to this program impossible.

In this tumultuous environment, the district considered how to respond to Judge Weigel's September order.[60] No action was taken until January, 1971, when Superintendent Shaheen appointed three committees to consider city-wide desegregation. The Citizens' Advisory Committee, originally intended to review the efforts of two committees comprised of district personnel, wound up doing most of the work. Neither the board nor the top-echelon bureaucrats wanted anything to do with the issue.

Each of the committees hoped for a rational, computer-aided method of sorting students on the bases of race, proximity, socioeconomic background, and academic achievement. Yet, as they soon learned, the district's antique record-keeping system rendered that expectation infeasible; it lacked even reliable data concerning students' residency (a sizeable number falsified their addresses) and school-building capacity.[61] The hoped-for creative programming turned into a less exciting and less successful effort to dig out basic information. On April 21, the citizens' committee reported that planning could not begin until early summer. In a memorandum to the superintendent, several senior administrators asserted that desegregation could not be accomplished before September, 1972, unless San Francisco chose to disregard all "we have learned about efforts toward orderly desegregation."[62] But the hope of "orderly desegregation" was shortly to be dashed by the district court.

The Search for a Constitutionally Acceptable Remedy

On April 20, 1971, the Supreme Court announced its long-awaited decision in the *Swann* case.[63] Rather than adopting nationwide constitutional standards, *Swann* addressed itself exclusively to school systems that prior to the 1954 *Brown* decision had been segregated by law. The Supreme Court did, however, set down guidelines concerning what was required "to eliminate from the public schools all vestiges of state-imposed segregation,"[64] and Judge Weigel could rely upon those, at least by analogy, in developing a cure for San Francisco's problem. While not insisting on precise racial balance, *Swann* did permit judges to use data concerning imbalance "as a starting point in the process of shaping a remedy."[65] Even more significantly, the district-wide busing scheme that it approved for Charlotte, North Carolina, was truly massive.

One week after the *Swann* opinion was handed down, Weigel ordered the desegregation of San Francisco's elementary schools in September, 1971. The April 28 order confined its discussion of the legal and factual issues to a footnote in which Weigel accepted all arguments advanced by plaintiffs, even those for which evidence was at best scanty or contradictory. Both inaction and action were the bases upon which the court found de jure segregation.[66] For example, the opinion embraced the conclusion that school-construction policies had "perpetuated and exacerbated" racial imbalance, ignoring the many racially neutral factors that led to those construction decisions; it also found discrimination in the drawing of unspecified attendance zones, failing to assess the legitimacy of the district's concern for a neighborhood-based school system.

Supplementary findings of fact, issued in June,[67] were somewhat more constitutionally persuasive: the court noted, for example, the discrimination implicit in the district's disproportionate assignment of minority teachers to identifiably Black schools.[68] But these findings, like the April opinion, treated plaintiffs' claims generously, and the district's rejoinders went undiscussed. Taken as a whole, the findings suggest that the court embraced an extremely expansive definition of unlawful desegregation, one which almost obliterated the distinction between de jure and de facto. Weigel said as much a week after his April 28 order was issued: "regardless of whether this is technically de jure or de facto, it is a situation of which no city should be proud. . . ." — a morally plausible proposition of questionable constitutional relevance. These findings of fact and conclusions of law were the bases upon which the next stage of the litigation, devising a remedy consistent with *Swann*, was to proceed.

Resolving the dispute was to be far more difficult than Judge Weigel intimated. For one thing, the Concerned Parents group reappeared, fortified by new counsel and eager to reopen the issue of legal wrong. For another, intervenors representing the Chinese community suddenly emerged to object to its inclusion in any desegregation plan. Finally, members of the board of education could not accept the conclusion that they or their predecessors had acted illegally. These parties moved to upset the orderly sequence of planning that Weigel anticipated.

The court's order posed a difficult dilemma for the board. The segregation of San Francisco's elementary schools was not, in the abstract, an unpleasant prospect, but several factors militated against compliance. The six-week planning period the judge had allowed seemed impossibly short to the board. Some members were unconvinced by the court's conclusion that San Francisco had engaged in de jure segregation; others had changed their views concerning the wisdom of city-wide desegregation. The board was also faced with the possibility of political extinction, and that may have influenced its judgment. A proposition inspired by anti-desegregation sentiment and calling for the creation of a popularly elected board to replace the appointed body was to appear on the November, 1971, ballot, and a showing of resistance to the court order may well have been thought politically prudent. The board moved to stay Weigel's April 28 order, a motion denied on May 6. Two weeks later, by a 4–3 vote, the board committed itself to appealing the decision.

Concerned Parents faced no such dilemmas. The intervenors had changed their lawyers: three talented attorneys, Willis and Vivian Hannawalt and Quentin Kopp, had taken on the case. On April 28, intervenors moved to reopen *Johnson* in order to elicit new evidence. The intervenors' lawyers eloquently — and sometimes wittily — expressed their opposition to the court's conclusion that San Francisco had acted improperly with respect to race. When the intervenors argued that the district was not legally to blame for its segregated schools since it had not caused the segregation, their words echoed those of Superintendent Spears ten years earlier:

> There is nothing whatsoever in either *Brown* or *Swann* which requires that justice be blind to the effects of the institutional racism implicit in the notions that children are fungible commodities and that Negro children must be in the company of White children before they may improve their achievement.[69]

The intervenors and the district both sought a stay of Weigel's September, 1971, desegregation deadline, pending the outcome of an appeal. On June 4, after a brief hearing, Weigel denied the motion, an action consistent with a decade of federal-district-court responses to similar motions. The case would go forward on schedule.

Desegregation versus integration. The task of courts had generally been viewed as limited to undoing the constitutional wrong of segregation; responsibility for bringing about integration has rested with school districts. In devising a remedy consistent with *Swann*, Weigel enlisted the district and, to its surprise, the NAACP. Each was ordered to prepare, within six weeks, a plan assuring that "the ratio of Black children to White children will be . . . substantially the same in each school."[70]

The two terms "desegregation" and "integration" are often used interchangeably, but it is useful to distinguish between them. Desegregation focuses exclusively on the reassignment of students to assure a racial mix. By contrast, integration takes a changed racial composition as the starting point for re-thinking the premises of the educational system. Desegregation deliberately brings together diverse cultures and diverse views of the mission of schooling. To make something of that new environment, to integrate the newly desegregated school, requires attention to, among other things, the attitude of teachers and students, devising situations in which people of different racial and ethnic groups confront each other as status equals, and the substance of the educational offering. Integration also demands an administrative structure that can responsibly accommodate what may well be convulsive change while adhering to some coherent sense of educational purpose. At least partly because of time pressures, both the district and the NAACP focused on busing students to achieve a greater racial mix; they produced desegregation, not integration, plans.

The district's plan was put together by the Citizens' Advisory Committee, almost by default: the board lacked the inclination and the staff lacked the time for the task.[71] The committee's schedule left little time for educational dreaming. The committee did consider such educational issues as the fit between desegregation and bilingual education, the need for greater choice among educational alternatives, and the involvement of parents in school policy making, but the primary focus was on producing a desegregation plan. The committee quickly dismissed the possibility of incorporating minor boundary adjustments, preservation of already desegregated schools, and voluntary busing arrangements into its scheme. While such an ad hoc approach might well have generated a solution tailored to San Francisco's needs, it was rejected both because it seemed unlikely to satisfy the court's ambiguous mandate and because the detailed evidence needed to evaluate such schemes was not at hand. In lieu of particularistic analysis, the committee relied on the formula of the California state guidelines for racial balance: the proportion of a given ethnic group in a racially balanced school must be no more than 15 percentage points above or below that group's proportion of the school-age population.[72] Since, for example, 28.7 percent of San Francisco's elementary-school children were Black, a school enrolling between 13.7 percent and 43.7 percent Black children would be racially balance with respect to Blacks. While this formula was admittedly arbitrary, it had already obtained official blessing, and any other formula could be — and was — attacked as equally arbitrary.

Within this broad framework, debate focused on two different approaches, "zone" and "city-wide." The zone approach, building upon the experience of the complexes, would divide the city into extended neighborhoods; busing distances would be minimized because the "neighborhoods" would be contiguous. The zone approach tried to preserve "political integrity," by which was meant something akin to neighborhood schools, and to minimize White unhappiness and any consequent flight to the suburbs. Under a zone concept, the California guidelines represented the maximum of politically tolerable desegregation. By contrast, the city-wide approach viewed the state guidelines as fixing the minimum permissible desegregation. Its advocates were less concerned with White acceptance of the plan or the preservation of neighborhoods than with the greatest possible socioeconomic and racial desegregation.

The Citizens' Advisory Committee, beset with continuing data problems, converted these broad notions into plans that could be put into effect the coming year. On June 1 they submitted the plans to the board of education. The committee recommended Horseshoe, a plan that divided the district into seven zones, left the Richmond Complex and the prospective Park South Complex largely intact, and barely satisfied the California 15-percent guidelines. Tri-Star, the leading "city-wide" alternative, was ranked fourth among seven plans. Proposals concerning nondesegregation questions were consigned to appendices in the committee report. The board of education quickly approved Horseshoe and submitted it to the court. A decade of public discussion and a court order had culminated in a desegregation plan hastily created by a small group of citizens and staff workers far from public purview. The board and Superintendent Shaheen, faced with other dilemmas, could not devote time to the planning process.

The NAACP was even less prepared than the district to undertake desegregation planning.[73] The outside consultants the NAACP retained were able to spend only forty-eight hours in San Francisco. Their Freedom Plan, completed in three weeks, resembled the citizens' committee's "city-wide" Tri-Star plan in many ways. It created six attendance areas, several of which were not contiguous. One of its zones required busing students between the northeast and southwest corners of the city, a substantial distance even given the compactness of San Francisco. Boundaries were drawn to provide for not only racial balance but also socioeconomic and achievement mixtures, insofar as the skimpy data available permitted such calculations. With respect to education-specific issues, the hastily drawn Freedom Plan was virtually silent. There just had not been time for serious consideration of anything other than student placement.

Both the NAACP's Freedom Plan and the district's Horseshoe Plan were submitted to the court on June 10, meeting the court's deadline and drawing the judge's praise. Weigel sought the help of all counsel in choosing the plan "which will meet the requirement of the law with minimum inconvenience to . . . the children and parents affected." Yet new intervenors were to upset the enterprise.

In May, 1971, the Chinese Big Six Companies, the clan-based private political and social organization that unofficially governs Chinatown, chose to become involved in the desegregation case.[74] They realized that what they had viewed as a squabble between Blacks and Whites might well disrupt their community-based public schools. The Six Companies organized a noisy protest against the Citizens' Advisory Committee's plans. The action stunned that group but otherwise had no effect. Neither did the appearance, at the June 3 board meeting, of what the press termed six hundred "booing, footstomping . . . shouting . . . Chinese-American parents — half the audience."[75] The Horseshoe Plan that was approved preserved most of Chinatown as part of a single zone but required the busing of many students into and out of Chinatown. The Six Companies decided to intervene directly in the litigation. They turned to Quentin Kopp, the attorney for the original Concerned Parents intervenors.

Kopp tried to bring this new group into the case literally days before a final decision concerning a desegregation remedy was anticipated. His "complaint of plaintiffs in intervention," filed on June 18, was explosive. The Chinese had an independent right to be heard, Kopp claimed. Although no one represented their interests, they were to be unwitting parties to court-ordered relief. Kopp attacked the *Johnson* suit as collusive: "The findings of fact and conclusions of law were obtained by negligence, acts of omission and obvious failure to present material evidence."[76] The Chinese community, Kopp declared, "should not without hearing be subjected to a 'cure' they neither need nor want. . . . " Even if posed at an awkwardly late moment, the argument that Chinese Americans were entitled to special consideration was not without legal plausibility. But to attend to that argument would almost necessarily have meant delaying desegregation, and that Weigel was unwilling to do. One June 30, the motion to intervene was denied and each of its arguments dismissed. Kopp, by no means finished, filed a motion for a stay of the court's order, reargued the issue before Weigel in August, and appeared before the Ninth Circuit when the case was heard on appeal. Meanwhile, he launched a successful campaign for a seat on the board of supervisors from the steps of Chinatown's Commodore Stockton School. However the case itself would ultimately be resolved, Kopp emerged politically a winner.

The Court's Dilemma: Maximum Desegregation or Institutional Legitimacy?

Judge Weigel had a difficult choice to make. Should he adopt the NAACP plan, which promised substantially more racial mixing of students, or the board's proposal, which could with some strain be described as embodying the wishes of a community whose choices concerning desegregation policy were constitutionally constrained? On June 21, 1971, Weigel scheduled an informal session on chambers, "to help the Court to fully understand the plans which [have] been submitted. . . ." and get the "unguarded cooperation" of all concerned.

In resolving the remedial issue, Weigel had first to deal with the Concerned Parents intervenors, who surprised everyone by arguing that if the court found de jure segregation to exist in San Francisco, the only permissible plan was one like the NAACP's that wholly desegregated the schools consistent with the Supreme Court's *Swann* guidelines. The Horseshoe Plan, they declared, imposed selective burdens in the name of political compromise, and they viewed that as its fatal defect. The intervenors still believed that San Francisco's segregation did not violate the Constitution. But, if they were wrong, they were greatly concerned that Horseshoe would only result in divisive annual petitions for further judicial relief and continuous pupil reassignment. Weigel resolved this dilemma by ruling that Concern Parents had no standing with respect to the nature of the remedy and forbidding them to call witnesses, at which point they declined further participation.

Most of the in-chambers session was devoted to a detailed review of the two plans submitted. Judge Weigel repeatedly expressed his unhappiness with the board "for having done very little until, on, or after April 28 . . . to get ready for the various contingencies that were . . . plainly foreseeable last September." Yet Weigel felt that he could not undo deficiencies in the district's planning. "I feel a sense of harassment by the tremendous number of problems on which I feel I have no grasp or expertise." The judge did not focus on remedial issues other than racial balance; indeed, until quite recently, judges have viewed broader integration questions as beyond the competency of the court. Weigel's opinion treated these matters as appropriately the responsibility of the district, noting only that the stress on desegregation did not "de-emphasize quality education."[77] He did urge, however, that Horseshoe be reshaped in order to minimize racial and ethnic imbalances; after the in-chambers session, the district undertook some modification.

Substantially less time was devoted to discussion of the Freedom Plan. The proposal had certain advantages: it provided for significantly more socioeconomic and racial desegregation, and it kept the residentially integrated Oceanside-Merced-Inglewood community intact. To the NAACP, the plan's authorship "by complete outsiders, who have no particular axes to grind," was also an advantage. The board, in its view, had "been just too interested in community participation. . . . " Action, not discussion, was what the NAACP wanted: "you go head and [desegregate] . . . and don't worry about selling it to the community."[78]

The court thought otherwise. In its view, the fatal defect of the NAACP Freedom Plan was the absence of even symbolic community involvement. That the NAACP's plan did a better job of reducing segregation was clearly apparent to the judge, but precisely *because* it was the NAACP's plan and not the board of education's it was less likely to gain community acceptance and hence to be fully implemented.

This difference was vital to a judge who recognized the controversial nature of any system-wide desegregation order and the importance of securing public acquiescence in, if not support for, this action. For this phase of the task, it was essential that he have some backing from the board of education. The primacy of this objective led Judge Weigel to his decision, announced on July 9, 1971. Both plans were approved.

> It is left to the choice of the school authorities to implement either one. Since the school authorities themselves submitted Horseshoe, it is anticipated that they will elect to carry out that plan. . . .While evidence of community sentiment or public feelings . . . cannot be the measure of compliance with the law, if both plans do qualify under the law — and both do — it is hardly ill-advised to permit implementation of that which the competent school authorities themselves have brought forward after extensive public hearings. . . .[79]

The Judge recognized that more than reassigning students was at issue. "[I]t is essential to have the good willed, open minded and genuine cooperation of school administrators, teachers, other school personnel, parents and the community at large."[80] Quite appropriately and quite self-consciously, Weigel was speaking to those who would be most affected by the decision, the citizens of San Francisco. How they would react remained uncertain.

The Protracted Appeals Process

Johnson was far from over. During July and August, 1971, the Chinatown intervenors sought unsuccessfully on several occasions to stay Judge Weigel's order until the Court of Appeals heard the case. The effort to postpone the inevitable came to an end when Supreme Court Justice William Douglas rejected Kopp's last request for a stay: "*Brown* . . . was not written for Blacks alone. . . . The theme of our school desegregation cases extends to all racial minorities treated invidiously by a State or any of its agencies. . . ."[81]

It would be almost three years before the Ninth Circuit decided the *Johnson* case. In the interval, plaintiffs' counsel Brunwasser pressed the district court to modify its order to assure that problems in implementing system-wide desegregation were corrected and to extend desegregation to the junior high schools. Weigel's only response was to order the district to report annually "all action taken to comply with the judgment, and to show plans for implementation in compliance with the letter and spirit of the decision." The judge subsequently denied a motion to consolidate the *Johnson* case with *O'Neill v. San Francisco Unified School District*,[82] a suit brought by the NAACP to desegregate San Francisco's junior and senior high schools. Any further trial-court action would await the appellate ruling.

On June 22, 1974, the Ninth Circuit Court of Appeals delivered its opinion in *Johnson*.[83] The 1973 Supreme Court decision in *Keyes v. School District No. 1, Denver*,[84] had set forth guidelines for judicial inquiry in non-southern desegregation cases. As the circuit court states, *Keyes* required a finding of "segregatory *intent*" to establish de jure segregation, which the district court had not made in *Johnson*. Hence, the case was remanded "to afford [the trial court] an opportunity to re-examine the record on the issue of intent."[85] The court also ordered that the Chinese intervenors be heard when the case was remanded.

The Ninth Circuit's reading of the "intent" requirement imposed on plaintiffs a heavier burden than have other circuit-court glosses on *Keyes*. Had the opinion been issued more expeditiously it might well have proved consequential. The Concerned Parents intervenors were prepared with a host of demands for data that, in their judgment, would have demolished the conclusion that San Francisco had practiced de jure segregation. By 1974, however, neither the Concerned Parents nor the district was disposed to re-open what had by then become a stale issue. Settlement of the dispute, ratified by a consent decree rather than a new trial, appeared in everyone's best interest. As of mid-1976, though, there has been neither a new trial nor a settlement. The Chinese intervenors have resisted any agreement that would legitimate the status quo. They may press for a plan which leaves Chinatown outside the embrace of Horseshoe; if they do, there may yet be another round of *Johnson* litigation.

The Aftermath: Implementing the Johnson Order

To announce a decision concerning desegregation is one thing; to secure its implementation is something altogether different and more difficult. Judge Weigel left implementation in the hands of those formally charge with the responsibility for running the school system; that choice, while not inevitable, conformed to traditional understandings of the demarcation between judicial authority and political and administrative authority.

In San Francisco, this expression of judicial laissez faire has had significant consequences. The management of desegregation has been a quintessentially political process which, while bounded by the terms of the decree, has been shaped far more by activity outside the courtroom. The process has reflected the political and organization realities of the district, specifically the low priority the post-*Johnson* board of education and administration gave to desegregation and their apparent disinterest in broader, integration-centered issues.

The desegregation issue has also been confounded by the emergence of newly politicized Third World groups pressing a competing educational-policy agenda. Their desire for bilingual-bicultural programs, like the concern for desegregation, has been phrased in terms of equal educational opportunity. But the separationist thrust of Third World groups' efforts collides directly with the assimilationist orientation of those seeking desegregation. The implementation of the *Johnson* decision has thus been marked by competition between these two understandings of the fundamental legal and ideological imperative and between the distinct claims that each makes on district priorities.

The Measures of Imperfect Success

By and large, the desegregation of San Francisco's elementary schools in September, 1971, was peaceful. Pockets of resistance were calmed by the energetic efforts of Mayor Alioto, who urged unhappy Whites to refrain from violence, to focus on the reversal of *Johnson*, and to support the ballot proposition for an elected school board.

Peace, however, did not mean smoothly managed desegregation. For one thing, district planning was haphazard. For another, segments of the White community staged quiet rebellions. Chinatown provided the most sustained and substantial opposition, organized and financed by the Big Six Companies. Approximately one thousand Chinese-American students enrolled in private "Freedom Schools" (named, ironically, for the schools established in the South as part of the fight for desegregation), and it took over a year to woo these students back into the public school system.[86]

Desegregation and education. In a more enduring sense, desegregation has not fulfilled its promise. Desegregation has increased, although not to the extent envisioned by the framers of Horseshoe. Five years after the decision, the far harder task of achieving an integrated environment has not even begun.

Elementary schools have become substantially more desegregated as a result of Horseshoe.[87] Prior to the decision, eighty of the ninety-six schools were imbalanced in terms of the state's guidelines. Horseshoe lessened but did not eliminate this imbalance: in December, 1971, one-third of the elementary schools were imbalanced with respect to one or more racial groups. By 1975–76, that number had climbed to almost one-half, but of these only seven schools were more than 50 percent Black. Ironically enough, Horseshoe itself was a contributor to imbalance. Several schools and, more seriously, several entire zones had been within a whisker of being racially imbalanced when the plan was adopted.

The loss of White students coincident with desegregation was one cause of this post-*Johnson* imbalance. Between 1965 and 1970, the year preceding *Johnson*, the percentage of elementary-school students in the district who were White declined from 42.8 percent to 34.5 percent; the average annual decline was 1.7 percentage points. During 1971, the first year of Horseshoe's implementation, the percentage of White students dropped an additional 4.1 points; Whites now constituted 30.1 percent of the student population. But such "flight," if it can be so called, occurred only during this initial year. Between 1971 and the present, the average rate of decline has been 1.2 percentage points, lower than in the years preceding Horseshoe. Yet one should not underestimate what these changes, coupled with an absolute decline in enrollment, mean in terms of actual numbers: only about half as many Whites attend elementary school in San Francisco today as in 1970.

The district made few efforts to couple desegregation with any educational programs designed to promote integration. Except for the Richmond and Park South Complexes, the zone boundaries did not allow for ongoing educational enterprises. During the late 1960s there had been attempts to develop a school-based program that would help keep the Oceanside-Merced-Inglewood area residentially mixed; when Horseshoe divided the schools between two zones, the program collapsed. The largely Black Hunter's Point region, which had begun to develop exemplary techniques for instructing minority-group children and involving parents, was also separated into two zones. A bilingual program sought by the Latino organizations was abandoned for lack of district money. The district's "educational lighthouse" school, which prior to *Johnson* had been staffed by teachers and students from San Francisco State College and had drawn a racially mixed student body from the entire city, collapsed in the wake of desegregation when it was absorbed into the regular system.

There are San Francisco public schools which, either by reputation or in terms of achievement-test scores, are "good." But the district itself can take little credit for encouraging this excellence. Some of the schools — Corbett and Rooftop, for example — are small "alternative public schools," set up at parental instigation. In other schools, highly motivated principals and superb teachers have produced good results despite central-office indifference. The *San Francisco Chronicle*'s longtime education reporter, Ron Moskowitz, spent three weeks in February, 1972, observing fourteen elementary schools and reported, "There are no longer good and bad schools . . . only good and bad classrooms . . . it all depends on the teacher."[88]

Administrative and electoral politics. That the district treated numerical desegregation as a complete solution to the issues raised in *Johnson* is partly traceable to the incapacity or unwillingness of school administrators and the board to go beyond legal literal-mindedness. Sustained indifference and un-productive politicking made a shambles of the integration aspiration.

Superintendent Shaheen tried to use the advent of desegregation as a ve-hicle for shaking up the administration, but he failed. Not that Shaheen was wholly blameless. He saw himself as a "facilitator," but he gave even staff loy-alists little support. He embraced too many new ideas at once and conse-quently gave all of them short shrift. His distrust of San Francisco's old-line administrators exacerbated tensions in the central office; he alienated the teachers' organizations by choosing encounter groups and public meetings over face-to-face bargaining; and he upset the board by proposing to take a vacation during the first two weeks of desegregation.[89]

"Shaheenigans" and desegregation were central issues in the 1971 mayor-alty campaign. Both Alioto and his conservative opponent urged Shaheen's replacement; both endorsed a charter amendment calling for an elected (and presumably less liberal) school board. Diane Feinstein, a member of the board of supervisors, a strong vote-getter, and the liberal candidate for mayor, spoke out for Shaheen and desegregation. Although many factors, among them Alioto's strong support from labor unions and minority groups, contributed to the outcome, the desegregation issue doomed Feinstein's campaign. The mayor won a smashing victory; Quentin Kopp, lawyer for the Chinatown intervenors, was elected to the board of supervisors. The charter amendment was approved; and the soon to be dissolved appointed board began to ease Shaheen out.

The board of education elected in June, 1972, after a campaign largely centered on busing, was more conservative than its predecessor; only two strong supporters of desegregation were among the seven winners.[90] But the problem that had persisted since Spears's retirement remained: could any-one intelligently run the schools? The departure of Shaheen in August, 1972, did not dramatically improve the quality of school administration. His successor, Steven Morena, tried and failed to reduce bureaucratic infighting. In 1975, Morena reported that he was unable to manage the district because of the board's incessant interference with and injection of political consider-ations into educational administration. Nor has Morena's successor, Robert Alioto (no kin to Mayor Alioto) had much better luck. Denying him the briefest of honeymoons, the board has turned down for political reasons several of his key administrative appointments.

In that political climate, integration has not interested those critically situ-ated to shape implementation of the court order. Currently no one really runs San Francisco's schools. The board's inability to establish priorities has spawned ceaseless struggles over programs and budget. Superintendent Alioto's concerns center primarily on gaining control over his unruly bu-reaucracy. With respect to desegregation, Alioto is most interested in relax-ation of the stringent racial-balance guidelines and substitution of a prohibition against predominantly one-race schools. If the superintendent prevails, he will merely have replaced one numerical standard with another, leaving more basic policy questions unaddressed.

After the *Johnson* decision, responsibility for desegregation was delegated to an Office of Integration. The office has devoted much of its energies to methodologically sophisticated analyses of enrollment data, but the statistical reports have not triggered policy changes. Nor has the office been able to address the manifold problems of integration. Effectively isolated from the rest of the administration, the office has been rendered bureaucratically impotent.[91]

The measures of its failure are evident. So-called "temporary attendance permits," issued first to Chinese American students to entice them back to the public schools and now to more than one-fifth of all district elementary students, have worked against racial balance without achieving any other compensating educational objective. As a result of special programs, resegregation has occurred within schools.[92] Classes for the gifted, hastily expanded with the adoption of the Horseshoe Plan, have a White-enrollment proportion twice the district-wide average and a correspondingly small Black enrollment. Blacks make up three-fifths, twice the district-wide average, of classes for the educable mentally retarded and the educationally handicapped, traditional dumping grounds for difficult-to-manage or slow-learning pupils.[93] These racially disproportionate enrollments clearly violate the *Johnson* court's prohibition against "educational techniques or innovations" which recreate segregation.[94]

San Francisco undertook voluntarily to desegregate its junior and senior high schools, but that process has not proceeded smoothly. Although in May, 1972, the NAACP had filed suit demanding immediate secondary school desegregation, [95] the case was not pursued vigorously, and the administration planned at its leisure. An attempt to devise an inventive plan that accomplished desegregation, while taking into account the needs of Chinese and Latino communities for special programs, encountered immense obstacles. Unless judicial modification could be secured, the district was compelled by the *Johnson* decision to use the Horseshoe Plan as its starting point. While the Horseshoe zone boundaries would predictably reproduce at the secondary level the racial imbalances existing in elementary schools, scrapping Horseshoe in favor of a new plan would only reopen the controversy concerning city-wide desegregation. Not surprisingly, the board invoked Horseshoe, at the cost of foregoing a more imaginative and equitable solution to secondary school desegregation.

In September, 1974, secondary school desegregation went into effect. New student assignments were coupled with a provision allowing students to transfer, for a variety of reasons, into other schools. In 1975–76, one-third of the district's approximately thirty-four thousand junior- and senior-high-school students exercised this transfer option, and many of them returned to neighborhood schools. The effects have been mixed: although there is less desegregation than the district's plan had contemplated, every secondary school is more desegregated than prior to desegregation. A proposal to dismiss the secondary-school suit was filed in August, 1976, by agreement of the parties. The more startling development is that few people care very much about the issue any longer. The administration will do what is expedient; the board is paralyzed by the prospect of doing anything; the NAACP is a much weaker organization today than in 1970. San Francisco's public-school enrollment continues to decline, from 82,033 in 1970–71 to 68,862 in 1975–76. Whites now make up only one-quarter of the school-age population. By 1979, the district projects a total enrollment of 59,082, with as many Chinese as White students in the public schools.[96] The original rationale for desegregation, to mix White and Black students, is becoming less and less demographically feasible in San Francisco.

Other Agendas

Between the filing of the *Johnson* complaint and the present, many White civil-rights supporters lost their intense commitment to desegregation. In part, this shift reflects changing perceptions concerning the value of the struggle, particularly in communities in which the preponderant population is non-White.

Blacks had never been directly involved, in substantial numbers, in the litigation; like most other desegregation suits, it was pressed by an elite. Looking back on the case, one of the participating attorneys saw this as a serious tactical error. "Unless an organization is prepared to do battle on all fronts relevant to a political litigation — and *Johnson* was a political litigation — it's best not to fight at all."[97] Black parents have had to live with a decision that in important respects has not improved their children's lives. A 1973 survey of San Francisco pupil and teacher attitudes suggests the depth of the problem.[98] In the argot of this survey, Black and Spanish-speaking children remain negative in their self-concepts and in their attitudes toward school and score higher on measures of school anxiety than their White or Asian counterparts. Desegregation has improved neither their motivation nor their achievement. Black and White students have little to do with one another. While teachers' attitudes toward multi-ethnic schools are generally positive, their expectations for Asian and White children are higher than for Black and Spanish-speaking students.

Black students have also not fared well in more readily measurable terms. Although modest improvement was noted in 1975–76, their achievement-test scores have remained relatively stable and well below those of Whites. They are also suspended substantially more often than Whites. In 1973–74, three-fifths of all suspended students at the secondary-school level were

Black.[99] Following desegregation, the number of sixth-grade suspensions almost doubled, and it was Black children who were suspended in three-quarters of the cases.[100]

This kind of evidence has prompted even those Blacks who had been enthusiastic about desegregation to question its value in improving educational opportunities for Black students.[101] Some middle-class Black families have followed the Whites into the suburbs; that phenomenon, coupled with declining birthrates, has led to a slight decline in Black enrollment since the *Johnson* decision. Several hundred Black families in the Hunter's Point community, whose residents lack the resources to leave the city, have requested that their children be reassigned to the neighborhood schools from which desegregation had promised them escape. There is no longer much talk about desegregation — or, for that matter, education generally — in the Black community.

In the other ethnic communities, notably Asian and Latino, there has been an awakening of interest in the public schools. Emerging ethnic pride, diligent efforts to overcome factionalism and present a more united political front, and the availability of federal funds for bilingual education encouraged this strong interest in the schools. The desegregation order also triggered these groups' concern for equality of opportunity with the Blacks and Whites. A turning point was the Supreme Court's 1974 decision in *Lau v. Nichols*,[102] which specifically ordered San Francisco to provide Chinese students who did not speak English a "meaningful opportunity to participate in the public educational program."[103] To the foreign-language communities of San Francisco, *Lau* was an invitation to sharpen their demands for bilingual-bicultural education.

Following *Lau*, Superintendent Morena appointed a Citizens' Bilingual Task Force, a group representing the most radical elements of the Latino and Asian communities, to shape a bilingual program. During the 1960s, civil-rights organizations had equated equal opportunity with desegregation, assuming that this remedy would produce an equal distribution of educational resources and help overcome the psychological harm of racial isolation. The bilingual task force held a decidedly different view:

> The burden should be on the school to adapt its educational approach so that the culture, language and learning style of all children in the school (not just those of Anglo middle-class background) are accepted and valued. Children should not be penalized for culture and linguistic differences, nor should they bear a burden to conform to a school-sanctioned culture by abandoning their own.[104]

The task-force report was more a political than an educational document. It clearly implied a new kind of "positive" or "affirmative" segregation which would cost a substantial amount of money to implement, and hence provoked sharply expressed opposition. Yet, however the bilingual issue is resolved in the near term, the report indicates that Chinese, Latinos, and Filipinos — largely excluded from the *Johnson* litigation — have become full participants in the struggle for political recognition in the schools.

Superintendent Alioto has objected to the racial-balance features of the *Johnson* remedy, as has the San Francisco Public Schools Commission, an august body appointed at the behest of California's Superintendent of Public Instruction to sort out the district's administrative tangles. Proposals for greater choice of school offering, including bilingual instruction, are bruited about. Perhaps the integration that *Johnson* hoped to achieve will result from these new forces; but, as a longtime observer put it, the resolution may instead represent "the ultimate insanity," the complete politicization of San Francisco's schools. As long-time board of education member Zuretti Goosby said: "I used to know what was right and what was wrong. I just don't know any more."

San Francisco and Beyond: The Dynamic of Desegregation

From the vantage point of 1976, what is most intriguing about San Francisco's efforts to wed racial justice with educational policy is how close the school district came to success. It is a story studded with "ifs": *if* the board of education and Superintendent Jenkins had been able to seize the day in the late 1960s, at a time when belief in the possibility of integration was perhaps strongest; *if* in 1970 the board and superintendent had firmly committed themselves to implementing the Park South and Richmond Complexes, irrespective of whether additional funds were forthcoming; *if*, in framing a remedy in *Johnson,* Judge Weigel had structured a process that could address the dilemmas of integration, rather than settling for racial balance; *if* San Francisco had been able to find a politically sophisticated superintendent able to turn the prevailing administrative anarchy into a working machine and thus make a go of integration after *Johnson.* None of these "ifs" became reality. And perhaps, given the changing character of the racial issue and the unique characteristics of particular urban communities, to imagine that these "ifs" offer lessons to other districts is to indulge in naive wishing.

Between 1960, when northern school desegregation first became politically salient, and the present, the character of the issue has dramatically altered. In the early years, the struggle for desegregation could be characterized along clear-cut liberal-conservative lines. Racial justice for Black schoolchildren formed an important part of Martin Luther King Jr.'s dream for a just republic; those who resisted that vision were held to do so out of bigotry, not principle.

Today, as the San Francisco case study suggests, the question has manifestly become more complex. The meaning of desegregation has changed: in place of largely symbolic gestures, intended primarily to demonstrate political good will, racial balance is sought by civil rights groups. The forum has shifted from the school board to the court. But the objective of legally coerced racial balance has been resisted for a variety of reasons. The educational evidence now in hand does not reveal racial balance to be a social panacea. Substantial numbers of Whites have opposed what is called "massive busing"; and some Blacks, recognizing both that opposition and the continuing departure of Whites from the cities, have opted for a stronger role in educational administration as a substitute for further efforts to achieve desegregation. These developments pose dilemmas for the courts. Even as judicial doctrine has come to treat northern and southern school segregation in nearly synonymous terms, lower-court judges have, as a practical matter, found themselves brokering solutions that have little to do with the new legal doctrine. What role the judiciary ought now to assume is a vital, unanswered question.

Change and Symbolism

Issues as ideologically volatile as segregation are never permanently resolved, for organizations whose primary concern is the furtherance of civil rights do not admit to final successes. They recognize only the stage-by-stage resolution of continuing controversies in which the meaning of the operant terms — here, equal educational opportunity — are constantly changing, the demands constantly expanding. The history of the desegregation controversy in San Francisco is no exception to this iron law of social movements.

The irresolvable quality of the issue is attributable in good part to its symbolic character. As Murray Edelman observes:

> In the field of race relations the talk . . . is in terms of liberty and equality on one side and in terms of the prevention of social disorder . . . on the other side. Neither of these ostensible goals . . . specifies a condition that is objectively definable in the sense that there can be a consensus that it has been achieved. . . . Their semantic ambiguity . . . is precisely what makes them potent symbols.[105]

In San Francisco, as elsewhere, desegregation has of course had more than symbolic impact. Most important among its instrumental effects has been the reassignment of thousands of schoolchildren. But critical to the drive for desegregation was a desire for official recognition that Black and Whites are formally equal, an end which it was felt only color consciousness in pupil assignment could accomplish. To obtain less would signal a civil-rights retreat, a surrender to racism.

If tangible equality rather than deference were the civil rights movement's primary goal, the consequences of symbolism could properly be minimized. The issue would then be converted into an evaluation of the relative merits of segregation as compared with other strategies for bringing about equality. Alternatively, were the whole matter irrelevant to the life of schools and schoolchildren, it could be dismissed as trivial. Neither is the case.

The kind of education that children in San Francisco and elsewhere presently receive is shaped by the reality of court-ordered desegregation. Yet those who achieved this "victory" have not been involved with the immensely more complicated business of providing an intelligent, humane, integrated educational program in racially and socioeconomically heterogeneous schools. It is tempting, but unhelpful and simplistic, to label such behavior as irresponsible. The point, rather, is to inquire how desegregation might be made to work in light of that sobering history, to raise questions and note policy choices, rather than advancing yet another set of "solutions."

The Evidence Concerning Desegregation: Its Effects on Policy

If the earlier advocates of desegregation believed that desegregation by itself would achieve great things, they have been sorely disappointed. Beginning with the publication of *Equality of Educational Opportunity* (the Coleman Report) in 1966,[106] the relationship between desegregation and benefit to students — measured variously in terms of achievement, self-perception, and racial attitudes — has undergone continuous and extensive scrutiny. The study of these issues has become, as Nathan Glazer notes, a matter of "Talmudic complexity,"[107] whose findings are at best equivocal. Nancy St. John, a careful student of this voluminous literature, concludes: "Biracial schooling must be judged neither a demonstrated success nor a demonstrated failure."[108] The apparent effects on students' achievement and racial attitudes vary from study to study. Such findings should not surprise, for they reflect the range of educational experiences that can be labeled "desegregation" or "integration."

The harder questions, with respect to which there has been less serious discussion, focus on the policy implications of these research conclusions. Does research support the proposition that desegregation is bad policy and should be abandoned, at least where it occurs involuntarily? Does it suggest that expectations concerning what desegregation can achieve should be lowered, if only to guard against disappointment? Or should the task of the primary policy-enforcing agency, the courts — giving meaning to the constitutional principle of equal protection — be undertaken without reference to the vagaries of social-science research?

The Politics of Desegregation

As desegregation came to be defined as racial balance rather than color-blind assignment of students, White opposition predictably increased. By the early 1970s, this opposition had crystallized around the scareword "busing." Although a substantial majority of Whites favors desegregation, a Gallup poll taken in October, 1971, reported that 76 percent of respondents opposed busing; there was almost no difference in reaction among the South, North, and West.[109] Whites were also expressing their unhappiness with their feet: the state of the schools was an apparently prominent factor motivating an increasing percentage of White families to leave the cities for the suburbs.[110]

Blacks, too, began to question desegregation brought about by court-compelled busing. Beginning in the late 1960s in New York City, the demand for community-controlled schools was regularly sounded.[111] Later, concern with remaking educational institutions was supplanted by a more pragmatic interest in managing presently existing, and increasingly Black, public-school systems of the large cities. The push for desegregation appeared quixotic in cities such as Washington, D.C., whose public-school population is 95 percent Black, or in Detroit, St. Louis, Newark, and Atlanta, whose student populations will resemble Washington's in a decade. To many Blacks, the possibility of creating desegregated metropolitan school systems by linking urban and surrounding suburban school districts was viewed not as a solution to the problem but rather as a means of diluting Blacks' newly acquired political influence over their schools.

This new attitude is reflected in the decision of the Atlanta NAACP, plaintiff in a suit against that city's school system, to forego further student desegregation in exchange for an increase in the number of Black teachers and administrators,[112] and in an agreement among the parties in a St. Louis desegregation suit to achieve similar objectives.[113] These agreements have been highly controversial. To their defenders — among them the Fifth Circuit Court of Appeals, which upheld the Atlanta consent decree — the resolution was a pragmatic necessity. Further efforts at desegregating students might well have prompted White departure; securing metropolitan-wide relief was neither pursued by the litigants nor legally very likely. In that context, it was argued, the local NAACP and Atlanta school officials had struck the only sensible bargain. Others saw the matter quite differently. The national NAACP, which intervened in the litigation, charged that the local civil-rights group had sold out Atlanta's Black children for the promise of a few jobs. Nor was it clear whether, in educational terms, the bargain was wise: were Black teachers, because of their race, clearly better equipped to educate Black students, as the decree suggested? Was this the kind of politics that decisions concerning racial justice should traffic in? And what had happened to an appellate court whose prior commitment to desegregation — at any political price — was previously unquestioned?

These are vital questions, not easily answered. One thing is, however, clear. To the extent that Atlanta and St. Louis mark an important change in the course of desegregation, we can anticipate considerably more ad hoc and less racial-balance-centered resolutions of the issue. The chosen resolution will depend more on the political vagaries of the particular community and less on constitutional doctrine than has thus far been the case.

Evolving Constitutional Doctrine

The 1973 Supreme Court decision in *Keyes* set forth standards to guide lower courts as they reviewed claims that northern and western school districts had engaged in deliberate segregation. But the touchstone of "intentional" segregation that the Court announced has puzzled judges and lawyers. The crucial, if quite technical, issue was the meaning of intent. In other legal contexts, it is frequently presumed that a person intends the natural and foreseeable consequences of his or her actions, and that presumption is embodied in *Keyes*. Under *Keyes*, could that presumption be rebutted by proof that a district's actions were innocently motivated and that the district's decisions were color-blind? Or would disclaimers of culpability — typically, arguments that student assignments faithfully adhered to a neighborhood-school policy — be unavailing; would courts treat the presumption of intentional segregation as irrebuttable? Justice Powell, concurring in the *Keyes* decision, criticized the intent standard as "nebulous,"[114] and subsequent events have borne out that judgment. Some circuit courts, among them the court reviewing the San Francisco case, have sought specific proof of intent; others have viewed intent as inferrable from actions whose predictable effect is additional segregation.[115] To the lay mind, the disparate conclusions of the lower courts concerning the constitutionality of segregation suggest arbitrariness.[116]

Justice Powell's *Keyes* concurrence urged that the distinction between constitutional de facto segregation and unconstitutional de jure segregation be abandoned in favor of a national standard: "local school boards will operate *integrated school systems* within their respective districts."[117] To Powell, the integration requirement meant an obligation to desegregate faculty and administration, equalize instructional opportunities throughout the district, and draw attendance zones and build new schools deliberately to encourage pupil desegregation. It did not, however, countenance court-ordered city-wide busing. Instead, the goal of the courts should be to "promote desegregation with other, equally important educational interests which a community may legitimately assert."[118]

While application of Justice Powell's "integration" approach would not be free of the interpretive difficulties that have bedeviled *Keyes*, the standard is more readily understandable. It also implicitly takes into account the political wisdom of restricting reliance on busing as a remedy. But Powell's approach presents a raft of new problems. It urges that courts somehow balance the Fourteenth Amendment requirement of equal protection with other "important educational interests" without specifying either what those interests might be or how the balance would be struck. Justice Powell's appraisal makes considerable sense if perceived as policy analysis. But that is not the usual cast of constitutional argument, and one wonders whether courts can employ such rhetoric while insisting that they are pursuing a constitutional, rather than a purely policy, objective.

The Courts: Monarchs, Mediators, or without Function?

In San Francisco, as in other communities, the trial judge exercised decisive responsibility for resolving a desegregation controversy. But the way in which that responsibility was exercised differed notably from the traditional role of courts. In classic court cases,[119] the trial judge describes a sequence of events and identifies a legal framework within which those events may be properly placed; the remedy, typically money damages, flows naturally from the determination of wrong. The dispute itself is clear and self-contained; its ramifications extend no farther than the parties before the court. The court's authority to control the parties' behavior is unquestioned (subject, of course, to the exhaustion of appeals). In that sense, the judge acts as monarch.

The scenario in desegregation cases — and, for that matter, a great many other public-law cases — is quite different. The precise legal basis for the court's ruling is often not clear, and the factual issues may be so complex that no single resolution can command consensus. The dispute is not solely between two parties with obviously opposed interests but spills over to involve a multiplicity of groups, each pressing an objective to which it attempts to give a constitutional anchor. In the San Francisco litigation, for example, not only the NAACP and the school district, but also the Chinese, those seeking a "color-blind" standard, and those interested in community-run Black schools all sought to be heard. The remedy, not legal wrong, occupies center state in the proceedings, for the remedy creates an ongoing regime of governmental duties rather than simply ordering a transfer of money. In such situations judges cannot be monarchical, for the effort to implement a remedy is of necessity outside their direct control.

How should courts respond to the dynamics of contemporary desegregation disputes? One alternative, epitomized by the Boston[120] and Detroit cases,[121] is for the judge to become increasingly involved in the details of a solution to the broader questions raised by such a suit. Judge Weigel was content with a plan that racially balanced San Francisco's elementary schools; the Boston and Detroit decisions treated the logistics of desegregation as merely the starting point for their analyses. They called for, among other things, teacher retraining, detailed student-rights codes, and instructional innovations.

Even in a judicial system which grants extraordinary remedial authority to judges, these decisions are unusual. The motivation for remedies whose scope extends well beyond matters of racial balance is clear enough: a remedy that focuses exclusively on student reassignment does not adequately respond to the myriad issues nascent in any desegregation suit. As Justice White pointed out, dissenting in *Milliken v. Bradley*:

> The [district court's] task is not to devise a system of pains and penalties to punish constitutional violations brought to light. Rather, it is to desegregate an *educational* system in which the races have been kept apart, without, at the same time, losing sight of the central *educational* function of the schools.[122]

True enough; but the question remains, are these matters properly the province of judges? Do they unfairly call upon school boards and school administrators to assume responsibility for managing an educational system over which they have only minimal authority? The Detroit and Boston decisions have led some to argue that the courts have gone too far and that, as Nathan Glazer asserts, "the judges should now stand back and allow the forces of political democracy in a pluralist society to do their proper work."[123]

But pluralist politics need not be equated with judicial abdication. It is conceivable that courts in desegregation cases can attempt to manage negotiations among many and diversely affected interests, shepherding an ongoing process of mutual accommodation within the broad framework laid down by the constitutional command to secure the equal protection of the laws. The Atlanta and St. Louis histories, recounted earlier, portend such a role. Those cases pose the essential question: is it institutionally legitimate for courts to function as mediators in constitutional litigation, or is that function too explicitly political for judges to assume? The response to that query, when it eventually comes, will powerfully influence the stance that courts of the future will assume in managing school-desegregation controversies.

** Research for the initial phases of this study was supported by a grant from the Ford Foundation to the Institute for Judicial Administration, New York University. A substantially different and lengthier version of this article will appear in *America in the Seventies: Problems, Policies, and Politics*, ed. Allan Sindler (Boston: Little, Brown, in press).

Notes

1. See James S. Coleman, "School Desegregation and Loss of Whites from Large Central-City School Districts," paper presented to the United States Commission on Civil Rights, Washington, D.C., 8 Dec. 1975; Thomas F. Pettigrew and Robert L. Green, "School Desegregation in Large Cities: A Critique of the Coleman 'White Flight' Thesis," *Harvard Educational Review*, 46 (1976), 1–53; "The Busing Dilemma," *Time*, 22 Sept. 1975, p. 1; James S. Coleman, "Response to Professors Pettigrew and Green," *Harvard Educational Review*, 46 (1976), 217–24; and Thomas F. Pettigrew and Robert L. Green, "A Reply to Professor Coleman," *Harvard Educational Review*, 46 (1976), 225–33.

2. See "Levi and Busing," *New Republic*, 12 June 1976, pp. 5–7.

3. This position is fully reflected in the symposium issue of *School Review*, 84 (1976), 309–517. See, for example, Alvin F. Poussaint and Toye Brown Lewis, "School Desegregation: A Synonym for Racial Equality," *School Review*, 84 (1976), 326–36; and Charles S. Bullock III, "Desegregating Urban Areas: Is It Worth It? Can It Be Done?" *School Review*, 84 (1976), 431–48.

4. The desegregation case study literature is modest in scope and, for the most part, predates the busing controversy. See, for example, Robert L. Crain, *The Politics of School Desegregation* (Chicago: Aldine, 1968); Anna Holden, *The Bus Stops Here: A Study of Desegregation in Three Cities* (New York: Agathon, 1974); Robert R. Mayer, Charles E. King, Anne Borders-Patterson, and James S. McCullough, *The Impact of School Desegregation in a Southern City: A Case Study in the Analysis of Educational Policy* (Lexington, Mass.: Lexington, 1974); and Lillian Rubin, *Busing and Backlash* (Berkeley, Calif.: Univ. of California Press, 1972). The best treatment of the interplay between bureaucratic poli-

tics and desegregation remains David Rogers, *110 Livingston Street: Politics and Bureaucracy in the New York City School System* (New York: Random House, 1968).

5. 339 F. Supp. 1315 (N.D. Cal. 1971), *vacated and remanded*, 500 F.2d 349 (9th Cir. 1974).

6. This case study relies heavily on primary source material — school district reports, board of education minutes, court transcripts and the like — in unraveling events surrounding the San Francisco desegregation controversy. More than fifty people — lawyers in the *Johnson* case, present and past board members, administrators, and community leaders — submitted to interviews; several provided unpublished material from their private libraries. In order to keep footnotes to a manageable number, these materials and interviews are cited only where essential to document an event or argument. For unpublished and inaccessible material, page references are not given here.

   Particularly valuable was the help of Doris Fine, Ph.D. candidate in the Department of Sociology and the School of Education, University of California, Berkeley, who conducted some of the interviews and ferreted out and analyzed data with remarkable proficiency.

7. See David J. Kirby, T. Robert Harris, Robert L. Crain, and Christine H. Rossell, *Political Strategies in Northern School Desegregation* (Lexington, Mass.: Lexington, 1973); and David L. Kirp and Mark G. Yudof, *Educational Policy and the Law* (Berkeley, Calif.: McCutchan, 1974), pp. 281–489.

8. See, in addition to the case studies noted in n. 4 above, Kaplan, "Segregation, Litigation and the Schools — Part II: The Gary Litigation," 59 *N.W.U.L. Rev.* 121 (1964).

9. The capitalization of "Blacks" and "Whites" as nouns is a *Harvard Educational Review* editorial policy and does not reflect the preference of the author.

10. On these background issues, see Frederick Wirt, *Power in the City: Decision-Making in San Francisco* (Berkeley, Calif.: Univ. of California Press, 1974); and Howard Becker, ed., *Culture and Civility in San Francisco* (Chicago: Aldine, 1971).

11. The census data are drawn from the 1950 and 1970 United States censuses and from 1974 estimates of the San Francisco Health Department. The category "White" does *not* include Spanish-surnamed persons, whose number is derived from "White foreign stock," "foreign-born" or "native of foreign or mixed parentage" data (for 1950) and from the 1970 census subject report.

12. San Francisco's 1905 decision to create separate schools for Chinese and Japanese students, ultimately reversed only through the personal intervention of President Theodore Roosevelt, reveals the historical roots of this prejudice. See David Brudnoy, "Race and the San Francisco School Board Incident: Contemporary Evaluations," *California Historical Quarterly*, 50 (1971), 295–312.

13. See Lee Dolson, "Administration of the San Francisco Public Schools," Diss. School of Education, Univ. of California, Berkeley, 1964.

14. Larry Cuban, "School Chiefs Under Fire: A Study of Three Big City Superintendents Under Outside Pressure," Diss. Stanford Univ. 1974, p. 130. Spears made this observation in 1957, contrasting the policies of Little Rock, Arkansas — then in the midst of racial turmoil — with those of San Francisco. In 1961, in the wake of a federal court decision striking down the boundary gerrymandering of a northern school district — *Taylor v. Board of Education*, 294 F.2d 36 (2d Cir. 1961), *cert. denied*, 368 U.S. 940 (1961) — Spears stated: "We have not manipulated boundaries to segregate racial groups nor to integrate them . . . .We . . . are trying to treat everyone fairly." *San Francisco Examiner*, 17 March 1961, p. 6, col. 1.

15. *Hearings of the United States Commission on Civil Rights*, San Francisco, 19 Sept. 1960, pp. 816–17.

16. This civil-rights history is recounted in Crain, pp. 81–94.

17. Harold Spears, "The Proper Recognition of a Pupil's Educational Background," unpublished paper, San Francisco Unified School District (SFUSD), 19 June 1962.

18. San Francisco Board of Education, Transcript, 18 Sept. 1962, is the primary source material for this section. See also Congress of Racial Equality, "Relationship Between Racial Balance and Sound Education in the San Francisco Unified School District," Unpublished paper, San Francisco, 1 Sept. 1962 (on file at the Alexander Meikeljohn Library, Berkeley, Calif.).
19. Brock v. Board of Education, No. 71034, (N.D. Cal., Oct. 2, 1962).
20. San Francisco Board of Education, "Final Report of the Ad Hoc Committee," Unpublished paper, 2 April 1963.
21. *San Francisco Chronicle*, 3 April 1963, p. 1, col. 7.
22. Transcript of the San Francisco Board of Education-San Francisco Human Rights Committee Joint Conferences, Vol. 1, 23 and 26 Aug. 1965, 51–54, 95–97.
23. Harold Spears and William L. Cobb, "Selected Data for Study in the Challenge to Effect Better Racial Balance in the San Francisco Public Schools," unpublished paper, SFUSD, Nov. 1965.
24. Crain, pp. 13–28, 75–84.
25. Two other related studies were undertaken at this time: the State Fair Employment Practices Commission and the San Francisco Human Rights Commission reviewed district employment practices, and the United States Commission on Civil Rights included San Francisco in its national assessment of *Racial Isolation in the Public Schools* (Washington, D.C.: GPO, 1967).
26 Stanford Research Institute, "Improving Racial Balance in the San Francisco Schools," Menlo Park, Calif., 1967.
27. Robert Jenkins, "EE/Q Report #1: Program Alternatives," Unpublished paper, SFUSD, 19 Dec. 1967.
28. Citizens' Advisory Committee, "EE/Q Progress Report," Unpublished paper, SFUSD, 19 May 1970, pp. 4–7.
29. Robert Jenkins, "EE/Q Schools for Living: An Adventure in Education," Unpublished paper, SFUSD, 15 Dec. 1969.
30. The recounting of Mayor Alioto's role derives largely from interviews with John DeLuca, executive deputy to the mayor, in San Francisco, 24 April 1975; Leroy Cannon, counsel to the board of education, in San Francisco, 8 April 1975; Terry Francois, NAACP board member and member, board of supervisors, in San Francisco, 28 March 1975; and Howard Nemerowski, former member, board of education, in San Francisco, 26 March 1972. Unsurprisingly, those interviewed offered markedly different assessments of Alioto's actions.
31. Wirt, p. 266.
32. *San Francisco Chronicle*, 4 Feb. 1970, p. 1, col. 1.
33. *San Francisco Chronicle*, 4 Feb. 1970, p. 1, col. 1.
34. Nelson v. San Francisco Unified School District, No. 618-643, San Francisco Super. Ct., June 15, 1970.
35. Interview with Robert Jenkins, former San Francisco superintendent of schools, in Redlands, Calif., 18 April 1975 (telephone interview).
36. *San Francisco Chronicle*, 6 Feb. 1970, p. 1, col. 6.
37. U.S. 483 (1954). This history is briefly chronicled in Read, "Judicial Evolution of the Law of School Integration Since *Brown v. Board of Education*," 39 *Law and Contemp. Probs.* 7 (1975).
38. 347 U.S. at 483, 495.
39. Brown v. Board of Education, 349 U.S. 294, 301 (1955).
40. 391 U.S. 430 (1968).
41. *Id.* at 439, 442.
42. 402 U.S. 1 (1971). That *Swann* should be read as limiting the remedial discretion of trial court judges is clear from a companion case, David v. Board of School Comm'rs,

402 U.S. 33 (1971), in which the lower court's failure to consider the possible use of busing and noncontiguous zoning in its desegregation order was basis for reversal.

43. The relevant doctrinal literature is immense. Among the best contributions are Goodman, "De Facto Segregation: A Constitutional Analysis," 60 *Calif. L. Rev.* 275 (1972); and Yudof, "Equal Educational Opportunity and the Courts," 51 *Tex. L. Rev.* 473 (1973).

44. Until the 1940s, several northern states had permitted school districts to maintain segregated schools at their option, a fact which no court appears to have found constitutionally relevant.

45. *See, e.g.,* Bell v. School City of Gary, 324 F.2d 209 (7th Cir. 1963), *cert. denied,* 377 U.S. 924 (1964); Deal v. Cincinnati Board of Education, 369 F. 2d 55 (6th Cir. 1966), *cert. denied,* 389 U.S. 847 (1967). *See also* Fiss, "Racial Imbalance in the Public Schools: The Constitutional Concepts," 78 *Harv. L. Rev.* 564 (1965).

46. *See, e.g.,* Dimond, "School Segregation in the North: There Is But One Constitution," 7 *Harv. Civ. Rts.-Civ. Lib. L. Rev.* 1 (1972).

47. *See, e.g.,* Davis v. School Dist., 309 F. Supp. 734 (E.D.Mich. 1970), *aff'd,* 443 F. 2d 573 (6th Cir. 1971); U.S. v. School Dist. No. 151, 301 F. Supp. 201 (N.D. Ill. 1969), *modified on other grounds,* 432 F. 2d 1147 (7th Cir. 1970). *See also* Fiss, "The Charlotte-Mecklenburg Case — Its Significance for Northern School Desegregation," 38 *U. Chi. L. Rev.* 697 (1971).

48. 413 U.S. 189 (1973).

49. This and subsequent quotations are drawn from the record, both of papers filed and transcripts of oral argument, which is available at the Office of the Clerk of the Court for the Northern District of California, San Francisco. Only references to published opinions of the court will be specifically footnoted.

50. Davis v. School Dist. 309 F. Supp. 734 (E.D. Mich. 1970).

51. James S. Coleman, Ernest Q. Campbell, Carol J. Hobson, James McPartland, Alexander M. Mood, Frederic D. Weinfeld, and Robert York, *Equality of Educational Opportunity* (Washington, D.C.: GPO, 1966). While the Coleman report was used by plaintiffs to demonstrate the educational benefits of racial desegregation, the report's broader conclusion, that the socioeconomic background of the individual student is the strongest predictor of school achievement, was not noted by plaintiffs, nor was the relevance of the report questioned by the defendant school district.

52. This and subsequent appraisals of the board of education are drawn from the record of board meetings and from interviews with both board of education members and knowledgeable students of educational politics in San Francisco. These include present commissioners: Lucille Abrahamson, in San Francisco, 7 April 1975; Zuretti Goosby, in San Francisco, 16 April 1975; and former commissioners: Laurel Glass, in San Francisco, 4 April 1975; Claire Lilienthal, in San Francisco, 14 March 1975; Howard Nemerowski, in San Francisco, 26 March 1975; and David Sanchez, in San Francisco, 7 April 1975. Perceptions of the board's role varied among those interviewed.

53. This assessment derives both from the record of the case and from an interview with George Krueger, in San Francisco, 20 March 1976.

54. This and subsequent analyses of Judge Weigel's role are based primarily on transcripts of oral argument and in-chambers conferences, secondarily on interviews with the lawyers who participated in the case. Because of the pendency of the *Johnson* litigation, Judge Weigel was not interviewed.

55. 402 U.S. 1 (1972).

56. Order Setting Aside Submission, Sept. 22, 1970.

57. This litany is drawn from Steven Weiner, "Educational Decisions in an Organized Anarchy," Diss. School of Education, Stanford Univ., 1972, pp. 437–70.

58. The discussion of school administration in San Francisco derives from interviews with ex-superintendents Thomas Shaheen, in Valley Cottage, New York, 23 March 1975 (telephone interview); and Robert Jenkins, in Redlands, California, 18 April 1975 (telephone interview); as well as board members, lower-echelon administrators (among them Irving Breyer, for forty years legal counsel to the school district, in San Francisco, 18 April 1976; and Donald Johnson, director of the Office of Integration, 1971–1973, in Sausalito, 20 March 1975); and such participants as James Ballard, president of the San Francisco American Federation of Teachers, in San Francisco, 14 March 1975.

59. Anderson v. San Francisco Unified Sch. Dist. 357 F. Supp. 248 (N.D. Cal. 1972). See also Earl Raab, "Quotas By Any Other Name," *Commentary*, Jan. 1972, pp. 41–45.

60. See generally Weiner.

61. See Equal Educational Opportunities Project, *Data Processing Requirements for School Desegregation: A Case Study of the San Francisco Unified School District* (Washington, D.C.: Council of Great City Schools, 1973).

62. Quoted in Weiner, p. 77.

63. 402 U.S. 1 (1971).

64. *Id.* at 15.

65. *Id.* at 25.

66. Johnson v. San Francisco Unified Sch. Dist., 339 F. Supp. 1315, 1-26-7, n. 3 (N.D. Cal. 1971).

67. *Id.* at 1329–39.

68. *Id.* at 1332.

69. "Intervenors' First Objections to Plan Filed on June 10, 1971," June 14, 1971, at 986.

70. 339 F. Supp. 1315 (N.D. Cal. 1971).

71. The analysis of the Citizens' Advisory Committee work draws on the documents the committee produced and on interviews with the one professional staff member, Donald Johnson, in Sausalito, 20 March 1975; and with committee members, including: Chairman Donald Kuhn, in San Francisco, 1 April 1975; and Nicki Salan, in San Francisco, 12 March 1975. See also Weiner.

72. Title V, Calif. Adm. Code, **14020–21. Sections 5002–3 of the Education Code, which had declared the state policy of eliminating racial balance in California schools and thus served as statutory warrant for the board of education's regulations, was itself repealed by initiative in 1972. That repeal was upheld by the California Supreme Court in Santa Barbara School Dist. v. Mullin, 13 Cal. 3d 315, 530 P. 2d 605 (1975).

73. Analysis of the NAACP's planning effort derives from the plan that organization produced, and from interviews with former NAACP Education Committee members: Lois Barnes, in Berkeley, 21 March 1976; and Ann Bloomfield, in San Francisco, 14 March 1976.

74. The observations concerning Chinatown and the Big Six Companies are drawn from a variety of sources, among them: Victor G. Nee and Brett de Bary Nee, *Longtime Californ'* (New York: Pantheon, 1973); and Stanford M. Lyman, "Red Guard on Grant Avenue," in *Culture and Civility in San Francisco*, ed. Howard Becker (Chicago: Aldine, 1971), pp. 20–52.

75. *San Francisco Examiner*, 4 June 1971, p. 1, col. 4.

76. Complaint of Plaintiffs in Intervention, June 18, 1971, at 1.

77. 339 F. Supp. at 1322.

78. Transcript, June 24, 1971, at 582.

79. *Id.* at 1321.

80. *Id.*

81. 404 U.S. 1214, 1216–7 (1971).

82. No. C-72-808 RFT (N.D. Cal., May 5, 1972).

83. 500 F. 2d 249 (9th Cir. 1974).
84. 413 U.S. 189 (1973).
85. 500 F. 2d at 352.
86. Tom Wolfe offered a somewhat romantic rendering of the Chinese Freedom School movement, "Bok Gooi, Hok Gooi and T'and Jen: Or, Why There Is No National Association for the Advancement of Chinese Americans," *New York*, 21 Sept. 1971, pp. 36–41. See also *Hearings of the Select Subcommittee on Equal Educational Opportunity of the United States Senate* (Washington, D.C.: GPO, 1971), part 9B, pp. 4223–28.
87. Except where specifically noted, the data for this section are drawn from the "status reports" of the Integration Department, SFUSD, published since 1965, and from the trial court opinion in Johnson v. San Francisco Unified Sch. Dist., 339 F. Supp. 1315 (N.D. Cal. 1971).
88. *San Francisco Chronicle*, 24 Feb. 1972, p. 15, col. 1.
89. *Report of the 1971 Grand Jury of the City and County of San Francisco* (San Francisco: n.d.).
90. While four incumbents were elected to the board, two had been appointed after the trial-court decision in *Johnson* was handed down, and both spoke out against busing. The other two elected incumbents supported the board's decision to appeal *Johnson*.
91. Discussion of the role of the Office of Integration (now Integration Department) is premised both on a reading of its reports, and on interviews with district administrators, among them the three successive directors of the office: Donald Johnson, in Sausalito, 20 March 1975; Carlos Cornejo, in San Francisco, 31 March 1975; and Margery J. Levy, in San Francisco, 10 April 1975.
92. Memorandum from Margery J. Levy, Director, Integration Department and ESAA, to Lane De Lara, Associate Superintendent, Operations and Research, "Evaluation of Elementary School Desegregation: Report #2, Resegregating Tendencies in Special Programs," SFUSD, 2 Oct. 1975.
93. Racial disproportionality in the programs for educable mentally retarded (EMR) students was successfully challenged in federal court. Larry P. v. Riles, 343 F. Supp. 1306 (N.D. Cal. 1972). As a result of that suit, student enrollment in EMR classes has dropped sharply — there are currently only 168 EMR students in the district — but the problem of racial disproportionality has not been solved.
94. 339 F. Supp. at 1325.
95. O'Neill v. San Francisco Unified Sch. Dist., No. C-72-808 RFT (N.D. Cal., May 5, 1972).
96. Andrew Moss, "A Five Year Projection of the Ethnic Composition of the San Francisco Unified School District Enrollment," Unpublished paper, SFUSD, April 1976.
97. Interview with James Herndon, co-counsel for plaintiffs in *Johnson*, in San Francisco, 8 April 1975.
98. Jane Mercer, "Evaluating Integrated Elementary Education," Unpublished paper prepared for SFUSD, Sept. 1973.
99. San Francisco Human Rights Commission, "Report on Suspensions," Unpublished paper, 7 Nov. 1974, p. 6.
100. San Francisco Unified School District, "ESAA Proposal," SFUSD, May 1973.
101. This evaluation is essentially based on interviews with school board commissioner Zuretti Goosby, in San Francisco, 16 April 1975; and Robert Fisher, education director of the Hunter's Point Southeast Educational Development (SEED) Program, in San Francisco, 31 March 1975. That Black enrollment in the district is declining is a demographic fact; the reasons for that decline are subject to speculation.
102. 414 U.S. 563 (1974).
103. *Id.* at 566.
104. "Report of the Citizens' Task Force for Bilingual Education," Unpublished paper, SFUSD, 21 Jan. 1975, p. 7.
105. Murray Edelman, *Politics as Symbolic Action* (Chicago: Markham, 1971), p. 16.

106. Coleman et al., *Equality.*
107. Nathan Glazer, *Affirmative Discrimination* (New York: Basic Books, 1975), p. 121.
108. Nancy St. John, *School Desegregation: Outcomes for Children* (New York: Wiley, 1975), p. 119. See also Frederick Mosteller and Daniel P. Moynihan, eds., *On Equality of Educational Opportunity* (New York: Random House, 1972); Weinberg, "The Relationship Between School Desegregation and Academic Achievement: A Review of the Research," 39 *Law and Contemp. Probs.* 240 (1975); Cohen, "The Effects of Desegregation on Race Relations," 39 *Law and Contemp. Probs.* 271 (1975); and Epps, "Impact of School Desegregation on Aspirations, Self-Concepts and Other Aspects of Personality," 39 *Law and Contemp. Probs.* 300 (1975).
109. Glazer, p. 84. Blacks and Whites hold different opinions on this issue. A 1974 Gallup survey found that 75 percent of "non-Whites" favored "busing school children to achieve better racial balance in schools." *Gallup Opinion Index Report* 113 (Princeton, N.J.: The American Institute of Public Opinion, Nov. 1974).
110. In referring to "the state of the schools," I have in mind something substantially more basic than their changing racial composition. With respect to this issue, data explaining the reasons for demographic shifts are largely unavailable; interpretations of the data have produced more heat than light.
111. See Alan Altschuler, *Community Control: The Black Demand for Participation in Large American Cities* (New York: Pegasus, 1970); and Leonard J. Fein, *The Ecology of the Public Schools: An Inquiry into Community Control* (New York: Pegasus, 1971).
112. Calhoun v. Cook, 362 F. Supp. 1249 (N.D. Ga. 1973), *aff'd*, 552 F. 2d 717 (5th Cir. 1975), *rehearing en banc denied*, 525 F. 2d 1203 (5th Cir. 1975).
113. Liddell v. Board of Education, No. 72C 100 (1) (E.D. Mo., Dec. 24, 1975).
114. 413 U.S. 189 (1973) at 227 (Powell, J., concurring).
115. Compare the decisions of the Ninth Circuit in Johnson v. Board of Education, 500 F. 2d 349 (9th Cir. 1974) and Soria v. Oxnard District Board of Trustees, 488 F. 2d 579 (9th Cir. 1973) with Hart v. Community School Board of Education, 512 F. 2d 37 (2d Cir. 1975) and United States v. Texas Education Agency, 532 F. 23 380 (5th Cir. 1976). See also United States v. School District of Omaha, 521 F. 2d 530 (8th Cir. 1975); Morgan v. Kerrigan, 509 F. 2d 580 (1st Cir. 1974).
116. In Diaz v. San Jose Unified School District, No. C-71-2130 REP, (N.D. Cal., Dec. 31, 1975), the District Court held that the San Jose school district had demonstrated that segregation resulted from adherence to a neighborhood-school policy, and that this demonstration overcame the presumption that the segregation was "intentional."
117. 413 U.S. 189, 226 (Powell, J., concurring).
118. *Id.* at 240.
119. The "classic" court model, and elements of its contemporary counterpart, are drawn from Chayes, "The Role of the Judiciary in a Public Law System," 89 *Harv. L. Rev.* 1281 (1976). Compare Nathan Glazer, "Towards an Imperial Judiciary?" *Public Interest*, 41 (1975), 104–23.
120. Morgan v. Kerrigan, 401 F. Supp. 216 (D. Mass 1975), *aff'd*, 530 F. 2d 401 (1st Cir. 1976).
121. Bradley v. Milliken, 402 F. Supp. 1096 (E.D. Mich. 1975), 411 F. Supp. 943 (E.D. Mich. 1975), *rev'd in part and remanded*, F. 2d (6th Cir. 1976). See also Thomas J. Flygare, "Can Federal Courts Control an Educational Program?" *Phi Delta Kappan*, 57 (1976), 550–51.
122. 418 U.S. 717, 764 (1974) (White, J. dissenting) (emphasis in original).
123. Glazer, *Affirmative Discrimination*, p. 129.

Bilingual Education:
The Legal Mandate

HERBERT TEITELBAUM
RICHARD J. HILLER

School districts are increasingly obliged to provide bilingual-bicultural education programs to their limited-English-speaking students. This obligation may derive from legislation, either federal or state, community pressure, or court order. Particularly influential in the growth of bilingual-bicultural programs were the federal Bilingual Education Act of 1968,[1] providing the first federal funds for bilingual education, and the Bilingual Education Act of 1974, in which Congress described such programs as those in which

> there is instruction given in, and study of, English and to the extent necessary to allow a child to progress effectively through the educational system, the native language of the children of limited English-speaking ability, and such instruction is given with appreciation for the cultural heritage of such children, and, with respect to elementary school instruction, such instruction shall, to the extent necessary, be in all courses or subjects of study which will allow a child to progress effectively through the educational system.[2]

This article traces recent developments in the courts' view of the responsibilities of school districts to offer educational programs for linguistic-minority students. While it does not delve deeply into the educational controversies over the merits of particular approaches, the discussion outlines various conceptions of appropriate instruction for these students. These conceptions range from English as a Second Language (ESL)[3] to bilingual bicultural programs.[4]

The landmark case in bilingual education was *Lau v. Nichols*.[5] It squarely presented to the courts the issue of whether non-English-speaking students who constitute national-origin minority groups receive an education free from unlawful discrimination when instructed in English, a language they do not understand. The Supreme Court's January 1974 ruling in *Lau* that federally aided school districts must address the needs of their non-English-speak-

Harvard Educational Review Vol. 47 No. 2 May 1977, 138–170
Copyright © Center for Applied Linguistics, Richard J. Hiller, Herbert Teitelbaum, 1977.
Reprinted with permission.

ing students continues to reverberate in the halls of educational institutions. Although it did not expressly endorse bilingual education, the *Lau* decision legitimized and gave impetus to the movement for equal educational opportunity for students who do not speak English. *Lau* raised the nation's consciousness of the need for bilingual education, encouraged additional federal legislation, energized federal enforcement efforts, led to federal funding of nine regional "general assistance *Lau* centers," aided the passage of state laws mandating bilingual education, and spawned more lawsuits.

Added to the arsenal of those seeking court-mandated bilingual programs are the "*Lau* remedies"[6] promulgated by the Department of Health, Education and Welfare (HEW). The *Lau* remedies may be valuable to litigants in suggesting to courts appropriate relief, but they have provoked controversy and criticism. Adherents of bilingual education find the *Lau* remedies too limited in scope, the discretion afforded local officials too broad, and HEW's enforcement efforts wholly inadequate. School authorities are displeased for very different reasons, arguing that the *Lau* remedies are ambiguous, unduly burdensome, and not amenable to implementation.

It is true that a court-ordered bilingual program often jars the educational system and may do little to persuade those who must carry out the decree of the merits of bilingual education. In fact, the antipathy of school personnel to bilingual education may intensify with judicial involvement. It is equally certain, however, that as long as school districts fail to meet the needs of linguistic-minority students, the jurisdiction of the courts will continue to be invoked. Litigation has served and will continue to serve as a necessary strategy for educational reform. Without this source of leverage, powerless communities often have no effective recourse when the educational hierarchy claims that problems like budget constraints and collective-bargaining agreements are insurmountable. Asserting the right to an equal educational opportunity tends to blunt those defenses, subjecting them to the scrutiny of the courts. *Lau* and related cases are convincing evidence that litigation is essential to secure compliance with the law where school systems are unresponsive to the call for educational reform.

But litigation need not and should not be the only tactic employed. Not all school districts must be threatened with court action or brought before the bar to be made to address the educational needs of linguistic-minority students. Efforts to pass state legislation mandating bilingual education or to apply community pressure on school officials have sometimes succeeded. These other avenues to securing bilingual education should be explored because both the legal process and the legal principles involved have inherent limitations. Even the most far-reaching decrees treat bilingual education as essentially compensatory education. For those who view bilingual education more expansively and chafe at the notion of remediation, lawsuits may produce less than satisfactory results.

Lau v. Nichols

Even the most prescient could not foresee at the time of its passage that Title VI of the Civil Rights Act of 1964[7] would become a principal weapon of linguistic minorities in their battle to establish bilingual programs and gain equal schooling. In 1964 the renaissance of bilingual education had barely begun, enactment of the Bilingual Education Act was still four years away, and a national consciousness of the need for bilingual education had not yet been evoked. Relatively few schools received federal monies in 1964, but by the time *Lau* was decided a decade later, virtually all of the nation's school districts were receiving federal aid[8] and fell within the prohibition of Title VI: "No person in the United States shall, on the ground of race, color or national origin, be excluded from participation in, be denied the benefits of, or be subjected to discrimination under any program or activity receiving Federal financial assistance."[9] Because each school district receiving federal monies must agree to comply with the antidiscrimination provision, Title VI has become an increasingly powerful lever for eradicating discrimination in education.

Two different developments were important in setting the stage for the application of Title VI in *Lau*. First, soon after passage of the statute, the right of private individuals to sue for enforcement was established.[10] Second, in 1968 HEW promulgated Title VI regulations and guidelines pertaining to the schooling of children of national-origin minority groups.[11]

The Lawsuit

Lau v. Nichols was brought by Chinese public school students against the San Francisco Unified School District in 1970. The parties did not dispute the critical facts that 1,790 Chinese students received no services designed to meet their linguistic needs and that these students suffered educationally.[12] What was in question was whether non-English-speaking students receive an equal educational opportunity when instructed in a language they cannot understand.

The plaintiffs claimed that the absence of programs designed to meet the linguistic needs of such students violated both Title VI and the Equal Protection Clause of the Fourteenth Amendment to the Constitution. They urged that equality in education go beyond providing the same buildings and books to all students and includes intangible factors.[13] Because they could not understand the language of the classroom, the Chinese students argued, they were deprived of even a minimally adequate education, let alone an education equal to that of other children. They claimed that their educational exclusion was a function of state action since school attendance was compulsory,[14] the use of the English language was mandated by the state,[15] and fluency in English was a prerequisite to high school graduation.[16] The difference in treatment, the plaintiffs contended, amounted to invidious discrimination because it affected a distinct national origin group.[17] They argued that the Constitution prohibited withholding from them the means of comprehending the language of instruction.

All these claims were rejected by the federal district court. The court ruled that the students' rights to an equal educational opportunity had been satisfied by their receipt of "the same education made available on the same terms and conditions to the other tens of thousands of students in the San Francisco Unified School District."[18] The Ninth Circuit Court of Appeals affirmed, with one dissent. That court ruled that the uniform use of English does not constitute unlawful discrimination and declared that English-language instruction must be paramount in the schooling process.[19]

The *Lau* petitioners then presented their case to the Supreme Court. At this point, because HEW was concerned with the impact of the lower-court decisions on its policies regarding non-English-speaking students and on its authority to govern the use of bilingual education funds, the United States requested and was granted permission to argue in support of the *Lau* petitioners as *amicus curiae*. Although the federal government raised the same constitutional arguments as the plaintiffs,[20] its presentation rested largely on Title VI guidelines and on its right to place reasonable conditions on the receipt of federal monies. The government reasoned that the Ninth Circuit had erred in dismissing the federal statutory claim based on Title VI as if it were no different from the claim of Fourteenth Amendment rights.[21] It stressed that the HEW regulations and guidelines construing Title VI were entitled to great weight according to prior Supreme Court decisions.[22] No matter how the Supreme Court might construe the principles of the Equal Protection Clause as applied to *Lau*, the government argued, HEW's interpretation of Title VI outlawed the actions of the San Francisco school district. The Supreme Court unanimously agreed, avoiding the constitutional issue and relying solely on Title VI.[23]

The *Lau* opinion touches on fundamental issues of what constitutes equal treatment, and it may be construed as going beyond the ruling that HEW can promulgate reasonable regulations and guidelines in implementing acts of Congress.[24] The Court considered whether students who do not understand English receive equal treatment when English is the sole medium of instruction and no additional steps are taken to teach them English. It reasoned: "Under these state-imposed standards there is no equality of treatment merely by providing students with the same facilities, textbooks, teachers, and curriculum; for students who do not understand English are effectively foreclosed from any meaningful education."[25]

The lower courts had ruled that offering identical services to all students is sufficient to meet the strictures of the Equal Protection Clause and implicitly of Title VI, even though students actually received disparate benefits because of significant differences in their opportunities to take advantage of those services. Rejecting this analysis, the Supreme Court relied on the Title

VI regulations and guidelines which speak to equality in the offering and receipt of benefits: "It seems obvious that the Chinese-speaking minority receives fewer benefits than the English-speaking majority from respondents'
school system which denies them a meaningful opportunity to participate in
the educational program — all earmarks of discrimination banned by the
regulations."[26]

A critical underpinning of the Court's decision was a memorandum issued
by HEW on May 25, 1970,[27] regarding children of national origin minority
groups with limited English-language skills. The memorandum informed
school districts that they must take affirmative steps to rectify English-language deficiencies — steps that would go beyond providing the same books
and teachers to all pupils. The Court reinforced this requirement. Construing Title VI broadly, it found that the statute proscribes treating different
people identically when the results will be unidentical. Any narrower view
might have led the Court to disregard the Title VI regulations and guidelines
as going beyond the scope intended by Congress for Title VI and, accordingly, as imposing an unauthorized condition on the disbursement of federal
money.[28]

Although bilingual education was the relief originally demanded in the
complaint, by the time *Lau* reached the Ninth Circuit Court this request for
specific relief had been abandoned, and all that was sought was effective affirmative steps on the part of the school district. The Supreme Court opinion did not mandate a specific approach to teaching national-origin students
with English-language problems. As Justice Douglas noted at the outset of
the Court's opinion:

> No specific remedy is urged upon us. Teaching English to the students of Chi-
> nese ancestry who do not speak the language is one choice. Giving instructions
> to this group in Chinese is another. There may be others. Petitioners ask only
> that the Board of Education be directed to apply its expertise to the problem
> and rectify the situation.[29]

In response to this Supreme Court mandate, the San Francisco Board of
Education approved a modified version of a master plan prepared by a citizens' task force. The district court entered a consent decree providing for a
bilingual-bicultural program for the Chinese, Filipino, and Spanish-language groups in the school district. The 10,903 students who comprised
these three groups constituted 82 percent of San Francisco students who
spoke little or no English. For students from other language groups, the decree required the implementation of ESL and other special programs, including, where feasible, bilingual instruction. Responsibility for monitoring
implementation of the decree was placed with a community council
established and given administrative support by the school district.

The Supreme Court has emphasized that neither the Constitution nor
federal law should or does convert courts into school boards.[30] Educational

policy is a state function, and the Court has declared itself "ill-equipped to determine the 'necessity' of discrete aspects of a state's program of compulsory education."[31] Even in cases that limit the power of the states to govern education, whether in the specific area of language instruction[32] or in the more general area of compulsory public-school attendance,[33] the courts are reluctant to interfere with the manner in which school authorities design and enforce minimal educational standards[34] or, indeed, pay for the education offered to students.[35] However, counterbalancing this deference to the policies of local school officials are the stringent standards courts imposed when discrimination on the basis of race or national origin is at stake. In *Lau* there is no question that the language discrimination perpetrated by the San Francisco school district was construed as national origin discrimination,[36] since Chinese children were involved.

In cases of language discrimination, as in other school-related discrimination cases involving race or national origin,[37] districts that have violated their duty to take affirmative steps to rectify language difficulties have the burden of presenting a plan and demonstrating to the courts its effectiveness in remedying their unlawful failure to open the instructional program to language-minority students.[38] The remedial standard that binds courts in desegregation cases — namely, whether the school district is offering a remedy that "promises to realistically work, and promises realistically to work now"[39] — may be equally applicable to cases brought under *Lau*. The HEW memorandum of May 25, 1970, is in accord with this standard and requires that a school district's affirmative steps "must be designed to meet . . . language skill needs as soon as possible."[40]

The Aftermath of *Lau*

The nationwide impact of the *Lau* ruling has been manifested in legislation at the federal and state levels and in several lawsuits. Seven months after the ruling, Congress codified the Court's holding in the Equal Educational Opportunity Act of 1974.[41] Significantly, the new federal legislation extended *Lau* to all public school districts, not just those receiving federal financial assistance: the proscription of *Lau* cannot now be circumvented by a school district spurning federal funds. Congress also recognized how important staffing is in any effort to fulfill the federal rights of linguistic minorities: although the act contained a general ban against discrimination in teacher hiring and assignment, it excepted from this ban staffing to fulfill the mandate to overcome the language barrier.[42] Also in the wake of *Lau*, numerous state legislatures have passed statutes mandating bilingual education.[43]

Two decisions since *Lau*, *Serna v. Portales Municipal Schools*[44] and *Aspira of New York, Inc., v. Board of Education of the City of New York*,[45] have resulted in court-mandated bilingual programs. A third decision, *Rios v. Read*,[46] discussed the school district's responsibilities, indicating that unless the district's bilingual program were effective, a *Lau* violation would be triggered the same as if no program were offered. A fourth, *Otero v. Mesa County Valley School District No. 51*,[47] rejected all claims of national-origin discrimination and, having found no *Lau* violations, never reached the knotty remedial problems. Two other cases raised issues of Native American bilingualism in the schools. Both ended in consent decrees, but neither case exclusively concerned bilingual education.[48]

Serna v. Portales Municipal Schools

1972, Chicano students challenged the English-only instructional program in the schools of Portales, New Mexico. After hearing testimony from teach ers, school administrators, and educational psychologists, the court found a violation of the students' constitutional rights to an equal educational opportunity and ordered that bilingual instruction be provided. The court rejected the school board's proposed program as tokenism and ordered the adoption of the bilingual-education program submitted by the plaintiffs. The Portales school officials, with the support of the New Mexico State Board of Education, appealed the decision.

Before the appeal was heard, the Supreme Court decided *Lau*. The Tenth Circuit Court of Appeals, noting that *Lau* and *Serna* were almost identical, affirmed the trial court's ruling under Title VI but, like the Supreme Court, declined to decide the constitutional claim. In upholding the trial court's adoption of the plaintiffs' plan for bilingual instruction, the Tenth Circuit held that the schoolchildren had a right to bilingual education.[49]

The amount of bilingual instruction ordered was not extensive compared to what has been implemented elsewhere. In the one elementary school where 86 percent of the students were Spanish-surnamed, all students in grades one to three were to receive sixty minutes of bilingual instruction per day, and students in grades four to six were to receive forty-five minutes per day. In the remaining three elementary schools, where the enrollment was predominantly Anglo, only thirty minutes of bilingual instruction was mandated for all grades. No minimum amount of bilingual instruction was ordered for students in junior high, and at the high-school level only the offering of ethnic studies was required. The plan was particularly significant in that English-dominant Chicano and Anglo students were required to receive some bilingual instruction.

Aspira of New York, Inc., v. Board of Education of the City of New York

Also in 1972, Puerto Rican and other Hispanic students in New York City sued the city board of education, claiming that the commitments of school officials to bilingual education remained largely unfulfilled.[50] Thousands of Hispanic students received instruction in ESL only, and tens of thousands received no instruction to meet their linguistic and cultural needs. Echoing the defense raised by the San Francisco school district in *Lau*, New York's board of education asserted that providing the same services to all students violates neither the Equal Protection Clause nor Title VI. The board also claimed that HEW and the state department of education were responsible for funding bilingual programs and, therefore, were indispensable parties to the lawsuit. The court rejected both defenses.[51]

After the *Lau* ruling, the *Aspira* plaintiffs moved for summary judgment. The court ordered the defendants to undertake an extensive survey of the needs of the Hispanic students and the special services and personnel available to them. The court also directed the parties to submit plans for meeting the students' educational needs.[52]

With the court's prodding, and after negotiations, the parties consented to a decree in August 1974. Under the consent decree the school board is required to design and implement an improved method for assessing Hispanic students' skills in English and Spanish in order to identify those students with English-language difficulties who, accordingly, have rights under *Lau*. For eligible students, instruction in core courses and other courses required for promotion and graduation must be offered in Spanish.[53] The decree also mandates programs designed to develop children's ability to speak, read, write, and understand English. It specifically rejects immersion as a technique of second-language acquisition and forbids pullout programs. So that segregation will not occur, students in the program must spend as much classroom time with students outside the program as their educational needs permit. Materials used in the program must reflect, where appropriate, the culture of the children involved. Recognizing the need for additional competent personnel, the decree calls for affirmative teacher recruitment and specifies the necessary teacher qualifications.[54]

The consent decree, in large measure, is not an educator's document. Although it describes a bilingual program, includes standards for identifying students entitled to the program, and sets forth teacher qualifications, it does not instruct educators in implementation — how to transform a plan on paper into a viable educational program. Furthermore, while the *Aspira* decree constitutes perhaps the most far-reaching court-ordered bilingual program since *Lau*, it does not reach all Hispanic students with rights under *Lau*. The *Lau* decision covers any students whose limited English-language skills exclude them from the regular instructional program. The *Aspira* consent decree, by contrast, applies only to those students who can participate in the learning process more effectively in Spanish than in English. Hispanic students who are no more proficient in Spanish than they are in English do not fall within the class defined in the consent decree and are not offered the program under its mandate.

Rios v. Read

The most recent decision related to *Lau* is *Rios v. Read*, rendered in 1977. In the context of a motion to compel a school district sued under *Lau* to disclose its students' records, the opinion in *Rios v. Read* probed the obligations imposed on school authorities toward their non-English-speaking students. Plaintiffs sought information concerning achievement levels, tenure in special ESL pullout classes, reading scores, and attendance rates in an effort to assess whether the programs of the school district of Patchogue-Medford, Long Island, effectively promoted academic progress and second-language fluency. Of the two principal defenses raised by the district in its effort to withhold the records, one focused on *Lau*.[55] Arguing that *Lau* requires only that a school district take affirmative steps to meet the needs of non-English-speaking students, the district maintained that an investigation of facts directed toward the effectiveness of those steps was irrelevant.

The district court acknowledged that the school district provided a remedial program for English-language-deficient children, that a bilingual department existed in the district, and that New York State's policy is to encourage bilingual education, but it nevertheless rejected the notion that *any* affirmative steps pursued by a school district satisfy *Lau*:

> It is not enough simply to provide a program for disadvantaged children or even to staff the program with bilingual teachers; rather, the critical question is whether the program is designed to assure as much as is reasonably possible the language deficient child's growth in the English language. An inadequate program is as harmful to a child who does not speak English as no program at all.[56]

For the first time, a district court amplified the holding of *Lau* by making reference to the legislative history of the federal Bilingual Education Act of 1974, in which Congress recognized the far-reaching implications of *Lau* and emphasized "the importance of bilingual education in the academic and personal growth of the language disadvantaged child."[57] The court observed that increasing the quantity of bilingual programs was "meaningless without a concomitant emphasis on the quality of instruction."[58]

Relying on *Serna*, the court summed up:

> To put a final perspective on the defendants' position, it could hardly be argued that if a school district was found to violate the standards of *Lau v. Nichols* because it had failed to provide any bilingual education for language disadvantaged children, a court would be required to accept without scrutiny whatever remedial program the school district then proposes simply because the district now could claim that it was taking "affirmative steps."[59]

For this district court, then, *Lau* is not a *carte blanche*; the standard of effectiveness governs for purposes of both liability and remedy when a school district is charged with offering inadequate programs.[60]

Otero v. Mesa County Valley School District No. 51

Otero presents the most resounding rejection of a claimed right to bilingual education since the lower-court decisions in *Lau*. The case demonstrated the judiciary's hesitancy to become involved in educational policy making, especially in the absence of the clear linguistic and educational evidence that would have proved critical to the plaintiffs' case.

To force the introduction of bilingual education, Chicano schoolchildren in Mesa County claimed that the programs provided to them were inappropriate and violated their rights under Title VI and the Equal Protection Clause. The plaintiffs sought to establish that the principal cause for Chicano students' poor performance in school was that "District 51 has created a school system oriented for middle-class, Anglo children, [and] has staffed the system with non-Chicano personnel who do not understand and cannot relate with Chicano students who are linguistically and culturally different."[61] In support of their claims, the plaintiffs relied heavily on the Cardenas-Cardenas Theory of Incompatibilities.[62]

While *Otero* was being prosecuted, the appeal in *Keyes v. School District No. 1, Denver, Colorado*,[63] involving the desegregation of the Denver schools, was decided by the Tenth Circuit. That appellate court reversed the district court's order that a bilingual-education program based on the Cardenas-Cardenas Theory of Incompatibilities be included in a Denver desegregation plan. The *Keyes* appellate court found that the Cardenas plan "would unjustifiably interfere with . . . state and local attempts to deal with the myriad economic, social, and philosophical problems connected with the education of minority students."[64] Relying heavily on *Keyes*, the *Otero* court held that the Fourteenth Amendment does not require school districts to offer bilingual-bicultural programs. It gratuitously added that the Cardenas plan, as applied to the defendant school district, was "illogical, unbelievable and unacceptable."[65] Low academic performance on the part of the Chicano students, the court found, was caused by socioeconomic factors and not the failings or unresponsiveness of the educational program.

With regard to the *Lau* claim, the court found that few if any students in the district had "real language deficiency" and that the school board was "making a real, conscientious effort to recognize, face, and solve any problem which may exist as to any student."[66] There was no discussion of the nature or the success of any special programs offered. In *Otero* the court merely found that plaintiffs did not prove the necessary facts to establish a violation of either Title VI or the Fourteenth Amendment.

Remedies

Establishing a *Lau* violation by proving that a school district offers no program to address the needs of limited-English-speaking students is easier than determining the type of program that will be sufficient to remedy a proven *Lau* violation. There is ample reason to believe that in judging a program's adequacy the courts will rely heavily on the standards set forth in HEW's *Lau* remedies,[67] since the *Lau* decision must be read not only as upholding the May 25 memorandum, but also as reaffirming the general authority of HEW to issue and enforce reasonable interpretive guidelines consistent with the purpose of Title VI.

In the summer of 1975, HEW's Office of Education and its Office of Civil Rights (OCR) jointly issued the findings of a task force set up after the *Lau* decision. Commonly referred to as the "*Lau* remedies,"[68] the findings outline, among other things, educational approaches found to be appropriate affirmative steps toward opening the instructional program to non-English-dominant students. School districts are required to develop quickly and then submit to OCR[69] specific voluntary compliance plans[70] if they are found to be noncompliant with Title VI and if they have twenty or more students of the same language group who have been identified as having a primary or home language other than English.[71] These twenty students need not all be students with limited English-language ability. School districts with a lone student with limited English-language skills are obliged to take affirmative steps, although these are not expected to be as extensive and comprehensive as they would be in other districts.

The *Lau* remedies do not mandate bilingual education. For example, they expressly endorse ESL as one of the five acceptable options at the high-school level. They also approve of ESL for students at the intermediate level who do not speak exclusively a language other than English. Even at the elementary level, where ESL is categorically rejected, bilingual education is not required. In fact, school authorities may propose and pursue educational approaches other than those outlined in the *Lau* remedies. The important stipulation is that they must demonstrate affirmatively that the educational program proffered — whatever it may be — will be equally effective in ensuring equal educational opportunity.[72]

Still, the significance of the *Lau* remedies should not be underestimated. In shifting to school authorities the burden of demonstrating that educational programs not conforming with programs contained in the *Lau* remedies are "equally effective," the *Lau* remedies at a minimum create a legal presumption in favor of bilingual education at the elementary and intermediate levels. This is a presumption that school districts may have great difficulty overcoming: it is particularly true of civil-rights litigation that the party able to shift the burden of proof is most often the party that prevails.

The Office of Civil Rights has stated that, although it does not look on the *Lau* remedies as "a regulation with the force of law," they are "entitled to weight as an agency interpretation" and are to be considered comparable to the May 25 memorandum.[73] Whether labeled a guideline, an agency interpretation entitled to great weight, or an agency regulation having the force of law, the *Lau* remedies clearly cannot be disregarded by school districts.[74] In dealing with courts, school districts will have difficulty asserting that the *Lau* remedies are unreasonable or inconsistent with Title VI, especially since program approaches are presented as options in the remedies, bilingual education is not mandated, and alternative programs are acceptable if shown to be equally effective. The flexibility and permissiveness of the *Lau* remedies, which some adherents of bilingual education have faulted, should save them from being struck down by the courts.

Enforcement

Compliance with the *Lau* remedies, as with any civil-rights law, is secured only to the extent that enforcement efforts are vigorous and the threat of sanctions is real.[75] The ultimate sanction for noncompliance, termination of federal funds, has rarely been invoked by HEW in recent years and has come to be regarded as a dead letter.[76] HEW is more likely to adopt the less extreme method for encouraging compliance that it used, for example, when the Seattle school district refused to submit a voluntary *Lau* compliance plan: deferral of future funding. HEW may also refuse to fund grant proposals submitted by districts suspected of noncompliance.

However, problems and delays in HEW's enforcement of Title VI suggest that the department is unlikely to act energetically on behalf of linguistic minorities. For example, Black students alleged, in *Adams v. Richardson*,[77] that HEW had consciously and expressly abdicated its enforcement responsibilities under Title VI to end segregation in southern public schools receiving federal funds. The court agreed, finding HEW derelict in its duty to investigate Title VI complaints promptly and to initiate enforcement proceedings if its attempts to achieve voluntary compliance failed. Two years later the court had to act again in *Adams v. Weinberger*.[78] Once again it found "an over-reliance by HEW on the use of voluntary negotiations over protracted time periods and a reluctance in recent years to use the administrative sanction process where school districts are known to be in noncompliance."[79] The court noted that HEW was still delaying in its investigations and failing to bring enforcement proceedings.

The attack on HEW broadened with *Brown v. Weinberger*[80] which challenged HEW's practice of continuing to provide federal funds to public schools in thirty-three northern and western states despite these schools' alleged violations of Title VI. *Brown v. Weinberger* went beyond *Adams v. Richardson* in that discrimination based on national origin, a well as race, was alleged. The decision in *Brown v. Weinberger* chronicled HEW's continuing failure to enforce Title VI. It found that some Title VI investigations had been pending for eight years, during which period HEW had neither determined whether the school districts involved were in compliance with Title VI nor initiated enforcement proceedings. In other school districts, where HEW had found noncompliance with Title VI (after investigations lasting up to seven years), the department had failed to achieve voluntary compliance yet had commenced no enforcement efforts; these school districts continued to receive federal funds. Still other school districts, although declared by HEW to be ineligible for Emergency School Aid Act assistance, nonetheless received substantial federal funds from HEW under other statutes. The court gave HEW sixty days to complete its investigations and commence enforcement proceedings against the school districts named.

Filing administrative complaints with HEW is one way of trying to obtain needed programs in bilingual education,[81] but this approach is fraught with problems and delays. Considering the dissatisfaction of minority groups with HEW's past enforcement efforts, it is to be expected that people seeking bilingual education for their schools will continue to turn to the courts. The threat of a lawsuit to compel local educational agencies to establish bilingual-education programs can be a deterrent to noncompliance. The lawsuit can come unexpectedly from a community too outnumbered or politically weak to influence local educational policies through traditional means. Defending a lawsuit costs money, and, with resources dwindling, school boards cannot ignore such costs. Although bringing lawsuits also costs money, reimbursement for attorneys' fees awaits plaintiffs who succeed in court or through settlement.[82]

Lawsuits may not only deplete the treasuries of school boards but also result in money damages against administrators. As the Supreme Court has said: "In some situations a damage remedy can be as effective a redress for the infringement of a constitutional right as injunctive relief might be in another."[83] It may be true that school officials who can demonstrate good faith and their own reasonable belief in the legality of their acts are insulated from suits seeking compensatory and punitive money damages. And it certainly is true that school officials are under no duty to anticipate unforeseeable developments in the law. But the well-worn adage that ignorance of the law is no excuse holds here: claimed ignorance of the *Lau* rights of students may not shield school officials who violate these rights.[84] Furthermore, if school officials fail to implement court orders, including consent decrees, they will be subject to the contempt powers of the court.[85]

Common Defenses of School Districts

As pressures mount from administrative proceedings and lawsuits to implement or augment bilingual programs, school officials generally seek to justify their inaction through certain standard defenses, citing budgetary constraints, provisions of collective-bargaining agreements, the limited number of students affected, and the undesirability of segregating minority students. The courts, however, have not been receptive to these defenses.

Budget

School boards frequently argue that budget constraints excuse their failure to provide bilingual programs. Underlying this defense is the assumption that bilingual programs cost more than the "regular" curriculum. This assumption has not been substantiated. The budgetary defense rests in most instances on the claimed need to hire more teachers. But unless a school system contemplates providing students in bilingual programs with more teachers per pupil than their English-monolingual counterparts have, the cost of personnel for bilingual programs should not impose a significant additional fiscal burden.[86] Even where school districts can show that bilingual programs require additional expenditures, the budget defense may not hold. Federal rights are not to be denied or deferred because of budget constraints, whether the rights flow from the Constitution or, like the claimed rights under *Lau*, from a federal statutory guarantee of equal educational opportunity.[87]

The Fifth Circuit Court of Appeals discussed the question of cost at length in *United States v. Texas Ed. Agency*,[88] the continuing desegregation litigation concerning the Austin public schools. Austin school officials argued that the determination of whether a constitutional violation exists should take into account the economic cost of dismantling a segregated school system, and that "root and branch desegregation" should not be ordered because of its cost. Rejecting both arguments, the court of appeals noted that cost is not relevant at the liability state and that, although cost is a factor to be considered in the balancing of interests at the remedy stage, a constitutional violation must be rectified.[89] Directly addressing the issue of funding bilingual programs, the court stated:

> The [Austin Independent School District] has an ongoing bilingual-bicultural education program that the Superintendent of Schools testified would continue "regardless of the level of federal funding." Indeed, state and federal law require as much. See 20 U.S.C.**1703(f); Tex. Educ. Code Ann. ** 21.451 et seq. (1975 pocket part). See also *Lau v. Nichols* [citation omitted]. The district court properly made this commitment a part of its decree.[90]

Similarly, in *Aspira*[91] the court rejected the argument that if a school district is required to implement bilingual programs, the state and HEW should share the financial burden. That court refused to make federal or state agencies indispensable parties to the lawsuit.

While federal courts may not have the power to order the levying of taxes and certainly lack power to alter a state's system for financial education,[92] they do have the authority to require public bodies to reallocate available resources to fund court-ordered remedies. In *Mills v. Board of Education* the court stopped short of ordering an increase in appropriations to provide immediate and adequate educational programs for handicapped children, but it did make the following ruling:

> If sufficient funds are not available to finance all of the services and programs that are needed and desirable in the system, then the available funds must be expended equitably in such a manner that no child is excluded from a publicly supported education consistent with his needs and ability to benefit therefrom. The inadequacies of the District of Columbia Public School System, whether occasioned by insufficient funding or administrative inefficiency, certainly can-

not be permitted to bear more heavily on the "exceptional" or handicapped child than the normal child.[93]

When a district claims that insufficient resources preclude instruction in a language that students understand, there may be grounds for a reordering of expenditures. Items of less educational importance may have to yield to programs necessary to meet effectively the mandate of Title VI.[94]

Finally, school officials should bear in mind that failure to reallocate resources could ultimately result in a cutoff of federal assistance for noncompliance with Title VI.[95] Thus, to deny non-English-speaking students their *Lau* rights on the grounds of fiscal plight may only reduce further the local education budget.

Contract Rights

School districts may also assert that contract rights of teachers clash with the implementation of a remedy under *Lau*. In asserting this claim, they raise issues on which federal courts have yet to rule. For example, should contract provisions concerning teacher qualifications, hiring, and retention frustrate the adoption of a program to meet the demands of *Lau*? Should unqualified monolingual teachers be retained and bilingual teachers with less seniority be laid off if the result is a curtailment of bilingual instruction to students in need? Basically, should teachers' contract rights prevail over students' needs? Several state courts have addressed contract or tenure disputes between bilingual and monolingual teachers but have not considered in such cases the rights of affected students.

It should be pointed out, though, that when school districts have used union contracts or state tenure statutes to resist orders to reassign faculty in faculty desegregation cases, their argument has failed consistently in federal court.[96] The same result should follow in bilingual education, since the Supremacy Clause of the Constitution requires that federal law (on which *Lau* was based) prevail when in conflict with state law.[97]

Number of Students

School districts commonly attempt to justify noncompliance with *Lau* by demonstrating, as in *Otero*, that the number of students not receiving appropriate programs is insignificant. How many limited-English-speaking students who receive no special language instruction must there be to establish a *Lau* violation and to obligate a school district to undertake remedial efforts? The opinion for the unanimous *Lau* court states no numerosity requirement. In a concurring opinion to *Lau*, though, Justice Blackmun and Chief Justice Burger concluded that special instruction would not be required where the case involved "a very few youngsters or . . . just a single child who speaks only German or Polish or Spanish or any other language other than English . . . [since] numbers are at the heart of this case."[98] In this view it was significant that the eighteen hundred Chinese students in *Lau* represented a "very substantial group."[99] The Blackmun view was echoed in *Serna* (where a "sizeable minority" of the school population won the right to bilingual education)[100] and followed in *Otero* (where the rights of a "tiny handful" of students were overruled).[101] Still, precisely what constitutes a "substantial group" to satisfy the Blackmun caveat is not fixed, although the outer perimeter may safely be drawn at eighteen hundred students.[102]

Title VI, however, speaks of individual rights in providing that "no person" in federally assisted programs shall be subject to discrimination. In codifying the holding in *Lau*, the Equal Educational Opportunity Act of 1974 adheres to the court's majority view as expressed by Justice Douglas. Under the act, no educational agency "shall deny equal educational opportunity *to an individual* on account of his or her . . . national origin" by failing "to take appropriate action to overcome language barriers" (emphasis added).[103]

On the matter of numbers, the *Lau* remedies seemingly seek to strike a balance. They recognize that even one limited-English-speaking student has rights under *Lau* and the Equal Educational Opportunity Act. Therefore, as we have seen, they stipulate that to satisfy those rights and address the child's educational needs, some affirmative steps must be taken, although the program adopted need not be as extensive or sophisticated as a program for twenty or more children of a particular national-origin group. Practical considerations, particularly the distribution of entitled students among schools within a district, will be the rule of thumb when a court is determining the feasibility of bilingual programs. More than likely the court will rely on the numerosity standards of the *Lau* remedies and the state bilingual education statute, if any.

Avoiding Minority-Student Segregation

Some skeptics see bilingual education as a precursor of political and ethnic separatism that threatens to divide communities along rigid lines.[104] Consequently, advocates of bilingual education often must give assurances that bilingual programs will not separate minority from non-minority students.

To avoid unlawful separation, programs can include non-minority students. Some methods for inclusion are grouping within classrooms; exchange, or a daily schedule of homogeneous grouping for bilingual instruction and heterogeneous grouping for other activities; staff differential, or highly individualized instruction by teacher aides, student teachers, paraprofessionals, and students; and individualized multimedia instruction.[105] Problems arise in these programs, though. For example, it has been argued that when the number of non-minority students in a bilingual program approaches or exceeds the number of minority students, the character of the program is jeopardized.[106] An opposite problem also occurs: sometimes not enough non-minority students are willing to participate in bilingual instruction. The fulfillment of a school district's duty to establish bilingual programs cannot await the success of recruiting non-minority volunteers. And while courts may direct non-minority involvement in bilingual programs,[107] the drawbacks of coerced attendance may outweigh the benefits.

Both HEW's 1968 regulations for the Bilingual Education Act and the May 25, 1970, HEW memorandum bar "segregation and separate treatment,"[108] but neither should be read as precluding bilingual programs in schools that are predominantly minority-attended. What they prohibit are programs that fail to rectify English-language deficiencies and instead separate and exclude students. The *Lau* remedies interdict the creation and, arguably, the perpetuation of ethnically identifiable schools in order to meet the special language needs of children of nation origin minority groups.[109] But they do not forbid maintaining existing bilingual programs in ethnically identifiable schools which have not been created or maintained through unlawful practices.

The *Lau* remedies also discuss classes within schools. They state that bilingual programs "do not justify the existence of racially/ethnically isolated or identifiable classes, *per se*." Further, they incorporate existing Emergency School Aid Act (ESAA) and Title VI regulations.[110] Under the applicable ESAA regulations,[111] schools which assign students to or within classes in a manner resulting "in the separation of minority group from non-minority group children for substantial portion of the school day" are ineligible for ESAA funding.[112] These regulations interpret "substantial" separation as separation "for more than 25 percent of the school day classroom periods."[113] Thus, where the separation lasts for more than 25 percent of the day, the presumption is raised that classroom or tracking assignments are impermissibly based on race, color, or national origin.[114] *Bona fide* ability groupings, however, are exempted from this presumption and prohibition.[115] A *bona fide* ability grouping must meet four requirements. First, placement in the group must be based on educationally relevant, nondiscriminatory, objective standards of measurement. Second, the grouping must be maintained during the school day for only as long as necessary. Third, it must be designed to meet the students' special needs and to improve academic achievement and performance through specially developed curriculums taught by specially trained instructional personnel. Finally, the grouping must be shown through objective testing to be educationally beneficial. Bilingual programs that separate minority from non-minority students for more than 25 percent of the school day should have no difficulty satisfying these ESAA requirements. There is one caveat, however: the regulations provide that the device used to group children of national origin minority groups must "not essentially measure English language skills."[116] This single provision cannot reasonably be read to rule out bilingual classes as *bona fide* ability groupings, however. The identification of students who need bilingual education obviously requires the measurement of English-language skills.[117]

In *Board of Ed. Cincinnati v. Department of HEW*, these ESAA regulations were held to be effective as a reasonable and proper exercise of HEW's regulatory authority and "well designed for the purpose of 'furthering federal education policy.' "[118] As the court observed, the ESAA regulations are consistent with established case law,[119] which permits student assignment to separate classes or tracks on the basis of ability provided such assignment "is not a subterfuge for racial discrimination."[120] In one desegregation case, *McNeal v. Tate County School District*, the Fifth Circuit said of ability grouping:

> If it does cause segregation, whether in classrooms or in schools, ability grouping may nevertheless be permitted in an otherwise unitary system if the school district can demonstrate that its assignment method is not based on the present results of past segregation or will remedy such results through better educational opportunities.[121]

Bilingual Education and Desegregation

The overriding mandate to desegregate will present formidable obstacles to organizing bilingual programs that are educationally viable and also meet the student-assignment guidelines fixed by the courts.[122] But bilingual education and desegregation need not be headed on a collision course; these educational goals are not necessarily mutually exclusive. Bilingual-education programs were first judicially mandated in 1970, four years before *Lau*, as part of the overall remedy in a Texas desegregation case.[123] Because of the broad remedial powers exercised by the courts to eliminate unlawful school segregation, desegregation cases continue to serve as convenient vehicles for court-ordered bilingual-education programs. Since a court's power to right unlawful school segregation (a constitutional wrong) may well be greater than its power to redress a *Lau* violation (a federal statutory violation), desegregation cases may provide the best hope for achieving comprehensive court-mandated bilingual-education programs.

The Courts' Remedial Powers

The expansion of the courts' powers to remedy school desegregation has been painstakingly slow. Despite the Supreme Court's declaration in 1955 in *Brown v. Board of Education (Brown II)* that a district court's remedial authority to desegregate is broad, the Court's use of the phrase "all deliberate speed" only invited delay.[124] Not until the 1960s did a series of Supreme Court decisions begin to close the gap between the time at which a school district was found to violate the principles of *Brown v. Board of Education (Brown I)* and the time for the implementation of an effective remedy. In 1963, the Court stated that a ruling calling for "deliberate speed" did not countenance indefinite delay.[125] The following year, it emphasized that "the time for mere 'deliberate speed' [had] run out,"[126] and, in 1965, it ruled that "delay in desegregating school systems [was] no longer tolerable."[127] By 1969, the Supreme Court was declaring that the "obligation of every school district is to terminate dual school systems at once and to operate now and hereafter only unitary schools."[128]

As it accelerated the schedules for desegregation, the Court also expanded the remedial authority of lower courts to insure complete and effective desegregation. In *Green v. County School Board of New Kent County, Virginia*, the Court announced that school officials found guilty of unlawful school segregation must take "whatever steps might be necessary to convert to a unitary system in which racial discrimination would be eliminated root and branch."[129] And in 1971, in *Swann*, the Court ruled that "all vestiges of state-imposed segregation" had to be removed and "once a right and violation have been shown, the scope of a district court's equitable powers to remedy past wrongs is broad, for breadth and flexibility are inherent in equitable remedies."[130]

In 1970, as the broad remedial powers of the courts were becoming firmly established, a federal district court in Texas required the implementation of the first desegregation plan to include curriculum changes designed to meet the needs of non-English-speaking students.[131] A subsequent decision in the same case required the inclusion of bilingual-bicultural programs. The court wrote:

> Having determined that the Mexican-American students . . . in the San Felipe Del Rio area may be and, indeed, for current educational purposes, must be considered as members of a cognizable ethnic or national origin group, the relief in this case becomes fundamentally similar to that which has been framed in school desegregation suits before this Court based on discriminatory treatment of Black students. The mandate, as directed by the Supreme Court, is to "eliminate discrimination root and branch," and to create a unitary school system "with no Black [Mexican] schools and no White schools but just schools."
>
> Just what is a unitary school system? The Supreme Court has offered as yet little explanation beyond saying that in such a system, no child will be effectively denied equal educational opportunities, and that the system shall exhibit the greatest amount of actual desegregation possible. Although these phrases are general and were made in the context of Black-White desegregation, this Court finds them to be useful guidelines in this case. [L]ittle could be more clear to the Court than the need . . . for special educational consideration to be given to the Mexican-American students in assisting them in adjusting to those parts of their new school environment which present a cultural and linguistic shock. Equally clear, however, is the need to avoid the creation of a stigma of inferiority akin to the "badges and indicia of slavery". . . . To avoid this result the Anglo-American students too must be called upon to adjust to their Mexican-American classmates, and learn to understand and appreciate their different linguistic and cultural attributes. The process by which all students participate in a joint learning and adjustment process will not only constitute an educational enrichment but, also, will bring the school system as a whole closer to that goal or state-of-being referred to by the Supreme Court as a "unitary system." [Citations omitted.][132]

Past Segregation of Non-Black Minority Students

Those who fear that bilingual education will promote separatism through segregated schools or classes should be reminded that many of the minority groups that now support bilingual education were themselves victims of segregation. Past segregation of non-Black minority students often was justified on the basis of purported English-language deficiencies, when the actual intent was clearly not compensatory education but rather the perpetuation of racism. The limited separation that may accompany the establishment of bilingual programs has neither the same intent nor the same effect as past practices.

In California, state law until 1947 permitted the establishment of separate schools for Chinese, American Indian, Japanese, and "Mongolian" students.[133] Although Mexican American students were not excluded by statute from White schools in California or in the Southwest generally, the absence of express legislative authority did not deter school officials from establishing and maintaining "Mexican-only" schools. In many school systems in the Southwest, Mexican Americans were "historically separated in fact from Anglos, although the separation never had a statutory origin."[134] Although some school authorities in these systems claimed that the Mexican-American students' English-language difficulties necessitated the establishment of separate schools,[135] the non-English-speaking children of recent immigrants from other countries were not separated in this way. In Uvalde, Texas, as early as 1907 there was a "Mexican school," established "apparently as the result of the language problem."[136] Arizona and California schools segregated Mexican American students in the same way.[137]

Tri-Ethnic Desegregation

Given the decades of persistent discrimination against Mexican American schoolchildren in the Southwest, one would have expected the Supreme Court to have begun well before the 1970s to try to untangle the problem of school segregation as it related to those children. In fact, though, it was not until 1973, when it decided its first "northern" desegregation case, *Keyes v. School District No. 1, Denver*[138] that the Court first outlined how Mexican American students were to be treated (or, more accurately, counted) in the context of desegregation. The *Keyes* court seemingly settled the question of whether Hispanic students in a tri-ethnic school system were to be considered minority students when it ruled that "schools with a combined predominance of Negroes and Hispanics [should be] included in the category of 'segregated' schools."[139] The *Keyes* directive to treat Mexican Americans as minority students turned on its finding that students of this group "suffer[ed] the same educational inequities as Negroes and American Indians."[140] A narrow reading of *Keyes* would limit this finding to Chicanos in the Southwest, and there is support for this view.[141] However, in applying *Keyes* the courts have interpreted this aspect of the holding expansively, neither restricting application of the term Hispanic to Chicanos in the Southwest nor requiring a showing of "identical discrimination." Other Hispanic persons, Asian Americans, and American Indians have been treated as minority students by courts at the liability and remedial stages of desegregation cases.[142]

Despite the more than a decade of authority that courts have had for reorganizing school systems to remove all vestiges of segregation, there are signs that the scope of a court's power to issue broad remedies in desegregation cases is being reconsidered.[143] The Tenth Circuit Court of Appeals in *Keyes* is a harbinger that the breadth of desegregation remedies, particularly as related to ordering bilingual education, may be come more narrowly circumscribed.[144]

A central feature of the desegregation plan adopted by the district court in *Keyes* was the so-called Cardenas plan, proposed by the Mexican American intervenors.[145] To implement the Cardenas plan on a pilot basis, the desegregation plan left intact four schools that were overwhelmingly Chicano. On appeal, however, the Tenth Circuit rejected the Cardenas plan. It found that, in approving the plea, the district court had "overstepped the limits of its remedial power"[146] and further found, on the authority of *San Antonio School District v. Rodriguez,* that the Cardenas plan would unjustifiably infringe upon state and local educational prerogatives.[147] According to the Tenth Circuit, no proof had been offered in the lower court to establish that the existing curricula discriminated against Chicanos, and the Denver public schools' failure to offer Hispanic students an "educational experience tailored to their unique cultural and developmental needs" did not violate the Fourteenth Amendment.[148] Nor had a *Lau* violation been established, since no proof of English-language disabilities had been presented to the district court.

Without the Cardenas plan, there was no justification for maintaining identifiably Chicano schools. To remove any doubts, the Tenth Circuit cautioned that bilingual education is no substitute for desegregation.[149] The court directed, though, that a determination be made of whether any *Lau* violations were present and what relief, if any, might be "necessary to ensure that Hispano and other minority children will have the opportunity to acquire proficiency in the English language."[150]

The decision in *Keyes* contains only two passing references to the Tenth Circuit's prior decision in *Serna* and the Supreme Court's decision in *Lau.*[151] According to the *Keyes* court, neither *Lau* nor *Serna* presented any obstacle to the *Keyes* ruling, since they concerned violations of Title VI and thus did not deal with the constitutional issue. Yet the restrictions the Tenth Circuit *Keyes* decision imposes on the scope of the district court's equitable authority seem inconsistent with its own approval of the remedial order in *Serna.* That case, initially forged on a finding of a Fourteenth Amendment violation and later, on appeal, upheld on the basis of Title VI, resulted in a relatively broad decree. The district court ordered a bilingual program including provisions for ethnic studies, recruitment of qualified bilingual teachers, and the inclusion of non-Chicano students in the program. The Tenth Circuit expressly acknowledged that the district court acted properly in going beyond the bilingual-bicultural plan recommended by the school district.[152]

Although the Tenth Circuit referred in *Serna* to "unique circumstances," neither it nor the lower court pinpointed the distinguishing aspects of the Portales schools. A comparison of the findings in *Serna* to those in *Keyes* raises questions as to whether Portales and Denver were substantively different in their treatment of Chicano students. Both district courts relied on achievement levels and IQ test results as indexes of inequality. Both accepted diminished self-concept as a contributor to inequality, and both related the need of improving self-concept to the need of imbuing the schools with aspects of the Chicano culture. Alienation of minority students was the central theme in both courts' conclusions that the Equal Protection Clause was violated. The nature of the proof offered and of the relief recommended in both cases makes the distinction drawn by the *Keyes* court unsatisfactory.

Why the Tenth Circuit adopted in *Keyes*, but not in *Serna*, the argument that the district court's relief "constituted an unwarranted and improper judicial interference in the internal affairs of the . . . school district"[153] can be explained only by the desegregation aspects of the Denver case and by the courts' increasing hesitancy to issue broad remedial decrees without clear poof of a correlative violation of law.[154] Whereas in *Serna* the violation was the failure of the school district to offer a curriculum to meet the educational needs of minority students, in *Keyes* the focus was segregation. Indeed, the Tenth Circuit found that the district court's plan was not sufficient to dismantle segregation in the Denver schools. The court could not be expected to approve identifiable minority schools, particularly when it was simultaneously ruling that the remedy had not gone far enough to desegregate the system as a whole. The ethnic groupings in the four pilot schools could not even be justified on the basis of the students' language disabilities, because evidence on that issue had not been proffered. Even with such evidence, it is doubtful whether this court would have ruled differently, since desegregation was its overriding concern.

Moreover, the thrust of desegregation is to offer the same education to all students regardless of race or national origin. To establish identifiable Chicano schools in the name of developing a greater sense of culture and self-concept may also permit the establishment of identifiable Black schools for the same reasons. Even if the creation of such schools might be educationally sound, it does not pass muster under the Constitution, especially when a system is found to be operating segregated schools and the mandate is to desegregate them. If bilingual programs are to be part of a desegregation remedy, they cannot jeopardize the court's paramount concern to integrate.

Another consideration in *Keyes* was that the addendum to the Cardenas plan would have brought about a major overhaul of the Denver educational system,[155] making the court nearly indistinguishable from a school board. The degree of detail in the addendum brought *Keyes* into conflict with the admonition of *Rodriguez* against judicial encroachment upon matters of educational policy. The equitable remedial powers of the courts to effect desegregation, though broad, are not limitless. In *Swann*, the Court noted that "the nature of the violation determines the scope of the remedy" and that in any formulation of relief the task is to "correct . . . the condition that offends the Constitution."[156] Applying this remedial standard to the metropolitan desegregation plan ordered in Detroit, the Supreme Court found in *Milliken v. Bradley*[157] that the lower court had exceeded its remedial powers by including in the plan suburban school districts which had not been shown to have offended the Constitution. Further evidence that the equitable remedial powers of the courts are circumscribed is provided by *Pasadena City Board of Education v. Spangler*, where the Supreme Court found that the district court exceeded its authority in requiring the "annual readjustment of attendance zones so that there would not be a majority of any minority in any Pasadena School."[158]

There should soon be some clarification of the courts' authority to fashion decrees that order particular educational programs. The Supreme Court will again consider the remedy ordered in *Milliken v. Bradley*, and the appeal presents precisely this issue.[159] The district court, in order to remedy effects of past segregation and to assure successful desegregation and avoid the possibility of resegregation, had directed the Detroit school board to institute widespread compensatory education programs. These programs were proposed by the board itself and went far beyond the mere fixing of ratios. Also included were programs in vocational education, remedial reading, in-service faculty training, unbiased testing, and counseling and career guidance. Although there was no showing of a constitutional violation in any of these specific areas, these aspects of the district court's order were upheld on appeal. The Sixth Court observed: "This is not a situation where the District Court 'appears to have acted solely according to its own notions of good educational policy unrelated to the demands of the Constitution.'"[160] The district court's plan also included a code of student conduct, a program of community relations, and — most important for our purposes — a bilingual-education component (independently required by state law). These components were not challenged on appeal, however.

Conclusion

When the issue of desegregation is raised, it is essential that those advocating bilingual education characterize the program as integrative, not segregative. As the Tenth Circuit underscored in *Keyes*, bilingual education is no substitute for desegregation. In other instances, such as the Boston case of *Morgan v. Kerrigan*,[161] courts have been persuaded that bilingual programs do not threaten desegregation and are necessary to secure equality in education. Moreover, even if bilingual programs for students with limited English-language abilities result in ethnic separation within schools, prevailing case authority and federal regulations may sanction them as *bona fide* ability groupings.

At the heart of the controversy over court-ordered bilingual programs is the effort to balance the command that unlawful discrimination must be swiftly and effectively remedied against the Supreme Court's admonition that judges are not educators. Passing upon the merits of particular instructional programs might seem to be the type of institutional metamorphosis *Rodriguez* sought to foreclose, but the nature of a *Lau* violation[162] will require courts to conduct this type of evaluation. Where school districts default in their responsibility to present effective programs to remedy *Lau* violations, courts will have no option but to develop their own programs.[163]

However, it is one thing to fault a particular program and another to propose a demonstrably better alternative. At a minimum, the courts and the school districts as well need reliable indexes for gauging programs by the standard of equal benefits, the touchstone of Title VI. Does bilingual education positively affect a student's self-concept? Does bilingual education hinder academic progress during the course of second-language acquisition? Does bilingual education improve achievement? The answers to these questions are significant in persuading a court to reject one remedy and adopt another.[164] Grades, scores on standardized achievement tests, and dropout and absentee rates are certainly probative as to whether a remedy is effective in securing equality of benefits. Expert testimony from linguists, psychologists, and educators knowledgeable in the instruction of non-English-speaking schoolchildren is essential. Surely significant, too, are HEW's *Lau* remedies and the prior expressions of "expertise" by local school officials, many of whom have gone on record as being committed to bilingual education and can be held to that commitment in considering issues of liability and remedy.

Undoubtedly, the law requires equality of educational opportunity, but the issue of bilingual education as a remedy tends to overshadow and subsume the issue of liability. While courts refrain from assuming the functions of school boards and avoid prescribing the day-to-day details of implementation of educational policy, the nature of a *Lau* violation will necessitate judicial scrutiny of the effectiveness of programs school districts offer to language-minority children. Under these circumstances traditional deference to a school district's authority to structure educational programs may give way to the courts' mandate to insure meaningful education for the children who fall under the protection of *Lau*.

Notes

1. 20 U.S.C. § 779 *et seq* (1970) (enacted Jan. 2, 1968).
2. 20 U.S.C. § 800 b-1(a)(4)(A)(i) (Supp. V 1975) (amending 20 U.S.C. § 880 b-1 (1970).
3. ESL is frequently, but mistakenly, considered a form of bilingual education. Although ESL as a component of a bilingual program may well be a useful tool for imparting English-language skills, its emphasis on single-language acquisition (English) prevents its acceptance as a substitute for bilingual education. See Bernard Spolsky, ed., *The Language Education of Minority Children* (Rowley, Mass.: Newbury House, 1972); Francesco Cordasco, *Bilingual Schooling in the United States: A Sourcebook for Educational Personnel* (New York: McGraw-Hill, 1976); and Susan Gilbert Schneider, *Revolution, Reaction or Reform: The 1974 Bilingual Education Act* (New York: Las Americas, in press).
4. Proponents of programs in bilingual-bicultural education consider them to be more than compensatory — that is, to do more than just make up for lack of English-language skills. Bilingual-bicultural education involves the use of two languages in a regular classroom curriculum which includes the students' historical, literary, and cultural traditions. The National Advisory Council on Bilingual Education in a 1975 report to the President and Congress defined bilingual education as "a process in which English and other languages and cultures that reflect the makeup of the community are used in instruction. It is designed to meet the unique language and culture needs of each student, regardless of origin." (National Advisory Council on Bilingual Education, "Annual Report," Washington, D.C., 1 Nov. 1975, p. 8). Significantly, the council deliberately accepted the substitution of "bilingual multicultural" education for "bilingual education" throughout its report.
5. 414 U.S. 563 (1974).
6. The "*Lau* remedies," not yet published in the *Federal Register*, bear the following title: "H.E.W. Memorandum on 'Task Force Findings Specifying Remedies Available For Eliminating Past Educational Practices Ruled Unlawful Under Lau v. Nichols, Summer, 1975.'"
7. 42 U.S.C. § 2000d (1970).
8. Federal expenditures for education increased dramatically with the passage of the Vocational Education Act of 1963, 20 U.S.C. § 1241 *et seq* (1970) (enacted Jan. 2, 1970), and the Elementary and Secondary Education Act of 1965, 20 U.S. C. §§ 236–44. As the level of federal funding for education rose to $4.2 billion in 1968 and to $16.5 billion in 1972, the number of schools receiving assistance multiplied. See Sar A. Levitan and Robert Taggart, *The Promise of Greatness* (Cambridge, Mass.: Harvard Univ. Press, 1976), p. 121.
9. 42 U.S.C. § 2000d (1970).
10. The legal theory justifying the right of affected private parties to sue is that they are third-party beneficiaries of the contractual assurances against discrimination given by school districts as a condition for receiving federal funds. Bossier Parish School v. Lemon, 370 F.2d 847 (5th Cir. 1967), *cert. denied*, 388 U.S. 911 (1967); Natonabah v. Board of Educ. of Gallup–McKinley County School Dist. 355 F. Supp. 716 (D.N.M. 1973) *See also* Gomez v. Florida State Employment Serv., 417 F. 2d 569 (5th Cir. 1969); Cook v. Ochsner Foundation Hosp., 319 F. Supp. 603 (E.D. La. 1970). *But see* Cannon v. Univ. of Chicago, 406 F. Supp. 1257, 1259 (N.D. Ill. 1976), *aff'd*, 45 U.S.L.W. 2149 (7th Cir. August 27, 1976), holding that victims of sex discrimination have no third-party beneficiary rights under Title IX, and that since *Lau* did not squarely address the issue as to Title VI, it would not be followed.
11. HEW regulation 45 C.F.R. § 80.3(b)(1) (1976) specifies that recipients of federal funds may not: "(ii) Provide any service, financial aid, or other benefit to an individual which is different, or is provided to others under the program. . . . (iv) Restrict an indi-

vidual in any way in the enjoyment of any advantage or privilege enjoyed by others receiving any service, financial aid, or other benefit under the program." Additionally, 45 C.F.R. § 80.3(b)(2) (1976) outlaws the use of methods or criteria which have the effect of discriminating against individuals on the basis of race or national origin. The guidelines state that "school systems are responsible for assuring that students of a particular race, color, or national origin are not denied the opportunity to obtain the education generally obtained by other students in the system" [33 Fed. Reg. 4956 (1968)].

12. The parties also agreed that 1,066 Chinese-speaking students received some form of compensatory education.

13. Relying on Brown v. Board of Ed., 347 U.S. 483 (1954), and its predecessors, Sweatt v. Painter, 339 U.S. 629 (1950), and McLaurin v. Oklahoma State Regents, 339 U.S. 637 (1950).

14. Cal. Ed. Code § 12101 (1971).

15. *Id.* § 71.

16. *Id.* § 8573.

17. Graham v. Richardson, 403 U.S. 365, 372 (1971); Oyama v. California, 332 U.S. 633, 643–44 (1948); Korematsu v. United States, 323 U.S. 214, 216 (1944); Hirabayashi v. United States, 320 U.S. 81, 100 (1943).

18. 483 F.2d 791,793 (9th Cir. 1973), *rehearing en banc denied* 483 F.2d 805, quoting from unreported district court opinion, Civil No. C-70, 627 LHB (N.D. Cal. May 26, 1970).

19. *Id.* at 798.

20. For an analysis of the constitutional arguments proffered see, "Note, The Constitutional Right of Bilingual Children to an Equal Educational Opportunity," 47 *S. Cal. L. Rev.* 943 (1974).

21. The Ninth Circuit dismissed the Title VI claim in a footnote, assuming that it was coterminous with the Equal Protection Clause: "Our determination of the merits of the other claims of appellants will likewise dispose of the claims made under the Civil Rights Act." (Lau v. Nichols, 483 F.2d at 794 n. 6).

22. *See* 414 U.S. at 571 where this concept is reflected.

23. The rule of avoiding constitutional determinations was first enunciated by Justice Brandeis in his concurrence in Ashwander v. Tennessee Valley Authority, 297 U.S. 288, 347 (1936).

24. 414 U.S. at 569.

25. *Id.* at 566.

26. *Id.* at 568.

27. This memorandum reflects HEW's findings that when English is the language of instruction but no special assistance is provided to non-English-speaking students, the local school district, upon these facts alone, has impermissibly excluded these students from participation in the district's educational program, denied them the benefits of that program, and subjected them to discrimination under that program, all on account of their national origin. The clarifying guidelines state in part: "Where inability to speak and understand the English language excludes national-origin minority-group children from effective participation in the educational program offered by a school district, the district must take affirmative steps to rectify the language deficiency in order to open its instructional program to these students."

28. "The critical question is, therefore, whether the regulations and guidelines promulgated by HEW go beyond the authority of § 601 Title VI. Last term, in Mourning v. Family Publications Servs., Inc., 411 U.S. 356, 369 [other citations omitted], we held that the validity of a regulation promulgated under a general authorization provision such as § 602 of Title VI 'will be sustained so long as it is "reasonably related to the purposes of the enabling legislation." Thorpe v. Housing Authority of the City of Dur-

ham, 393 U.S. 268, 280-81 (1969) [footnotes and other citations omitted]' I think the guidelines here fairly meet that test." [414 U.S. at 571 (Stewart, J. concurring)]. The significance of Title VI and its effect-oriented proscription may be dramatically increased in the wake of Washington v. Davies, 426 U.S. 429 (1976), which held, in an employment-discrimination case brought under 42 U.S.C. § 1983, that discriminatory effect without discriminatory intent is not sufficient to constitute a violation of the Equal Protection Clause. *Cf.* Village of Arlington Heights v. Metropolitan Housing Development Corp, 97 S.Ct.455 (1977).

29. 414 U.S. at 564–65. It is wholly consistent with Supreme Court doctrine that no specific remedy was ordered in *Lau*. Remedies are almost always left to the trial court. *See* Swann v. Charlotte-Mecklenburg Board of Educ., 402 U.S. 1, 28 (1971); Brown v. Board of Educ., 349 U.S. 294, 298, 300 (1955) (Brown II).

30. San Antonio Independent School Dist. v. Rodriguez, 411 U.S. 1 (1973); Wood v. Strickland, 420 U.S. 308 (1974).

31. Wisconsin v. Yoder, 406 U.S. 205, 213–14, 239 (1972). *See* Kurland, "Equal Educational Opportunity: The Limits of Constitutional Jurisprudence Undefined," 35 *U. Chi. L. Rev.* 583, 596–99 (1968); *Accord*, Swann, 402 U.S. 1 at 16.

32. Meyer v. Nebraska, 262 U.S. 390 (1923). *Meyer* and its companion cases Bartels v. Iowa and Bohning v. Ohio, both reported at 262 U.S. 404 (1923), arose in the aftermath of World War I. As part of the effort to expunge any German influence, legislation was passed in several states, including Nebraska, Iowa, and Ohio, forbidding teachers in both public and private schools to offer instruction in a foreign language. Although the Supreme Court in *Meyer* declared the statute to be an unconstitutional infringement on the due-process rights of the teacher and the parents involved, the opinion was almost apologetic: "The desire of the legislature to foster a homogeneous people with American ideals prepared readily to understand current discussions of civic matters, is easy to appreciate" (Meyer, *supra* at 402). For cases raising similar issues, *see also* Farrington v. Tokushige, 11 F.2d 710 (9th Cir. 1926), *aff'd*, 273 U.S. 284 (1927); Mo Hock ke Loc Po v. Stainback, 74 F. Supp. 852 (D. Hawaii 1947), *rev'd on other grounds*, 336 U.S. 368 (1949). The facts in *Meyer* concerned a private school. Accordingly, the *Meyer* court did not pass upon the state's authority to restrict foreign-language teaching in a public-school setting.

33. Yoder, 406 U.S. at 239.

34. *Id.*; Lemon v. Kurtzman, 403 U.S. 602, 613 (1971).

35. 411 U.S. 1.

36. Language discrimination was first equated with national-origin discrimination by the Supreme Court in Yu Cong Eng v. Trinidad, 271 U.S. 500 (1925). The case involved a Philippine criminal statute, "The Chinese Bookkeeping Act," which outlawed the keeping of account books in a language other than English, Spanish, or any local dialect. Since the legislative history revealed that the act was aimed at Chinese merchants, the Court found that it violated both the Due Process and Equal Protection Clauses. *See* Hernandez v. Erlengusch, 368 F. Supp. 752 (D. Ore. 1973), where a tavern owner's policy of forbidding foreign languages from being spoken at the bar was found to be national-origin discrimination and was successfully challenged as a violation of the Equal Protection Clause. Courts have not been consistent, however, in correlating language and national origin. In the area of equal employment opportunity, the Sixth Circuit in Frontera v. Sindell, 522 F2d 1215 (6th Cir. 1975), held that administering a civil-service examination for the job of carpenter in English only did not violate the equal-protection rights of the Spanish-speaking plaintiff. In Commonwealth v. Olivo, Mass., 337 N.E.2d 904 (1975), involving the imposition of a fine for failing to comply with an English-language notice to vacate a dwelling, the court distinguished language discrimination from national-origin discrimination, ruling that the non-English

speakers were not treated differently because of the language they spoke or because of national origin per se. As a result, in neither case did the court find inequality in treatment drawn on racial or national-origin lines.

37. Swann, 402 U.S. 1.

38. *See* Serna v. Portales Municipal Schools, 351 F. Supp. 1279 (N.D. Mex. 1972), *aff'd*, 499 F.2d 1147 (10th Cir. 1974).

39. Green v. School Bd. of New Kent County, 391 U.S. 430, 439 (1968).

40. 35 Fed. Reg. 11595 (1970).

41. 20 U.S.C. § 1703 (Supp.V 1975).

42. 20 U.S.C. § 1703(d) (Supp. 1975).

43. The terms of these state laws differ, but the first, the Massachusetts Transitional Bilingual Education Law of 1971 (*Mass. Gen. Laws* ch. 71A), served as a prototype for laws in other states. A brief description of this and other statutes appears in *Bilingual-Bicultural Education: A Handbook for Attorneys and Community Workers* (Cambridge, Mass.: Center for Law and Education, 1975), pp. 251–80. Substantial growth of bilingual education is in large measure a consequence of the proliferation of state legislation. When bilingual-education lawsuits are brought in states with bilingual-education statutes, it is likely that courts will not go beyond the terms of the legislation in fashioning remedial decrees. *See* Milliken v. Bradley, 402 F. Supp. 1096, 1144 (E.D. Mich. 1975), *aff'd*, 540 F.2d 229 (6th Cir.), *cert. granted*, _____U.S._____, 45 U.S.L.W. 3359 (Nov. 16, 1976). *But see* Morgan v. Kerrigan, 401 F. Supp. 216, 242 (D. Mass. 1975), *aff'd*, 530 F.2d 401 (1st Cir. 1976), *cert. denied sub nom.* White v. Morgan, 426 U.S. 935 (1976), _____U.S._____, 44 U.S.L.W. 3719 (June 15, 1976), in which the district court in desegregating the Boston public schools required that bilingual education be offered to kindergarten students despite the fact that state law left bilingual education to the option of the school district.

44. 351 F. Supp. 1279 (N.D. Mex. 1972), *aff'd* 499 F.2d 1147, 1154 (10th Cir. 1974).

45. 72 Civ. 4002 (S.D.N.Y. Aug. 29, 1974) (unreported consent decree); 58 F.R.D. 62 (S.D.N.Y. 1973).

46. 75 C.296 (E.D.N.Y. Jan. 14, 1977) (Memorandum of Decision and Order).

47. 408 F. Supp. 162 (D. Colo. 1975).

48. Sinajini v. San Juan School Dist., Civil No. 75-346 (D. Utah 1975); Denetclarence v. Board of Educ. of Independent School Dist. No. 22, N. 8872 (D.N.M. Feb. 15, 1974). The spread of bilingual education in reservation schools has resulted not so much from litigation related to bilingualism as from the efforts of the Indian nations, both in and out of court, to establish and strength their political sovereignty. The trend towards community-operated or tribally operated schools and away from schools run by the Bureau of Indian Affairs, public-school systems, and the church has sustained the growth of bilingual-education programs on the reservations. See A. John Waubaunsee, *Indian Control of Schools and Bilingual Education* (Arlington, Va.: Center for Applied Linguistics, 1976),

49. 499 F.2d at 1154.

50. Beginning in 1963, the chief educational officers of the New York City schools had publicly endorsed bilingual-bicultural education. Superintendent Calvin E. Gross urged in 1963 that "Puerto Rican children and other new arrivals to the City be enabled to develop biculturally and bilingually," and he deplored "the melting pot approach in which new arrivals are made over in our own image" (*New York Times*, 2 May 1963, p. 37, col. 1). Two years later, the board of education stated: "Bilingualism and biculturalism will be encouraged for all pupils, and particularly Spanish-speaking ones, as an aspect of excellence which will benefit our community and nation in their relationship to a multicultured world" ("Statement of Policy of Board of Education of

New York City," adopted 18 April 1965, issued 28 April 1965, p. 602). And in 1967, New York City's endorsement of bilingual education was declared to Congress: "We are dedicated to the bilingual approach to this educational program. Although we stress the importance of full command of the English language, we also believe in the maintenance and strengthening of the child's language skills in the native tongue of the pupil or his parents. Bilingual programs can provide superior educational bene-fits" ("Testimony given by Dr. Bernard E. Donovan, Superintendent of Schools, New York City, before the House General Subcommittee on Education of the House Com-mittee on Education and Labor on H.R. 9840 and H.R. 10224," press release #451-66/ 67, New York City Board of Education, 7 July 1967).

51. 58 F.R.D. at 64.
52. 72 Civ. 4002 (S.D.N.Y. April 30, 1974) (unreported Memorandum and Order). See *Bi-lingual Dicultural Education*, pp. 71–105 and 155–172 for the parties' plans.
53. The court rules that although the board is required to offer the program to all eligible students, a parent may withdraw a child at any time. *See* 72 Civ. 4002 (S.D.N.Y. July 11, 1975) (unreported Memorandum).
54. Professionals in the program must: (a) be fluent in the Spanish language and able to comprehend fully, and express themselves effectively in, written Spanish; (b) possess the requisite content and knowledge skills in the substantive courses they teach; (c) possess the requisite pedagogical skills; and (d) be capable of reading, writing, and speaking English.
55. The other defense to disclosing student records was the Family Educational Rights and Privacy Act of 1974, 20 U.S.C. § k232g, which under certain circumstances bars disclosure of the contents of student records.
56. Rios v. Read, 75 C. 296 at 15.
57. *Id.* at 16 referring to *H.R. Rep. No.* 93-805, 93rd Cong., 2nd sess. 66, reprinted in (1974) *U.S. Code Cong. and Admin. News* 4148.
58. *Id.* at 16.
59. *Id.*
60. In addition, the court, citing Griggs v. Duke Power Co. [401 U.S. 424 (1971)], sug-gested that the plaintiff's burden of proof might be similar to the burden in an em-ployment-discrimination case brought under Title VII of the 1964 Civil Rights Act. That is, plaintiffs would first have to prove that the school district's programs and poli-cies create a discriminatory situation in that they allow significant numbers of His-panic students to lag behind English-speaking students in academic progress because of problems with the English language. Once this was shown, school-district officials would have the burden of demonstrating "that their bilingual program is genuinely designed and administered to meet the needs of English-language-deficient children and that alternative approaches would not produce results or would be unfeasible." *See* McDonnell-Douglas Corp. v. Green, 411 U.S. 792 (1973).
61. 408 F. Supp. At 164.
62. This theory is premised on the hypothesis that the educational failure of minority chil-dren is attributable to a lack of compatibility between their characteristics and the characteristics presupposed by typical instructional programs tailored for a White, An-glo-Saxon, English-speaking, middle-class school population. Rather than changing the child to fit the instructional program, the theory proposes changing the instruc-tional program to fit the child.
63. 521 F.2d 465 (10th Cir. 1975).
64. *Id.* at 482.
65. 408 F. Supp. at 170.
66. *Id.* at 171.

67. Formerly, in the context of school-desegregation cases, courts relied heavily on analogous HEW standards in formulating relief. HEW's Office of Education first issued desegregation guidelines in April 1965. These guidelines "fixed the minimum standards to be used in determining the qualifications for schools applying for federal financial aid" [Singleton v. Jackson Municipal Separate School Dist., 348 F.2d 729, 730 n.6 (5th Cir. 1965)]. School districts were given several choices of ways to satisfy Title VI requirements. The courts consistently attached great weight to these guidelines. In 1966 and again in 1968, HEW issued revised guidelines relating to school desegregation, and again courts accorded them "serious judicial deference, respectful consideration, and real weight," albeit refusing to abdicate their constitutional responsibilities to HEW entirely [United States v. Jefferson County Bd. of Educ., 372 F.2d 836 (5th Cir. 1967), *cert. denied sub nom.* United States v. Caddo Parish Bd. of Educ., 389 U.S. 840 (1967)]. *See also* Kemp v. Beasley, 389 F.2d 178, 185 (8th Cir. 1968); Whittenberg v. Greenville County School Dist., 298 F. Supp. 784 (D.S.C. 1969).

68. *See* note 6, *supra.*

69. Because school districts which have substantial numbers of recent Indochinese immigrants have specifically been granted relief from the requirement to test immediately, one can reasonably infer that all other covered districts must respond immediately.

70.. Memorandum for chief state school officers accompanying the *Lau* remedies.

71. *Lau* remedies, Part I, "Identification of Students' Primary or Home Language," sets forth the manner in which this identification is made.

72. "Conceivably, other methods of achieving the goals set by the '*Lau* remedies' may exist, but the Office of Civil Rights will accept an alternative approach only if there is a reasonable basis to believe that it is at least as effective as the guidance set in the '*Lau* remedies'" (letter from Lloyd R. Henderson, Director, Elementary and Secondary Education Division, Office for Civil Rights, to Rosa Castro Feinberg, *Lau* General Assistance Center B, School of Education, University of Miami, 15 March 1976). However, Seattle's plan, dated 11 June 1976, indicates that HEW will settle for less than full adherence to the *Lau* remedies. For example, the plan permits schools to offer programs other than bilingual education to non-English monolinguals in primary grades without any showing of equality in effectiveness.

73. Letter from Peter E. Holmes, Director of OCR, to Dr. J. Loren Troxel, Superintendent, Seattle Public Schools, 24 Nov. 1975. The "force of law" generally connotes that which has the force and effect of a statute, creating legally binding rights and obligations.

74. The fact that the *Lau* remedies have not been published in the *Federal Register* does not render them, as some have argued, without the "force of law." Considering that the *Lau* remedies have been widely disseminated, it is difficult to imagine that an offending school official will be able to assert lack of actual notice with any success. *See* Thorpe v. Housing Authority of the City of Durham, 393 U.S. 268, 276 (1969); Andrews v. Knowlton, 509 F.2d 898, 905 (2d Cir. 1975); Like v. Carter, 448 F.2d 798, 803–04 (8th Cir. 1971); Kessler v. F.C.C., 326 F.2d 673, 690 (D.C. Cir. 1963); United States v. Aarons, 310 F.2d 341, 346 (2d Cir. 1962); Rodriguez v. Swank, 318 F. Supp. 289, 295 (N.D. Ill. 1970), *aff'd*, 403 U.S. 901 (1971).

75. Within the first month of the Carter administration, the threat of cutoff of federal funds was resurrected by HEW secretary Califano when he ordered the reopening of six school-desegregation cases in Arkansas and Texas that the earlier administration "had left in limbo," *New York Times*, 18 Feb. 1977, p. A16, col. 1. See "In the Matter of Chicago Public School District #299, *et al.*," No. 5-120, HEW, Feb. 15, 1977.

76. All of OCR's compliance reviews follow a similar scenario: regional offices select school districts for review; conduct onsite investigations; collect, review, and analyze

pertinent data; prepare findings; issue letters of noncompliance; seek voluntary corrective action; and, if all else fails, initiate administrative or judicial proceedings. This review process is predictably protracted.

77. 356 F. Supp. 92 (D.D.C. 1973), *aff'd in pertinent part*, 480 F.2d 1159 (D.C. Cir. 1973).

78 391 F. Supp. 269 (D.D.C. 1975).

79 *Id.* at 271.

80. Civil Action No. 75-1068 (D.D.C. July 20, 1976) (preliminary injunction issued *sub nom.* Brown v. Matthews).

81. 45 C.F.R. § 80 (1976).

82. Aspira, 65 F.R.D. 541 (S.D.N.Y. 1975); 423 F. Supp. 647, 660 (S.D.N.Y. 1976). Congress authorized as part of the Education Amendments of 1972 the award of attorneys' fees to prevailing parties in educational rights cases [§ 718 of Title VII (20 U.S.C. § 1617) (supp. V 1975)]. In so doing, Congress intended to encourage private individuals to redress discrimination in schools through litigation.

83. Scheuer v. Rhodes, 416 U.S. 237, 238 (1974).

84. Wood v. Strickland, 420 U.S. 308; *see also* O'Connor v. Donaldson 422 U.S. 563 (1975).

85. Aspira, 423 F. Supp.

86. Where state laws require that pupil/teacher ratios be lower for bilingual classes than for regular classes, there will be additional costs.

87 Griffin v. School Bd. of Prince Edward County, 377 U.S. 218, 253 (1964); United States v. School Dist. 151 of Cook County, Illinois, 301 F. Supp. 201, 206, *aff'd*, 432 F.2d 1147, *cert. denied*, 402 U.S. 943 (1971).

88. 532 F.2d 380 (5th Cir. 1976), *rev'd on other grounds*, _____U.S._____, 45 U.S.L.W. 3413 (Dec. 7, 1976).

89. *Id.* 532 F.2d at 398.

90. *Id. But see* Serna, 351 F. Supp. at 1283, where the court made implementation of the bilingual program a precondition for receipt of additional federal funds after HEW represented that such funds would be forthcoming.

91. 58 F.R.D. at 64.

92. See Rodriguez, 411 U.S. 1; Wheeler v. Barrera, 417 U.S. 402 (1974); New York State Ass'n for Retarded Children, Inc., v. Rockefeller, 357 F. Supp. 752, 764 (E.D.N.Y. 1973). *But see* Robinson v. Cahill, 118 N.J. Super. 223, 287 A.2d 187 (1972), *cert. denied sub nom.* Dickey v. Robinson, 414 U.S. 976 (1973); Serrano v. Priest, 5 Cal. 3d 584, 487 P.2d 1241 (1971).

93. 348 F. Supp. 866, 876 (D.D.C. 1972). *See* Jones v. Wittenberg, 330 F. Supp. 707, 713 (N.D. Ohio 1971), *aff'd sub nom.* Jones v. Metzger, 456 F.2d 854 (6th Cir. 1972), a prisoners' rights case in which the court ordered a reallocation of appropriations to meet the court's mandate to improve prison facilities. And, in Rhem v. Malcolm, 507 F.2d 333, 341 n. 19 (2d Cir. 1974), claims of insufficient funds notwithstanding, the court required that unless inadequate prison facilities were remodeled, the prisoners were to be released. *See also* Finney v. Arkansas Bd. of Corrections, 505 F.2d 194, 200–204 (8th Cir. 1974); Rozecki v. Caughan, 459 F.2d 6 (1st Cir. 1972).

94. *See* Justice v. Board of Educ. 351 F. Supp. 1252, 1261 n. 27 (S.D.N.Y. 1972).

95. 42 U.S.C. § 2000d (1970).

96. Lee v. Macon, 483 F.2d 242, 243 (5th Cir. 1973); United States v. Greenwood Municipal Separate School Dist., 406 F.2d 1086, 1094 (5th Cir. 1969), *cert. denied*, 396 U.S. 1011 (1970); United States v. Board of Educ. of the City of Bessemer, 396 F.2d 44, 51 (5th Cir. 1968); Bradley v. Milliken, 402 F. Supp. 1096, 1144 (E.D. Mich. 1975), *aff'd*, 540 F.2d 229 (6th Cir.), *cert. granted*, _____U.S._____, 45 U.S.L.W. 3359 (Nov. 16, 1976); Berry v. School Dist. of City of Benton Harbor, _____ F. Supp._____ (W.D. Mich. 1971), *rev'd as to other parts*, 505 F.2d 238, 240–41 (6th Cir. 1974).

97. Art. VI, § 2.
98. 414 U.S. at 571–72.
99. *Id.*
100. 499 F.2d at 1149. Spanish-surnamed pupils constituted 25 percent of the Portales school population, a "sizeable minority," most of whom were deficient in the English language. In affirming the trial court's order to implement bilingual programs, the Tenth Circuit sought to allay the concerns expressed by the New Mexico State Board of Education: "It is suggested that bilingual programs will not be necessitated throughout the state wherever a student is found who does not have adequate facility in the English language. We do not share [the State Board of Education's] fears. As Mr. Justice Blackmun pointed out in his concurring opinion in *Lau,* numbers are at the heart of this and only when a substantial group is being deprived of a meaningful education will a Title VI violation exist" (*Id.* at 1154).
101. In *Otero* 1,063 students, only 8.2 percent, were Mexican American. The *Otero* court concluded that inability to speak or understand the English language excluded "no more than a tiny handful." Thus, the numbers of students with valid claims of *Lau* violations were "extremely small" (408 F. Supp. at 165, 172).
102. In Evans v. Buchanan, 416 F. Supp. 328, 360 (D.Del. 1976), (three-judge), a desegregation case involving Black plaintiffs and Hispanic intervenors, the court, citing *Lau,* prohibited the reduction of existing bilingual programs that served only 375 Hispanic students, less than 1 percent of the total pupil enrollment. In Morgan v. Kerrigan, 401 F. Supp. 216 (D. Mass. 1975), *aff'd,* 530 F.2d 401 (1st Cir. 1970), *cert. denied,* _____U.S._____, 44 U.S.L.W. 3719 (June 15, 1976), while Hispanic students found to need bilingual instruction numbered over 3,600, the plan adopted by the court also required bilingual programs for other less numerous linguistic-minority students: 370 Italian, 519 Chinese, 160 Greek, 190 French Haitian, and 60 Portuguese.
103. 20 U.S.C. § 1703(f) (Supp. V 1975); *see* Hernandez v. Porter, Civil Action No. 5-71532 (E.D. Mich. March 19, 1976).
104. Editorials, "Divisive Languages," *New York Times,* 28 Oct. 1975, p. 32; "Bilingual Danger," *New York Times,* 22 Nov. 1976; "Bilingual Issue, Cont'd," *New York Times,* 11 Dec 1976; but see Herbert Teitelbaum, "Bilingual Education Here," *New York Times,* 26 May 1975, p. 15, col. 4.
105. Jose Cardenas, "Bilingual Education, Segregation, and a Third Alternative," *Inequality in Education,* 19 (1975), 19.
106. Judicial recognition of this concept is reflected in the desegregation plan adopted by the court in Boston, where a citywide bilingual (Spanish-English) magnet school was exempted from the ethnic/racial student assignment guidelines (Morgan v. Kerrigan, 530 F.2d at 423 n. 33). The regulations governing bilingual programs funded under the Bilingual Education Act expressly caution against excessive participation of students who are not of limited English ability and require that priority for placement in the programs must be given to students with limited English ability [45 C.F.R. § 123.02(g)(2)(i) (1976)].
107. United States v. State of Texas, 321 F. Supp. 1043 (E.D. Tex. 1970), *supplemented by* 330 F. Supp. 235 (E.D. Tex. 1971); Serna, 351 F. Supp. 1279 (N.D. Mex. 1972), *aff'd,* 499 F.2d 1147 (10th Cir. 1974).
108. The 1968 regulations provide, in part, that a recipient of federal funds may not on the grounds of race, color, or national origin "subject an individual to segregation or separate treatment" [45 C.F.R. § 80.3(b)(iii)(1976)] or discriminate "in the availability or use of any academic . . . or other facility . . . of the recipient." [*Id.,* § 80.5(b)]. The May 25, 1970, memorandum directs that: "any ability grouping or tracking system employed by the school system to deal with the special language needs of national-origin

minority-group children must be designed to meet such language skill needs as soon as possible and must not operate as an educational dead-end or permanent track."

109. "It is not educationally necessary nor legally permissible to create racially/ethnically identifiable schools in order to respond to student language characteristics as specified in the programs described herein." *Lau* remedies, Part VI (A).

110. *Id.* at Part VI (B).

111. ESAA provides federal financial assistance to local educational agencies which seek to eliminate minority-group segregation and discrimination in elementary and secondary schools and to overcome the educational disadvantages resulting from minority-group isolation. 20 U.S.C. § 1607(c)(1)(A) (Supp. V. 1975); 20 U.S.C. § 1606(a)(6) (Supp. V 1975).

112. 20 U.S.C. § 1605(d)(1)(C) (Supp. V 1975).

113. 45 C.F.R. § 185.43(c) (1976).

114. 45 C.F.R. § 185.43(d)(5) (1976).

115. 45 C.F.R. § 185.43(c) (1976); 20 U.S.C. § 1605(d)(1)(C) (Supp. V 1975).

116. 45 C.F.R. § 185.43(c)(1) (1976).

117. Significantly, the ESAA regulations bar funding under the act to local educational agencies "denying equality of educational opportunity . . . on the basis of language or cultural background" [45 C.F.R. § 185.43(d)(2) (1976)].

118. 396 F. Supp. 203, 238 (S.D. Ohio 1975).

119. Berkelman v. San Francisco Unified School Dist., 501 F.2d 1264, 1267–68 (9th Cir. 1974); Murray v. West Baton Rouge Parish School Bd., 472 F.2d 438, 444 (5th Cir. 1973); George v. O'Kelly, 448 F.2d 148, 150 (5th Cir. 1971); Moore v. Tangipahoa Parish School Bd., 304 F. Supp. 244, 249 (D. La. 1969), *app. dismissed*, 421 F.2d 1407 (5th Cir. 1969); Hobsen v. Hansen, 269 F. Supp. 401, 442–92 (D.D.C. 1967), *aff'd sub nom.* Smuck v. Hobson, 408 F.2d 175 (D.C. Cir. 1969); United States v. Norcome, 375 F. Supp. 270, 286, 287–88 (D.D.C. 1974); Larry P. v. Riles, 343 F. Supp. 1306, 1312 (N.D. Cal. 1972); Pennsylvania Ass'n. for Retarded Children v. Commonwealth of Pa., 334 F. Supp. 1257 (E. Pa. 1971) (consent decree); Swann v. Charlotte-Mecklenburg Bd. of Educ., 300 F. Supp. 1358, 1367 (W.D.N.C. 1969); Miller v. School Dist. No. 2, Clarendon, S.C., 256 F. Supp. 370, 375 (D.S.C. 1966).

120. 396 F. Supp. at 238.

121. 508 F.2d 1017, 1020 (5th Cir. 1975).

122. *See* Orfield, "How To Make Desegregation Work: The Adaptation of Schools to Their Newly Integrated Student Bodies," 39 *Law & Contemp. Prob.* 336 (1975).

123. United States v. State of Tex., 342 F. Supp. 24, 28 (E.D. Tex. 1971), *aff'd per curiam*, 446 F.2d 518 (5th Cir. 1972).

124. Brown II, 349 U.S. 299.

125. Watson v. City of Memphis, 373 U.S. 526, 529 (1963).

126. Griffin, 377 U.S. at 234.

127. Bradley v. School Bd. of Richmond, 392 U.S. 103, 105 n. 31 (1965).

128. Alexander v. Holmes County Board of Education, 396 U.S. 19, 20 (1969).

129. 391 U.S. 430, 437–38 (1968).

130. 402 U.S. 1, 15 (1971); see also Wright v. Council of City of Emporia, 407 U.S. 451, 463 (1972).

131. United States v. State of Texas, 321 F. Supp. 1043 (E.D. Tex. 1970), 330 F. Supp. 235, 247–49 (E.D. Tex.) *modifying, aff'd in part*, 447 F.2d 441, 448 (5th Cir.), *cert. denied* 407 U.S. 1206 (1972).

132. *Id.*, 342 F. Supp. at 27–28. Forty years earlier, Chicano children had challenged the segregated schools of the San Felipe Del Rio School District, arguing that to separate them from "other White" students violated the Constitution. The courts upheld the

segregated schooling on the grounds that separation was justified by a rational reason — English-language deficiency [Salvatieria v. Independent School Dist., 335 S.W.2d 790 (1930), *cert. denied*, 284 U.S. 580 (1931)]. *See* Delgado v. Bastrop, Civ. No. 388 (W.D. Tex. 1948); Mendez v. Westminster School Dist., 64 F. Supp. 544 (S.D. Cal. 1946), *aff'd*, 161 F.2d 774 (9th Cir. 1947); Gonzalez v. Sheely, 96 F. Supp. 1004 (D. Ariz. 1951); Hernandez v. Driscoll Consolidated Independent School Dist., 2 Rel. L. Rep. 329 (S.D. Tex. Jan 11, 1957); Chapa v. Odem Independent School Dist., Civil No. 66-c-72 (S.D. Tex. July 20, 1967).

133. § 8003 and 8004 Cal. Ed. (repealed 1947).

134. Cisneros v. Corpus Christi Independent School Dist., 467 F.2d 142 (5th Cir. 1972) *affirming and modifying* 324 F. Supp. 599 (S.D. Tex. 1970), 330 F. Supp. 1377 (S.D. Tex. 1971) *(en banc)*, *cert. denied*, 413 U.S. 920 (1973).

135. A Texas education survey made in 1925 observed: "On pedagogical grounds a very good argument can be made for segregation in the early grades. In the opinion of the survey staff, it is wise to segregate, if it is done on educational grounds, and results in distinct efforts to provide non-English speaking pupils with specially trained teachers and the necessary special training resources" [Quoted in Arnold H. Leibowitz, "English Literacy: Legal Sanction for Discrimination," 39 *Revista Juridica de la Universidad de Puerto Rico* 313, 367 n. 242 (1970)]. Texas school officials continue to attempt to justify existing segregation of Mexican-American students as vestiges of past efforts to remedy English-language difficulties. As late as 1976, in United States v. Texas Educ. Agency, 532 F.2d 380, 391 (5th Cir. 1976), the Austin school board contended "that Mexican-Americans were segregated before 1950 not because of their ethnic background, but because they had language difficulties or were children of migrant workers and needed special educational considerations."

136. Morales v. Shannon, 516 F.2d 411 (5th Cir. 1975).

137. Gonzalez v. Sheely, 96 F. Supp. 1004; Méndez v. Westminster School Dist., 64 F. Supp. 544.

138. 413 U.S. 189 (1973).

139. *Id.* at 195. No longer could school officials engaging in purposeful segregative policies escape a finding of unlawful segregation simply by classifying Hispanic students as "White" and claiming that a school predominantly Black and Hispanic was not segregated. Nor could officials desegregate Black schools by reassigning only Hispanic students to these schools. As the court noted in Arvizu v. Waco Independent School District: "All too often, the practical effect of the desegregation of tri-ethnic school systems has been that Black students are mixed with Mexican-American students, thus denying to both groups the benefit of any meaningful desegregation" [373 F. Supp. 1264, 1270 (W.D. Tex. 1973) *aff'd in part, rev'd as to other issues*, 495 F.2d 499 (5th Cir. 1974)].

140. 413 U.S. at 197. In so ruling, the Supreme Court adopted the reasoning of the Fifth Circuit Court of Appeals, which had previously held Hispanic persons to be part of a separate identifiable ethnic group. United States v. Texas Educ. Agency, 467 F.2d 848 (5th Cir. 1972) *(en banc)*; Cisneros, 467 F.2d 142.

141. In combining Blacks and Hispanos "for the purposes of defining a 'segregated' school," the High Court relied on evidence that "in the Southwest Hispanos and Negroes have a great many things in common . . . [suffering] identical discrimination in treatment" (413 U.S. at 197–98).

142. Hart v. Community School Bd. of Brooklyn, NYC Sch. D. #21, 383 F. Supp. 699, 733 (E.D.N.Y.), *aff'd*, 512 F.2d 37 (2d Cir. 1975); Morgan v. Hennigan, 379 F. Supp. 410, 415, n. 1 (D. Mass. 1974) *aff'd sub nom.* Morgan v. Kerrigan, 509 F.2d 580 (1st Cir. 1975), *cert. denied*, 421 U.S. 963 (liability), and 401 F. Supp. 216 (remedy), where

Puerto Ricans, Cubans, Dominicans, and other non-Whites were collectively accorded separate legal status as "other minorities."

143. Austin Independent School Dist. v. United States, _____U.S._____, 45 U.S.L.W. 3413 (Dec. 7, 1976); Milliken v. Bradley, 402 F. Supp. 1096 (E.D. Mich. 1975), *aff'd*, 540 F.2d 229 (6th Cir.), *cert. granted*, _____U.S._____, 45 U.S.L.W. 3359 (Nov. 16, 1976); Brinkman v. Gilligan, 539 F.2d 1084 (6th Cir. 1976), *cert. granted*, 45 U.S.L.W. 3489 (Jan. 18, 1977).

144. 521 F.2d 465.

145. *See* note 62, *supra*.

146. 521 F.2d at 481.

147. *Id.* at 482.

148. *Id.*

149. *Id.* at 400.

150. *Id.* at 483. See Hon. William E. Doyle, "Social Science Evidence in Court Cases," in *Education, Social Science and the Judicial Process* (Washington, D.C.: National Institute of Education, 1976).

151. 521 F.2d at 480, 483.

152. *Id.* at 1154.

153. *Id.*

154. *But see*, Morgan V. Kerrigan, 530 F.2d at 416 n. 19: "A remedy may sometimes properly 'exceed the violation' in that it may do more than eradicate the constitutional wrong. To the extent that 'overbreadth' in the remedy is necessary to ensure that the constitutional violation is corrected, it is not at all unusual. There are many instances in the law in which remedial law places greater restrictions on primary activity than did the substantive law that had been violated."

155. Specific recommendations contained in the addendum included: eliminating special costs for such items as gym shoes; taking field trips to museums, libraries, department stores, and tortilla factories and other minority-run enterprises; and engaging theater and ballet groups to reinforce cultural recognition. Admittedly, these aspects of the addendum are extreme examples, but the district court never clarified whether it was adopting them and others in its order, and the Tenth Circuit was clearly troubled by this portion of the order [Keyes, 380 F. Supp. 673, 697 (D. Colo. 1974)].

156. 402 U.S. at 16.

157. 418 U.S. 717 (1974).

158. _____U.S._____, 49 L. Ed. 2d 599, 608 (1976).

159. 45 U.S.L.W. 3359.

160. 540 F.2d 241-42.

161. 401 F. Supp. 216 (D. Mass. 1975), *aff'd*, 530 F.2d 401 (1st Cir. 1976), *cert. denied*, _____U.S._____, 44 U.S.L.W. 3719 (June 15, 1976).

162. *See also* Morales v. Shannon, *supra*, where the Fifth Circuit gave the opinion that "it strikes us that this entire question [of bilingual education] goes to a matter reserved to educators," and cautioned that "on the off chance that defendants are engaging in discriminatory practices in the program as it currently exists, we pretermit decision here and remand to the district court for further consideration there on a fresh record in the event appellants determine to pursue the question. It is now and unlawful educational practice to fail to take appropriate action to overcome language barriers."

163. Serna, 351 F. Supp. 1279 (N.D. Mex. 1972), *aff'd*, 499 F.2d 1147 (10th Cir. 1974).

164. Several of these issues are addressed in *A Better Chance to Learn: Bilingual Bicultural Education* (Washington, D.C.: U.S. Commission on Civil Rights Clearinghouse, 1975); *see also* Grubb, "Breaking the Language Barrier: The Right to Bilingual Education," 9 *Harv. Civil Rts.-Civ. Lib. L. Rev.* 52 (1974).

The authors wish to express their appreciation to the Center for Applied Linguistics for creating a forum, with the support of the Carnegie Corporation of New York, for discussion of the issues presented in this article. For providing them the opportunity to litigate several of the cases discussed in this article, the authors are indebted to the Puerto Rican Legal Defense and Education Fund, Inc.

From the Treaty of Guadalupe Hidalgo to *Hopwood:* The Educational Plight and Struggle of Mexican Americans in the Southwest

GUADALUPE SAN MIGUEL JR.
RICHARD R. VALENCIA

February 2, 1998, marked the sesquicentennial of the signing of the Treaty of Guadalupe Hidalgo, a treaty that brought an end to the Mexican American War (1846–1848) and the annexation, by conquest, of over 525,000 square miles of territory by the United States (including present-day Arizona, California, western Colorado, Nevada, New Mexico, Texas, and Utah). To many contemporary Mexican Americans, the Treaty of Guadalupe Hidalgo signaled the beginning of persistent discrimination, and oppression (Rendón, 1971).[1] In the field of Mexican American Studies, 1848 has become a major point of demarcation in that 150 years ago, Mexicans living in the United States became a conquered people. Although Articles VIII and IX of the Treaty explicitly respected and guaranteed the civil and property rights of Mexicans who elected to remain in the United States, such provisions proved illusory and were unfulfilled (Griswold del Castillo, 1990). To many Mexican Americans, the Treaty of Guadalupe Hidalgo is but another broken agreement, analogous to the U.S. government's violation of treaties it entered into with various Native American tribes.

In this article, we offer some insights into the schooling of Mexican Americans over the last 150 years. We examine how the foundation of conflict, hostility, and discrimination, as symbolized by the Treaty, shaped the emergence, expansion, and changing character of public education for the Mexican American people of the Southwest. This analysis is not intended to be a complete history of Mexican American education. That has yet to be written. Rather, this article is a synthesis of Mexican American public education in the U.S. Southwest over the last 150 years. We interpret these experiences by focusing on major themes, trends, and developments.

From a historiographic perspective, we draw from the two approaches suggested by San Miguel (1986) to study the history of Mexican American edu-

Harvard Educational Review Vol. 68 No. 3 Fall 1998, 353–412

cation. The first approach — which we refer to as the "plight" dimension of Mexican American education — examines what schools have done to or for Mexican American students, and how these students have fared. The second approach — which we refer to as the "struggle" dimension — explores how Mexican Americans have developed campaigns for the attainment of equal educational opportunity.[2]

Using these two approaches, we discuss the schooling of Mexican Americans in the United States in four sections: 1) the origins of schooling for Mexican children in the "American" Southwest, 1848–1890s; 2) the expansion of Mexican American public education, 1890–1930; 3) the changing character of public education, 1930–1960; and 4) Mexican American education in the contemporary period.

Origins of Schooling in the "American" Southwest, 1848–1890s

After the signing of the Treaty of Guadalupe Hidalgo in 1848, the world in which the Mexican-origin population found itself changed dramatically. Education also changed dramatically in the post-1848 decades, as formal instruction or schooling assumed an increasingly important role in the Southwest in general and in the Mexican-origin community in particular.[3]

Emergence of Diverse Forms of Schooling

Schooling was not a novel innovation in the Southwest. Prior to the arrival of the Anglos, political leaders in this area, known then as the far northern frontier of Mexico, established schools. They were not widespread nor permanent ventures, but where they existed, these schools were part of community life and contributed to the promotion of literacy and culture in these frontier regions (Gallegos, 1991).

After the Mexican American War, the number, longevity, and sponsorship of schools increased. Up to that time, schooling for the general population had been sponsored primarily by the Catholic Church.[4] In the post-1848 period other groups also established schools. Among the most important of these were Protestant denominational groups and public officials.[5] The following traces the origins and evolution of these diverse forms of schooling in the new "American" Southwest.

— Catholic Schools

Catholic schooling was very much a part of Mexican culture in the Southwest before the U.S. conquest.[6] After 1848 it expanded significantly, as the Church proceeded to strengthen its role in the emerging U.S. social order. As part of this effort, the Church rebuilt its churches, reaffirmed its authority over religious practices, and reestablished control over its "flock."[7] It also established educational institutions in the Southwest, including academies and convents for girls, colleges and seminaries for boys, and parish schools for working-class children. In New Mexico, between fifteen and twenty schools in as many cities were established between 1853 and 1874 (Avant, 1940). In California, an undetermined number of schools were established for Mexican boys and girls in several cities, including Santa Barbara, Ventura, and Los Angeles.[8] In Texas, a handful of schools for Mexican children were also established in cities such as El Paso, Brownsville, Corpus Christi, and San Antonio (Castañeda, 1976).

The primary reasons the Catholic Church built schools throughout the region were to strengthen the religious tenets promoted during the years prior to U.S. annexation and to ensure that the large and increasing numbers of newcomers acquired the Catholic faith (North, 1936). The proselytizing efforts of various Protestant denominations, the increasing secularization of American institutions — especially the emerging public school systems — and attacks against the Catholic Church in various parts of the country also encouraged the addition of parishes and schools by which a U.S. Catholicism could be propagated.[9]

— Protestant Schools

Protestants, especially the Presbyterians, also established schools for Mexican-origin children in the Southwest. The purposes of these schools were to convert the Mexican-origin population, to train a Christian leadership that would contribute to this process, and to promote Americanization (Banker, 1993; Rankin, 1966).

Although some schools for Mexican-origin children were founded in the 1850s, the majority were not established until the post–Civil War years.[10] Protestants increased schooling for Mexican-origin children due to several factors, including the concerted efforts of missionaries who believed that schools would enable them to better reach the natives (Banker, 1993); the Presbyterian church's new evangelization policy favoring the establishment of schools for members of the "exceptional" populations in areas without any public education facilities;[11] the lack of public schooling in many areas of the Southwest; and the vigorous financial and moral support of the newly established Women's Executive Committee of the Presbyterian Church (Agnew & Barber, 1971; Presbyterian Panorama, 1952). In all, Presbyterians established approximately fifty mission or plaza schools for Mexican-origin children between 1878 and 1896.[12] Their number decreased significantly in the 1890s due to the establishment of public education facilities in these communities, but new elementary schools continued to be founded during the next two decades.[13] Protestant ministers and laypersons also organized secondary schools, especially after the Civil War (Brackenridge, García- Tretor, & Stover, 1971). Between 1868 and 1896 they established approximately nine boarding schools in New Mexico, Texas, and California. The Presbyterians established seven of these schools, the Methodists two.[14]

These secondary schools were occasionally labeled "industrial," but they were aimed at providing Mexican-origin individuals with instruction suitable for mobility in the economy and for leadership positions in the larger society. Protestant secondary schools were similar to the post-bellum mission schools and colleges established in the South by northern philanthropists and religious organizations, especially the American Missionary Association. These southern mission schools assumed the training of a Black professional elite and an educated leadership after most southern states failed to provide integrated and quality public education for Blacks in the late 1860s.[15] Despite the label of "college," the vast majority of these mission schools focused on pre-college instruction (Weinberg, 1977). Protestant schools in the Southwest were similar to these post-bellum schools in the South, as they provided Mexican-origin children with some trade training, a traditional academic curriculum, and experience in civic affairs.

— Public Schools

Local officials such as city council and school board members also established schools for Mexican-origin children in this post-1848 period, but since they were more interested in first providing White children with school facilities, the Mexican schools were few.[16] Local and state political leaders' lack of commitment to public schooling, racial prejudice, and political differences among Anglos and Mexicans accounted for this phenomenon (Atkins, 1978; Friedman, 1978; Hendrick, 1977; Weinberg, 1977).

After the 1870s, the number of schools for Mexican-origin children increased dramatically due to popular demand, legal mandates, increasing financial ability, and a greater acceptance of the ideal of common schooling by local and state political leaders (Atkins, 1978; Eby, 1925; Ferris, 1962). However, this educational access occurred in the context of increasing societal discrimination and a general subordination of Mexican Americans.

Out of this relationship between society and education there emerged a pattern of institutional discrimination that was reflected in the establishment of segregated schools for Mexican-origin children. In New Mexico, for instance, officials began to establish segregated schools in 1872. By the 1880s, more than 50 percent of the territory's school-age population, most of whom were Mexican children, were enrolled in these segregated schools (Chaves, 1892). In Texas, officials established segregated schools for Mexican working-class children in the rural areas during the 1880s and in the urban areas in the 1890s. The need to maintain a cheap labor source in the ranches probably accounted for the earlier presence of Mexican schools in the rural areas (Friedman, 1978; Weinberg, 1977). Despite the influx of Mexican immigrant students, California officials did not build any additional schools for Mexican children until the turn of the century. Those that already existed continued to be segregated and, in some cases, were inferior to the Anglo schools (California Superintendent of Public Instruction, 1869).

In this period, then, the number of schools and their sponsors increased significantly. Among the most important sponsors of these schools were the Catholic Church, Protestant denominational groups, and public officials. These sponsors had various reasons for establishing schools, including conversion, religious competition, legal mandates, and desires for learning. Their establishment indicated that Mexican-origin children were not excluded from education per se, but were provided varying degrees of access to different types of schooling. It also indicated that schooling in general, and public education in particular, was becoming increasingly important in the new U.S. social order.

Americanization and the Schools in the Nineteenth Century

The schools established in the Southwest during the late nineteenth century were also more diverse in the goals that they pursued. In the decades prior to U.S. rule, most schools in general were primarily responsible for teaching literacy and some religion. But beginning at mid-century, as Handlin (1982) notes, schools underwent a significant transformation and assumed a new task — that of transforming the cultural identities of groups perceived to be foreigners. Handlin argues that this impulse to reform was not due to class imposition or to urbanization and industrialization, but to the "vague aspirations" of those Americans interested in conversion, that is, in persuading those in "darkness" to walk "in the way of light" (1982, p. 7). These schools, in other words, assumed a new social goal and became responsible for Americanizing the Mexican-origin population.

In the historical literature, "Americanization" usually refers to an organized national political movement that compelled immigrants during the second decade of the twentieth century to adopt certain "Anglo-American ways while remaining at the bottom of the socioeconomic strata of American society" (Tamura, 1994, p. 52). But Americanization was much more than simply a coercive twentieth-century political movement aimed at promoting the adoption of U.S. economic, political, religious, and cultural forms. It was, rather, a complex social and institutional process that originated in the colonial period. Its purpose was not only to inculcate American ways, but also to discourage the maintenance of immigrant and minority group cultures (Carlson, 1975). Occasionally, however, Americanization promoted the maintenance of these so-called "foreign" group cultures, but this was rare. We refer to the former process as subtractive Americanization and to the latter as additive Americanization.[17]

Subtractive and additive Americanization were integral aspects of school development. The former occurred when the schools devalued particular minority groups and their specific cultural heritages, when they sought to re-place these groups' distinct identities with an idealized American one, or when they sought to remove minority communities, languages, and cultures from the school content and structures.[18] Additive Americanization took place when schools promoted maintenance of minority cultures and specifi-cally when they valued minority participation in education, when they en-couraged the development of students' bicultural identity, or when they pro-moted minority communities, languages, and cultures in their curriculum and operations.[19]

Catholic Schools

Most of the Mexican schools of the Southwest promoted either subtractive or additive Americanization, but significant differences existed among them. Catholic schools, for instance, took a stand in favor of Mexican Americans and their cultural heritage. For the most part they validated, rather than disparaged, this group and their cultural heritage in the pro-cess of teaching them U.S. social, economic, and political ideals (Camp-bell, 1987). The Catholic Church's approach to Americanization — due primarily to official Church policy on national parishes and influenced by demography, geography, community desire, as well as the threat of Protestant evangelization efforts — was reflected in the schools' operations and practices. Catholic authorities, for instance, used Spanish as a tool of instruction in the schools, named these institutions after well-known Mexi-can religious figures, and encouraged Mexican-origin participation in their support and maintenance.[20]

Because of this accommodative stance, Mexican Americans, despite their distrust of formal Church policies and practices, strongly supported the es-tablishment of Catholic schools in the Southwest. They donated materials, volunteered their labor, and generously gave money to establish and main-tain them (Campbell, 1987).

Protestant Schools

Unlike Catholic schools, the Protestant schools took a hostile position toward Mexican Americans and their identity. Protestant school leaders viewed Mexican people as illiterate, perversely immoral, superstitious, "densely ignorant," and lacking in "civilized" customs. Their culture was also viewed in largely negative terms. As we shall see later, these views (i.e., deficit thinking) were highly influential in shaping perceptions of Mexican Ameri-cans' educability. One of the central purposes of Protestant schools was to transform this group into "Americans" by stamping out their distinct identity and replacing it with an idealized, Protestant-based American identity.[21]

Notwithstanding their hostility, Protestant schools in time became more accommodating (Banker, 1993). This was due, in large part, to Mexican

American resistance to Protestant teachings. Their resistance eventually led to the acquisition of a more favorable but still paternalistic view of this group and its cultural heritage, and to the selective use of its language and culture in the schools. Many of these schools, for instance, occasionally used Spanish-language materials and instruction in the classroom. They also used secular aspects of the Mexican cultural traditions in the curriculum and promoted certain secular patriotic celebrations, such as *el dieciséis de Septiembre* or *el cinco de Mayo* (Banker, 1993).[22]

The primary reason for the use of the Spanish language and Mexican culture in the schools, we suggest, was not to preserve them, but, rather, to encourage a more rapid, albeit less painful, method of Americanization. Language and cultural maintenance, if it occurred, was probably an unintentional outcome of Protestant methods.

Public Schools

Public schools, like Catholic schools, originally promoted additive Americanization. In the early years of U.S. rule, they promoted the use of Spanish in the schools, included the Mexican cultural heritage in the curriculum, and encouraged members of the Mexican American community to participate in public schooling. The major reason for this accommodation was structural. Public schools, unlike those established by religious groups, were local institutions controlled by members of the local communities. In many parts of the Southwest, the local communities were comprised primarily of Mexican Americans and Catholic Church officials. These two groups therefore assumed important governance, administrative, and instructional positions in the schools and made decisions favoring the use of Spanish as the language of instruction and the use of Catholic materials, including the Bible, in the curriculum.[23]

The use of Spanish-language and Catholic materials in the curriculum and the presence of Mexican Americans and Catholic officials in the schools, however, made public education suspect in the eyes of many southwestern Anglo officials. Because of these alleged "foreignisms," many of them felt that public education was not really "American" in character. The primary task of these individuals, then, was not to Americanize Mexican children, but to Americanize the public school. The public school needed to be transformed into an essentially American institution before it could successfully embark on its historic task of transforming the ethnic identities of those perceived to be foreigners. In practical terms, this meant that minority and Catholic individuals, as well as the language they spoke or the culture they embraced, had to be removed and replaced by American (i.e., Anglo) individuals and cultural forms, including the English language and non-sectarianism. In acquiring these American characteristics, the public school itself became an increasingly subtractive institution.

The Americanization of Public Education in the Southwest

The process of transforming an accommodative public school system in the Southwest into an essentially American institution was a constant and uneven one that began at mid-century and continued late into the nineteenth century. It was achieved through a process of subtraction — that is, a process that involved the removal of all minority communities, languages, and cultures from the governance, administration, and content of public education. Occasional opposition from Mexican American individuals, concerned Catholic officials, and sympathetic educators slowed down, but did not halt, these efforts. Because of demographic and political reasons, the schools in Texas and California were more rapidly transformed than those in New Mexico.

The schools removed the ethnic and religious community, as well as two significant aspects of the Mexican heritage — the Spanish language and the Mexican culture. First, Mexican American individuals and Catholic officials were removed from the public schools. Both had supported the establishment of public schools and to varying degrees assumed important decision-making positions in their governance structures, administration, and instruction.[24] In many cases, they had made decisions in favor of the use of Spanish, Spanish-language texts, and Catholic materials in the classroom. But their participation in the schools significantly decreased over the years. The former decreased primarily because of demographic reasons and racial discrimination; the latter because of stiff opposition from Protestant Anglos. Most U.S. historians refer to the campaign to separate church and state as the "school question" (see, for instance, Atkins, 1978). Mexican Americans, however, viewed this as an attack against their centuries-old heritage and against individuals who shared their cultural values (Ketz, 1997). By the end of the nineteenth century, most Mexican Americans and Catholic officials were removed from the public schools.

Public officials also removed Spanish as a means of instruction from the public schools. The campaign to "subtract" Spanish from public education was part of a general nativist sentiment that affected all non-English languages and cultures and all public institutions throughout the country. This campaign was, in large part, a response to the increasing racial/ethnic diversity found in the United States due largely to westward expansionism and European immigration. The presence of diverse groups created immense problems in terms of their incorporation into American culture and raised a variety of anxieties and fears among the (native) White population, including the impact that they could have on American culture, on social and political unity in this country, and on the political hegemony of White America.[25] In response to these concerns, White educators and other policymakers initiated a campaign against diversity. The primary goals of this campaign were to promote the purity of Anglo-American culture, unify the country on the basis of a common culture and language, and maintain the political dominance of native Whites (Banks, 1986; Leibowitz, 1971). In many ways, then, the campaign to remove Spanish from the public schools in the Southwest was the regional expression of a national campaign.

The subtraction of Spanish from public education was accomplished through the enactment of English-language policies at the state and local levels, which not only prescribed English as the medium of instruction in the schools, but also discouraged, inhibited, or prohibited the use of Spanish (Leibowitz, 1976). In some cases, language designation was usually accompanied by other discriminatory legislation and practices against the minorities who spoke their native languages (Leibowitz, 1976).

Restrictions on the use of Spanish in the schools did not have an immediate impact on Mexican Americans or on public officials, as many of them simply continued to use Spanish.[26] These restrictions did, however, affect the status of Spanish in the schools and attitudes toward this language. In most cases, they reaffirmed the primacy of only one language — English — at the expense of others (Macías, 1983). They also violated the Treaty of Guadalupe Hidalgo, which guaranteed Mexican Americans "the enjoyment of all the rights of citizens of the United States," including the right to maintain their language (Original Text of Treaty of Guadalupe Hidalgo, Art. 9, excerpted from Miller, 1937).

The subtraction of Spanish from the schools occurred in two phases. In the first phase, mostly during the 1850s, Spanish was usually only limited as a medium of instruction in the schools. Both Texas and California, for instance, enacted legislation in this decade mandating the use of English in the schools and restricting the use of Spanish.[27] Anglo officials in New Mexico tried to enact an English-only law for the public schools during the 1850s, but were unsuccessful because of the large and politically strong Mexican American population.[28]

During the second phase, from 1870 to the early 1890s, Spanish was prohibited in the public schools. In 1870, for instance, Texas and California passed English-language laws prohibiting its use.[29] A similar English-only law was passed in New Mexico in 1891.[30] Anglos' increased anxieties over the continued growth of minority groups and their increased impact on U.S. religion, culture, politics, and social life was the impetus for the passage of these laws (Calvert & De León, 1990; Hendrick, 1977, 1980; Macías, 1984). The passage of these English-language laws did not immediately remove Spanish from the schools, but it laid the legal framework for its successful removal over the next several decades.

Most Mexican Americans opposed English policies that failed to value the importance of Spanish to the Mexican-origin population or that favored its removal from the schools (*El Clamor Público*, 1856). Because of the size and influence of the Mexican American community there, the strongest opposition came from New Mexico, where Mexican Americans consistently opposed the establishment of a public school system that did not support the use of Spanish as a language of instruction (Meyer, 1977; Milk, 1980). This opposition also occurred in California and Texas (Griswold del Castillo, 1979; Leibowitz, 1971).

Finally, between 1850 and 1880, school officials eliminated Mexican culture from the public school curriculum by removing classes pertaining to Catholic topics and Mexican history. Due to the small size of the Mexican American population and the relatively weak position of the Catholic Church in both states, public officials in California and Texas successfully removed these courses from their public schools by the mid-1850s. Some schools in these states, however, did not fully remove Catholic heritage classes until the early 1880s. For instance, in Los Angeles, which had the largest Mexican community in California, the public schools taught "La doctrina Católica" as part of its curriculum until 1882 (Griswold del Castillo, 1979; Pitt, 1968). Similarly, in New Mexico, school officials encountered significant opposition due to combined efforts of the politically influential Catholic Church and the numerically large Mexican American statewide leadership. Both fought to have Catholic topics in general and Mexican history courses in particular taught in the public schools until the 1890s.

The replacement of Mexican heritage classes with new courses and instructional materials that reflected the Anglo-American experience gave rise to the emergence of an Anglo-centric curriculum. This shift can be seen in the history textbooks used in the schools by the 1870s. These books, which began to appear a decade after the Mexican American War, contained only disparaging comments about the Mexican presence in the Southwest. These books consistently denounced the character of the Mexican people and stressed the nobility of the Anglos and their actions (Castañeda, 1943). One of the history books, for instance, described the Battle of Mier, which Mexican troops won in the 1830s, in the following manner:

> At this point, where Mexican valor failed, Mexican trickery succeeded. . . . They indicated that a reinforcement of eight hundred fresh men were expected every moment; that the general admired the bravery of the Texans and wished to save them from the certain destruction. . . . It seems strange that the Texans had not learned by this time never to trust the Mexicans, promises or no promises. (Pennybacker, 1895, p. 229)

Most of the late nineteenth- and even early twentieth-century history textbooks had a narrow scope of Texas history and either omitted or minimized the cultural contributions of Spain and Mexico to the state's development. According to the authors of these history textbooks, little or nothing occurred in Texas worthy of record before the coming of the first Anglo settlers from the United States.[31]

As a consequence of these interpretive shifts in the curriculum, the Mexican American presence in the Southwest was now presented through the eyes of the dominant Anglo group. This interpretation generally tended to omit the contributions of Mexican Americans and to provide a distorted and stereotypical view of Mexican-origin people and their cultural heritage (Cameron, 1976; García, 1981).

Expansion of Mexican American Public Education, 1890–1930

During the early twentieth century, public education changed dramatically — largely in response to the tremendous social, economic, political, and cultural changes underway in American life. Between 1890 and 1930, education, in some form, was extended to individuals from all racial, national, gender, and age groups, governance structures were altered to benefit middle-class individuals, and new innovations in educational administration such as testing were introduced. (Later, we discuss in some detail the curricular impact of mass intelligence testing on Mexican American students.) The curriculum was diversified to meet the needs of the heterogeneous student population, educational programs were standardized, and instructional methodology was revolutionized through the introduction of a new psychology and more sophisticated learning theories. One-room schools in rural areas were consolidated into larger units for efficiency, and schools became articulated from elementary to the post-secondary grades (Pulliam, 1987).[32]

The Mexican American population also changed during the early twentieth century. Between 1890 and 1930, Mexican Americans became more socially differentiated, economically diverse, and politically active. Although diverse in many ways, Mexican Americans, as a group, were politically powerless, economically impoverished, and socially alienated. Most of them lived in highly segregated communities, in dismal housing conditions, and Spanish was the dominant language. Mexicans were predominantly a cheap source of labor for U.S. industry (Meier & Stewart, 1990).

The subordinate position of Mexican Americans posed significant challenges for public schools over the decades. The schools and those who shaped them, however, ignored and/or misconstrued the multiple needs of the heterogeneous Mexican-origin student population. In many cases, the schools responded not to the genuine needs of this diverse group of children, but to those of other stronger political and economic interests.[33] Due to these contextual realities, the nineteenth-century pattern of inequitable, segregated, and subtractive schooling was extended and strengthened over time, much to the detriment of education for Mexican Americans.

School Access

In the early twentieth century, Mexican Americans were provided increasing albeit inequitable access to the public schools. Increased enrollment was due, in large part, to a mixture of contrary forces such as the increasing availability of school facilities; the passage of child labor and school attendance laws; immigration; urbanization and concentration in rural pockets; and greater economic stability and increased economic exploitation (Eby, 1925;

Ferrier, 1937). In 1900, for example, the enrollment of Mexican-origin school-age children between the ages of five and seventeen ranged from a low of 17 percent in Texas to about 50 percent in New Mexico (De León, 1982; Territorial Superintendent's Report, 1891, 1892). By 1930, enrollment rates increased, but only moderately. The state with the lowest percentage of Mexican American children enrolled was Texas, with 50 percent; the highest was New Mexico, with approximately 74 percent (U.S. Bureau of the Census, 1961a, 1961b). Comparative data on the enrollment of Mexican Americans and Anglos is lacking, but figures from Texas suggest an incredible enrollment gap. In 1900, the percent of Mexican American and Anglo school-age children enrolled in the public schools stood at 17 percent and 39 percent, respectively. By 1928, and despite the increased enrollment for both, the gap between them widened. In that year, the relative percentages of Mexican American and Anglo school-age children stood at 49 percent and 83 percent, respectively (Manuel, 1930).

Despite the increasing access to education, a large proportion of these students still did not attend schools due in large part to poverty, mobility associated with rural employment, and discrimination on the part of educational policymakers. Three major groups of Mexican American students were denied full access to public education during the first half of the twentieth century: agricultural migrants, secondary school-age students, and post-secondary school-age students. School officials either actively excluded these children from the public schools or took little positive action to encourage their enrollment (Weinberg, 1977).

Quality of Education

Notwithstanding their increased access to public schools, Mexican American children received an inferior quality education, as evidenced by segregated facilities and administrative mistreatment, among others. Segregation expanded significantly after the 1890s because of increased nativist sentiments towards the growing presence of Mexican-origin children in the schools. Segregation in the early decades of the twentieth century was primarily confined to the elementary grades, due to the high withdrawal rates of Mexican children before reaching secondary public schools. But once they began to seek access to secondary schooling, local officials established segregated facilities in these grades as well (González, 1990; San Miguel, 1979).

Politics and prejudice were key in establishing segregated facilities, but culture and class became crucial in maintaining and extending this practice over time. State officials played an important role in the expansion of educational segregation by sanctioning its presence and by allocating state funds for the maintenance of these locally segregated schools. Local school officials throughout the Southwest established separate facilities for Mexican children and then asked the state to fund these schools.[34] Residential segregation, demographic shifts in the population, and economic conditions also greatly influenced the expansion of segregation in the twentieth century (González, 1990).

These separate schools were unequal in many respects to those provided for Anglo children. In relation to Anglo schools, Mexican schools were older, their school equipment was generally less adequate, per pupil expenditures were generally lower, and the staff were less appropriately trained, qualified, and experienced. In many cases, the teachers were sent to the Mexican schools as a form of punishment or to introduce them to the teaching profession (Manuel, 1930; Reynolds, 1933).[35]

In many instances Mexican Americans vociferously protested school segregation. In 1910, in San Angelo, Texas, for example, the Mexican American community staged a "blowout" (school walkout). Its charge was that the segregated Mexican school was inferior in physical facilities and quality of instruction. The Mexican community demanded that its children be allowed to attend the White schools. The school board, after hearing the charges and demands, decided against integration. Subsequently, the Mexican parents boycotted their school altogether. The boycott lasted through 1915, but to no avail. Some of the Mexican children attended the local Catholic school and the Mexican Presbyterian Mission school (De León, 1974).

Local officials also developed administrative measures that were discriminatory towards Mexican Americans. For example, Mexican American children, similar to other working-class, immigrant, and ethnically different children, were consistently diagnosed as being intellectually inferior, channeled into low-track classes, and deprived of opportunities for success (González, 1990; Valencia, 1997c). These policies and practices served to stratify the student population according to various categories and to reproduce the existing relations of domination in the classroom and in society in general (González, 1990).

Curricular Policies

In the early twentieth century, the public school curriculum underwent significant changes as it sought to meet the diverse needs of a heterogeneous student population (Kliebard, 1987). As part of this process, public school officials provided Mexican American children with an academically imbalanced and culturally subtractive curriculum. Originally comprised of the "3Rs" and some socialization, the curriculum for Mexican American school children in the early decades of the twentieth century became increasingly imbalanced. It emphasized socialization and non-academic concerns at the expense of academics. At the elementary level, curricular emphasis shifted from the 3Rs to focus on the "3Cs," common *cultural* norms, *civics* instruction, and *command* of the English tongue (Carter & Segura, 1979). At the secondary level, the emphasis was shifted to vocational and general education. Although comprised of some elements of the 3Rs, the curriculum for Mexican Americans in the secondary grades came to have larger doses of more practical instruction (González, 1990).

As was the case at the end of the nineteenth century, in the early twentieth century the curriculum remained linguistically and culturally subtractive because of the continuing influence of assimilationist ideology and nativism (Banks, 1986; Leibowitz, 1971; Macías, 1983). Instructional materials and school textbooks, for the most part, continued to either omit or distort the Mexican cultural heritage. Linguistic subtraction continued to be reflected in the English-only policies and anti-Spanish practices found in most public school systems throughout the country during this period (Anderson, 1969; O'Brien, 1961).

Minority groups and committed educators opposed the subtractive curriculum and tried to reintroduce language and culture into the schools, but without much success. For instance, restrictive English-only laws were challenged in the courts during the mid-1920s by a variety of religious, racial, and minority groups. These challenges eventually led to the repeal of proscriptive laws by the U.S. Supreme Court in the 1920s (Anderson, 1969; O'Brien, 1961). Mexican Americans in Texas also challenged the English-only law in the state legislature and successfully promoted changes in this bill (Anderson, 1969; O'Brien, 1961; San Miguel, 1987).

Pattern of School Performance

The major educational consequence of inferior schooling was a pattern of skewed academic performance, characterized by Mexican American students' poor achievement and little school success. This pattern of poor school performance was reflected through measures such as low test scores, high withdrawal rates from school, and low median number of school years completed. Although their performance scores improved over the decades, the gap between Anglo and Mexican American students did not change significantly over time (Little, 1944; Manuel, 1930; U.S. Commission on Civil Rights, 1971b).

Not all Mexican American students, however, did poorly in school. Contrary to popular and scholarly opinion, some of them experienced school success. This group included those individuals who completed both secondary and post-secondary school during the years from the 1890s to the 1930s. Although no specific figures exist indicating the degree of academic success, evidence from published sources on religious and public high schools suggests the existence of a group of school achievers. Manuel, for instance, noted that in the late 1920s, approximately 10 percent of the Mexican American school-age population in Texas completed high school (Manuel, 1930; see also Little, 1944). Several studies of religious schools such as St. Michael's Catholic school in Santa Fe, New Mexico, Central High Catholic School in Los Angeles, California, and Menaul High School in Albuquerque,

New Mexico, have been graduating Mexican American students since their establishment in the late nineteenth or early twentieth century (Becklund, 1985; Menaul School Centennial, 1981; St. Michael's College, 1959). Several studies also indicate that while the number of Mexican American students attending college in the early twentieth century was extremely small, usually less than one percent, the existence of such college students indicates an unexplored tradition of Mexican-origin school success (Muñoz, 1989; Weinberg, 1977).[36] Although data on secondary and post-secondary enrollment is lacking, existing sources refute the myth of unprecedented poor achievement and suggest exceptions to the patterns of school performance in the Mexican origin community.

Mexican Americans, then, have had a checkered pattern of academic performance, not merely one of low achievement. Any patterns of success, be they individual or on a small scale, should be explored further in order to better understand how these students overcame what were obviously tremendous odds.

The Changing Character of Public Education, 1930–1960

Public education for Mexican American students during the period 1930–1960 was one of entrenchment and expansion of both segregation and inferior schooling. This era was also characterized by considerable change and concerted struggle, as the Mexican American community made major initiatives in their quest for educational equality.

Central to the changing character of public education for Mexican American students in this period were the evolving nature of "deficit thinking," the entrenchment and rise of school segregation and inferior schooling conditions and outcomes promoted by racial/ethnic isolation, and Mexican American efforts to improve schools through legal challenges of segregation and cultural critiques of intelligence testing.

The Evolving Nature of Deficit Thinking

Deficit thinking refers to the notion that students (particularly of low-income, racial/ethnic minority background) fail in school (e.g., perform poorly on standardized tests) because such students and their families have internal defects, or deficits, that thwart the learning process (Valencia, 1997b). For example, this thinking maintains that Mexican American students who experience school failure do so because of limited educability, poor motivation, and inadequate familial socialization for academic competence.[37] Deficit thinking is founded on racial and class bias that "blames the victim," rather than examining how schools are structured to prevent students from learning.[38]

Deficit thinking has had a considerable impact on shaping perceptions of Mexican American students' educability and subsequent schooling prac-

135

tices. In the 1920s, when state administrators in parts of the Southwest first expressed official interest in providing public education for Mexican Americans (San Miguel, 1987), hereditarianism was hitting its zenith in educational thought and practice (Cravens, 1978; Valencia, 1997c). Hereditarian theory posits that genetics largely accounts for individual differences such as intellectual performance in the behavior of human beings, as well as differences between groups.[39]

With the advent of the first intelligence test (the Binet-Simon scale), developed in 1905 in France, and its subsequent importation and cultural appropriation by U.S. scholars, the intelligence testing movement rapidly swept through the 1920s (Valencia, 1997a). Based on numerous "race psychology" studies of this era (see, e.g., review by Garth, 1925), the lower intellectual performance of certain groups (such as poor and working-class African American and Mexican American students) was deemed genetically based. Valencia (1997c), drawing from Sánchez (1932), identified eight studies between 1922 and 1929 that included Mexican American students as participants.[40] In all eight studies the author(s) concluded, either explicitly or suggestively, that the lower intelligence-test performance of Mexican American children compared to their White peers in the investigations or White normative data was due to heredity.

It is important to underscore that deficit thinking also contains a *prescriptive* element, that is, the advancement of certain curricular interventions based on the perceived educability of low-socioeconomic status (SES) children of color (Valencia, 1997b). From the race psychology studies of the 1920s, specific deficit thinking schooling practices such as outright school segregation, dead-end classes for the allegedly mentally retarded, and low-level vocational education emerged. With group intelligence testing available, many thousands of schoolchildren were tested and subsequently grouped for instructional purposes commensurate to their *innate* ability (Valencia, 1997c).

In 1920s California, a state in which the Mexican American population was growing rapidly, there was considerable mass intellectual assessment of schoolchildren. For example, in addition to large-scale testing in the San Jose area (Young, 1922), by 1923 there were 50,000 students in the Oakland and Berkeley school systems that had been tested and classified on ability (Dickson, 1923). The institutionalization of mass intelligence testing, counseling programs, and differentiated curriculum in Los Angeles were used in ways that effectively stratified students along racial/ethnic and SES lines (González, 1974a, 1974b, 1990). In Los Angeles, by decade's end, a total of 328,000 tests had been administered at the elementary level alone (González, 1974a). Based in part on IQ test results, González (1974a) has suggested that almost 50 percent of Mexican American elementary students were placed in classes for the mentally sub-average (slow learners) and mentally retarded. It has been estimated that Mexican American elementary-age students comprised only 13 percent of the student population in 1927 in Los Angeles City and County (Taylor, 1929, cited in González, 1974a). Consequently, these numbers suggest an enormous over-representational disparity of 285 percent in the labeling and placement of Mexican American students in special education classes in Los Angeles during this period.

Foley (1997) has commented that, beginning around 1930 and lasting through the early 1960s, there was a shift among social scientists from a deficit thinking model based on genetics to one relying on cultural attributes and behaviors.[41] These "new" deficit theorists frequently turned to the works of anthropologist Lewis (e.g., 1959, 1965), who popularized the "culture of poverty" theory. On the culture of poverty construct, Foley (1997) notes: "Lewis argues that the poor create an autonomous, distinct subculture or way of life that becomes encapsulated and self-perpetuating over generations" (p. 115). The major implication is that if the culture of poverty is autonomous, then the poor *create* their *own* problems. As Foley has discussed, low-SES Mexican Americans were viewed in ways that evoked extremely negative images (e.g., fatalistic, present-time orientation, violent, and dysfunctional in familial relations and socialization).

The appropriation of the culture of poverty model by deficit thinkers laid the foundation for the cultural deprivation or disadvantagement theory that reached its apex in the 1960s (see Pearl, 1997). The psychological literature of the 1960s gushed with the new social constructions of the "culturally deprived" or "culturally disadvantaged" family, home, and child (see, e.g., Frost & Hawkes, 1966; Hellmuth, 1967). These cultural-familial variants of deficit thinking in this period were clearly not conducive to promoting school success for Mexican American students. Rather, these negative, blame-the-victim perceptions served as the dominant means by which to view Mexican American youngsters' educability as quite limited.

Segregation and Inferior Education: On the Rise

By the beginning of the 1930s, the template for the future of Mexican American education was formed. Forced and widespread school segregation and inferior schooling of Mexican American children became the norm — although there were no legal statutes that mandated such racial/ethnic isolation (see González, 1990; San Miguel, 1987). In California and Texas, the Mexican American population increased dramatically, and local school boards instituted practices that led to the segregation of Mexican American students from their White peers.

By 1931, 85 percent of California school districts surveyed by Leis (1931) reported segregating Mexican American students either in separate schools or separate classrooms (Hendrick, 1977). Leis, with the cooperation of the County Superintendent of San Bernardino (California), surveyed thirteen school districts in California. These districts had nearly 88,000 students enrolled — 25 percent of whom were Mexican American. Leis reported that

eleven (85 percent) of the thirteen districts surveyed stated that they segregated Mexican American students for the first several grades. Reasons given
for the separation of White and Mexican American children was "entirely or
partly . . . for educational purposes" (p. 25). More specifically, Leis reported
that generally

> segregation ends in the fourth, fifth, or sixth grade because the language hand-
> icap has practically disappeared and social adaptation has fitted the Mexican
> child to go into the grades with the White children if he remains in school. Ex-
> cessive dropping out at these levels is a large factor in discontinuing
> segregation. (1931, p. 66)

In Texas, by 1930, 90 percent of the schools were racially/ethnically segregated (Rangel & Alcala, 1972). Increased segregation was largely due to the
growth in the Mexican American school-age population and the failure of
schools to heed desegregation compliance policies, despite landmark desegregation cases in which Mexican Americans proved victorious. For example,
as San Miguel (1987) has noted:

> During the 1930s it was estimated that over 40 school districts established sepa-
> rate schools for Mexicans. By 1942, Wilson Little reported that approximately
> 122 districts in fifty-nine widely distributed and representative counties across
> the state [of Texas] maintained separate schools for Mexican students. (p. 56)

Weinberg (1977, citing Penrod, 1948) has commented that Mexican
American students attended twenty-eight mandated segregated schools in
Los Angeles and one in San Diego — thus demonstrating the persistence of
school segregation in post–World War II years. As Weinberg has underscored, "Segregation continued in force almost everywhere" (p. 160).

Mexican American education from 1930 to 1960 was not only characterized by the rise of school segregation, but also by the inferior nature of such
schooling during the pre- and postwar years. For example, in 1934 the
League of United Latin American Citizens (LULAC) issued a report on the
condition of schools in the West Side barrio of San Antonio, Texas (San
Miguel, 1987), which noted that the teacher-student ratio in the West Side
schools was 1:46, while the ratio in the Anglo schools was 1:36.[42] The report
also stated that the per pupil expenditures were $24.50 and $35.96, respectively, for the Mexican American and Anglo schools.[43] Conditions were so
bad that community activist Eluterio Escobar described (in 1947) the temporary wooden classroom buildings as "fire traps" (García, 1979).

The inferior conditions in Mexican American schools were further documented by Calderón (1950) in his master's thesis, which consisted of case
studies of two Mexican American schools and one Anglo school in Edcouch-
Elsa, Texas (lower Rio Grande Valley). Calderón reported that average class
sizes in the Mexican American schools were in the high thirties and low for-
ties, while the average class size in the Anglo school was thirty-three. Regarding promotion practices, he noted that the Mexican American "children

were compelled to spend two years in the first grade without regard to the ability of the student to do the work" (p. 20). The Anglo school had a band, a cafeteria, and students had regular access to dental and medical services. In 1950's Texas, the Mexican American schools did not have access to these facilities and services. Additionally, Calderón noted that Anglo and Mexican American children traveled to school together, but the latter students "were traditionally seated in the rear of the bus" (p. 40). Calderón's thesis is particularly insightful, as his report contains stark, highly detailed photographs of facility conditions at the schools. The Anglo school had inside lavatories, with walls separating the commodes and tile floors. Water fountains, electrically cooled, were also located inside the school building. Classroom light bulbs were shielded, thus providing diffuse lighting. In sharp contrast, the Mexican American schools had lavatories outside the building, no walls separating stalls, and bare concrete floors. Drinking fountains with non-cooled water were also located outside. Finally, bare light bulbs hung from the ceilings.

It is not surprising that during the 1930–1960 time period, segregated and inferior schooling conditions for Mexican Americans would frequently lead to poor academic performance, progress, and attainment.[44] Drake (1927), for example, compared the relative academic performance of Mexican American and White seventh- and eighth-graders in Tucson, Arizona. Based on results from the Stanford Achievement Tests, the Mexican American group's mean score (60.2) was about a standard deviation lower than the mean score (68.9) of the White group. Further, in a comprehensive report titled "The Education of Spanish-Speaking Children in Five Southwestern States," Reynolds (1933) quoted an Arizona study as follows: "In general, the type of Mexican child taken into the Arizona school tends to be backward in rate of mental development, lags a year behind other pupils, shows a heavy failure percentage, and an early elimination from school" (p. 38). An example of such school failure was the finding that for every "100 Mexican children in grade 1 there are 7 in grade 8, while for 100 non-Mexican children in grade 1 there are 52 in grade 8" (p. 39).

The Reynolds (1933) study was sponsored by the Office of Education of the U.S. Department of the Interior. Though ambitious in scope, the study provided scattered information about schooling conditions of "Mexican" (i.e., Mexican American) students attending schools in the Southwest (Arizona, California, Colorado, New Mexico, and Texas). Major findings were:

1. Mexican American children frequently attended segregated schools, and such isolation, it was noted, was based on "instructional" reasons (usually to learn English). Reynolds noted, "In the opinion of the many experienced teachers and supervisors the fourth or fifth is the grade at which separate instruction for Mexican pupils should end" (p. 11). Reynolds also commented: "Practically, however, so few Mexican pupils

reach the upper elementary grades that the opinion has not to date received much of a test."

2. "Teaching materials adequate in amount and of the right kind for Mexican children are conspicuously absent" (p. 13).

3. "Teachers, even experienced ones, reported they were ill equipped to teach the Mexican American students (particularly Spanish-speakers), and received "little supervisory guidance" (p. 22).

4. The percentage of Mexican American teachers was extremely small; based on a survey of seven selected counties in the five states, "the total number of teachers . . . is 2,320. This number includes 26 [1.1 percent] Mexicans" (p. 23).

5. Mexican American pupils "are not attending school to anything like the extent to which English-speaking [i.e. White] pupils living in the same sections attend" (p. 37).

6. The percentage of Mexican American students who were pedagogically retarded (average for their grade) was very high.

Although Reynolds's study appeared to be objective in reporting the details of inferior schooling conditions faced by Mexican American children in the Southwest, one suggestion for curricular focus was far from being the rigorous, cognitively demanding instruction these students surely needed. Reynolds, who apparently bought into the stereotype of the time that Mexican American children have special talents in art, recommended the following:

> In conclusion: Evidence available strongly suggests that pupils so eager, as are practically all members of the group concerned in this study, to undertake pictorial representation should be given every opportunity to develop their potentialities, be they few or many. Here is a phase of education in which Spanish-speaking pupils are certainly not handicapped. Here they feel equal to others and quickly demonstrate their equality. As a means to arouse their enthusiasm for a more extended period of school attendance than that of which they at present avail themselves, emphasis on art instruction in the case of Spanish-speaking pupils seem to be indicated. (p. 22)

In his analysis of Census data, Chapa (1988) found that in 1940, Mexican Americans in California (ages 25–64) completed an average of 7.5 years of schooling, while Whites finished an average of 10.5 years — a gap of three years. In 1979, nearly forty years later, the mean for Mexican Americans was 11.0 years and 13.4 for Whites — a gap of 2.4 years. Cromack's (1949) study of schools in Austin, Texas, provides yet another example of Mexican American school failure. Referring to Cromack's investigation, Weinberg (1977) commented:

> Academically, Mexican-American students in Austin lagged seriously. In 1947–48, they constituted nearly three-fourths of all elementary students, one fifth of junior high students, and only one-thirteenth of senior high students. Mexican-

American students made up from one-sixth to one-fifth of the city's enrollment during 1943–1947, but only one-sixtieth of all graduates. (p. 162)

In sum, there is evidence that Mexican American students experienced massive school inequalities. This inferior and segregated schooling led to considerable school failure for many of these students (e.g., very early exiting from the schooling process, poor academic performance). It is not surprising that the Mexican American community mounted a campaign for educational equality, a topic we cover next.

The Mexican American Struggle for Educational Equality, 1930s–1950s

Viewed collectively, the decades of the 1930s, 1940s, and 1950s represent a major campaign by Mexican Americans in their quest for the realization of educational equality: landmark litigation, the founding of advocacy organizations, the grassroots organizing of individual activists, and the research and writings of individual scholars were particularly prominent in this era of the concerted agitation for quality education for Mexican American students.

The School Segregation Struggle

> Mexican Americans and others . . . identified school desegregation as the most despicable form of discrimination practiced against Spanish-speaking children. . . . After the war, school desegregation continued to be viewed as *the major factor* impeding the educational, social, and economic mobility of the Mexican American population. (San Miguel, 1987, p. 117; italics added)

This passage underscores the historical struggle and significance of the campaign against school segregation.[45] Accordingly, Mexican American plaintiffs filed numerous lawsuits during this era. We focus on four cases that are particularly important in providing insight to plaintiffs' legal strategies and the courts' findings: *Independent School District v. Salvatierra* (1930, 1931); *Alvarez v. Lemon Grove School District* (1931); *Méndez v. Westminister School District* (1946, 1947); *Delgado et al. v. Bastrop Independent School District of Bastrop County et al.* (1948).[46]

The legal struggle for school desegregation was initiated in Texas and California in the early 1930s. The *Salvatierra* case, which was brought about by Mexican American parents in Del Rio, Texas, was significant for several reasons (San Miguel, 1987). First, the constitution of the State of Texas, adopted in 1875 and ratified in 1876, allowed for the segregation of White and "colored" children — colored meaning only "Negro."[47] Thus, *Salvatierra* was a landmark case in determining the constitutionality of separating Mexican American children on racial grounds. Second, the findings of the court would serve as the basis for future legal challenges of segregation of Mexican American students. Third, the counsel for the plaintiffs in *Salvatierra* were lawyers of LULAC, the newly established Mexican American advocacy organization, which had its first opportunity to flex its muscles in this important test case.

The court ruled in *Salvatierra* that the school district illegally segregated Mexican American students on the basis of race (Rangel & Alcala, 1972), although they were considered to be members of the White race — a strong point argued by plaintiffs' lawyers.[48] The judgment, however, was overturned by the appellate court on the basis that the school district did not intentionally, arbitrarily segregate the Mexican American children by race, and, given that the children had special language needs (i.e., to learn English), the school district had the authority to segregate Mexican American students on educational grounds. This latter ruling would serve as a major obstacle in desegregation rulings for years to come. The Texas Court of Appeals decision in *Salvatierra* was appealed by LULAC to the U.S. Supreme Court, but the case was dismissed for lack of jurisdiction (Balderrama, 1982, cited in Alvarez, 1986).

In *Alvarez v. Lemon Grove* (1931), the school board of the Lemon Grove School District (Lemon Grove, California, near San Diego) sought to build a separate grammar school for the Mexican American children, claiming overcrowding at the existing school where both Anglo and Mexican American students attended (Alvarez, 1986). Mexican American parents organized a protest, forming the Comité de Vecinos de Lemon Grove (Lemon Grove Neighborhood Committee). The parents instructed their children not to attend the so-called new school, which the children called *La Caballeriza* (the stable). Judge Claude Chambers, Superior Court of California in San Diego, ruled in favor of the plaintiffs on the basis that separate facilities for Mexican American students were not conducive towards their Americanization and retarded the English-language development of the Spanish-speaking children. Judge Chambers also found that the school board had no legal right to segregate Mexican American children, as California law had no such provisions.[49] Although the Alvarez case was deemed the nation's first successful desegregation court case, "it was isolated as a local event and had no precedent-setting ruling affecting either the State of California or other situations of school segregation in the Southwest" (Alvarez, 1986, p. 131). Nevertheless, *Alvarez* is noted as the first successful legal challenge to school segregation in the country (Alvarez, 1986; González, 1990)

The *Méndez v. Westminster* (1946, 1947) case in California, which preceded the 1954 *Brown v. Board of Education of Topeka* by nearly a decade, was the *first* federal court decision in the area of school segregation and marked the end of de jure segregation in California (González, 1990). In this class action lawsuit, Gonzalo Méndez et al. claimed their children were denied access to a White school simply because they were Mexican (i.e., in appearance, Spanish surname). The importance of this landmark case rests on the judge's ruling regarding a new interpretation of the Fourteenth Amendment (i.e., a break with the prevailing *Plessy* doctrine of "separate but equal"), as well as his decision on the legality of segregating Mexican Americans on linguistic grounds. The court concluded that the school board had segregated Mexican American children on the basis of their "Latinized" appearance and had gerrymandered the school district in order to ensure that Mexican American students attend segregated schools. The court concluded that this was an illegal action, as there was no constitutional or congressional mandate that authorized school boards in California to segregate Mexican American students. Judge Paul McCormick stated that the Fourteenth Amendment had guaranteed Mexican Americans equal rights in the United States (Donato, Menchaca, & Valencia, 1991). Particularly significant about Judge McCormick's ruling is that it differed substantially from the rulings in *Salvatierra* and *Delgado* regarding the nature of segregation: "McCormick contended that no evidence existed that showed segregation aided in the development of English proficiency, that on the contrary, evidence demonstrated that segregation retarded language and cultural assimilation. Consequently, the segregation of Mexican children *had no legal or educational justification*" (González, 1990, p. 153; italics added). According to González (1990), Judge McCormick broke with the prevailing separate but equal doctrine of *Plessy v. Ferguson* (1896):

> In so stating, the Judge broke with *Plessy* and clearly defined a distinction between physical equality (facilities) and social equality. In this case, separate but equal facilities were unconstitutional because they created a social inequality. Thus, rather than acting as a protection for the practice of segregation, the Fourteenth Amendment served to repeal segregation. (p. 153)

Although the *Méndez* case helped to end de jure segregation in California, the school segregation of Mexican American students remained widespread (Hendrick, 1977) and, in fact, increased over the following decades. Moreover, as González (1990) has noted when speaking of *Mendez* and its aftermath, "Eventually, de jure segregation in schools ended throughout the Southwest, but not before an educational policy reinforcing socioeconomic inequality severely victimized generations of Mexican children" (p. 29).

In 1948, the centennial of the Treaty of Guadalupe Hidalgo, *Delgado et al. v. Bastrop Independent School District of Bastrop County et al.* was litigated in the U.S. District Court for the Western Division of Texas, and was backed by a cadre of powerful Mexican American individuals and organizations.[50] Minerva Delgado and twenty other plaintiffs sued several school districts in Central Texas, asserting that "school officials . . . were segregating Spanish-speaking [Mexican American] children contrary to the [Texas] Constitution" (San Miguel, 1987, p. 123). It appears that the catalyst for bringing forth *Delgado* was the momentous victory in *Méndez* (González, 1990; San Miguel, 1987), as the plaintiffs believed that *Delgado* would do for Texas what *Méndez* did for California — bring an end to school segregation. Judge Ben

Rice ruled that segregation of the Mexican American students was discriminatory and illegal, and violated the students' constitutional rights as guaranteed by the Fourteenth Amendment (see San Miguel, 1987). However, the court also ruled that the school district could segregate first-grade Mexican American students who had English-language deficiencies. Such segregation was to be within the same school attended by all other students.

Initially viewed by plaintiffs as the decision that could bring an end to segregation in Texas, these hopes were never realized (San Miguel, 1987). In what Allsup (1979) describes as the clash of White obstinacy and Mexican American determination, school districts throughout Texas failed to comply with the *Delgado* decision. This was made easy, in part, by the State Board of Education and its creation of a complex bureaucratic system of grievance and redress and the non-compliance of the *Delgado* proviso through evasive schemes designed at the local level. As San Miguel (1987) has noted:

> The mid and late 1950s can probably be called the *era of subterfuge*, since it was during this period that a multitude of practices — for example, freedom of choice plans, selected student transfer and transportation plans, and classification systems based on language or scholastic ability — were utilized by local school districts to maintain segregated schools. (p. 134; italics added)

Cultural Critiques of Intelligence Testing: George I. Sánchez[51]

In the 1920s there were no Mexican American intellectuals to criticize mental testing research on Mexican American students.[52] Given that Mexican American students in the Southwest were subject to frequent intelligence testing and resultant curricular ability grouping and tracking, this situation was lamentable. This changed, however, with the emergence of the work of George Isidore Sánchez, one of the first Mexican American academics to challenge contentions that Mexican American children were innately inferior to White children in intelligence, and who exposed the inferior schooling they received via curriculum differentiation. Sánchez's academic career — from his master's thesis challenging the measurement of mental ability based on just one test through his later work on the fallacy of IQ being constant and the effects of language development on academic and mental ability — focused on exposing the shortcomings and failures of traditional standardized intelligence testing and measures on Mexican American children.

Soon after joining the faculty at the University of Texas (UT) at Austin in 1940 (where he served as chair of the Department of History and Philosophy of Education from 1950 to 1959), Sánchez became a champion of Mexican American civil rights, challenging school segregation and discrimination in housing and employment. So illustrious was his career that in 1994 UT Austin named the College of Education building after him. Sánchez's pioneering work as an academician and Chicano activist from the 1930s until his death in 1972 set a groundbreaking path through which Chicano-based scholarship and activism developed and flourished in the contemporary era.

Mexican American Education in the Contemporary Period, 1960–1998

Mexican American education has undergone immense transformations during the contemporary era, from 1960 through the present. There has been a virtual explosion of research and publications targeting the Mexican American schooling experience (e.g., the seminal works by Carter, 1970; Carter & Segura, 1979; followed by San Miguel, 1987; González, 1990; Valencia, 1991b; and, most recently, Donato, 1997).

In addition to a sharp rise in Mexican American scholarship, this period is also characterized as an era of continuing struggle in the Mexican American campaign for equality in education. As in the past, the contemporary Mexican American struggle has expressed itself via litigation, advocacy organizations, individual activists, political demonstrations, and legislation. For example, Mexican American enrollments in higher education have dramatically increased since the 1960s, bilingual education has been established, and school retention at the high school level has considerably improved (Valencia, 1991b, 1997f; Valencia & Chapa, 1993).

Notwithstanding these gains, a myriad of schooling problems still abound for Mexican American students. School segregation is on the rise; limited-English-proficient students are under-enrolled in bilingual education classes; the Mexican American high school dropout rate compared to the rate of their White peers is scandalously high; academic achievement (e.g., reading performance) of Mexican Americans continues to lag behind their White peers; inequities in school financing are pervasive; and curriculum differentiation, a historical reality, continues (Valencia, 1991a). Exacerbating the educational plight of Mexican Americans is the current political climate in which anti-bilingual education, anti-affirmative action, and anti-diversity policies characterize discourse. The 1990s will go down in history as a decade of oppression and regressive social laws and policies vis-à-vis Mexican Americans and other Latinos, as seen in the voter approval of Propositions 187, 209, and 227 in California, and the *Hopwood v. University of Texas* (1996) decision in Texas.

The Educational Plight of Mexican Americans: Problems Abound

The decade of the 1970s was a time in which Mexican Americans began to garner considerable attention to their numerous educational problems, population growth, and overall status as an economically disadvantaged minority. Accompanying this national attention in the 1970s, Mexican Americans received the frequently stated claim that the 1980s would be the "decade of the Hispanic" (Valencia, 1991a). Such expectations within and outside the larger Latino community were that Mexican Americans (and Puerto Ricans) would benefit from their growing presence along educational, economic, and political lines. Contrary to the anticipated gains, the 1980s left many Latinos — particularly Mexican Americans and Puerto Ricans — worse off (Miranda & Quiroz, 1989). For example, in 1978, 12.5 percent of Latino families with heads of household who completed high school lived in poverty. By 1988, the figure climbed to 16 percent. In short, Latinos continued to experience unequal benefits from education (Miranda & Quiroz, 1989). The decade of the 1990s has, in general, not fared well for Mexican Americans, as evidenced by the current educational crisis.

The Mexican-American Education Study (MAES) Report, by the U.S. Commission on Civil Rights, is the most comprehensive investigation of Mexican American schooling conditions and outcomes ever undertaken. Initiated by members of Congress who were sensitive to the educational plight of Mexican Americans, and pursuant to Public Law 85-315, this massive study was published in the early 1970s and consisted of reports on six topics: 1) school segregation (U.S. Commission on Civil Rights, 1971a); 2) academic performance and school retention (1971b); 3) language suppression and cultural exclusion (1972a); 4) inequities in school financing in Texas (1972b); 5) teacher-student classroom interactions (1973); 6) grade retention, ability grouping, enrollment in classes of the educable mentally retarded, and availability of Mexican American counselors (1974).

The MAES focused on five states in the Southwest (Arizona, California, Colorado, New Mexico, and Texas) — the area, with some exception, that was annexed by the United States via the Treaty of Guadalupe Hidalgo. At the time of the study, about 70 percent of all Mexican American students attended schools in the Southwest (U.S. Commission on Civil Rights, 1971a). As such, this study serves as a benchmark for the nature of education of Mexican Americans about 125 years after the Treaty, and a baseline from which to compare current schooling conditions and outcomes. In the sixth and final report, a powerfully castigating conclusion was drawn regarding the grave condition of Mexican American education:

> In all . . . aspects of their education, Mexican American students are still largely ignored. . . . In the face of so massive a failure on the part of the educational establishment, drastic reforms would, without question, be instituted, and instituted swiftly. These are precisely the dimensions of the educational establishment's failure with respect to Mexican Americans. Yet little has been done to change the status quo — a status quo that has demonstrated its bankruptcy.
>
> Not only has the educational establishment in the Southwest failed to make needed changes, it has failed to understand fully its inadequacies. The six reports of the Commission's Mexican American Educational Study cite scores of instances in which the actions of individual school officials have reflected an attitude which blames educational failure on Chicano children rather than on the inadequacies of the school program. Southwestern educators must begin not only to recognize the failure of the system in educating Chicano children, but to acknowledge that change must occur at all levels — from the policies set in the state legislatures to the educational environment created in individual classrooms. (U.S. Commission on Civil Rights, 1974, p. 69)

The MAES brought these students' plight into the national limelight. This exposure was assisted by the publication of a comprehensive book, *The Mexican-American People: The Nation's Second Largest Minority* (Grebler, Moore, & Guzman, 1970);[53] and coincided with the aspirations of the incipient Chicano Movement — a struggle born out of the social plight and inequities of Chicano communities — and of which education was a cornerstone. Thus, by the early 1970s the Mexican American people, and their educational plight, had finally garnered national attention. The status quo described by MAES, however, would continue to prevail.

Segregation

The MAES report on the ethnic isolation of Mexican American elementary and secondary students in the Southwest (U.S. Commission on Civil Rights, 1971a) confirmed that the historical segregation of Mexican American students has persisted into the contemporary period. In 1968, one in two Mexican American students attended schools in which they comprised the predominant ethnic group (i.e., 50 to 100 percent Mexican American enrollment). One in five Mexican American students attended schools that were 80 to 100 percent Mexican American.

Later studies revealed that Mexican American student segregation actually increased from the MAES 1968 baseline date. For example, Orfield (1988) compared Latino student segregation regionally and nationally from 1968 to 1984.[54] For this sixteen-year period, Orfield's analysis of national data revealed that the percentage of Latinos enrolled in predominantly White schools dropped by 36 percent. For Latino students enrolled in 90 to 100 percent minority schools, Latino enrollment increased 35 percent. For the West, Latino enrollment in predominantly White schools declined by 45 percent; in 90 to 100 percent minority schools, Latino enrollment soared by 92 percent.

The isolation of Mexican American students has grown to such a degree that Latino students in California and Texas schools experience greater isolation than do African American students in Alabama and Mississippi (Orfield & Montfort, 1992; see also Orum, 1986; Donato et al., 1991). In Texas — a state that has forcefully segregated its Mexican American students since it established public education — school segregation of Mexican American and other Latino students is particularly severe. In the 1993–1994 school year, nearly two in three (64 percent) of *all* Mexican American (and other Latino) school-age students attended schools in which 70 percent or greater of the students were racial/ethnic minorities. About 49 percent of all African American students and only 7 percent of White students attended such schools (Brooks & South, 1995).

What has led to the intensification of Mexican American school segregation? Why have the court orders of the 51-year-old *Méndez* (1947) and 44-

year-old *Brown* (1954) decisions — which struck down the then 60-year-old *Plessy* (1896) "separate but equal" doctrine — become shattered visions for school desegregation proponents? Orfield, Montfort, and George (1987) contend that a great deal of the failure in desegregation struggles is associated with opposition at the national political level since the early 1970s:

> Three of the four Administrations since 1968 were openly hostile to urban desegregation efforts and the Carter Administration took few initiatives in the field. There have been no important policy initiatives supporting desegregation from any branch of government since 1971. (p. 1)

Why segregation of Mexican American students has increased is, of course, also related to continued and escalated residential segregation (Rivkin, 1994) and other factors, such as stagnation in economic mobility for Mexican Americans and other Latinos (see, e.g., Pérez & De La Rosa Salazar, 1993). It appears, however, that the principal driving forces against desegregation have been a national political policy and a judiciary reluctant to mandate desegregation orders (see, e.g., Orfield & Eaton, 1996). There is ample research that demonstrates the relation between the increase of Mexican American student isolation and achievement problems. As Donato et al. (1991) have commented: "segregated Chicano schools tend to be schools characterized by low funding, high dropout rates, low achievement test scores . . . and few college preparatory courses" (p. 32).[55] This is not to suggest that Mexican American students in segregated schools are incapable of learning and performing at satisfactory or high levels of academic achievement. Rather, the reality is that such schools are typically neglected and are low priorities for school districts.

Academic Performance

The MAES report on reading achievement (U.S. Commission on Civil Rights, 1971b) also confirmed that the historically poor academic performance of many Mexican American students continues during the contemporary era. In the five southwestern states (at grade levels 4, 8, and 12), for example, the *majority* of Mexican American students read *below* grade level. In contrast, about one-fourth to one-third of Anglo students performed below grade level.

Data from the National Assessment of Educational Progress (NAEP) show that between 1975 and 1996, Latino students on the average scored substantially below White students in mathematics, reading, and science. These NAEP scale point differences, in these three subject areas, demonstrate large educational gaps between White and Latino students that remain persistent and pervasive (Campbell, Voekl, & Donahue, 1997, cited in Valencia, 1997d).

A further example of the persistence of large White-Latino gaps in academic achievement into the 1990s is in highly segregated Texas schools. On the current state-mandated Texas Assessment of Academic Skills (TAAS), data for the 1996 school year show that 83 percent of all White sixth-graders passed all parts of TAAS (reading, writing, and mathematics). In sharp contrast, only 55 percent of all Latino sixth-graders (overwhelmingly of Mexican origin) passed all parts of the test (Fikac, 1996). The most recent TAAS data (spring 1998) show that White students (grades 3, 7, 10) continue to pass the test at considerably higher percentages than their Latino peers (Brooks, 1998).[56]

High School Retention

One of the more tragic findings of the MAES was the information on retention rates (U.S. Commission on Civil Rights, 1971b). Rather than using the term "dropout," the Commission used "school holding power" — which was defined as "A basic measure of a school system's effectiveness . . . to hold its students until they have completed the full course of study" [i.e., kindergarten through grade twelve] (p. 8). By placing the onus for retention on the schools, the Commission advocated an anti-deficit-thinking perspective. With respect to comparative school holding power rates within the five southwestern states for White and Mexican American students, the MAES reported rates of 86 percent and 60 percent, respectively. When disaggregated by state, Arizona showed the highest Mexican American school holding rate (81 percent), and Texas — as expected — the lowest (53 percent). The school holding rates for the other southwestern states were: California, 64 percent; Colorado, 67 percent; and New Mexico, 71 percent. The MAES did not offer a discussion of possible reasons for the differences in school holding power among the five states. As to why Texas had the lowest retention rate, we surmise this was largely due to Texas having a longer and more pronounced history of inferior education vis-à-vis Mexican Americans.

Although completion rates for both Whites and Mexican Americans have risen, current data on school holding power or dropout rates show that the gap strongly persists. Trend analysis from 1975 to 1995 for people age twenty-five to twenty-nine reveal that the Latino high school completion rate, as well as the rate for Whites, has increased (Carter & Wilson, 1997). The White-Latino gap, however, has remained relatively constant, on the average, about thirty percentage points over the twenty-year period.

For instance, in 1975 the White and Latino high school completion rates were, respectively, 65 percent and 38 percent — a gap of twenty-seven percentage points. In 1995, the White and Latino rates were, respectively, 83 percent and 53 percent — a gap of thirty percentage points. Given that Mexican Americans have been reported to have the *lowest* high school graduation rate of any Latino subgroup (Chapa & Valencia, 1993), this White-Latino gap is likely to be larger for a White-Mexican American comparison.

Curriculum Differentiation

The MAES report on ability grouping revealed that curriculum differentiation has continued to prevail into the contemporary period (U.S. Commission on Civil Rights, 1974). Drawing from survey data of 1,100 schools in the Southwest, the Commission found clear evidence of unfavorable curriculum differentiation vis-à-vis Mexican American students. The majority of Whites and Mexican Americans were placed in the medium-ability group level and enrolled in average classes or provided average-level instruction. The MAES suggested that medium-ability groups and average classes were of a standard curricular type. However, Mexican American students were over-represented (more than twofold) in low-ability classes/instruction and under-represented (by about twofold) in high-ability classes/instruction. Current data on curriculum differentiation are hard to come by, as there are no national or state data bases on Mexican American students and ability grouping in elementary schools and tracking in secondary schools. As a result, one must rely on analyses of local districts.

In an analysis of 1995 enrollment patterns by race/ethnicity of students in a school district in Arizona, Valencia (1997e) calculated 685 individual disparity analyses for all levels of mathematics, science, and English courses.[57] The most significant pattern observed across the eight high schools and across the three types of courses was that Mexican American students were substantially *under-represented* in the college preparatory courses, particularly "honors courses." In contrast, White students were substantially *over-represented* in the college preparatory courses, especially honors courses. Such findings are disturbing, given that the school district had been under a court-ordered desegregation plan for ten years at the time of the study. The implications of the study are that desegregation, without true integration, is destined to create inequalities in access to the knowledge necessary for Mexican American students' matriculation to college.[58]

Language Exclusion

As previously noted, the exclusion of Spanish as a language of instruction is historically rooted.[59] The MAES report on language suppression and cultural exclusion found that less than 7 percent of the schools in the southwestern U.S. offered bilingual education (U.S. Commission on Civil Rights, 1972a).

Although bilingual education has contributed much to the improvement of schooling for limited-English-proficient (LEP) Mexican American students (e.g., August & Hakuta, 1997; Meyers & Feinberg, 1992; Willig, 1985), there are still a substantial portion of these students whose language-learning needs have gone unmet. For example, Olsen (1988) reported that in California there were over 613,000 LEP students in spring of 1987 (about 73 percent Latino, overwhelmingly of Mexican origin), yet less than 25 percent were being served in bilingual education classes. The other 75 percent were provided little, if any, instruction in their first language. In a more recent analysis, Macías (1993) reported that in California (in 1992) there were 1.1 million kindergarten through grade-12 LEP students (77 percent Spanish language). Of the total, "barely half of all LEP students . . . received some instruction in the non-English language. . . . Half of all LEP students . . . received all their instruction only in English" (pp. 251–252).

For decades, most Mexican American students whose mother tongue was Spanish and who were not proficient in English have faced the sink-or-swim pedagogical practice of English-only instruction. Although some Mexican American students survived this submersion, many did not. The establishment of bilingual education in the 1970s has proven, over the years, to be a contributor to Mexican American school success (see, e.g., August & Hakuta, 1997). But only a small portion of students actually have access to bilingual education, and its very existence is currently in jeopardy.

Enrollment in Higher Education

In the 1920s, 1930s, and up to the mid-1940s, a Mexican American presence in college was rare. At the end of World War II, however, Mexican American enrollment in college increased as some returning veterans took advantage of the G.I. Bill of Rights that provided them with low-interest loans to attend college (Morín, 1963). Notwithstanding these increases in higher education enrollment, the MAES report on academic achievement found Mexican American students to be severely under-enrolled in college relative to their presence in the college-age population and compared to their White peers (U.S. Commission on Civil Rights, 1971b). For the five southwestern states, 49 percent of White students entered college and 24 percent completed. In contrast, 23 percent of Mexican American students entered college, with only 5 percent finishing and earning bachelor's degrees.

Many recent studies confirm that the low college enrollment and completion rates reported by the MAES report persist (e.g., Keller, Deneen, & Magallán, 1991; Olívas, 1986; Pérez & De La Rosa Salazar, 1993). Recent analyses by Carter and Wilson (1997) have underscored the persistence of low college completion rates for Latinos (Mexican Americans, Puerto Ricans, and other Latinos). Based on a trend analysis from 1975 to 1995 of persons twenty-five to twenty-nine years old, the Latino completion rate in 1975 was about 6 percent, rising to 9 percent in 1995. In sharp contrast, the White completion rate was 15 percent in 1975 and 24 percent in 1995 — thus showing a sharp increase in the White-Latino gap. Again, this gap is likely larger for a White-Mexican American comparison, as Mexican Americans have the lowest college completion rate of the various Latino subgroups (Chapa & Valencia, 1993).

The Contemporary Campaign for Educational Equality: The Struggle Escalates

Given the many educational adversities that Mexican Americans face in the contemporary era, it is not surprising that their struggle for educational equality during this period has greatly escalated. Here we focus on three aspects of this struggle: key litigation, the emergence of advocacy organizations, and key legislation. We conclude with a brief discussion on the mounting oppression and crises in California and Texas — as evidenced by a trilogy of voter-initiated propositions that have been passed in the former and the *Hopwood* decision in the latter.

Litigation

There has been an enormous amount of litigation brought about by Mexican American plaintiffs in the contemporary period. Our focus here is on those lawsuits that we feel have most influenced education for Mexican American communities in this era — cases regarding desegregation, school finance, undocumented schoolchildren, special education, and school closures.

A landmark case in the history of desegregation lawsuits initiated by Mexican Americans, *Cisneros v. Corpus Christi Independent School District* (1970), set off a flood of similar cases (Salinas, 1971). Prior to *Cisneros,* some school districts in the Southwest were desegregating their schools by pairing African American and Mexican American students, given that the latter group was considered "other White." In *Cisneros,* the judge ruled that Mexican Americans were an ethnically identifiable minority group, and thus were entitled to the protection of the *Brown* (1954) decision (see, e.g., Salinas, 1971; San Miguel, 1987). As such, the court found, the mixing of African Americans and Mexican Americans for purposes of desegregation did not produce a unitary school system. In *Ross v. Eckels* (1970), a desegregation case in Houston, Texas, in which Mexican American students were similarly paired with African Americans, the Fifth Circuit Court of Appeals held that Mexican Americans were not an identifiable minority group for purposes of desegregation. Ironically the *Cisneros* and *Ross* rulings were made by the same court.

This confusion was finally settled in *Keyes v. School District Number One* (1973) by the U.S. Supreme Court. In *Keyes,* which involved a desegregation case in Denver, Colorado, the Court was compelled to make a decision on "how to treat Mexican American children in the desegregation process" (San Miguel, 1987, p. 180). The Court decided that Mexican Americans were an identifiable minority group, and thus could not be paired with African Americans in the desegregation process.

Rodríguez et al. v. San Antonio Independent School District et al. (1971), which dealt with school finance equity, was the longest running legal case in the history of Mexican American education. The plaintiffs sued the San Antonio Independent School District, charging that the Texas school finance system violated the U.S. Constitution under the equal protection clause of the Fourteenth Amendment. After more than two decades of litigation that included a failed trip to the U.S. Supreme Court (see O'Connor & Epstein, 1984), the reestablished case (*Edgewood v. Kirby*, 1989) found itself at the Texas Supreme Court. The Court's 9-0 decision found that the state's public school finance system violated the Texas state constitution and ruled it unconstitutional (Graves, 1989). The Court ordered state legislators to prepare a new, comprehensive funding plan by May 1990. After a litany of appeals and legislative squabbles, the Texas Supreme Court (in a 5-4 decision) upheld the final school finance law that was passed ("School-Finance Law Upheld," 1995). The basic element of the new finance law, approved by the Texas Supreme Court, Senate Bill 7, was that property-rich school districts had to share their local tax money with property-poor school districts.

Plyer v. Doe (1982), another landmark lawsuit was initiated by Mexican American plaintiffs on behalf of undocumented Mexican immigrant students, who, pursuant to a 1975 revision in the Texas public school admission and funding statute, would no longer be eligible to attend public schools (Cardenas & Córtez, 1986). The U.S. Supreme Court ruled in a 5-4 decision that Texas could not exclude undocumented children from tuition-free enrollment in the state's public schools. The Court's decision upheld the lower court rulings and agreed that the State of Texas could not provide convincing evidence of adverse fiscal impact (the state's primary argument against providing public education for these children) caused by the enrollment of undocumented students (Cardenas & Cortez, 1986).

A trio of cases dealing with special education — *Diana v. State Board of Education* (1970),[60] *Covarrúbias v. San Diego Unified School District* (1971), and *Guadalupe v. Tempe Elementary School District* (1972) — collectively addressed the longstanding issue of over-representation of Mexican American students in classes for mildly mentally retarded students (see Henderson & Valencia, 1985). These cases, all settled by consent decree, led to major changes in the promotion of nondiscriminatory assessment of Mexican American and other minority students (requiring, e.g., assessment of dominant language, IQ testing in child's dominant tongue, greater use of performance and nonverbal tests, assessment of adaptive behavior, due process, and use of multiple data sources in assessment). These cases helped shape the nondiscriminatory mandate of Public Law 94-142 (Federal Register, 1977), the Education for All Handicapped Children Act of 1975.[61]

Other Mexican American initiated litigation focused on school closures. In the 1970s, declining enrollment, runaway inflation, and fiscal austerity led to the closure of over seven thousand public schools, affecting 80 percent of the nation's school districts (Scott, 1983). Predictably so, politically and economically powerless working-class and racial/ethnic minority schools were targeted for closure (Valencia, 1984a). The fear of White flight was considered by some school boards in deciding which schools to close. For instance, in Santa Barbara, California, the school board voiced the following when considering closing one of the high-enrollment White schools:

> The school's residential area is one of the highest socioeconomic areas in the city. Maintaining this area as a predominantly public school attendance area is important to the District. Unless the District can attract and hold these upper middle class areas the entire Elementary School District is in danger of becoming more ethnically and socioeconomically segregated. (Quoted in Valencia, 1980, p. 10)

Although the high-enrollment White schools were experiencing declines in student enrollments, high-enrollment Mexican American schools were pegged for closure by local school boards (see Valencia, 1980, 1984a, 1984b). This board's rationale for not closing any White schools in Santa Barbara did not sit well with groups of Mexican American parents, who sued the school district in *Angeles et al. v. Santa Barbara School District* (1979). The plaintiffs' lawyer argued that such a rationale was arbitrary and discriminatory based upon the suspect classification of wealth (see Valencia, 1980). Refusing to have their neighborhood schools closed, Mexican Americans filed suits. Plaintiffs lost in *Angeles* (Valencia, 1980, 1984b), but were victorious in other lawsuits, such as *Castro et al. v. Phoenix Union High School District No. 210 et al.* (1982) (Valencia, 1984c). Although the *Angeles* and *Castro* cases are likely to go down as mere footnotes in the history of Mexican American educational litigation, they are still important cases, for they represent, according to Valencia,

> a new form of denial to education . . . that was not there previously. . . . In the past, whatever difficulties Chicanos were experiencing in the school, they at least had neighborhood schools. Now, it appears that even neighborhood schools for Chicanos are in jeopardy. The implication of this new form of denial could be disastrous. By denying neighborhood schools to the Chicano community, school district officials are creating conditions that will hamper and even prevent Chicano parents from becoming involved in the education of their children. Rather than building upon strengths existing within Chicano schools and communities in terms of academic achievement gains, school-community cohesiveness, bilingual education, and so forth, the school district through this new form of denial will be setting in motion an erosion and disintegration of the very recent and small educational gains Chicanos have made. (1980, pp. 17–18)

Fortunately, school closures are no longer an issue due to population increases, especially among Latinos and other minority groups; instead, new schools are steadily being built. But past closures still serve as painful reminders of the uneven power relations and injustices that often shape educational decisionmaking.

Advocacy Organizations

Mexican American advocacy organizations have historically been extremely important in pursuing equal educational opportunities. The Mexican American community has continued this tradition into the contemporary period by forming such organizations. Two of the most significant organizations in the contemporary period are the Mexican American Legal Defense and Educational Fund (MALDEF), founded in 1968, and Movimiento Estudiantil Chicano de Aztlán[62] (Chicano Student Movement of Aztlán, known as MEChA), founded in 1969.[63]

MALDEF was formed in 1968 by Pete Tijerina, a Mexican American lawyer from San Antonio, Texas. MALDEF designed itself around the highly successful Legal Defense Fund (LDF) of the National Association for the Advancement of Colored People (NAACP; see O'Connor & Epstein, 1984).[64] After several years of defining its mission, the organization, with Vilma Martínez as its leader, was reoriented in 1973 to become the interest group litigator it was intended to be (O'Connor & Epstein, 1984). During its early years (1970–1981), MALDEF filed ninety-three lawsuits dealing with education; of this total, seventy-one (76.3 percent) were desegregation cases (San Miguel, 1987). Its most important desegregation case was *Cisneros* (1970), which, as discussed earlier, led to the 1973 U.S. Supreme Court decision in *Keyes v. School District Number One, Denver, Colorado*, that Mexican Americans were an identifiable minority group for purposes of desegregation. Over the last three decades, MALDEF has evolved into a chief source of successful education litigation for the Mexican American community, winning many lawsuits and setting highly influential case law (e.g., *Plyer*).

In the late 1960s, Mexican American students enrolled in college in the greatest numbers ever (Muñoz, 1989), many of whom were first-generation college students. To a large degree, this unprecedented increase in Mexican American college enrollment was the result of the efforts of the Chicano Movement, of which the Chicano Student Movement was a powerful arm (Muñoz, 1989). At a 1969 statewide meeting in Santa Barbara, California, Chicano college students, professors, staff, and community activists drafted a master plan of higher education, *El Plán de Santa Bárbara*, that discussed three major subjects: 1) student recruitment and retention strategies; 2) the mechanics for establishing Chicano Studies programs, including curricular content; and 3) the means to increase Chicano student presence in community activities (Chicano Coordinating Committee on Higher Education, 1969). The Santa Barbara meeting was also significant in that it brought together a number of Chicano student organizations in California (e.g., MASC, Mexican American Student Confederation; UMAS, United Mexican American Students), which united at the meeting forming one collective organization — MEChA — to implement *El Plán de Santa Bárbara* (Muñoz, 1989).[65]

MEChA's political role was in part to raise the consciousness of entering Chicano/a students to the plight of the Chicano community. This was largely done through MEChA meetings, forums, and teach-ins. MEChA chapters also worked in their local communities through activities such as film showings, speakers, picnics, support of local candidates running for office, and holding rallies and protests when injustices occurred. MEChA's educational role was to work in the areas of student recruitment, expansion of Chicano Studies curricula, development of a major in Chicano Studies on their campuses, and hiring of Chicano/a faculty.

The struggle for educational equality was enhanced by the gradual development of Mexican American scholarly research. With the establishment of Chicano Studies in some universities in the Southwest, many Mexican American students were introduced to the many facets of the Mexican American experience (e.g., literature, history, political science, and sociology). In Mexican American history courses, the Mexican American War and the Treaty of Guadalupe Hidalgo were focal points of study. In general, Chicano Studies provided a space where applied research, knowledge, and theories could be developed for the improvement of Chicano communities.[66] MEChA's impact on the struggle for educational equality has been considerable. In the last thirty years, MEChA has produced many individuals who have pursued political activism in their professional careers (see Muñoz, 1989). Currently, there are many MEChA chapters in universities across the Southwest, and "MEChistas" continue to be at the vanguard of educational struggles in higher education.

Legislation

Although the legislative process (both state and federal) can lead to bills that result in powerful educational reform (e.g., G.I. Bill of Rights, Public Law 94-142), it is interesting that Mexican American legislators have sparingly used legislation to improve education for Mexican Americans. Why this is so is not clear. One interpretation is that the school reform movement has been driven and dominated by powerful conservative forces whose agendas, ideologies, and reform efforts have had counterproductive effects on Mexican Americans and other students who experience school failure (see Reyes & Valencia, 1993, for a sustained analysis). This is not to say that Mexican Americans have not used the legislative process in producing school reform.

Mexican American-initiated legislation during the contemporary period has been heavily concentrated on the struggle for bilingual education. This struggle has great historical importance, in that the Mexican American call for instruction in Spanish, the mother tongue, can be contextualized as an issue of language rights within the scope of the Treaty of Guadalupe Hidalgo. As Rendón (1971) states in his *Chicano Manifesto*, "The Treaty of Guadalupe Hidalgo is the most important document concerning Mexican Americans that exists. From it stem specific guarantees affecting our civil rights, *language,* culture, and religion" (p. 81; italics added). We briefly examine the contemporary legislative struggle for bilingual education in Texas, which we interpret as a clash between Mexican American determination and Anglo obstinacy.

The long, drawn-out struggle for bilingual education in Texas lasted from 1969 to 1981 (see San Miguel, 1987; Vega, 1983). The main players in the struggle were two Democrats — State Senator Joe Bernal and State Representative Carlos Truan. Over more than a decade, a number of bilingual education House Bills (H.B.s) and Senate Bills (S.B.s) were introduced by these two men and their colleagues. Some made law, but others were passed at committee level and then watered down by the plenary. Some never made it past the committee level (San Miguel, 1987; Vega, 1983).[67] Finally, in 1981, twelve years of political struggle resulted in the passage of S.B. 477, a landmark bill mandating bilingual education for the first time in Texas history. Its many features included provisions for language proficiency assessment of students prior to enrollment in bilingual classes; exit criteria from bilingual education classes; and provisions for the Texas Educational Agency (TEA) to oversee all operations of bilingual education (Vega, 1983).

In sum, the historical educational plight of Mexican Americans has continued well into the contemporary period. Through litigation, advocacy organizations, and legislation, Mexican Americans have continued their long tradition of asserting their rightful claim to a just and equitable education.

The Current Educational Crises in California and Texas

Scholars have focused on a host of educational concerns, particularly in California and Texas, the two most populous states, as well as where the vast majority of the Mexican American school-age populations reside. It is also in these two states where a proliferation of attacks on educational issues have directly affected the quality of Mexican American schooling. In this last section we focus on ballot initiatives and litigation in California and Texas that have had an impact on the access to equal education opportunities, and could have far-reaching implications nationwide.[68]

California

The passage of Proposition 187 in November 1994, Proposition 209 in November 1996, and Proposition 227 in June 1998 had one common effect on the Mexican American community: all three propositions seriously limit access to equal educational opportunities. These initiative are not only oppressive, but also regressive. In effect, they endanger much of what has been gained through decades of struggle for educational equality.

Proposition 187 was "designed to restrict public schooling, welfare, and non-emergency medical services to persons who are not able to prove their legal immigration or nationality status in the U.S." (Macías, 1994, p. 3). Mexican Americans took action even before the proposition passed. Less than a week before the November 1994 vote on Proposition 187, about ten thousand middle and high school students (mostly Latinos) walked out of thirty-two California schools and hit the streets in a mostly peaceful protest (Suro & Balz, 1994). Given the anti-Latino sentiment of Proposition 187, it was not surprising that the voting was racially/ethnically polarized. Macías (1994), referring to the *Los Angeles Times* exit poll, noted that 63 percent of Whites voted for the proposition while only 23 percent of Latinos voted as such. After the proposition passed, legal challenges were promptly filed. In November 1995, Judge Mariana Pfaelzer issued a ruling stating, in part, that California was illegally attempting to regulate immigration. She also struck down the proposition, which she stated violated the U.S. Supreme Court's landmark decision in *Plyer* (1982). In March 1998, Judge Pfaelzer disemboweled what remained of Proposition 187 (e.g., denial of educational and social services to "illegal immigrants"), asserting that the law was completely unconstitutional (Associated Press, 1998a). If the state of California does appeal Judge Pfaelzer's decision, the case is likely to be heard before the U.S. Supreme Court.

In November 1996, Proposition 209 — the self-labeled "Civil Rights Initiative" — was passed by 54 percent of those who voted (Epstein, 1997). Prior to passage of this referendum, in 1995, the Regents of the University of California adopted a new admissions policy (SP1) that ended affirmative action in the University of California system (Pachón, Mejía, & Bergman, 1997). Proposition 209 went much further, prohibiting local and state agencies from granting "preferential treatment" to racial/ethnic minorities and/or women in the areas of state contracting, employment, and education (Epstein, 1997). The ironically labeled "Civil Rights Initiative" brought an end to affirmative action in public higher education throughout California.

The impact of SP1 and Proposition 209 on Mexican American and other Latino student access to the University of California (UC) is only slowly emerging. The analyses presented by Pachón et al. (1997) show that in the UC system, Latino freshman enrollment rates increased from 1985 to 1989, were relatively stable through 1995, and have declined from 1995 through the present.[69] Even more dramatic enrollment decreases have occurred at law schools in the UC system, including Boalt, Davis, and Los Angeles, where Mexican American/Latino enrollments dropped by 50 percent between 1994 and 1997, from 14.6 percent to 7.2 percent, while White enrollments in these law schools increased from 54.5 percent to 73.5 percent during the same period. These decreases are clear signs of the negative effects SP1 and Proposition 209 are having on Mexican American/Latino access to one of the premiere public university systems in the nation.

The third part of the California anti-civil rights trilogy — Proposition 227 — was passed with a vote of 61 percent "yes" to 39 percent "no" on June 2, 1998 (Associated Press, 1998b). Proposition 227, which is a direct attempt to dismantle bilingual education in the state, presents major obstacles to educational equality for limited-English-proficient (LEP) and non-English-proficient (NEP) Mexican Americans and other Latino students, as well as other non-English-speaking students. It eliminates instruction in the native language of these students and replaces it with "structured immersion" in English for one year (euphemism for the "sink-or-swim" practice of decades past). Baker and Hakuta (1997) describe the workings of Proposition 227 as such:

> As opposed to other measures that have been widely interpreted as "immigrant bashing," however, the Unz proposal [Proposition 227] recognizes the rights of immigrant students as a group. However, it focuses almost solely on their right to learn English, as opposed to content matter. In addition, it severely limits the availability of bilingual instruction: under the terms of the initiative, parents will have to go personally to their child's school site to enroll them in bilingual education, and children would have to meet eligibility criteria, such as minimum age and fluency in English. Also, parents will be able to sue school districts and teachers if they provide native language instruction in a manner that does not comply with the proposed law. That is, they will be able to file against districts if their students receive anything other than English-only instruction. (p. 6)

Proposition 227, through its pedagogically unsound English-only mandate that was the status quo before the 1970s, is likely to have a profoundly adverse impact on the education of California's 1.3 million and growing LEP students — 79 percent of whom are Spanish-speakers (the vast majority of these are of Mexican origin; see Baker & Hakuta, 1997). Legal challenges to Proposition 227 have been initiated. Immediately after the bill's passage, "Civil rights groups represented by the Mexican American Legal and Educational Fund filed the suit charging that the law violated the civil rights of youngsters who speak little English" (Lelyveld, 1998, p. A2). On July 15, 1998, Federal Judge Charles Legge ruled that Proposition 227 did not discriminate against minorities or violate federal law that requires schools to help LEP students overcome their language barriers. It is expected that Judge Legge's decision will be appealed to the Ninth Circuit Court of Appeals (Wire Services, 1998). Passage of Proposition 227 represents one of the greatest ironies in Mexican American educational history: The passage of this anti-bilingual education law occurred in 1998, the sesquicentennial of the Treaty of Guadalupe Hidalgo, a treaty that agreed to protect the civil rights — including the language rights — of Mexicans living in the newly conquered area (Rendón, 1971).

Texas

In 1992, Cheryl Hopwood, a White woman, was not admitted to the University of Texas School of Law. Hopwood, along with three other White plaintiffs who were also denied admission, filed suit against the university, claiming reverse discrimination as a result of the use of race in the law school's admission process. In 1994, U.S. District Judge Sam Sparks ruled in *Hopwood v. State of Texas* (1996) that although the University of Texas School of Law violated Cheryl Hopwood's (and three other White plaintiffs') constitutional rights to equal protection under the Fourteenth Amendment, it did not have to ban its affirmative action policies. The plaintiffs appealed Judge Sparks's decision to the Fifth Circuit Court of Appeals, and, to the shock and dismay of affirmative action proponents, the appellate court, in March 1998, reversed Judge Sparks's ruling (Phillips, 1996a).[70] Thus, the appellate court's decision in *Hopwood* made illegal the use of race/ethnicity and gender (i.e., affirmative action) in undergraduate and graduate admissions in institutions of higher education within the jurisdiction of the Fifth Circuit Court of Appeals, which includes Texas, Louisiana, and Mississippi.

The two major findings by the Fifth Circuit Court of Appeals in its reversal of *Hopwood* were: 1) that the UT School of Law did not present any compelling justification for elevating one race over another in the admissions process, and, as such, it violated the plaintiffs' rights under the Fourteenth Amendment: therefore, any use of race in the admissions process was proscribed; and 2) that state-supported schools may reasonably consider a host of other factors in the admissions process (e.g., extracurricular activities, socioeconomic status, if applicants' parents were alumni, applicants' home state) (Phillips, 1996b). The Fifth Circuit Court of Appeals ruling could also have an impact in schools in Mississippi and Louisiana, some of which use affirmative action admissions similar to those of UT (Roser, 1996).

Although the impact of *Hopwood* on Mexican American and other Latino students' enrollment in higher education is just emerging, preliminary data and analyses indicate that access is declining.[71] Chapa (1997) found that admissions and enrollment of Mexican Americans declined at the University of Texas at the undergraduate level and in first-year law and medical school students. Some of his findings are as follows:

- Although the enrollment of first-year UT Austin undergraduate Mexican American and other Latino students increased from 772 in 1996 to 807 in 1997, their relative percentages of all first-year undergraduates declined from 14 percent in 1996 to 12.1 percent in 1997.
- First-year Mexican American and other Latino students at the UT School of Law declined in absolute and relative numbers (i.e., in 1996 there were forty-two students, and twenty-six in 1997 — relative percentages of 8.6 percent and 5.6 percent, respectively). For African American students, the enrollment decline was far worse — thirty-one students (6.4 percent) in 1996, and only four (0.9 percent) in 1997.
- Data for all Texas public law and medical schools also showed declines for Mexican American and other Latino first-year students for the 1996–1997 period. For Latino law school students, the decrease was 14.6 percent; for medical school students the enrollment decline was 23.8 percent. White

law school students increased by 2.1 percent; White medical school students by 7.6 percent.

• The amount of financial aid in the form of scholarships also sharply decreased for Latino students. Prior to *Hopwood,* there was specific financial assistance at UT Austin for Latino and African American students. In 1996, they received 100 percent of these race-based scholarships. In 1997, however, only 55 percent of this aid was given to Latino and African American students, while the other 45 percent was given to Whites and Asian Americans.

In addition, Chapa cites Attorney General Dan Morales's broad interpretation of the *Hopwood* decision as a further threat to the status of Mexican American access to higher education. Morales's interpretation took *Hopwood* from a decision on admissions to "Hopwood prohibits the use of race in admissions decisions, financial aid, scholarships, and student and *faculty* recruitment and retention" (1997, p. 6).

Conclusion

What does this survey of the educational plight and struggle of Mexican Americans from the Treaty of Guadalupe Hidalgo to *Hopwood* lead us to conclude?

First, the Mexican American people have been extremely resolute in their quest for educational equality. From the 1910 "blowouts" (school walkouts) of Tejanos in San Angelo (De León, 1974) to the political demonstrations, scholarship, and litigation of today, Mexican Americans have shown fierce determination in their campaign to attain equality in education. Their struggles have taken a variety of forms: litigation, the efforts of advocacy organizations, the leadership of individual activists, confrontational and peaceful political demonstrations, and Mexican American-initiated legislation.

Second, although there has been important progress in the educational status of Mexican Americans — including access to higher education and graduation from institutions; establishment of bilingual education; the founding of Mexican American/Chicano Studies; improvements in school financing allocations; growth in scholarship on Mexican American education — many obstacles continue to threaten Mexican Americans' quest for educational equality. As we have discussed, there have been major setbacks in some areas — bilingual education and higher education, in particular.

Third, as Mexican American and Latino populations grow dramatically, their educational conditions are, in fact, worsening (see Valencia & Chapa, 1993). The Mexican American and overall Latino populations (general and school age) are increasing at unprecedented rates. By the year 2010, a mere twelve years from now, Latinos will become the largest U.S. racial/ethnic minority group (Bovee, 1993). A June 1996 U.S. Census Bureau report estimated that Latino children (at 12 million) surpassed African American children (at 11.4 million) for the first time in demographic history ("Facts and Figures," 1996). This dramatic increase — of which more than 60 percent is Mexican origin — is clearly seen in California and Texas. Projections are that the White population in California could dip under 50 percent as early as the year 2000 (Bouvier, 1991). In Texas, Whites are expected to lose their numerical majority status sometime between 2009 and 2026 (Eskenazi, 1994). Among school-age children in California, White students lost their plurality to Latinos in 1997 (Hurtado & García, 1997).

Fourth, given the passage of Propositions 187, 209, and 227, and the *Hopwood* decision, the future of educational progress and equality looks bleak for Mexican Americans. For example, in early November 1997, the U.S. Supreme Court refused to hear a legal challenge from opponents of Proposition 209. This denial will have a profound impact on Mexican Americans' equal access to higher education, an impact that will be felt beyond California's borders. The Court's decision could encourage other states to follow California's path. Measures similar to Proposition 209 have already been proposed in twenty-five states (Epstein, 1997). In the aftermath of Proposition 227, a House committee approved a bill in June 1998 (sponsored by California Republican Frank Riggs) that would radically curtail federally funded bilingual programs, including prohibiting schools from keeping any students in bilingual programs for more than three years (Cooper, 1998). Scholars and policymakers are referring to the current atmosphere as a "Latino civil rights crisis" (Aguilar, 1997; McDonnell, 1997; also, see endnote number 68).

Fifth, although educational discrimination against Latinos is widespread, there is an ongoing persistent lack of attention to these matters by most policymakers. Yzaguirre and Kamasaki (1997) contend that "the problem is not so much the lack of information but the ability to 'process' the information that is already quite widely available" (p. 10). They argue for a paradigmatic shift to better understand and address the diminution of civil rights among Mexican Americans and other Latinos. The authors contend:

> The principal issue, we believe, is that the Hispanic experience in this country exists outside the most widely understood paradigm about race. The traditional "Black-White" paradigm rests on two concepts. The first is the legacy of *slavery;* the second is the "demarcation line" of *skin color.* In this paradigm, the rationale for discrimination has its roots in the practice of slavery, and the continuing basis for discrimination is skin color. For Latinos, however, the rationale for discrimination has its roots in *conquest* — the acquisition of California and the American Southwest, possessions formerly held by Mexico in 1848; and Puerto Rico (and for a time, Cuba and the Philippines), from Spain after the Spanish-American War in 1898. The continuing basis for discrimination against Hispanics includes skin color in some cases, but also includes *culture* — characteristics such as surname, language, and speech accent. (p. 10)

Our analysis of the educational plight and struggle of Mexican Americans follows Yzaguirre and Kamasaki's paradigm and leads to our basic conclusion: The Treaty of Guadalupe Hidalgo, which came about through the conquest of a culturally distinct people, serves as the taproot for understanding Mexican American educational history.

What does this history of Mexican American education help us predict about the immediate and long-term future for the Mexican American community and its struggle for educational equality? The clash between White obstinacy and Mexican American determination will certainly continue. Athough the struggle ahead is unquestionably formidable, given the Mexican American community's historical resolve for the pursuit and attainment of educational equality, we dare say that this resoluteness will continue, and even escalate, in the difficult years ahead.

Notes

1. In the text, "Mexican," "Mexican American," and "Mexican-origin" are used interchangeably. "Anglo" is a common term used to refer to Anglo-Americans and European immigrants in the Southwest. It is important to note, as does Montejano (1987), that the use of "Mexican" and "Anglo" conceal considerable diversity in the way members of these groups have identified themselves. Mexicans, for instance, have called themselves Mexicano, Castilian, Spanish, Hispano, Latin American, Chicano, and Hispanic. Each of these identities has reflected a class character as well as the political climate of the time. Likewise, Anglo-Americans and European immigrants, including such "non-Anglo" subgroups as Irish, Italian, and Jewish, were referred to by many in the Southwest as simply "Anglos" or "Whites."

2. Valencia and Solórzano (1997) have identified five historical and contemporary processes in which Mexican Americans have struggled for better education: 1) litigation, such as *Méndez v. Westminister* (1946); 2) advocacy organizations, such as the League of United Latin American Citizens (LULAC) (Márquez, 1993); 3) individual activists like George I. Sánchez (Rómo, 1986); 4) political demonstrations, such as the East Los Angeles high school "blowouts" [walkouts] of 1968 (Rosen, 1974); and 5) legislation, such as Senate Bill 477, the 1981 bilingual education law of Texas (San Miguel, 1987).

3. For a recent study of schooling and literacy in the colonial period, see Gallegos (1991).

4. Some schools were established by Mexican officials as early as the 1790s, but without much success. For examples of these early state-sponsored schools, see Gallegos (1991).

5. The Mexican community established a variety of tuition and free secular schools in selective urban and rural areas. However, evidence is lacking on the extent to which this occurred in the Southwest. Still, the presence of these schools suggests a strong community desire for schooling among Mexican Americans. More research needs to be conducted in this area.

6. Catholicism was introduced in the Southwest during the Spanish colonial period and remained the only official religion until the U.S. conquest. For a brief history of the Catholic Church's impact on Mexican Americans, see Dolan and Hinojosa (1994) and Sandoval (1990).

7. The Catholic Church hierarchy in the 1850s expressed dismay over the moral and religious beliefs and practices of the Mexican-origin population. It initiated a program of

reform aimed at strengthening its role in the emerging U.S. social order. As part of this effort, it expelled Mexican-origin priests and replaced them with European ones, and eliminated Mexican traditions within the Church. It also condemned the Penitentes, a religious lay organization of Mexican men, for their lack of regular church attendance, and the Mexican community for its failure to support the Church's new policies of taxation and moral regeneration. The Church's view of Mexican Americans and their religious practices led to many misunderstandings and conflicts between the institutional Church and the Mexican community. Despite these misunderstandings, the Mexican community continued to support the Church and its teachings. For more on this topic, see Dolan and Hinojosa (1994), Faulk (1966), and Castañeda (1976).

8. These schools were also state supported, but in 1852 a new law prohibited religious schools from sharing in state funds (see California Superintendent of Public Instruction, 1866). Several years later, additional measures aimed at eliminating public funding and support of private religious schools were enacted (see Pitt, 1968). For a history of these policies, see North (1936).

9. For a history of efforts to revitalize the Catholic Church during the early decades of U.S. rule in the territories of the Southwest and in Texas, respectively, see Faulk (1966) and Castañeda (1976).

10. The primary means for evangelizing among the Mexican-origin population before the Civil War was not education, but preaching and congregation-building. See Brackenridge, García-Treto, and Stover (1971).

11. For an elaboration of these policies, see Presbyterian Church (1878).

12. The vast majority of these schools were in the New Mexico Territory because of the lack of public education, high illiteracy rates, the strong presence of the Catholic Church, and Presbyterian policies. They lasted anywhere from three months to eighty years. The average length was probably one to three years. (Agnew & Barber, 1971; Banker, 1993; Zeleny, 1944). In 1889 there were over thirty-three schools in New Mexico with a total enrollment of 1,131. See *Home Mission Monthly* (1889), cited in Agnew and Barber (1971). On Texas schools, see Rayburn (1966), Rankin (1966), and Chatfield (1893).

13. By 1908, the Board of Home Missions reported that they were responsible for establishing over sixty schools in the territory, enrolling over 1,500 students (Atkins, 1978).

14. For more on these schools, see Agnew and Barber (1971), Atkins (1978), Buck (1949), Rankin (1966), Chatfield (1893), and Brackenridge, García-Tretor, and Stover (1971).

15. Although public schools were provided for African American students, they were segregated and inferior and "failed to give Negroes even the rudiments of an adequate education" (Meier & Rudwick, 1966, p. 145). Anderson has argued that this type of education, based on the "Hampton-Tuskegee Idea," was an ideological force aimed at incorporating African Americans into the economy as a subordinate group and at reinforcing a racial hierarchy in the Southeast. For a history of industrial public education for Blacks in the South, see Anderson (1988).

16. At least one school was founded in San Antonio, Texas, and at least two in California. Commitment to teaching and to assimilation on the part of individual educators contributed to this early type of access for Mexican-origin students to both integrated and segregated schooling (Friedman, 1978; Pelton, 1891; Weinberg, 1977).

17. The literature on Americanization usually refers to our "subtractive" concept as "coercive." Coercive, however, implies imposition — to repress or compel. The subtractive notion, in our view, is less judgmental. For an overview of Americanization as applied to education, see Montalto (1982).

18. Sánchez (1993) refers to the adoption of American values or to the alteration of values and habits as part of this Americanization in the 1920s.

19. The notion of subtractive and additive Americanization is taken from similar concepts applied to bilingual education. For further elaboration of these concepts, see Lambert (1981) and Hernández-Chavez (1984).

20. For an overview of the Church's relationship to Mexican-origin communities during the period from 1836 to 1890, see Sándoval (1990).

21. This view was applied to all of the "anomalous" peoples encountered by Protestants in the Southwest, and included Mexicans, Native Americans, and the Mormons of Utah. See Banker (1993) and Bender (1993). Official policy listed several other anomalous groups, including "Aztecs," Chinese, and the "natives of Alaska." See Presbyterian Church (1878).

22. The 16th of September is Mexican Independence Day. *El cinco de Mayo*, the 5th of May, celebrates a successful battle by Mexican troops against an invading French army in 1860. For further information on the struggle for independence and on the French invasion, see Meyer (1983) and Sherman (1983).

23. For example, in New Mexico, where the vast majority of Mexican-origin individuals were concentrated during the nineteenth century, over 90 percent of the territorial legislators responsible for enacting school legislation from the 1850s to the 1880s were Mexican Americans. Approximately 80 percent of the total number of county superintendents in the 1870s were Mexicans. In Los Angeles, Mexican Americans comprised close to half of the school board members during the 1850s, they supported bilingual instruction in the schools, the participation of Catholic officials, and the use of Catholic materials in the instructional process (Los Angeles City Council, 1938; "Message of the mayor," 1853; Padilla & Ramírez, 1974).

24. Both of these groups served in various capacities in state or territorial legislatures, county school boards, and local school decisionmaking structures in California, New Mexico, and Texas. For an example of the extensive participation of Mexican Americans in local government positions in Los Angeles, see *Chronological Records of Los Angeles City Officials, 1850–1938* (Los Angeles City Council, 1938).

25. Many of these Whites believed that the infusion of ethnic and racial minority cultures, most of which were "inferior," could transform Anglo-American culture and lead to its decline. Others believed that the maintenance of non-English languages could lead to the replacement of English and to possible social and political fragmentation. Many others, especially politicians, found diversity especially troubling, since racial and ethnic groups tended to vote for their own kind. For a history of this campaign against diversity, see Brice Heath (1977), Banks (1986), and Macías (1984).

26. See, for instance, Ketz (1997), chapter two, for examples of how Mexican Americans continued using Spanish despite official English-only policies. For similar examples among Germans in the Midwest during the nineteenth century, see Schlossman (1983).

27. This 1858 bill stipulated that no school would receive state funding unless English was "principally taught" in it (*School Law of 1858,* in Eby, 1919). In the 1850s, California suspended the 1849 Constitutional provision allowing the state government to publish its laws in Spanish. In 1855, the State Bureau of Public Instruction formalized the campaign against Spanish and all other non-English languages when it issued an administrative ruling requiring all schools to teach strictly in English (Beck, 1975; Kloss, 1977; Pitt, 1968).

28. Governor William Lane, for instance, proposed in the early 1850s that, for efficiency's sake, the legislature should replace Spanish with English as the official state language. Due to fierce resistance by the large Spanish-speaking community, his proposal was

soundly defeated in the territorial legislature. Anglo legislators in 1856 proposed the establishment of an English-only public school system. Mexican American voters rejected the monolingual public school system by a wide margin. See Eiband (1978).

29. On the Texas law, see *School Law of 1870,* in Eby (1919). For the law in California, see *California Statutes* (1870). The California provision was strengthened and broadened to include all public institutions with the passage in 1879 of a new constitution that made English the only "official language of the state" (California Constitution, 1879).

30. School Law of 1891, cited in Meyer (1977). For a Mexican American response to this law and its aftermath, see Espinosa (1917).

31. The trivialization of Spanish and Mexican contributions to Texas in the history books existed into the 1930s. Castañeda quotes from a popular state-adopted history text to illustrate the continuity of this narrow scope of Texas history. *Lone Star State* was written by Clarence Wharton and published in 1932. The author's view of early Texas history is reflected in the following comment on Anglo-American colonization: "We are now at the real beginning of Texas history. All that happened in 300 years after Piñeda sailed along our shores and Cabeza de Vaca tramped from Galveston Island to the Rio Grande was of little importance" (Castañeda, 1943, pp. 99–103).

32. See also Katz (1973), who argued that at least four of the following characterized school changes in the twentieth century: 1) the attempt to alter the political control of education; 2) the reformulation of educational thought (child-centered, reformist, scientific); 3) the introduction of educational innovations; 4) the promotion of pedagogical change; and 5) the injection of scientific management into administrative practice.

33. Taylor (1930, 1934/1971) notes many examples of schools responding more to the needs of politically influential farmers and growers in rural south Texas than to those of Mexican children.

34. For an example of the establishment, funding, and challenge of a separate school in Lemon Grove, California, see Alvarez, (1986).

35. There is no adequate study of the evolution of segregated and unequal facilities in the Mexican American community. For representative samples of some segregation studies at different points in time and for different areas, see Sánchez (1934), Leis (1931), Homes (1950), and U.S. Commission on Civil Rights (1971a).

36. There are many examples of Mexican American college graduates. They include George I. Sánchez, a recipient of a Ph.D. from the University of California, Berkeley, in 1934, and Jovita González, a recipient of a Master's degree from the University of Texas at Austin, in 1930. On Sánchez, see García (1989). On González, see Limón (1994).

37. See Pearl (1997) and Valencia (1997c) for discussion of these assertions.

38. See Valencia (1997a) for a history of deficit thinking from the American colonial period to the present.

39. For analyses of early hereditarian thought, see also Blum (1978) and Degler (1991).

40. These eight studies are: Garretson (1928); Garth (1923, 1928); Goodenough (1926); Koch and Simmons (1926); Paschal and Sullivan (1925); Sheldon (1924); Young (1922).

41. Foley (1997) discusses five developments that may have accounted for the collapse of the genetic pathology model (e.g., in light of the rise of Hitler and Nazism, many U.S. scholars did not want to align themselves with the genetic pathology model, a theory that was clearly racist).

42. The League of United Latin American Citizens (LULAC) was founded in 1929 in Corpus Christi, Texas. LULAC's membership was largely middle class, exclusively male (for years), and emphasized assimilation. "LULAC proposed to integrate the [Mexican American] community into the political and social institutions" (San Miguel,

1987, p. 69). LULAC, still active today with many chapters nationwide, has always had equality of education as a major goal. For a history of LULAC, see Márquez (1993).

43. Inequities in school financing between segregated Mexican American and Anglo schools were quite common during this time period (see, e.g., Gilbert, 1947).

44. The discussion that refers to the Drake (1927), Reynolds (1933), and Chapa (1988) studies are excerpted, with minor modifications, from Valencia (1991a).

45. Given the important role of school segregation in the history of Mexican American students, it is not surprising that this subject has been the interest of a number of contemporary scholars (e.g., Donato, 1997; Donato, Menchaca, & Valencia, 1991; Gonzáles, 1990; Hendrick, 1977; Menchaca, 1995; Menchaca & Valencia, 1990; San Miguel, 1986, 1987; Weinberg, 1977; Wollenburg, 1978).

46. Discussions of these four desegregation court cases are excerpted, with minor modifications, from Donato et al. (1991).

47. See Section 7, Article VII of the Texas Constitution.

48. Rangel and Alcala (1972) have commented that the "other White" strategy argued in *Salvatierra* rested on the prevailing doctrine of the *Plessy v. Ferguson* (1896) case. As Weinberg (1977) has noted: "In the absence of a state law requiring segregation of Mexican-Americans, they claimed equal treatment with all other `Whites.' The crucial point was to leave little leeway to be treated as Blacks under both state law and U.S. Supreme Court ruling" (p. 166). The other White strategy would be used in Mexican American desegregation cases for four decades, but was finally abandoned in *Cisneros* (1970).

49. Although there were no de jure provisions for segregating Mexican American children under the California School Code of this era, the state did have the power to establish separate schools for "Indian," "Chinese," "Japanese," and "Mongolian" children (Alvarez, 1986).

50. Included in this cadre were attorney Gus García, Dr. Hector García, and Professor George Sánchez, and the organizations LULAC and the G.I. Forum, a newly founded Mexican American veterans advocacy group.

51. This section on Sánchez is excerpted, with minor modifications, from Valencia (1997c).

52. The genetic pathology era of deficit thinking, which hit its stride in the 1920s, did not prevail uncontested (Valencia, 1997c). African American scholars of this era, for example, were not silent on the allegations of deficit thinkers who asserted that African Americans were innately inferior in intelligence. African American intellectuals did not take lightly these frequent racial pronouncements of hereditarianism. Examining pointed hypotheses and using clever research designs and methodological rigor, a cadre of African American scholars of this period joined the rising heterodoxy (see Guthrie, 1976; Thomas, 1982; Valencia, 1997c). Although their research, rejoinders to the orthodoxy of hereditarian thought, and dissent have gone unrecognized by many scholars, the African American intellectual critique of early mental testing is a vital part of the history of challenges to deficit thinking in educational thought and practice.

53. *The Mexican American People,* a 777-page book, was the first comprehensive report on the condition and position of the Mexican American people in the United States. The book covers numerous facets — for example, demographic trends, educational attainment, socioeconomic status, residential segregation, the family, intermarriage patterns, and political interactions.

54. Orfield (1988) reported data for Latinos as a whole, not disaggregated by Latino subgroups (e.g., Mexican American, Puerto Rican). Given that Mexican American students comprise the strong majority of Latino students, any findings about Latinos as a whole in the present article can safely be generalized to Mexican Americans.

55. For empirical studies documenting this relation, see Espinosa and Ochoa (1986), Jaeger (1987), Orfield (1988), Orum (1986), and Valencia (1984c).
56. TAAS is taking its toll on Mexican American (and other Latino) and African American high school students. The TAAS failure rate and subsequent diploma denial rate of many of these students are so much higher than their White peers that in October 1997, MALDEF filed a lawsuit against the Texas Education Agency and other defendants (Brooks, 1997a). The allegation is that TAAS is discriminatory and unfair, resulting in considerably higher failure rates for Mexican American and African Americans compared to their White peers. As such, many Mexican American students are forced to traverse an obstacle-filled path in their attempts to achieve some semblance of school success. High-stakes testing programs like TAAS that are used to determine graduation from high school is one such obstacle.
57. Valencia (1997e) is an unpublished study about tracking in a southwestern high school district (eight comprehensive schools; grades 9 to 12; about 21,000 students; Latino enrollment is 55 percent [overwhelmingly Mexican American]; White, 27 percent; African American, 12 percent; and "Other," 6 percent.). The school district has been under a desegregation plan via a 1985 Consent Decree and Desegregation Order. A disparity analysis produces a quantifiable index of over-representation and under-representation patterns when, for example, race/ethnicity is a factor of concern. For a brief reference to this investigation, see Valencia (1997g).
58. For a discussion of the distinction between desegregation and integration, see Donato et al. (1991).
59. For a history and evolution of bilingual education in the United States, see the following: Arias and Casanova (1993), Crawford (1989), Fishman and Keller (1982), Hakuta (1986).
60. *Diana* was a class action lawsuit filed against the State of California on behalf of Mexican American children in Monterey.
61. Public Law 94-142, designed to protect the assessment and placement rights of special needs children, contains a number of mandates (e.g., due process, confidentiality, use of multiple data sources in assessment, in-service training of teachers). The mandate most important to Mexican American children states, "Testing and evaluation materials and procedures used for the purposes of evaluation and placement of handicapped children must be selected and administered so as not to be racially or culturally discriminatory" (Federal Register, 1977, p. 42496). In 1990, Congress retitled the Education for All Handicapped Children Act the Individuals with Disabilities Act.
62. According to Rendón (1971), the term "Aztlán" was first employed by Chicano activists at a youth conference in Denver, Colorado, in 1969. Aztlán is best thought of as the place of origin of the Mexican Indian peoples. Muñoz (1989) notes:

Aztlán was the name used by the Aztecs to refer to the place of their origin. Since the Aztecs had migrated to Central Mexico from "somewhere in the north," Chicano activists claimed that Aztlán was all the southwestern United States taken from Mexico as a result of the Mexican-American War. (p. 77)

63. The criteria we used for selecting MALDEF and MEChA as two of the most significant advocacy organizations pursuing equal educational opportunities are their ability to sensitize the Mexican American community and others to the educational plight of Mexican American students, and to create educational and social change. MALDEF, as the chief litigator of Mexican American educational concerns, clearly fits these criteria, as does MEChA, which has produced numerous intellectuals and professionals devoted to educational improvement for Mexican Americans (see Muñoz, 1989, for a discussion).
64. The LDF, an independent arm of the NAACP, relied on three critical strategies in litigating civil rights cases: 1) employ attorneys highly skilled in civil rights law; 2) litigate

potentially good test cases with far-reaching implications; 3) seek support from other attorneys (Vose, 1959, cited in O'Connor & Epstein, 1984).

65. Chicano college students from the Bay Area, Central Valley, and Sacramento region came together to form one student organization, MASC, which was founded in 1966 by Armando Váldez at a meeting in San Jose, California (A. Valdez, personal communication, May 30, 1998). In 1967, a Chicano student conference was held at Loyola University in California at which UMAS was founded (Rosen, 1974).

66. In addition to MEChA and Chicano Studies, there were other groups that sought to bring attention to the violation of the treaty. In the 1960s, Reies Lopez Tijerina organized La Alianza Federal de Mercedes in New Mexico, in an attempt by Hispanos (Mexican Americans in New Mexico) to regain community land grants taken away after the 1848 treaty. Furthermore, the Brown Berets — a paramilitary urban youth sector of the Chicano Movement — in September 1972, started a 42-day occupation of Santa Catalina Island. The Berets claimed that this island (off the Southern California coast) was not included in the treaty, and therefore still belonged to Mexico (Griswold del Castillo, 1990).

67. In 1969, Bernal and Truan introduced H.B. 103. This bill, which was passed, repealed a 1918 law, H.B. 218, that made English the exclusive language of instruction in all public schools. H.B. 218 was actually an iteration of S.B. 218, which was passed in 1905 and made English the exclusive language of instruction (Vega, 1983). But, although H.B. 103 was the first bilingual education bill passed in Texas, it lacked authority, as it made implementation of bilingual education voluntary. Given its voluntary nature, H.B. 103 provided no state funds for implementation of bilingual education.

68. In our discussion we draw in part from several papers presented in December 1997 at the research conference entitled "The Latino Civil Rights Crisis," held in Los Angeles and Washington, DC, and cosponored by the Civil Rights Project of Harvard University and the Tomas Rivera Policy Institute in Claremont, California.

69. UC Berkeley released its fall 1998 admissions data in late March 1998 (Burdman, 1998). It appears that the combined impact of Proposition 209 and SP1 on minority admissions was devastating. Admissions officials reported that the number of African American, Chicano/Latino, and Native American freshman admits fell from 1,678 in 1997 to 610 in 1998 — a 64 percent decline. The decline for Mexican American students was 61 percent; drops for African Americans and Native Americans were 70 percent and 63 percent, respectively. On other campuses, reports varied considerably. For example, UC Riverside reported a 42 percent increase in Mexican American freshmen, while UC San Diego reported a 40 percent drop in Mexican American freshman admittees (Burdman, 1998).

70. The Fifth Circuit Court of Appeals, in its stunning reversal of Judge Sparks's ruling, also overturned U.S. Supreme Court Justice Powell's statement on the well-known *Bakke* decision (*Regents of the University of California v. Bakke,* 1978) — which had been the basis for universities' using race/ethnicity as a factor in admissions.

Allan Bakke, the plaintiff in the nation's first affirmative action case, was a White applicant denied admission to the UC Davis Medical School. He asserted that the school's annual sixteen set asides (out of one hundred seats) for minority admissions was reverse discrimination. The UC Davis program was found to be unconstitutional because of its quotas. Justice Powell did note, however, that it would not violate the U.S. Constitution if universities paid *some* attention to race in admissions ("Affirmative action: Is it needed or has it outlived its purpose?", 1995) In its two-to-one decision, the Fifth Circuit Court ruled in 1996 that Justice Powell's was a "lonely opinion," and thus held no substance and did not reflect the other justices' opinions.

71. In an attempt to reverse declines of minority admissions at the undergraduate level in Texas public universities, H.B. 588 (authored by Mexican American State Representa-

tive Irma Rangel) and its Senate companion S.B. 177 (authored by Mexican American State Senator Gonzalo Barrientos) were passed into law. Coined as the "Top Ten Percent Plan," high school students who graduate in the top 10 percent of their classes will be automatically admitted to one of Texas's premier institutions, such as UT or Texas A&M. "The intended effect of the automatic admissions policy, which does not allow standardized test scores or other criteria to be used in admissions, is for ethnic and racial minorities who attend [high] schools with high concentrations of minorities to be admitted" (Chapa, 1997, p. 11). The Top Ten Percent Plan will go into effect in fall 1998.

Texas law and medical schools, in response to *Hopwood,* are taking the lead in deemphasizing testing in admissions decisions (Brooks, 1997b, 1997c). Most recently, the Texas A&M medical school has decided to drop altogether the requirement that prospective students take the Medical School College Admissions Test. Students' undergraduate grade point average and coursework taken will be the major criteria in admissions decisions (Roser, 1998).

References

Affirmative action: Is it still needed or has it outlived its purposes? (1995, March 26). *Austin American-Statesman,* p. C1.

Agnew, E. J., & Barber, R. K. (1971). The unique Presbyterian school system of New Mexico. *Journal of Presbyterian History, 49,* 197–224.

Aguílar, L. (1997, December 18). Latinos: An afterthought in D.C. *Austin American-Statesman,* p. A23.

Allsup, C. (1979). Education is our freedom: The American G.I. Forum and the Mexican American school segregation in Texas, 1948–1957. *Aztlán, 8,* 27–50.

Alvarez, R. (1986). The Lemon Grove incident: The nation's first successful desegregation court case. *Journal of San Diego History, Spring,* 116–135.

Alvarez v. Lemon Grove School District, Superior Court of the State of California, County of San Diego, 1931, Petition for Writ of Mandate, No. 66625.

Anderson, J. D. (1988). *The education of Blacks in the South, 1860–1935.* Chapel Hill: University of North Carolina Press.

Anderson, T. (1969). *Foreign languages in the elementary school: A struggle against mediocrity.* Austin: University of Texas Press.

Angeles et al. v. Santa Barbara School District et al., case no. 127040, Superior Court, Santa Barbara, CA (August, 1979).

Arías, M. B., & Casanova, V. (Eds.). (1993). *Bilingual education: Politics, practice, and research.* Chicago: University of Chicago Press.

Avant, L. (1940). *History of Catholic education in New Mexico since the American occupation.* Unpublished master's thesis, University of New Mexico, Albuquerque.

Associated Press. (1998a, March 19). Judge kills California immigration law. *Austin American-Statesman,* p. A3.

Associated Press. (1998b, June 3) Measure to end bilingual education approved. *Los Angeles Times,* p. A1.

Atkins, J. C. (1978). *Who will educate?: The schooling question in territorial New Mexico, 1846–1911.* Unpublished dissertation, University of New Mexico, Albuquerque.

August, D., & Hakuta, K. (1997). *Improving schooling for language-minority children.* Washington, DC: National Academy Press.

Baker, S., & Hakuta, K. (1997, December). *Bilingual education and Latino civil rights.* Paper presented at the Harvard University Civil Rights Project Conference on the Latino Civil Rights Crisis, Los Angeles, CA, and Washington, DC.

Balderrama, F. E. (1982). *In defense of La Raza.* Tucson: University of Arizona Press.

Banker, M. T. (1993). *Presbyterian missions and cultural interaction in the far Southwest, 1850–1950.* Chicago: University of Illinois Press.

Banks, J. A. (1986) *Multiethnic education: Theory and practice* (2nd ed.). Boston: Allyn & Bacon.

Beck, N. P. (1975). *The other children: Minority education in California public schools from statehood to 1890.* Unpublished doctoral dissertation, University of California, Los Angeles.

Becklund, L. (1985, May 1) Catholic high school backers sue L.A. diocese to halt school sale. *Los Angeles Times,* pp. 1, 6.

Bender, N. (1993). *Winning the West for Christ.* Albuquerque: University of New Mexico Press.

Blum, J. M. (1078). *Pseudoscience and mental ability: The origins and fallacies of the IQ controversy.* New York: Monthly Review Press.

Bouvier, L. F. (1991). *Fifty million Californians?* Washington, DC: Center for Immigration Studies.

Bovee, T. (1993, September 9). Hispanics to become largest U.S. minority. *Austin American-Statesman,* pp. A1, A11.

Brackenridge, D. R., García-Treto, F. O., & Stover, J. (1971). Presbyterian missions to Mexican Americans in Texas in the nineteenth century. *Journal of Presbyterian History, 49,* 103–132.

Brice Heath, S. (1977). Language and politics in the United States. In M. Saville-Troike (Ed.), *Georgetown University round table on language and linguistics* (pp. 267–296). Washington, DC: Georgetown University Press.

Brooks, A. P. (1997a, October 20). MALDEF sues, state listens on Texas graduation exam. *Austin American-Statesman,* pp. A1, A7.

Brooks, A. P. (1997b, October 17). Law, medical schools hunting for minorities. *Austin American Statesman,* pp. B1, B7.

Brooks, A. P. (1997c, October 26). Texas colleges looking past test scores. *Austin American-Statesman,* pp. A1, A16.

Brooks, A. P. (1998, May 22). Many more students are passing the TAAS. *Austin American-Statesman,* pp. A1, A7.

Brooks, A. P., & South, J. (1995, April 9). School-choice plans worry segregation critics. *Austin American-Statesman,* pp. A1, A18–19.

Brown v. Board of Education of Topeka, 347 U.S. 483, at 494 (1954).

Burdman, P. (1998, March 31). UC Berkeley to see drop in minorities. *San Francisco Chronicle,* p. A1.

Calderón, C. I. (1950). *The education of Spanish-speaking children in Edcouch-Elsa, Texas.* Unpublished master's thesis, University of Texas at Austin.

California Constitution, Art. 4, sec. 24, (1879).

California Statutes, ch. 556, sec. 55 (1870).

California Superintendent of Public Instruction. (1866). *First biennial report.* Sacramento, CA: Author.

California Superintendent of Public Instruction. (1869). *Third biennial report, 1868 and 1869.* Sacramento, CA: O. P. Fitzerald.

Calvert, R. A., & De León, A. (1990). *The history of Texas.* Arlington Heights, TX: Harlan Davidson.

Cameron, J. W. (1976). *The history of Mexican public education in Los Angeles, 1910–1930.* Unpublished doctoral dissertation, University of Southern California, Los Angeles.

Campbell, F. (1987). Missiology in New Mexico, 1850–1900: The success and failure of Catholic education. In C. Guerneri & D. Alvarez (Eds.), *Religion and society in the American West* (pp. 59–78). Lantham, MD: University Press of America.

Campbell, J. R., Voelkl, K. E., & Donahue, P. L. (1997). *Report in brief, NAEP 1996 trends in academic progress.* Princeton, NJ: Educational Testing Service.

Cardenas, J. A., & Córtez, A. (1986). The impact of *Plyer v. Doe* upon Texas public schools. *Journal of Law & Education, 15,* 1–17.

Carlson, R. A. (1975). *The Quest for conformity: Americanization through education.* New York: Wiley and Sons.

Carter, D. J., & Wilson, R. (1997). *Minorities in higher education.* Washington, DC: American Council on Higher Education.

Carter, T. (1970). *Mexican Americans in schools: A history of educational neglect.* New York: College Entrance Examination Board.

Carter, T. P., & Segura, R. D. (1979). *Mexican Americans in school: A decade of change.* New York: College Entrance Examination Board.

Castañeda, C. E. (1943). The broadening concept of history teaching in Texas. In *Proceedings of the Inter-American Conference on Intellectual Inter-Change.* Austin: University of Texas, Institute of Latin American Studies.

Castañeda, C. E. (1976). *Our Catholic heritage in Texas, 1519–1936: Vol. VII. The church in Texas since independence, 1836–1950* (pp. 285–347). New York: Arno Press. (Original work published in 1958)

Castro et al. v. Phoenix Union High School District #210 et al., case no. CIV 82-302 PHX VAC, United States Court, District of Arizona, Phoenix, AZ (August, 1982).

Chapa, J. (1988). The question of Mexican American assimilation: Socioeconomic parity or underclass formation? *Public Affairs Comment, 35,* 1–14.

Chapa, J. (1997, December). *The* Hopwood *decision in Texas as an attack on Latino access to selective higher education programs.* Paper presented at the Harvard University Civil Rights Project Conference on the Latino Civil Rights Crisis, Los Angeles, CA, and Washington, DC.

Chapa J., & Valencia, R. R. (1993). Latino population growth, demographic characteristics, and educational stagnation: An examination of recent trends. *Hispanic Journal of Behavioral Sciences, 15,* 165–187.

Chatfield, W. H. (1893). *The twin cities of the border and the country of the Lower Rio Grande.* New Orleans: E. P. Brandao.

Chaves, A. (1892). *Report of the Superintendent of Public Instruction.* Santa Fe: New Mexican Printing.

Chicano Coordinating Committee on Higher Education. (1969). *El Plán de Santa Bárbara: A Chicano plan for higher education.* Oakland, CA: Author.

Cisneros v. Corpus Christi Independent School District, 324 F. Supp. 599 (W.D. Tex. 1970), appeal docketed, No. 71-2397 (5th Cir. July 16, 1971).

Cooper, R. T. (1998, June 5) U.S. bill seeks bilingual education limit. *Austin American-Statesman,* p. A2.

Covarrúbias v. San Diego Unified School District, Civil Action No. 70-30d (S.D. Cal. 1971).

Cravens, H. (1978). *The triumph of evolution: American scientists and the heredity-environment controversy, 1900–1941.* Philadelphia: University of Pennsylvania Press.

Crawford, J. (1989). *Bilingual education: History, politics, theory, and practice.* Trenton, NJ: Crane.

Cromack, I. W. (1949). *Latin-Americans: A minority group in the Austin public schools.* Unpublished master's thesis, University of Texas at Austin.

Degler, C. N. (1991). *In search of human nature: The decline and revival of Darwinism in American social thought.* New York: Oxford University Press.

De León, A. (1974). Blowout 1910 style: A Chicano school boycott in West Texas. *Texana, 12,* 125–140.

De León, A. (1982). *The Tejano community, 1836–1900.* Albuquerque: University of New Mexico Press.

Delgado et al. v. Bastrop Independent School District of Bastrop County et al., docketed, No. 388 (W.D. Tex. June 15, 1948).

Diana v. State Board of Education, Civil Action No. C-70-37 (N.D. Cal. 1970).

Dickson, V. E. (1923). *Mental tests and the classroom teacher.* Yonkers-on-Hudson, NY: World Book.

Dolan, J. P., & Hinojosa, G. M. (Eds.). (1994). *Mexican Americans and the Catholic Church, 1900–1965* (pp. 13–30). Notre Dame, IN: University of Notre Dame Press.

Donato, R. (1997). *The other struggle for equal schools: Mexican Americans during the civil rights era.* Albany: State University of New York Press.

Donato, R., Menchaca, M., & Valencia, R. R. (1991). Segregation, desegregation, and integration of Chicano students. In R. R. Valencia (Ed.), *Chicano school failure and success: Research and policy agendas for the 1990s* (pp. 27–63). London, Eng.: Falmer Press.

Drake, R. H. (1927). *A comparative study of the mentality and achievement of Mexican and White children.* Unpublished master's thesis, University of Southern California, Los Angeles.

Eby, F. (1919). *Education in Texas: Source materials.* Austin: University of Texas Press.

Eby, F. (1925). *The development of education in Texas.* New York: Macmillan.

Edgewood Independent School District v. Kirby, 777 S.W.2d 391 (Tex. 1989).

Eiband, D. M. (1978). *The dual language policy in New Mexico.* Unpublished master's thesis, University of Texas at Austin.

El Clamor Público. (1856, November 1).

Epstein, A. (1997, November 4). Affirmative action ban stands. *Austin American-Statesman,* pp. A1, A12.

Eskenazi, S. (1994, January 25). Minority groups are growing share of Texas population. *Austin American-Statesman,* pp. A1, A5.

Espinosa, A. M. (1917). Speech mixture in New Mexico: The influence of the English language on New Mexican Spanish. In H. M. Stephens & H. E. Bolton (Eds.), *The Pacific Ocean in history* (pp. 408–428). New York: Macmillan.

Espinosa, R., & Ochoa, A. (1986). Concentration of California Hispanic students in schools with low achievement: A research note. *American Journal of Education, 95,* 77–95.

Facts and figures. (1996, November). *Hispanic,* p. 12.

Faulk, O. B. (Ed.). (1966). *John Baptist Salpointe: Soldier of the cross.* Tucson, AZ: Diocese of Tucson.

Federal Register. (1977, August 23). Education of Handicapped Children. Regulations Implementing Education for All Handicapped Children Act of 1975, pp. 42474–42518.

Ferrier, W. W. (1937). *Ninety years of education in California, 1846–1936.* Berkeley, CA: Sather Gate Book Shop.

Ferris, D. F. (1962). *Judge Marvin and the founder of the California public school system.* Berkeley: University of California Press.

Fikac, P. (1996, June 6). Students' TAAS results improve. *Austin American-Statesman,* pp. B1, B5.

Fishman, J., & Keller, G. (Eds.). (1982). *Bilingual education for Hispanic students in the United States.* New York: Teachers College Press.

Foley, D. E. (1997). Deficit thinking models based on culture: The anthropological protest. In R. R. Valencia (Ed.), *The evolution of deficit thinking: Educational thought and practice* (pp. 113–131). London, Eng.: Falmer Press.

Friedman, M. S. (1978). *An appraisal of the role of the public school as an acculturating agency of Mexican Americans in Texas, 1850–1968.* Unpublished doctoral dissertation, New York University, New York City.

Frost, J. L., & Hawkes, G. R. (Eds.). (1966). *The disadvantaged child: Issues and innovations.* New York: Houghton Mifflin.

Gallegos, B. P. (1991). *Literacy, society and education in New Mexico, 1693–1821.* Albuquerque: University of New Mexico Press.

García, M. T. (1979). *Mexican Americans: Leadership, ideology, and identity, 1930–1960.* New Haven, CT: Yale University Press.

García, M. (1981). *Desert immigrants.* New Haven, CT: Yale University Press.

García, M. (1989). *Mexican Americans.* New Haven, CT: Yale University Press.

Garretson, O. K. (1928). Study of the causes of retardation among Mexican children. *Journal of Educational Psychology, 19,* 31–40.

Garth, T. R. (1923). A comparison of the intelligence of Mexican and mixed and full blood Indian children. *Psychological Review, 30,* 388–401.

Garth, T. R. (1925). A review of race psychology. *Psychological Bulletin, 22,* 343–364.

Garth, T. R. (1928). The intelligence of Mexican school children. *School and Society, 27,* 791–794.

Gilbert, E. H. (1947). *Some legal aspects of the education of Spanish-speaking children in Texas.* Unpublished master's thesis, University of Texas at Austin.

González, G. G. (1974a). *The system of public education and its function within the Chicano communities, 1920–1930.* Unpublished doctoral dissertation, University of California, Los Angeles.

González, G. G. (1974b). Racism, education and the Mexican community in Los Angeles, 1920–1930. *Societas, 4,* 287–301.

González, G. G. (1990). *Chicano education in the era of segregation.* Philadelphia: Balch Institute Press.

Goodenough, F. L. (1926). Racial differences in the intelligence of school children. *Journal of Experimental Psychology, 9,* 388–397.

Graves, D. (1989, October 3). Court strikes down school finance plan: Justices set May 1 deadline for equitable system. *Austin American-Statesman,* pp. A1, A6.

Grebler, L., Moore, J. W., & Guzman, R. C. (1970). *The Mexican-American people: The nation's second largest minority.* New York: Free Press.

Griswold del Castillo, R. (1979). *The Los Angeles barrio, 1850–1890.* Los Angeles: University of California Press.

Griswold del Castillo, R. (1990). *The Treaty of Guadalupe Hidalgo: A legacy of conflict.* Norman: University of Oklahoma Press.

Guadalupe v. Tempe Elementary School District, No. 3, Civ. No. 71-435 (D. Ariz., 1972).

Guthrie, R. V. (1976). *Even the rat was White: A historical view of psychology.* New York: Harper & Row.

Hakuta, K. (1986). *Mirror of language: The debate on bilingualism.* New York: Basic Books.

Handlin, O. (1982). Education and the European immigrant, 1820–1920. In B. J. Weiss (Ed.), *American education and the European immigrant: 1840–1940* (pp. 3–16). Chicago: University of Illinois Press.

Hellmuth, J. (Ed.). (1967). *Disadvantaged child* (vol. I). New York: Brunner/Mazel.

Henderson, R. W., & Valencia, R. R. (1985). Nondiscriminatory school psychological services: Beyond nonbiased assessment. In J. R. Bergan (Ed.), *School psychology in contemporary society* (pp. 340–377). Columbus, OH: Charles E. Merrill.

Hendrick, I. (1977). *The education of non-Whites in California, 1848–1970.* San Francisco: R&E Associates.

Hendrick, I. G. (1980). *California education: A brief history.* San Francisco: Boyd Fraser.

Hernández-Chavez, E. (1984). The inadequacy of English immersion education as an educational approach for language minority students in the United States. In *Studies of immersion education* (pp. 144–183). Sacramento: California State Department of Education.

Homes, F. G. (1950). *Close the breach: A report of the study of school segregation in Arizona.* Phoenix: Arizona Council for Civic Unity.

Hopwood v. State of Texas, 78 F. 3d 932, 5th Cir. (1996).

Hurtado, A., & García, E. E. (1997). Student's pathways to higher education: Lessons learned from the Latino Eligibility Study. In M. Yepes-Baraya (Ed.), *ETS Invitational Conference on Latino Educational Issues: Conference proceedings* (pp. 67–86). Princeton, NJ: Educational Testing Service.

Independent School District v. Salvatierra, 33 S.W. 2d 790 (Tex. Civ. App. — San Antonio 1930), cert. denied, 284 U.S. 580 (1931).

Jaeger, C. (1987). *Minority and low income high schools: Evidence of educational inequality in metro Los Angeles* (Report No. 8). Chicago: University of Chicago, Metropolitan Opportunity Project.

Katz, M. (1973). *Class, bureaucracy, and schools.* New York: Praeger.

Keller, G. D., Deneen, J. R., & Magallán, R. J. (1991). *Assessment and access: Hispanics in higher education.* Albany: State University of New York Press.

Ketz, L. M. (1997). *Schools of their own: The education of Hispanos in New Mexico, 1850–1940.* Albuquerque: University of New Mexico Press.

Keyes v. School District Number One, Denver Colorado, 380 F. Supp. 673 (D. Colo. 1973), 521 F. 2d 465 (10th Cir. 1975).

Kliebard, H. M. (1987). *The struggle for the American curriculum, 1893–1958.* New York: Routledge & Kegan Paul.

Kloss, H. (1977). *The American bilingual tradition.* Rowley, MA: Newberry House.

Koch, H. L., & Simmons, R. (1926). A study of the test performance of American, Mexican, and Negro children. *Psychological Monographs, 35,* 1–116.

Lambert, W. E. (1981). Bilingualism and language acquisition. In H. Wintz (Ed.), *Native language and foreign language acquisition* (pp. 9–12). New York: New York Academy of Sciences.

Leibowitz, A. (1971, March). *Educational policy and political acceptance: The imposition of English as the language of instruction in American schools.* (ERIC Document Reproduction Service No. ED 047 321)

Leibowitz, A. (1976). Language and the law: The exercise of power through official designation of language. In W. O'Barr & J. O'Barr (Eds.), *Language and politics* (pp. 449–466). The Hague: Mouton.

Leis, W. (1931). *The status of education for Mexican children.* Unpublished master's thesis, University of Southern California, Los Angeles.

Lelyveld, N. (1998, June 4). California's voters opt for traditional choices. *Austin American-Statesman,* p. A2.

Lewis, O. (1959). *Five families: Mexican case studies in the culture of poverty.* New York: Basic Books.

Lewis, O. (1965). The culture of poverty. *Scientific American, 215,* 19–25.

Limón, J. E. (1994). *Dancing with the devil.* Madison: University of Wisconsin Press.

Little, W. (1944). *Spanish speaking children in Texas.* Austin: University of Texas Press.

Los Angeles City Council. (1938). *Chronological records of Los Angeles city officials, 1850–1938.* Los Angeles: Author.

Macías, R. F. (1983). *Institutionalizing democratic language rights.* Unpublished manuscript.

Macías, R. F. (1984). *Cauldron-boil and bubble: United States language policy towards indigenous language groups during the nineteenth century.* Unpublished manuscript.

Macías, R. F. (1993). Language and ethnic classification of language minorities: Chicano and Latino students in the 1990s. *Hispanic Journal of Behavioral Sciences, 15,* 230–257.

Macías, R. F. (1994). California adopts Proposition 187. *Linguistic Minority Research Institute News, 4,* 1–4.

Manuel, H. T. (1930). *The education of Spanish-speaking children in Texas.* Austin: University of Texas Press.

Márquez, B. (1993). *LULAC: The evolution of a Mexican American political organization.* Austin: University of Texas Press.

McDonnell, P. J. (1997, December 4). Latinos face civil rights crisis, panel told. *Los Angeles Times,* pp. B1, B10.

Meier, A., & Rudwick, E. M. (1966). *From plantation to ghetto.* New York: Hill & Wang.

Meier, K. J., & Stewart, J., Jr. (1990). *The politics of Hispanic education.* New York: State University of New York Press.

Menual School Centennial, 1881–1981. (1981). Albuquerque, NM: Menual Historical Library.

Menchaca, M. (1995). *The Mexican outsiders: A community history of marginalization and discrimination in California.* Austin: University of Texas Press.

Menchaca, M., & Valencia, R. R. (1990). Anglo-Saxon ideologies and their impact on the segregation of Mexican students in California, the 1920s–1930s. *Anthropology and Education Quarterly, 21,* 222–249.

Méndez v. Westminister School District, 64 F. Supp. 544 (S.D. Cal 1946), affirmed 161 F. 2d 774 (9th Cir 1947).

Message of the mayor. (May 14, 1853). *Los Angeles Star.*

Meyer, M. C. (1983). *The course of Mexican history* (2nd ed.). New York: Oxford University Press.

Meyer, D. L. (1977). The language issue in New Mexico, 1880–1900: Mexican American resistance against cultural erosion. *Bilingual Review, 4*(1/2), 99–106.

Meyers, M., & Feinberg, S. (1992). *Assessing evaluation studies: The case of bilingual education strategies.* Panel to Review Evaluation Studies of Bilingual Education, Committee on National Statistics, National Research Council. Washington, DC: National Academy Press.

Milk, R. (1980). The issue of language in education in territorial New Mexico. *Bilingual Review/Revista Bilingue, 7,* 212–221.

Miller, H. (1937). *Treaties and other international acts of the United States of America* (vol. 5). Washington, DC: Government Printing Office.

Miranda, L., & Quiroz, J. T. (1989). *The decade of the Hispanic: A sobering economic retrospective.* Washington, DC: National Council of La Raza.

Montalto, N. V. (1982). *A history of the intercultural education movement, 1924–1941.* New York: Garland.

Montejano, D. (1987). *Anglos and Mexicans in the making of Texas, 1836–1986.* Austin: University of Texas Press.

Morín, R. (1963). *Among the valiant: Mexican Americans in WWII and Korea.* Los Angeles: Borden.

Muñoz, C. (1989). *Youth, identity, power: The Chicano movement.* New York: Verso.

North, W. E. (1936). *Catholic education in Southern California.* Unpublished doctoral dissertation, Catholic University of America, Washington, DC.

O'Brien, K. B. (1961). Education, Americanization, and the Supreme Court: The 1920s. *American Quarterly, 13,* 161–171.

O'Connor, K., & Epstein, L. (1984). A legal voice for the Chicano community: The activities of the Mexican American Legal Defense and Educational Fund, 1968–1982. *Social Science Quarterly, 65,* 245–256.

Olívas, M. A. (Ed.). (1986). *Latino college students.* New York: Teachers College Press.

Olsen, L. (1988). *Crossing the schoolhouse border: Immigrant students and the California public schools.* Boston: California Tomorrow.

Orfield, G. (1988, July). *The growth and concentration of Hispanic enrollment and the future of American education.* Paper presented at the National Council of La Raza Conference, Albuquerque, NM.

Orfield, G., & Monfort, F. (1992). *Status of school desegregation: The next generation* (Report to the National School Boards Association). Alexandria, VA: Council of Urban Boards of Education.

Orfield, G., Monfort, F., & George, R. (1987). *School segregation in the 1980s: Trends in the states and metropolitan areas.* Chicago: University of Chicago, National School Desegregation Project.

Orfield, G., & Eaton, S. (1996). *Dismantling desegregation.* New York: New Press.

Orum, L. S. (1986). *The education of Hispanics: Status and implications.* Washington, DC: National Council of La Raza.

Pachón, H. P., Mejía, A. F., & Bergman, E. (1997, December). *California Latinos and collegiate education: The continuing crisis.* Paper presented at the Harvard Civil Rights Project Research Conference on the Latino Civil Rights Crisis, Los Angeles, CA, and Washington, DC.

Padilla, F. V., & Ramírez, C. B. (1974). Patterns of Chicano representation in California, Colorado, and Nuevo Mejico. *Aztlán, 5,* 189–234.

Paschal, F. C., & Sullivan, L. R. (1925). Racial differences in the mental and physical development of Mexican children. *Comparative Psychology Monographs, 3,* 1–76.

Pearl, A. (1997). Cultural and accumulated environment deficit models. In R. R. Valencia (Ed.), *The evolution of deficit thinking: Educational thought and practice* (pp. 132–159). London, Eng.: Falmer Press

Pelton, J. C. (1891). First public school and its founders. *Golden Era, 40,* 845–850.

Pennybacker, J. H. (1895) *A new history of Texas for schools.* Palestine, TX: Palestine.

Pérez, S. M., & De La Rosa Salazar, D. (1993). Economic, labor force, and social implications of Latino educational and population trends. *Hispanic Journal of Behavioral Sciences, 15,* 188–229.

Phillips, J. (1996a, March 21). College officials reel over UT ruling. *Austin American-Statesman,* pp. A1, A8.

Phillips, J. (1996b, March 23). Judge says rule on preferences was never a rule. *Austin American-Statesman,* pp. A1, A11.

Pitt, L. (1968). *The decline of the Californios: A social history of the Spanish-speaking Californians, 1846–1890.* Berkeley: University of California Press.

Plessy v. Ferguson, 16 S.Ct. 1138 (1896).

Plyer v. Doe, 457 U.S. 202, 210 (1982).

Presbyterian Church. (1878). *Minutes of the general assembly.* New York: Presbyterian Church of the USA.

Presbyterian Panorama. (1952). New York: Presbyterian Church of the USA.

Pulliam, J. D. (1987). *History of education in America* (4th ed.). Columbus, OH: Merrill.

Rangel, S. C., & Alcala, C. M. (1972). Project report: De jure segregation of Chicanos in Texas schools. *Harvard Civil Rights-Civil Liberties Law Review, 7,* 307–391.

Rankin, M. (1966). *Texas in 1850.* Waco, TX: Texian Press.

Rayburn, J. C. (1966). Introduction. In M. Rankin (Ed.), *Texas in 1850.* Waco, TX: Texian Press.

Regents of the University of California v. Bakke, 438 U.S. 265 (1978).

Rendón, A. B. (1971). *Chicano manifesto.* New York: Macmillan.

Reyes, P., & Valencia, R. R. (1993). Educational policy and the growing Latino student population: Problems and prospects. *Hispanic Journal of Behavioral Sciences, 15,* 258–283.

Reynolds, A. (1933). *The education of Spanish-speaking children in five southwestern states* (Bulletin 1933, No. 11). Washington, DC: Government Printing Office.

Rivkin, S. G. (1994). Residential segregation and school integration. *Sociology in Education, 67,* 279–292.

Rodríguez et al. v. San Antonio School District et al., 337 F. Supp. 280 (W.D. Tex 1971), 36 L. Ed. 2d 1b, 93 S. Ct. 1278 (1973).

Rómo, R. (1986). George I. Sánchez and the civil rights movement: 1940 to 1960. *La Raza Law Journal, 1,* 342–362.

Rosen, G. (1974). The development of the Chicano movement in Los Angeles from 1967 to 1969. *Aztlán, 4,* 155–183.

Roser, M. A. (1996, March 21). UT policy ruling decried. *Austin American-Statesman,* p. A8.

Roser, M. A. (1998, February 4). To draw minorities, A&M drops test. *Austin American-Statesman,* pp. B1, B6.

Ross v. Eckels, 434 F 2d. 1140 (5th Cir. 1970).

Salínas, G. (1971). Mexican-Americans and the desegregation of schools in the Southwest. *Houston Law Review, 8,* 929–951.

San Miguel, G. (1979). From a dual to a tripartite school system: The origins and development of educational segregation in Corpus Christi, Texas. *Integrated Education, 17,* 27–38.

San Miguel, G., Jr. (1986). Status of the historiography of Mexican American education: A preliminary analysis. *History of Education Quarterly, 26,* 523–536.

San Miguel, G., Jr. (1987). *"Let all of them take heed": Mexican Americans and the campaign for educational equality in Texas, 1910–1981.* Austin: University of Texas Press.

Sánchez, G. I. (1932). Scores of Spanish-speaking children on repeated tests. *Journal of Genetic Psychology, 40,* 223–231.

Sánchez, G. I. (1934). Bilingualism and mental measures. *Journal of Applied Psychology, 18,* 765–772.

Sánchez, G. J. (1993). *Becoming Mexican American: Ethnicity, culture, and identity in Chicano Los Angeles, 1900–1945.* New York: Oxford University Press.

Sándoval, M. (1990). *On the move: A history of the Hispanic church in the United States.* New York: Orbis Press.

Schlossman, S. L. (1983). Is there an American tradition of bilingual education? German in the public elementary schools, 1840–1919. *American Journal of Education, 91,* 139–186.

School-finance law upheld. (1995, January 31). *Austin American-Statesman,* p. A1.

Scott, H. H. (1983). Desegregation in Nashville: Conflicts and contradictions in preserving schools in Black communities. *Education and Urban Society, 15,* 235–244.

Sheldon, W. H. (1924). The intelligence of Mexican children. *School and Society, 19,* 139–142.

Sherman, W. L. (1983). *The course of Mexican history* (2nd ed.). New York: Oxford University Press.

St. Michael's College, 100 years of service. (1959). Santa Fe, NM: St. Michael's College.

Suro, R., & Balz, D. (1994, November 3). Proposition 187 dominates, divides California races. *Austin American-Statesman,* p. A9.

Tamura, E. H. (1994). *Americanization, acculturation, and ethnic identity: The Nisei generation in Hawaii.* Chicago: University of Illinois Press.

Taylor, P. S. (1929). *Mexican labor in the United States: Racial school statistics.* Los Angeles: University of California Publications in Economics.

Taylor, P. (1930). *Mexican labor in the United States: Dimmit County, Winter Garden District, South Texas.* Los Angles: University of California Press.

Taylor, P. (1971). *American-Mexican frontier: Nueces County, Texas.* New York: Russell. (Original work published 1934)

Territorial superintendent's annual report. (1891). Santa Fe: New Mexican Printing.
Territorial superintendent's annual report. (1892). Santa Fe: New Mexican Printing.
Thomas, W. B. (1982). Black intellectuals critique of early mental testing: A little known saga of the 1920s. *American Journal of Education, 90,* 258–292.
U.S. Bureau of the Census. (1961a). *Vol. 1, Part 33* (New Mexico). Washington, DC: Government Printing Office.
U.S. Bureau of the Census. (1961b). Table 45: School enrollment, by age, for the state: 1930–1960. In *Vol. 1, Part 33* (New Mexico). Washington, DC: Government Printing Office.
U.S. Commission on Civil Rights. (1971a). *Mexican American education study, report 1: Ethnic isolation of Mexican Americans in the public schools of the Southwest.* Washington, DC: Government Printing Office.
U.S. Commission on Civil Rights. (1971b). *Mexican American education study, report 2: The unfinished education. Outcomes for minorities in the five southwestern states.* Washington, DC: Government Printing Office.
U.S. Commission on Civil Rights. (1972a). *Mexican American education study, report 3: The excluded student. Educational practices affecting Mexican Americans in the Southwest.* Washington, DC: Government Printing Office.
U.S. Commission on Civil Rights. (1972b). *Mexican American education study, report 4: Mexican American education in Texas. A function of wealth.* Washington, DC: Government Printing Office.
U.S. Commission on Civil Rights. (1973). *Mexican American education study, report 5: Teachers and students.* Washington, DC: Government Printing Office.
U.S. Commission on Civil Rights. (1974). *Mexican American education study, report 6: Toward quality education for Mexican Americans.* Washington, DC: Government Printing Office.
Valencia, R. R. (1980). The school closure issue and the Chicano community. *Urban Review, 12,* 5–21.
Valencia, R. R. (1984a). *School closures and policy issues* (Policy Paper No. 84-C3). Stanford, CA: Stanford University, Institute for Research on Educational Finance and Governance.
Valencia, R. R. (1984b). The school closure issue and the Chicano community: A follow-up study of the *Angeles* case. *Urban Review, 16,* 145–163.
Valencia, R. R. (1984c). *Understanding school closures: Discriminatory impact on Chicano and Black students* (Policy Monograph Series, No. 1). Stanford, CA: Stanford University, Stanford Center for Chicano Research.
Valencia, R. R. (1991a). The plight of Mexican American students: An overview of schooling conditions and outcomes. In R. R. Valencia (Ed.), *Chicano school failure and success: Research and policy agendas for the 1990s* (pp. 3–26). London, Eng.: Falmer Press.
Valencia, R. R. (Ed.). (1991b). *Chicano school failure and success: Research and policy agendas for the 1990s* (pp. 3–26). London, Eng.: Falmer Press.
Valencia, R. R. (Ed.). (1997a). *The evolution of deficit thinking: Educational thought and practice.* London, Eng.: Falmer Press.
Valencia, R. R. (1997b). Conceptualizing the notion of deficit thinking. In R. R. Valencia (Ed.), *The evolution of deficit thinking: Educational thought and practice* (pp. 1–12). London, Eng.: Falmer Press.
Valencia, R. R. (1997c). Genetic pathology model of deficit thinking. In R. R. Valencia (Ed.), *The evolution of deficit thinking: Educational thought and practice* (pp. 41–112). London, Eng.: Falmer Press.
Valencia, R. R. (1997d). Latino demographic and educational conditions. *ETS Policy Notes, 8,* 1–4, 11.

Valencia, R. R. (1997e). *Course enrollments by race/ethnicity in a Southwestern high school district: An analysis of access.* Unpublished manuscript.

Valencia, R. R. (1997f). Latinos and education: An overview of sociodemographic characteristics and schooling conditions. In M. Yepes-Baraya (Ed.), *ETS Invitational Conference on Latino Educational Issues* (pp. 13–37). Princeton, NJ: Educational Testing Service.

Valencia, R. R. (1997g, December). *Latino students and testing issues: Perspectives on the Great Gatekeeper.* Paper presented at the Harvard University Civil Rights Project Research Conference on the Latino Civil Rights Crisis, Los Angeles, CA, and Washington, DC.

Valencia, R. R., & Chapa, J. (Eds.). (1993). Special issue: Latino population growth and demographic trends. Implications for education. *Hispanic Journal of Behavioral Sciences, 15,* 163–284.

Valencia, R. R., & Solórzano, D. G. (1997). Contemporary deficit thinking. In R. R. Valencia (Ed.), *The evolution of deficit thinking: Educational thought and practice* (pp. 160–210). London, Eng.: Falmer Press.

Vega, J. E. (1983). *Education, politics, and bilingualism in Texas.* Washington, DC: University Press of America.

Vose, C. E. (1959). *Caucasians only.* Berkeley: University of California Press.

Weinberg, M. (1977). *A chance to learn: The history of race and education in the United States.* Cambridge, Eng.: Cambridge University Press.

Wharton, C. (1932). *Lone star state.* Austin: University of Texas Press.

Willig, A. (1985). A meta-analysis of selected studies on the effectiveness of bilingual education. *Review of Educational Research, 55,* 269–317.

Wire Services. (1998, July 16). English-only initiative upheld. *Austin American-Statesman,* p. A2.

Wollenberg, C. (1978). *All deliberate speed: Segregation and exclusion in California schools, 1855–1975.* Berkeley: University of California Press.

Young, K. (1922). *Mental differences in certain immigrant groups: Psychological tests of South Europeans in typical California schools with bearing on the educational policy and on the problems of racial contacts in this country* (No. 11). Eugene: University of Oregon Press.

Yzaguirre, R., & Kamasaki, C. (1997, December). *Comment on the Latino Civil Rights Crisis, a Research Conference.* Paper presented at the Harvard University Civil Rights Project Conference on the Latino Civil Rights Crisis, Los Angeles, CA, and Washington, DC.

Zeleny, C. (1944). *Relations between the Spanish-Americans and Anglo-Americans in New Mexico: A study of conflict and accommodation in a dual ethnic situation.* Unpublished doctoral dissertation, Yale University, New Haven, CT.

Both authors contributed equally to this article. Their names are listed alphabetically. Correspondence concerning this article can be addressed to either author: Guadalupe San Miguel Jr., Department of History, University of Houston, Houston, TX 77204-3785; Richard R. Valencia, Department of Educational Psychology, George I Sánchez Building, University of Texas at Austin, Austin, TX 78712-1296.

The Economy of Literacy:
How the Supreme Court Stalled
the Civil Rights Movement

CATHERINE PRENDERGAST

Until the middle of the twentieth century, the dominant U.S. educational policy was to use whatever means possible, including the force of law, to restrict access to literacy for African Americans and to preserve it for Whites. Throughout much of the nineteenth century, these restrictions included making it a crime to teach enslaved people to read or write and providing only a second-class education to the newly freed (Cornelius, 1991). Until the mid–twentieth century, educational policy continued to deny equal education to African Americans and restricted their access to higher education. Furthermore, segregation in public schools was enforced well after passage of the Fourteenth Amendment, which mandates equal protection under the law for all citizens (Royster, 2000).

According to Anderson (1988), it was an American tradition rather than an aberration to provide unequal education to Whites and African Americans. Ostensibly, the U.S. Supreme Court's 1954 decision in *Brown v. Board of Education* was intended to end this tradition by discontinuing legalized segregation in schools. However, a number of African American literacy scholars have noted a recent resurgence of segregation as well as persistent disparities in educational opportunity along racial lines (Delpit, 1988; Fordham, 1988; Foster, 1997; Willis, 1995). Observing that students of color and White students in the 1990s were in many ways more segregated than they were before the civil rights movement and legalized desegregation, Ladson-Billings and Tate (1995) have called for a reexamination of *Brown*.

At stake in *Brown* was the question of whether or not segregated public education violated the Equal Protection Clause of the Fourteenth Amendment. As part of its effort to define "equal protection," the Court also took up the task of defining the importance of education. In this the Court thought on a grand scale: the rationale in *Brown* for ending legalized segregation rested on defining public education as the precursor to good citizenship, cultural values, professional preparation, and even normalcy, a "right which must be made available to all on equal terms":

Harvard Educational Review Vol. 72 No. 2 Summer 2002, 206–229

Today, education is perhaps the most important function of state and local governments. . . . It is the very foundation of good citizenship. Today it is a principal instrument in awakening the child to cultural values, in preparing him for later professional training, and in helping him adjust normally to his environment. In these days it is doubtful that any child may reasonably be expected to succeed in life if he is denied the opportunity of an education. Such an opportunity, where the state has undertaken to provide it, is a right which must be made available for all on equal terms. (*Brown*, 1954, p. 493)

This language in the *Brown* decision linking public education to citizenship, opportunity, professionalism, and undefined normalcy is representative of what Cook-Gumperz (1986) has termed the late–twentieth century "ideology of literacy" (p. 33). According to Cook-Gumperz, as the twentieth century progressed, schooling came to be seen more and more as the principle vehicle for ensuring both "social stability and economic advancement" and the transformation of individuals into "members of the wider society" (pp. 33–34). At the same time, Cook-Gumperz maintains, literacy, conceptually conjoined to mass schooling, came to be seen as both a basic human right and the building block of modern society. In order to render what in the mid–twentieth century was seen as a potentially volatile decision with broad social implications, the Court supported its decision in *Brown* largely on this ideology of literacy. The repeated use of "today" in the Court's language emphasizes the modern imperative of schooling. As the twentieth century drew to a close, however, literacy scholars began to point out flaws in the governing ideology of literacy. Through the study of changing historical and cultural conditions, literacy scholars have shown that the outcomes that are claimed for both literacy and education do not necessarily result in the opportunities imagined (Brandt, 1999; Graff, 1995; Street, 1984). Further, Cook-Gumperz (1986) argues that the notion that mass schooling provides a kind of functional literacy, which in turn provides equal opportunity, has the effect of blaming individuals for the social stratification that modern schooling, with ranking devices like tracking, actually facilitates.

Scholars have also observed that the designation of literacy and education as "rights" is more rhetorical than real. Though the *Brown* decision initiated desegregation by determining that an education free of segregation and inequality is a right, this right has proven to be all too fungible in practice, as literacy scholars have documented (Kozol, 1991; Ladson-Billings & Tate, 1995). A 1988 conference entitled The Right to Literacy, sponsored by the Modern Language Association, spawned a volume of essays questioning the notion of literacy as a right. In this volume, the editors suggest that formulating literacy in terms of rights is inevitably problematic because literacy "is not in itself a panacea for social inequity" or a way to "grant more influence or power to those who have been disempowered by their race" (Lunsford, Moglen, & Slevin, 1990, p. 2).

It is no accident that literacy scholars began to wrestle with the rhetorical enmeshment of rights, equal opportunity, education, and literacy in the late 1980s, following a period of diminished government enforcement of civil rights laws against discrimination in housing, education, and employment (Lipsitz, 1998). In response to this same governmental neglect, critical race theorists — predominantly legal scholars of color — have come to consider rights and equal opportunity to be ultimately race dependent (e.g., Bell, 1992a; Crenshaw, Gotonda, Peller, & Thomas, 1995; Delgado, 1995; Williams, 1991). They argue that civil rights, intended to ensure life and liberty, have generally been sacrificed for property rights, intended to protect ownership. Further, White identity has been legally recognized as having property value. Harris (1993) explains: "Whiteness . . . meets the functional criteria of property. Specifically, the law has accorded 'holders' of Whiteness the same privileges and benefits accorded holders of other types of property. The liberal view of property is that it includes the exclusive rights of possession, use, and disposition" (p. 1731). Bell (1987) points out that the property value of White identity was established when a fundamental contradiction presented by the Declaration of Independence — that all men were created equal and are entitled to liberty, except those enslaved — was resolved by labeling African Americans as property. Harris demonstrates that the property value of White identity was reinforced in the 1896 Supreme Court case *Plessy v. Ferguson*, which established the "separate but equal" doctrine that *Brown* would later overturn. Plessy argued that in being barred from a White streetcar, he had been denied the reputation of being White and thus its pecuniary value (Harris, 1993, p. 1747). The Court decided that Plessy did not meet Louisiana's legal criteria for being White and thus was not deprived of property (*Plessy*, 1896).

As Lamos (2000) points out, critical race theorists reveal not only the property value given to White identity, but also the complicity of the justice system in maintaining education as White property. Harris (1993), for example, extends her discussion of White property to suggest that legal challenges to affirmative action in educational settings are predicated on the notions of White entitlement to education. Bell (1980, 1992a, 1992b) offers his critique of the race-dependent nature of rights in part through a review of desegregation litigation. The analysis of critical race theorists suggests that there is a sound historical reason to believe that insights from both legal and literacy studies might inform how ideologies of literacy and the course of racial justice intersect in the latter half of the twentieth century. Major cases that defined public and legal notions of racism also dealt with education and literacy. *Brown*, a case most obviously about education, resulted in defining racism as school segregation. Because it was such a high-profile case that mobilized mass interests, *Brown* ensured that ideologies of literacy would continue to inform legal definitions of racial discrimination and remedy.

The 1976 ruling in *Washington v. Davis* defined racial discrimination as being necessarily intentional. Although on the surface an employment discrimination case, at issue in *Washington* was a written entrance exam to the Washington, DC, police force that African American applicants failed at twice the rate of Whites. The question of racial bias in literacy testing was therefore discussed at great length in the oral arguments before the Supreme Court. During these arguments, the justices reinforced the rhetoric of "literacy crisis" that subsequently defined public discourse on literacy during the mid- to late-1970s (Graff, 1979). I argue that this rhetoric provided fertile ground for subsequent challenges to affirmative action. The decision in *Washington* informed one of the most prominent and legally significant cases over racial justice and literacy, *Regents of the University of California v. Bakke,* which was argued in 1977 and decided in 1978. Alan Bakke, rejected twice by the University of California at Davis Medical School, charged that as a White man he was discriminated against by the school's affirmative action policies. As I will argue, the majority of the Court in this case seemed more concerned with upholding certain conceptions of literacy standards than with ensuring the equality of education that had eluded the country even after *Brown*.

For many observers, *Brown* and *Bakke* bookend the legal struggle for civil rights in the Supreme Court, the first case holding the great promise that the later case definitively showed to be unfulfilled. However, looking at the conceptions of literacy informing these cases, I argue that the continuities between the two are as important to consider as the discontinuities. Despite the lofty prose equating education with equal opportunity, the ideologies of literacy informing these crucial decisions were consistent with the maintenance of education as White property. Through the *Brown* decision, the Court formulated education as a specifically racialized attribute. The arguments, the decision, and the remedies proffered in *Brown* constructed equal education as the opportunity to be educated among Whites. Encoded, then, in the ideology of literacy that *Brown* presented was a privileging of White identity. This privileging remained consistent throughout *Washington* and *Bakke*. Examination of the records of these cases, the justices' decision, the counsels' arguments, and the expert witnesses' testimony demonstrates that the definition of literacy as White property that had preceded *Brown* survived in it, and subsequently survived through *Bakke*. These cases were unable to condemn fully the caste system of segregation and unable to remedy sufficiently inequities in educational resources. Instead, they continued rather than reversed the equation between Whiteness and literacy that had occurred for centuries by reinforcing the cultural belief in literacy as White property.

How these cases racialized notions of literacy is significant in understanding a period of struggle to improve the material conditions of the lives of African Americans. The *Brown* decision represents a moment when the NAACP's legal defense team, hemmed in by White supremacy, had little choice but to use the master's tools — bigotry — to attack the master's house — legalized segregation (Tushnet, 1994). A historically sensitive analysis of *Brown* reveals the constraints under which Marshall and his team of NAACP lawyers labored, and the ability of White supremacists to thwart even the most pressing moral imperative — to remove legalized segregation, the country's most visible symbol of White supremacy. Although problematic, the ideology of literacy advanced in and emerging from *Brown* played a great role in generating energy for all kinds of demands that eventually had little to do with literacy. It has not, however, assured equality of education, as Carter (1980), one of the chief architects of the NAACP's strategy in *Brown*, has noted. The absence of equality in education after *Brown* has prompted investigation into the cultural climate surrounding the decision. Bell (1980) argues, for example, that the Court's desire to placate Whites ultimately took precedence in the decision over the well-being of African American school-children. Dudziak (1988/1995) suggests that from the beginning the Court and the nation sought to eliminate only those signs of oppression that were causing the nation economic and political harm. She argues that segregation was a weakness the United States could ill afford during its Cold War efforts to expand its influence internationally in countries where people of color were in the majority. The mixture of interests and motives leading up to *Brown* suggests that a lukewarm attack on segregation might have been all the country and the Court were willing to embrace at that time.

By the late 1970s the Court's commitment to racial justice had cooled even further. While Justice Marshall was disturbed by the slow progress of actual change and the laissez-faire attitude of his colleagues, the oral arguments of the *Washington* and *Bakke* cases suggest that many of the justices were disturbed by the demands for actual change generated by the civil rights movement. The rhetoric of "literacy crisis" served to slow the progress of the civil rights movement even further as the discussion about improving the conditions of African American lives was displaced by laments over declining literacy standards. Review of the arguments in all three cases reveals that the public education that had been the gold standard of literacy as equal opportunity in *Brown* was denigrated in *Washington* and *Bakke*. I argue that this denigration occurred because people of color were perceived to have unrestricted access to public education. In the economy of literacy as White property, once previously segregated racialized groups were granted relief in one literacy environment, that environment was denigrated to lower its value (see Lamos, 2000).

To show this gradual denigration, I begin with a discussion of the faith in public education that the *Brown* decision reflected — a faith based in the notion that those public schools would remain mostly White. In the oral argument of *Washington,* justices no longer had that faith and would question the value of a public high school education for professional advancement or even minimal literacy attainment. The following year, the *Bakke* decision would reveal a further rejection of public education in a more subtle form, as the most influential opinion in that case — that of Justice Powell — would employ Harvard's admissions policy to deligitimize and in fact render unconstitutional the University of California at Davis affirmative action admissions policy. In examining these cases, I look not only at the legal precedents that might inform any given decision, but also at the historical contexts surrounding the decisions, the biographies of the justices, and the cultural biases that seem to inform their approach to literacy. As such, my analysis joins other recent work questioning the neutrality of the justice system and the objectivity of the justices who embody the law (see Amsterdam & Bruner, 2000).

Brown: Equal Education in an Unequal Society

Mark V. Tushnet, who clerked for Thurgood Marshall in the 1970s, observed that Marshall's stories describing successful civil rights litigation embodied the Trickster figure of African American oral tradition, illustrating how to use a racist system against itself. According to Tushnet, Marshall told a story about Whites who got a court injunction against the local African American church forbidding the church to use property that had been donated to it for a cemetery. The church was allowed to keep the land, however, and eventually a developer offered to buy it:

> "After some brief negotiations, the church agreed to sell the land at a price that not only would allow it to purchase land for a cemetery anywhere in the city, but also would pay off the mortgage, repair the building, and generally do just about anything else it wanted." Marshall would conclude this story with its moral "Thank God for prejudice." (Tushnet, 1994, p. 4)

Tushnet uses this anecdote to explain that the original strategy of civil rights litigation to desegregate schools was to "work within a racist system to combat racism" (p. 3). The fight to end segregation, he points out, began by relying indirectly on *Plessy v. Ferguson* and its establishment of "separate but equal," not by disputing it. Tushnet's analysis suggests the degree to which the NAACP's lawyers depended on the available strategies within a racist system to arrive at *Brown*, a watershed moment of the civil rights struggle in the courts.

Brown v. Board of Education refers to the four school segregation cases from Delaware, Kansas, South Carolina, and Virginia that the Supreme Court considered as a body. Two decisions, customarily known as *Brown I* and *Brown II*, were handed down by the Court. *Brown I* refers to the May 17, 1954, decision in which segregated schools were found to be unconstitutional. On May 31, 1955, *Brown II* ordered the dismantling of segregated education "with all deliberate speed." By condemning segregation, the first decision rendered a critical moral statement, although, as I will show, it did so in terms that would prove problematic. The second decision, many have argued, fell just short of retracting the previous condemnation of segregation, and certainly sapped the decision of a good deal of practical effectiveness (Lawrence, 1980; Patterson, 2001). To understand why *Brown* turned out as it did, it is necessary to examine the strategies for implementing school desegregation leading up to *Brown* that suggest the climate of racial assumptions in which the NAACP's lawyers were forced to negotiate.

In the late 1920s and early 1930s, the NAACP legal team's strategy was to bring about the end of segregation by default. They argued for equities in funding, physical structures, and faculty between African American and White schools, which they felt could not possibly be satisfied. This attack on inequities in educational funding did not include a direct attack on segregation as unconstitutional because it was feared that a direct push at overturning segregation's legal support, *Plessy*, might result in the decision being upheld. Instead, their arguments alleged violation of civil rights by showing gross disparities in educational resources available to African Americans and Whites, indirectly relying on *Plessy*'s separate but equal clause — though they never directly called on *Plessy* for support (Tushnet, 1994). Graduate and professional schools became obvious targets for this strategy because almost none of these schools in the southern states served African Americans. Over time, cases evolved from arguing the inadequacies of physical facilities and faculty to arguing the inadequacies of intangible attributes of the curriculum. The NAACP argued, for example, that the ability to associate in extra-curricular activities and engage in social networks comprised a professional education as much as the official curriculum (Patterson, 2001). Once education could be articulated as a matter of both tangible and intangible factors, including unrestricted social interaction, it only remained to argue that the act of segregation itself was the source of harm (Whitman, 1993).

By the 1950s, the national climate had changed significantly enough to make overturning *Plessy* less the impossible goal it had seemed in the 1930s. As the United States sought to expand its influence internationally at the beginning of the Cold War, it faced scrutiny for its hypocrisies at home. Newspapers in Asia and Africa carried stories condemning segregation as a failure of the United States to support democracy on its own soil (Dudziak, 1988/1995). African American veterans of World War II were less patient with the second-class citizenship that the country they had risked their lives defending was offering them. Meanwhile, businesses and industries within the United States were finding the cost of maintaining segregated facilities or hiring only White workers in southern cities increasingly burdensome. Thurgood Marshall and others began to see that an attack on segregated education at all levels, and even a challenge to segregation itself as unconstitutional, might have greater support. By 1950, Marshall had begun to make it clear to those who sought improvement in segregated facilities that the NAACP would not involve itself in pursuing cases along those lines. He began the push to overturn *Plessy*, sculpting with Robert Carter a controversial approach based on proving that segregated schools caused Black children psychological harm (Tushnet, 1994).

The most compelling arguments supporting this approach were those presented by psychiatrists, including Kenneth Clark of the City College of New York. His now famous research measured the effects of segregation on children's psychological health by asking African American children in segregated and nonsegregated schools questions about their feelings toward Black and White dolls (Clark, 1950). Using Clark's findings, the NAACP advanced the argument that no segregated school could ever be considered equal because segregation itself fosters feelings of inferiority that impede learning. This argument was the most influential expert evidence supporting the condemnation of separate but equal education in *Brown I*. Although the argument was controversial at the time both in and outside of the NACCP, it might have been attractive to a Supreme Court looking not to offend Whites. The argument of psychological harm, as construed in *Brown I*, provided the grounds for overturning separate but equal without challenging White supremacy. In fact, the argument relied on White supremacy as its foundation. The testimony of David Krech, a professor of psychology at the University of California and an expert witness for the plaintiffs in the South Carolina case, affirms White supremacy even as it decries segregation by citing the "inadequate education we build into the Negro" as the reason for White superiority:

> I would say that most White people have cause to be prejudiced against the Negro, because the Negro in most cases is indeed inferior to the White man, because the White man has made him [that] through the practice of legal segregation. . . . As a consequence of inadequate education we build into the Negro the very characteristic, not only intellectual, but also personality characteristics, which we then use to justify prejudice. (Whitman, 1993, p. 64)

Krech's excuse for White prejudice is an example of using bigotry to fight bigotry. The pathologizing of African American children represented by the testimony of Krech and others proved to be an intractable part of understanding the harm of segregation. In their decision, the Court quoted the following language from the district court decision of the Kansas case (*Brown*, 1951), which alleges even cognitive deficiency in African American children as a result of segregation:

> Segregation of White and colored children in public schools has a detrimental effect upon the colored children. The impact is greater when it has the sanction of the law; for the policy of separating the races is usually interpreted as denoting the inferiority of the Negro group. A sense of inferiority affects the motivation of the child to learn. Segregation with the sanction of law, therefore has a tendency to [retard] the educational and mental development of the Negro children and to deprive them of some of the benefits they would receive in a racial[ly] integrated school system. (*Brown*, 1954, p. 494)[1]

According to critical race theorists, many of the problems with the *Brown* decision are rooted in the Court's problematic normalizing of a segregated society (Lawrence, 1980). Lawrence (1980) argues that the Court's reasoning was flawed because it failed to acknowledge that the only purpose of segregation was to denote White superiority. With a sideways acknowledgement of the harm of segregation, the *Brown I* decision overturned *Plessy* while at the same time leaving the property value of Whiteness that *Plessy* established intact (Bell, 1987; Harris, 1993).

The assumption of Whiteness as property informed the educational expert's testimony for the NAACP's legal defense in the *Brown* trial. Picking up on the arguments over equity in intangible elements of the curriculum, which had succeeded in the graduate and professional school cases, Hugh Speer, professor of education at the University of Kansas City, argued that African American children were harmed by being denied the opportunity to associate with White people — a vital part of the curriculum in what he termed our multicultural society:

> The more heterogeneous the group in which the children participate, the better [they] can function in our multi-cultural and multi-group society. For example, if the colored children are denied the experience in school of associating with White children, who represent 90% of our national society in which these colored children must live, then the colored child's curriculum is being greatly curtailed. (Whitman, 1993, p. 71)

Speer's argument assumed that students of color would remain a minority in a society overwhelmingly dominated by Whites. The argument neglected the various legal and cultural machinations that operate to maintain that ratio (see López, 1996). Additionally, it assumed that participation in a heterogeneous group necessarily meant better functioning in a heterogeneous society. Yet at the time Speer made his remarks, there was no indication that an end to segregation in educational settings would mean an end to segregation in all areas. In order to be credible, Speer's argument had to sidestep the actual nature of the national society in which this education takes place, including the limitations placed on heterogeneity by Jim Crow laws and northern residential segregation. Similarly, in order to be accepted, the NAACP had to limit its attack on racism to educational segregation in the South (Carter, 1980). Regardless of the assumptions underlying Speer's argument, accepting it means believing that a setting devoid of White children becomes by default an educationally poorer setting, a reasoning that confirms the property value of being White.

If, despite its shortcomings, the Court's decision in *Brown I* impressed the country as a firm condemnation of segregation, the effect of that condemnation was quickly muted by *Brown II*. Threats of a radical and even violent reaction to desegregation hung over the entire proceedings of *Brown I*, from considering the verdict to devising the remedy. In 1951, for example, former Supreme Court Justice James Byrnes became governor of South Carolina and announced that his state would abolish public schooling before it would desegregate (Patterson, 2001; Tushnet, 1994). Muse (1964) records that, in contrast, the initial southern reaction to *Brown II* was relief — a feeling that the Court had come to its senses. The qualification of "with all deliberate speed," as well as lack of clarity as to whether *Brown I* outlawed segregation or merely race-based school assignment, led to the virtual unenforceability of the desegregation mandate in the face of resistance. Considering the Court's failure to act decisively, Lawrence (1980) suggests that after *Brown II,* de jure, or legal, segregation has remained as what is popularly imagined as de facto, or actual, segregation, which has been sanctioned by law as neglect.

Bell (1987) argues that the racial-balance remedy proposed by *Brown II* inevitably failed African American schoolchildren because it failed to improve education, and, as a former attorney for the NAACP, he regrets that the pursuit of equality of resources was so readily abandoned by the legal defense team. He writes: "The racial-balance goal can be met only in schools where Whites are in the majority and retain control. The quality of schooling Black children receive is determined by what Whites (they of the group who caused the harm in the first place) are willing to provide — which, as we should not be surprised to learn, is not very much" (p. 116). Faced with the loss of control over the schools, many in the African American community wondered about the wisdom of the approach taken in the *Brown* case. There were petitions to maintain all–African American schools, a move the integrationists saw as a betrayal (Bell, 1980). Many African American teachers in Topeka, Kansas, opposed the *Brown* suit from the very beginning, fearing that they would be replaced by White teachers in integrated schools (Whitman, 1993). Their fears turned out to be well founded. In the first eleven years after desegregation, over thirty thousand African American teachers were dismissed; many of those who weren't dismissed were relocated to desegregated schools where they were marginalized and poorly treated (Foster, 1997). Black principals and administrators were demoted as well (Bell, 1987).

Lawrence (1980) suggests that, while *Brown* effectively spawned the civil rights movement, it also determined in many ways the terms and scope of that movement, which eventually failed to engage the reality of racism directly. The decision in *Brown* and the remedy of desegregation changed the way in which racism was expressed and discussed in the United States. However, ending legalized segregation and ending discrimination would prove to be two different challenges. Bell (1992a) describes the situation faced by people of color:

> Racial bias in the pre-*Brown* era was stark, open, unalloyed with hypocrisy and blank-faced lies. . . . Today, because bias is masked in unofficial practices and "neutral" standards, we must wrestle with the question whether race or some individual failing has cost us the job, denied us the promotion, or prompted our being rejected as tenants for an apartment. (p. 6)

According to many critical race theorists, the decision in *Brown* actually made fighting these forms of discrimination a more difficult task (Freeman, 1980, 1995; Lawrence, 1980). First, it problematically defined discrimination narrowly as segregation (Lawrence, 1980). Second, by establishing educational opportunity as an end in itself, rather than concerning itself with equality of result, it gave no provisions for improving the conditions of schools that were underfunded and made efforts to remedy educational inequity difficult to pursue in any terms other than racial balancing. Lastly, as Freeman (1980, 1995) observes, *Brown* laid the groundwork for subsequent challenges to antidiscrimination legislation by bolstering many doctrinal abstractions — chiefly equal opportunity, legal neutrality, and color-blindness. These abstractions serve to dehistoricize the concept of racial discrimination. Freeman (1995) argues that the failure to consider discrimination in the history of race relations in the United States opened the door for later reversals of the gains of the civil rights movement. In short, the ideologies of literacy supporting the *Brown* decision may have propelled the Court to condemn segregation, but the goal of ensuring equality of education remained elusive and the true character of racial discrimination remained unrecognized.

Washington: Invoking the "Literacy Crisis"

Washington v. Davis (1976) is generally acknowledged as one of those later reversals of the gains of the civil rights movement. The case dealt a near fatal blow to antidiscrimination legislation by narrowly defining racism as necessarily intentional, effectively invalidating the notion of unequal outcomes as racism. Although an employment discrimination case, questions of reading and writing ability were debated at great length to determine the validity of a charge of racial bias in literacy testing. The Court called into question whether a high school education was sufficient to prepare people for professional training. In this case, applicants who were denied admittance to the District of Columbia's Metropolitan Police Department alleged that Test 21, a written test that African American applicants failed at twice the rate of White applicants, discriminated against African Americans. The city argued that verbal ability was needed to enforce the law and that Test 21 was predictive of performance on the Recruit School training test taken during the training period. The Court sided with the city by ruling that Test 21 "serves the neutral and legitimate purpose of requiring all applicants to meet a uniform minimum standard of literacy" (*Washington*, 1976, p. 255). However, as Justice Brennan, joined by Justice Marshall, noted in his dissent, the Court never examined the training test to determine how it might be related to job performance. The city's argument that Test 21 was predictive of success on the training test was unsupported by proof of any correlation between Test 21 and "performance of the job of being a police officer" (*Washington*, 1976,

p. 267). Justice Brennan argued that the burden of proof should not fall on those attempting to prove discrimination, but on the city to establish the usefulness of the test.

Justice Brennan's dissension, while too strict in its interpretive framework to challenge directly the notion that literacy can be characterized as a uniform minimum standard, does call into question the notion of transferability of literacy skills from one task to another that undergirds the decision of the majority. Since then, literacy scholars have conducted research that has challenged this notion more directly. Ethnographic investigations, including Scribner and Cole's (1981/1988) study of the Vai people of Liberia, Heath's (1983) study of working-class communities in the Carolina Piedmont, and Street's (1984) study of literacy practices in Iran, revealed the multifaceted nature of literacy in practice. These studies all concluded that the abilities to read, write, and memorize are highly contextual and task dependent with limited transferability to new contexts and tasks, and hence it is not possible to speak of a single, normative literacy. Historical studies of literacy by Cook-Gumperz (1986) and Graff (1979, 1995) challenged the notion of literacy as an abstract and neutral set of skills consistent over time and place. As a field, literacy scholars have come to a near consensus that acultural conceptions of literacy, such as those that the city argued in *Washington* and that were accepted by the Supreme Court, are flawed. Of course, these ethnographic and historic literacy studies were not available at the time the Court was deliberating. However, other expert conceptions of literacy as context dependent were available — for example, studies that measured the construct validity of the entrance test to the need of the job — and their relevance was debated in the case.

Listening to the oral arguments it becomes clear that members of the Court were concerned that "expert" testimony might replace the "commonsense" notion that police officers need to have reading and writing skills.[2] The counsel for the city, David Sutton, appealed to these commonsense notions of literacy in arguing that verbal ability was necessary to learn basic tools of the police trade. He argued that police work takes place in an evolving legal context that requires basic understanding of the components of criminal offenses, the laws of arrest, search and seizure, and elements of report writing. He referred to Test 21, a general test given to many civil servants — not just police officers — as "a straightforward test of verbal ability" (*Complete Oral Arguments*, 1980, p. 8). Justice Stevens asked repeatedly if any of the counsels were contending that verbal ability was not necessary for the job of being a police officer (p. 32).[3]

Counsel for the respondents in this case, Richard Sobol, argued in return that the city had not met its burden under the Equal Protection Clause of the Fourteenth Amendment to the Constitution to establish proof that Test 21 was not an excessive test of verbal ability. He offered the *Washington Post* crossword puzzle as an example of a test of verbal ability and asked whether it was an appropriate test of verbal ability for this situation. He further asked why the requirement of a high school diploma, which all applicants had to meet in order to fill out an application, was not considered enough evidence of verbal ability. In order to prove appropriateness, he maintained, a "construct validation" study, as he termed it — that is, a study measuring a trait (in this case, verbal ability) against an analysis of the actual tasks of the job — needed to be conducted (*Complete Oral Arguments*, 1980, p. 58). Although such a test was routine in employment discrimination cases, it was not conducted in this case, nor were any experts brought in to testify to the complexity of reading and writing tasks on the job.

Even though Sobol argued that expert notions might have revealed literacy to be context dependent, he appeared unable to treat literacy contextually. Instead, both the attorneys and the justices often discussed literacy in quantitative rather than qualitative terms. Sobol focused on "how much" rather than "what kind" of verbal ability was deemed necessary for the job of being a police officer. The conception of literacy as a quantifiable skill in the *Washington* case was in many ways what allowed literacy to be positioned as endangered by antidiscrimination legislation. Sutton, counsel for the petitioner, played on fears of declining literacy standards. In response, Sobol argued that forcing employers to meet the burden of proof for their literacy requirements did not involve lowering standards if discriminatory effects were in evidence. He protested Sutton's approach: "There is an underlying current in the briefs in this case that there is something about the *Griggs*[4] test which requires putting incompetents in jobs" (*Complete Oral Arguments*, 1980, p. 60). However, in his rebuttal, Sutton strengthened the rhetoric of declining standards by charging that Sobol would have the department "tap the ocean's depths" (p. 82) to determine the lowest workable cutoff score for the test. One justice remarked that "the problem is we live in an age if one can believe what he hears and reads, that many high school graduates don't have high school educations" (p. 83). Another justice offered that Test 21 could be seen as a necessary measure to sort out the part of the high school crop without a high school education. These comments echoed an earlier remark by Justice Rehnquist, who offered that "Test 21 obviously adds something since many high school diplomates failed it" (p. 63). This remark reinforced the necessity of the test and the inadequacy of a high school education, as well as the notion that literacy skills could be measured in terms of an amount.

After lamenting the precipitous decline in educational standards, Sutton, speaking directly to Justice Marshall, argued for the Metropolitan Police Department's record of equal opportunity employment, pointing out that the African American population of the Metropolitan Police Department had spiraled to 41 percent. Justice Marshall responded, comparing the current state of the department now to its state in 1866: "I don't get anything out of how much it's grown. The question is, is it constitutional now?" (*Complete*

Oral Arguments, 1980, p. 84). Sutton maintained that the test had no adverse impact and that the Metropolitan Police Department had complied with the Civil Rights Act. He repeatedly argued that the police department could do no more than they had already done to increase African American presence on the force, and therefore no redress of potential racial imbalance should be imposed and no back pay could be demanded. At this point, Sutton invoked the various remedies demanded since the Civil Rights Act to remedy discrimination, and on that note the case was closed.

Following the rhetoric of declining standards with the discussion of remedy was significant. In *Washington,* a high school diploma had ceased to be sufficient for professional advancement in the minds of many of the justices, and it had ceased to be the bearer of equal opportunity that it was thought to be when the Court decided *Brown.* Here, knowledge and literacy were separated from the act of getting a public education, whereas in *Brown* these had all been conflated. In *Washington,* the arguments did not center on the relevance of public education but rather on its irrelevance. Ironically, once African Americans were nominally granted remedy in the form of admittance to formerly all-White schools in *Brown,* the value of that education diminished in the eyes of the members of the Court. This ideological shift in the value of public education only mirrored the physical shifting of the populations in the schools, as "White flight" had become a feature of the post-*Brown* era.[5]

The racializing of education that was reinforced through demographic shifts and court decisions is significant for thinking about a cultural view of literacy. In analyzing the *Washington* case, Lawrence (1987) focuses not on literacy primarily but on the acultural conception of racism in the case. Nevertheless, his conclusions inevitably lead him to discuss literacy. He suggests that, had racism been understood as a systemic and pervasive feature in U.S. culture, rather than as an aberrant act of intention, the outcome of the decision might have been different. The Court might have considered that the test did not measure features of communication at which African American applicants might excel. For example, African American police might be better skilled at communicating in their own neighborhoods where White police are seen as an invading military presence. Lawrence argues that, by failing to account for the socially pervasive influence of racism, the decision reinforced the cultural myth that Whites are more intelligent than African Americans. He points out that the more the test can be seen as neutral, the more the lower performance of African Americans becomes a confirmation of this myth.

Lawrence (1987) further discusses the significance of the case being about the job of a police officer. Police officers are representatives of state authority, and in a systemically racist country, authority is vested in White people. Whites, from employees of the civil service commission to Supreme Court justices, he suggests, were uncomfortable and unaccustomed to seeing African Americans in positions of authority. It became necessary, then, to rationalize, however unconsciously, a way to legitimize an overwhelming White presence in positions of authority.

Conceptions of literacy as White property, I argue, were put in service of this rationalization. The problem with the decision in *Washington* was not simply that it held up literacy to be abstract and neutral rather than socially situated, but that it did not take into account the economics of literacy as White property as part of the social situation. Test 21 failed in numerous ways. It failed to provide equal opportunity by not measuring people with culturally appropriate standards; in other words, it failed to test communicative skills that African Americans might have that Whites did not. Additionally, Test 21 failed to take into account the historically unequal education African Americans and Whites received prior to the test. Test 21 served to confirm the equation of literacy and Whiteness already established and entrenched in the minds of the White majority to rationalize the exclusion of African Americans from authority positions.

Lawrence's explanation of the justices' decision becomes even more plausible because, not only were the justices presented with no evidence establishing Test 21's relationship to job performance, they were presented with evidence from a study appendixed to the brief filed for the petitioner that there was little to no relationship. Passing Test 21 had a "positive but low relationship to job performances" for White officers, but for African American officers "Test 21 . . . does not predict differences in on-the-job performance" (Brief for Petitioner, 1975, p. 99). This study, conducted by the Standards Division of the U.S. Civil Service Commission, correlated job performance ratings with performance on Test 21 and the Recruit School's training test.[6] The city was forced to argue that Test 21 was predictive of success on the training test because that was all the test could predict. Therefore, as Justice Brennan noted in his dissent, the argument that Test 21 was predictive of success on the training test was irrelevant because all officers were tutored until they passed the training test. In the particular cultural context in which it appeared, Test 21 actually had no purpose except as a replacement of legalized segregation.

In terms of the civil rights movement, the result of the *Washington v. Davis* decision was disastrous, coming at the moment when it was most crucial to recognize the systemic nature of racism in keeping people of color as members of a perpetual underclass. The Court reinforced the notion of racial discrimination as the discrete "faults" of "atomistic individuals whose actions are outside of and apart from the social fabric without historical continuity" (Freeman, 1995, p. 30). This conception of racism is the one that Freeman (1995) identifies as most hampering antidiscrimination efforts. I would argue that it has similarly hampered efforts to provide equality of education as a remedy for historic discrimination. In the oral argument to the *Washington* case, Justice Marshall attempted to revive the goal of providing equal education by asking Sutton, "Suppose the high schools of this area are very low.

Would anything be done about that?" (*Complete Oral Arguments*, 1980, p. 83) Sutton dodged the implication of societal responsibility to provide decent education to all citizens, arguing that it had no relationship to the right of a community to a "competent police force" (p. 84). The issue of providing equality of education was not pursued, as the discussion in the end was dominated by Sutton's contention that no discrimination existed that needed to be addressed. The notion that it was the responsibility of the state to provide equality of education was further eroded in the case the Supreme Court heard a year after *Washington, Regents of the University of California v. Bakke.*

Bakke: *"Well, I come from Harvard ..."*

Alan Bakke, a White applicant to the University of California at Davis Medical School who had been rejected twice, charged that a special admissions program with sixteen seats set aside for minority students instituted by faculty to improve minority recruitment was discriminatory. The *Bakke* case generated intense public interest, with more than 130 organizations filing *amicus* briefs (Gormley, 1997).[7] *Bakke* differed significantly from *Brown* and *Washington* in that the interests of groups of color were not represented in the case itself, even though the outcome stood to affect greatly the fate of admissions programs geared at redressing past discrimination. Recognizing the potential significance of the case, several groups of color petitioned the Regents not to bring their appeal to the U.S. Supreme Court because the record had been so poorly prepared, as some of the justices for the Supreme Court noted in their internal memos (Ball, 2000). No attempt had been made to document the history of discrimination in California state schools, and no attempt had been made to challenge the criteria for admission — grades and the MCAT (Bell, 1992b). Additionally, UC Davis claimed that Bakke would have been admitted if he had not been White, even though the medical school had rejected other White applicants with higher scores (Selmi, 1999). This problematic claim placed the African American and Chicano/a students served by the special admissions programs in an unfavorable light. In a memo to Justice Marshall dated September 13, 1977, law clerk Ellen Silberman pointed out that the case was an "unfortunate one" on which to base the fate of affirmative action (Ball, 2000). If heard by the Supreme Court, Silberman observed, the case could end any legal attempts to pull people of color in general and African Americans in particular "out of the lowest occupations and into the mainstream of America" (Ball, 2000, p. 91).

The overall tone of Sutton's final words in *Washington*, which suggested that the civil rights movement had gone too far, characterized the discussion of discrimination and remedy of the oral arguments in *Bakke*. Here, the members of the Court took a more active role in invoking the "slippery slope" of a remedy's costs to Whites by asking how many Blacks in the medical school would be enough to ensure diversity. Justice Rehnquist asked,

"What if the UCD had decided that . . . they would set aside 50 seats, until that balance were redressed and the minority population of doctors equaled that of the population as a whole?" (Ball, 2000, p. 93). Justice Powell also asked whether the number of seats should be related to the population. At this, Regent's counsel, Archibald Cox, whose job it was to defend the special admissions program, balked, suggesting that,

> as the number gets higher, the finding of invidiousness increases and social purposes are diminished. . . . I think one of the things which causes all of us concern about these programs is the danger they will give rise to some notion of group entitlement to numbers, regardless either of the ability of the individual or of their potential contribution in society. (Ball, 2000, p. 93)

In using the term *invidiousness*, Cox made reference to the new understanding of racism forged in the *Washington v. Davis* decision, which determined that "disproportionate impact is not irrelevant, but it is not the sole touchstone of invidious discrimination" (*Washington*, 1976, p. 242). After Justice Stevens pressed the issue, Cox later defined invidious discrimination as "classifying a person as inferior" (Ball, 2000, p. 94). However, Cox was unable to explain what test would differentiate the case of fifty set-aside seats from the case of sixteen, given that the motivation was the same. Cox's argument suggests that the mere presence of more people of color in the educational environment is cause not only to question their qualifications and their utility to society, but also to investigate whether Whites had been stigmatized or classified as inferior in an effort to meet that goal. His argument also creates a damning equation where the greater the quotient of racialized others, the greater burden those individuals have to produce evidence of their literacy and social usefulness. Certainly such sentiments poorly represent the cause of racial justice if redressing racism in the social fabric of the nation is to be taken seriously.

Derrick Bell, in analyzing *Bakke*, suggested that the poor arguing of the issues in the case meant that they were "treated more like a law school exam or an exercise in moral philosophy than a matter of paramount importance to Black citizens still striving for real citizenship in all these years" (1992b, p. 651). Yet I believe that the manner in which the case was argued illustrates that the matters involved, far from being trivial, were of paramount importance to Whites as well, in terms of maintaining the investment in literacy as White property in the face of perceived threat. At stake in the case, even if not directly challenged, were the standards used to judge literacy attainment as racially and culturally neutral — standards whose arbitrary nature had not been examined even in the face of a racially disparate impact.[8] The chairman of the admissions committee testified that everyone admitted to Davis' medical school, regardless of whether they were admitted under the special admissions program with lower cutoff scores or the regular admissions program, was qualified. The performance of students of color at the medical school was shown to be satisfactory or better than White students, suggesting that admission test scores do not accurately predict performance.

Bell (1992b) suggests that if groups of color had been represented in the case, the neutrality of literacy standards would certainly have been called into question. From the standpoint of people of color, generating information on discrimination in California schools or questioning the neutrality of the scores would have been crucial. He argues that the people who were arguing both sides of this case had benefited from those standards and had everything to lose by questioning their legitimacy and neutrality. Rather than question the legitimacy of standards, Cox and some members of the Supreme Court took advantage of their shared connections to elite literacy institutions to identify those institutions as maintaining the standards under threat. They were invested in doing so because their reputations were in part tied to the reputation of Harvard University — the literacy institution to which they were affiliated or from which they had received degrees.

These investments in the standards of their own literacy institutions were evident in seemingly incidental aspects of the oral argument and the decision. For example, Justice Blackmun asked Cox whether the special admissions policy might be viewed in the same way as an athletic scholarship, since attracting students demonstrating athletic prowess is the aim of most institutions. Cox responded with a chuckle, "Well, I come from Harvard, sir. I don't know whether it's our aim, but we don't do very well." General laughter enveloped the courtroom. Justice Blackmun remarked, "I can remember the time when you did" (Kurland & Casper, 1978, p. 628).[9] Dreyfuss and Lawrence (1979) remark that this exchange restored "the special kinship of those on the bench and the attorney for the university in this lament for Harvard football and their common interest in preserving the quality of higher education. One exception to the laughter was Justice Thurgood Marshall" (p. 184).

In his biography of Cox, Gormley (1997) writes that the purpose of this joke was strategic. Cox had planned to liken the special admissions program to athletic scholarships, but the regents of the University of California had asked him not to because they felt such a comparison would trivialize special admissions. Gormley maintains that Cox used the joke to get the Court off the topic, and in that way it worked. But the fact that the joke worked is nonetheless significant in understanding how investments in literacy institutions played a role in the argument and decision of the case. Cox, as an alum and one of the most prominent members of the Harvard Law School faculty, embodied Harvard as an institution and was in a position to invoke its literacy value. Since one-third of the Court had received degrees from Harvard and thus shared an investment in the institution, it is not surprising that the joke worked. Although the motive of Cox's comment may have been to put himself in a position to argue the case the way the regents wanted, the effect was a subtle elevation of Harvard. In having failed to ensure athletic success, Harvard could be seen as having literacy standards unclouded by other criteria.

Harvard's appearance in the case was ultimately more than incidental. Harvard College's admissions program was in the appendix to the opinion of Justice Powell in the decision. Powell, another Harvard Law School alum, found Harvard's undergraduate admissions policy, in which race is taken into account along with other criteria, laudable even though he found Davis' special admissions program of set-asides unsupportable. Justices Brennan, White, Marshall, and Blackmun pointed out in their dissenting opinion that there was no distinction between Davis' and Harvard's programs in constitutional terms. However, a distinction existed for the counsel and for some of the justices based on the recognition of Harvard as the pinnacle of literacy attainment. Most problematic, Harvard moved from being the bearer of standards to being the determiner of constitutionality. Introducing Harvard as a model is significant because it shows that Harvard's admissions policies trumped the formulations of the writers of the Fourteenth Amendment and the convention of legal precedent. In *Bakke*, Harvard, and not the Constitution, was invoked to legitimate affirmative action, with the result that the notion of "quota" became anathema to the considerations of racial justice remedy, and Alan Bakke was admitted to the UC Davis Medical School.[10]

Several opinions were written for *Bakke*, but Justice Powell's opinion, trumpeting Harvard's admissions policy, was to become effectively the law of the land for universities looking to avoid a challenge to their affirmative action programs. However, challenges to affirmative action were not put to rest by *Bakke*. As a result of *Bakke's* formulations, which deny remedy where clear past discrimination by particular institutions on particular people of color cannot be proven, or where particular Whites not related to the discriminatory policies might be harmed, *Bakke* left affirmative action vulnerable (Bell, 1992b). Justice Marshall attempted during the oral argument to redirect the discussion away from the focus on harm to Whites toward a discussion of the lives of the people affirmative action was intended to benefit. During an exchange with Colvin, the counsel for Alan Bakke, on the issue of the constitutionality of "set-aside seats" as a remedy for historic discrimination, Justice Marshall charged, "You are talking about your client's rights. Don't these underprivileged people have some rights?" (Ball, 2000, p. 97).

Justice Marshall wrote his own opinion to *Bakke*, in which he asserted the continuing effects of racism in the social fabric of the nation and suggested the importance of literacy institutions in placing individuals in influential and prosperous positions:

> It is because of a legacy of unequal treatment that we now must permit the institutions of this society to give consideration to race in making decisions about who will hold the positions of influence, affluence, and prestige in America. . . . I do not believe that anyone can truly look into America's past and still find that a remedy for that past is impermissible. (*Bakke*, 1978, p. 402)

Meanwhile, the director of admissions at Harvard Law School and the dean of admissions at Harvard College reacted to the announcement of the *Bakke* decision by denying that they gave minority students any preference in the admissions process (Nadel, 1978). The *Harvard Law Record* reported that, while Cox had advanced "the Davis position favoring quotas in his Supreme Court brief and oral argument, he would vote against quotas at Harvard" (Nadel, 1978, p. 4).

The Economy of Literacy as White Property

Bakke and *Washington*, both products of the late 1970s, were decided in a vastly different national climate than the one that surrounded *Brown*. By the 1970s, opposition to busing was intense. Public support for many civil rights measures had eroded and the Supreme Court itself was more conservative. Residential segregation had increased in many areas. In its most literal sense, the property value of White identity is revealed in a story told by critical race theorist Patricia Williams (1997) about her attempts to buy a house in a virtually all-White neighborhood. Her financial matters were conducted over the phone because the house was in another state. Her loan was approved immediately, but when she received the paperwork from the bank, she noticed that the loan officer had checked off that she was "White" on the Fair Housing form. She amended the form, checking off "Black," and returned it to the bank:

> Suddenly the deal came to a screeching halt. The bank wanted more money as a down payment, they wanted me to pay more points, they wanted to raise the rate of interest. Suddenly I found myself facing great resistance and much more debt. (p. 40)

The reason the bank gave for wanting more money was that property values in the area had started to decline. Williams was puzzled, as prices there had remained stable since World War II. Finally, after a conversation with her real estate agent, she understood that *she* was the cause of falling prices, the start of the "tipping point" when Whites would begin to move out.

The *Washington* and *Bakke* cases reveal that literacy is governed by a similar economy. When African American applicants are admitted, whether to a high school or the police force or a medical school, literacy standards are perceived to be falling or in peril of falling. In many situations, when this perception of declining standards has occurred, Whites simply go elsewhere, to attend other schools or take other jobs. The case in *Bakke* is interesting because it is more difficult to go "up" from such a distinguished place as the UC Davis Medical School. By fleeing to Harvard as the model and bearer of literacy standards, Justice Powell enacted a kind of White flight, away from the public toward the private sphere. The public education that had meant so much to the Supreme Court justices of the *Brown* decision as a means to equal opportunity is case by case denigrated until it is almost as devalued as the active pursuit of racial justice. Once remedy is granted in one literacy environment, that literacy environment is denigrated to devalue its worth. This is the economy of literacy as White property, an economy that served the White majority in the Supreme Court in its efforts to bring the course of racial justice to a halt.

Notes

1. Brackets reflect the Supreme Court justices' amendments to the language of the district court judge in *Brown* (1951).
2. Recordings of the oral argument were accessed online (Goldman, 2002).
3. Although transcripts of Supreme Court oral arguments do not reveal which justice is speaking, Justice Stevens is clearly identified in the context of the discussion as having asked this question.
4. The decision in the *Griggs* case established that employers must show that a standard for employment is necessary if it results in a racially disparate impact, hence the *Griggs* test (see *Griggs*, 1971).
5. According to Douglas (1995), the flight of White students from public schools in the South, where desegregation actually was enforced, was massive: "The average southern school system under a court-imposed desegregation order lost 38 percent of its White population between 1970–1984" (p. 246).
6. Applicants to the Recruit School must pass Test 21 in order to be admitted. Students at the Recruit School take the Recruit School training test during their training.
7. *Amicus* briefs are submitted by nonparties who have an interest in the outcome of the case.
8. When the UC Davis Medical School opened its doors in 1968 with no special admissions policy, it admitted no Blacks or Chicanos (*Bakke*, 1978, p. 21).
9. While laughter is documented in this written transcript, see also audio of the oral argument in Goldman (1999). For identification of the speakers, see Dreyfuss and Lawrence (1979, p. 184).
10. The decision in *Bakke* reads, "Held: The judgment below is affirmed insofar as it orders respondent's admission to Davis and invalidates petitioner's special admissions program, but is reversed insofar as it prohibits petitioner from taking race into account as a factor in its future admissions decisions" (1978, p. 267).

References

Amsterdam, A., & Bruner, J. (2000). *Minding the law*. Cambridge, MA: Harvard University Press.

Anderson, J. D. (1988). *The education of Blacks in the South, 1860–1935*. Chapel Hill: University of North Carolina Press.

Ball, H. (2000). *The* Bakke *case: Race, education, and affirmative action*. Lawrence: University Press of Kansas.

Bell, D. (1980). *Brown* and the interest-convergence dilemma. In D. Bell (Ed.), *Shades of Brown: New perspectives on school desegregation* (pp. 90–107). New York: Teachers College Press.

Bell, D. (1987). *And we are not saved: The elusive quest for racial justice.* New York: Basic Books.

Bell, D. (1992a). *Faces at the bottom of the well.* New York: Basic Books.

Bell, D. (1992b). *Race, racism and American law* (3rd ed.). Boston: Little, Brown.

Brandt, D. (1999). Literacy and economic change. *Harvard Educational Review, 69,* 373–394.

Brief for Petitioner in Support of Certiorari, at 99, Washington v. Davis, 512 F.2d 956 (D.C. Cir. 1975), petition for cert. filed, 44 U.S.L.W. 3035 (U.S. May 28, 1975) (No. 74-1492), cert. granted, 423 U.S. 820 (1975).

Brown v. Board of Education of Topeka, Shawnee County, Kansas, 98 F. Supp. 797 (1951).

Brown v. Board of Education I, 347 U.S. 483 (1954).

Brown v. Board of Education II, 349 U.S. 294 (1955).

Carter, R. (1980). A reassessment of *Brown v. Board of Education.* In D. Bell (Ed.), *Shades of* Brown: *New perspectives on school desegregation* (pp. 21–28). New York: Teachers College Press.

Clark, K. B. (1950). *Effect of prejudice and discrimination on personality development.* Paper presented at the Midcentury White House Conference on Children and Youth, Washington, DC.

Complete oral arguments of the Supreme Court of the United States: A retrospective 1969 term through 1979 term. (1980). Frederick, MD: University Publications of America.

Cook-Gumperz, J. (Ed.). (1986). *The social construction of literacy.* New York: Cambridge University Press.

Cornelius, J. D. (1991). *"When I can read my title clear": Literacy, slavery, and religion in the antebellum South.* Columbia: University of South Carolina Press.

Crenshaw, K., Gotanda, N., Peller, G., & Thomas, K. (Eds.). (1995). *Critical race theory: The key writings that formed the movement.* New York: New Press.

Delgado, R. (Ed.). (1995). *Critical race theory: The cutting edge.* Philadelphia: Temple University Press.

Delpit, L. D. (1988). The silenced dialogue: Power and pedagogy in educating other people's children. *Harvard Educational Review, 58,* 280–298.

Dreyfuss, J., & Lawrence, C. (1979). *The Bakke case: The politics of inequality.* New York: Harcourt Brace Jovanovich.

Douglas, D. (1995). *Reading, writing, and race: The desegregation of the Charlotte schools.* Charlotte: University of North Carolina Press.

Dudziak, M. L. (1995). Desegregation as Cold War imperative. In R. Delgado (Ed.), *Critical race theory the cutting edge* (pp. 110–121). Philadelphia: Temple University Press. (Original work published 1988)

Fordham, S. (1988). Racelessness as a factor in Black students' school success: Pragmatic strategy or Pyrrhic victory? *Harvard Educational Review, 58,* 54–84.

Foster, M. (1997). *Black teachers on teaching.* New York: New Press.

Freeman, A. D. (1980). School desegregation law: Promise, contradiction, rationalization. In D. Bell (Ed.), *Shades of* Brown: *New perspectives on school desegregation* (pp. 70–89). New York: Teachers College Press.

Freeman, A. D. (1995). Legitimizing racial discrimination through antidiscrimination law: A critical review of Supreme Court doctrine. In K. Crenshaw, N. Gotanda, G. Peller, & K. Thomas (Eds.), *Critical race theory: The key writings that formed the movement* (pp. 29–46). New York: New Press.

Goldman, J. (Ed.). (1999). *The Supreme Court's greatest hits* [CD-ROM]. Evanston, IL: Northwestern University Press.

Goldman, J. (Ed.). (2002). *The OYEZ project* [On-line]. Available: http://oyez.nwu.edu/cases/cases.cgi?command=show&caseid=434

Gormley, K. (1997). *Archibald Cox: Conscience of a nation*. Reading, MA: Addison-Wesley.

Griggs v. Duke Power Co., 401 U.S. 424 (1971).

Graff, H. (1979). *The literacy myth: Literacy and social structure in the nineteenth-century city*. New York: Academic Press.

Graff, H. J. (1995). *The labyrinths of literacy: Reflections on literacy past and present*. Pittsburgh: University of Pittsburgh Press.

Harris, C. (1993). Whiteness as property. *Harvard Law Review, 106*, 1707–1791.

Heath, S. B. (1983). *Ways with words*. Cambridge, Eng.: Cambridge University Press.

Kozol, J. (1991). *Savage inequalities: Children in America's schools*. New York: Crown.

Kurland, P., & Casper, G. (Eds.). (1978). *Landmark briefs and arguments of the Supreme Court of the United States: Constitutional law* (1977 term supplement, vol. 100). Washington, DC: University Publications of America.

Ladson-Billings, G., & Tate, W. (1995). Toward a critical race theory of education. *Teachers College Record, 97*, 47–68.

Lamos, S. (2000). Basic writing, CUNY, and "mainstreaming": (De)racialization reconsidered. *Journal of Basic Writing, 19*(2), 22–43.

Lawrence, C. R. (1980). "One more river to cross"—Recognizing the real injury in *Brown*: A prerequisite to shaping new remedies. In D. Bell (Ed.), *Shades of Brown: New perspectives on school desegregation* (pp. 48–69). New York: Teachers College Press.

Lawrence, C. R. (1987). The id, the ego, and equal protection: Reckoning with unconscious racism. *Stanford Law Review, 39*, 317–388.

Lipsitz, G. (1998). *The possessive investment in Whiteness: How White people profit from identity politics*. Philadelphia: Temple University Press.

Lopéz, I. H. (1996). *White by law: The legal construction of race*. New York: New York University Press.

Lunsford, A., Moglen, H., & Slevin, J. (Eds.). (1990). *The right to literacy*. New York: Modern Language Association.

Muse, B. (1964). *Ten years of prelude: The story of integration since the Supreme Court's 1954 decision*. New York: Viking Press.

Nadel, M. (1978). Supreme Court raps gavel: *Bakke*. *Harvard Law Record, 65*(2), 4, 6.

Patterson, J. T. (2001). Brown v. Board of Education: *A civil rights milestone and its troubled legacy*. New York: Oxford University Press.

Plessy v. Ferguson, 163 U.S. 537 (1896).

Regents of the University of California v. Bakke, 438 U.S. 265 (1978).

Royster, J. J. (2000). *Traces of a stream: Literacy and social change among African American women*. Pittsburgh: University of Pittsburgh Press.

Scribner, S., & Cole, M. (1988). Unpackaging literacy. In E. Kintgen, B. Kroll, & M. Rose (Eds.), *Perspectives on literacy* (pp. 57–70). Carbondale: Southern Illinois University Press. (Original work published 1981)

Selmi, M. (1999). The life of *Bakke*: An affirmative action retrospective. *Georgetown Law Journal, 87*, 981–1022.

Street, B. (1984). *Literacy in theory and in practice*. Cambridge, Eng.: Cambridge University Press.

Tushnet, M. (1994). *Making civil rights law: Thurgood Marshall and the Supreme Court, 1936–1961*. New York: Oxford University Press.

Washington v. Davis, 426 U.S. 229 (1976).

Whitman, M. (1993). *Removing a badge of slavery: The record of* Brown v. Board of Education. New York: Markus Wiener.

Williams, P. (1991). *The alchemy of race and rights*. Cambridge, MA: Harvard University Press.

Williams, P. (1997). *Seeing a color-blind future: The paradox of race.* New York: Farrar, Straus & Giroux.

Willis, A. I. (1995). Reading the world of school literacy: Contextualizing the experience of a young African American male. *Harvard Educational Review, 65,* 30–49.

This article would not have been possible without Jane Williams and Thomas Mills of the University of Illinois Law School Library, who were so generous with their expertise. Carrie LaManna and Steve Lamos provided additional research assistance. Michael Heller and Michelle Hong read earlier versions of this article and shared their invaluable perspectives. Many thanks as well to the fabulous editorial board of the *Harvard Educational Review.*

PART TWO
INTRODUCTION
The Practice of Integration

Fifty years after the *Brown v. Board of Education* decision, Americans are keenly aware of the deplorable conditions and inequities that exist in schools intended for African Americans and those for Whites.[1] However, similar inequities existed for other people of color. In several court cases and social uprisings in the twentieth century, Asian Americans (*Gong Lum v. Rice*),[2] Mexican Americans (the battle for community control of the schools in Crystal City, Texas),[3] and Native Americans (the establishment of the Rough Rock Demonstration School)[4] argued that the schooling opportunities available to them were far from adequate. In these prominent cases, attention, and in some instances relief in the form of case law or policy, improved educational opportunities for students of color. As U.S. society becomes increasingly multiracial and multiethnic, we are compelled to explore how the post-*Brown* environment shaped the educational practices for, and experiences of, students within and beyond the Black-White racial dichotomy.

This section focuses on the practice of integration inside schools and classrooms. The essays highlight the voices and experiences of teachers, students, administrators, and educational researchers who continuously grapple with the daily realities of the failed promises of *Brown*. This section is significant for its examination of the experiences of some students who are often overlooked in research literature and court decisions.[5] The authors in this section remind us that the simple physical presence of students of diverse social locations does not equal an environment in which authentic experiences of learning, appreciating, celebrating, and even challenging the experiences and perspectives of others, are acknowledged and valued. Indeed, as Michelle Fine, Lois Weis, and Linda Powell write, the integrated school environment should be one that "self-consciously creates intellectual and social engagement across racial and ethnic groups." These authors illustrate that the acknowledgment and celebration of difference is an essential ingredient to any truly integrated educational setting. These accounts of schooling in the urban Northeast, northwestern Alaska, public and private environments, and in institutions of higher education are chronicles of significant challenges to the goal of equitable education for traditionally marginalized students. Similarly, there are individual accounts of communities, parents, teachers, administrators, and especially students resisting the status quo and redefining what it means to be educated in late-twentieth-century America.

The first essay in this section provides a framework for analyzing the experiences of educators and students in three racially desegregated schools who are struggling with unquestioned racial differences and uninterrupted racist discourse. Fine, Weiss, and Powell introduce a continuum that moves from desegregated school spaces where differences are ignored to one in which teachers are actively working toward creating a space where differences are acknowledged and valued. The authors examine what components must be in place to build a community of difference within a given school context. For example, in one school the authors detail an unchallenged co-construction of Whiteness and the Other by White males, both students and teachers. They reinforce a hegemonic structure in which White female students are placed on a pedestal and not considered equal, Black males are vilified, Black females are not considered attractive and are insulted, and Yemeni students are ignored and clearly regarded as inferior to Whites. The importance of maintaining a democratic structure in which all members of the learning community can contribute equally is one among many innovations in this article.

In the second essay, Leona Okakok examines a common struggle of communities of color — the struggle to maintain one's primary culture while accommodating the dominant culture. Okakok, a community activist in the Point Barrow school district serving Native American students, analyzes differences between the northwest Alaska Inupiat and the Western worldview of education. She recounts a Native people's resistance to Western colonialism, as Inupiat children risk punishment to maintain their native language and customs. This article's uniqueness lies in the illustration of the Native school board's takeover of the educational system in an effort to adapt a foreign educational system to contemporary Inupiat culture. Through community organization, a curricular model is created that respects the culture and customs of the Inupiat people. This schooling simultaneously endows students with the skills necessary to succeed in a social milieu where Western education is also valued. Okakok illustrates that the curricular and pedagogical innovation brought about by a community is a strong shift toward an integrated philosophy of learning — a philosophy that incorporates Western and Inupiat cultural ways of learning.

The third essay in this section challenges the orthodoxy in which Latino students are studied by focusing specifically on the experiences of Puerto Ricans in U.S. schools. Sonia Nieto documents the colonial relationship between Puerto Rico and the United States, noting that U.S. imperialism led, and continues to contribute to, the migration of Puerto Ricans to the U.S.

mainland. In an excellent piece for classroom teachers, Nieto combines the research on Puerto Rican students in U.S. schools with the power of a growing body of fiction written by Puerto Ricans to bring the experiences of Puerto Rican students to life. Nieto identifies four themes from the literature and fiction: colonialism/resistance, cultural deficit/cultural acceptance, assimilation/identity, and marginalization/belonging. She concludes with the assertion that the essential ingredient for improving the experience of Puerto Rican children in U.S. schools is the creation of caring communities, and challenges the community of educators and policymakers to help create such environments. The experiences of Puerto Rican students and their families in both the research literature and fictive accounts clearly indicate that schools are de jure desegregated. However, students and community members are still resisting substandard educational facilities, disengaged educators, and weak curricula. Nieto gives readers a ray of hope by pointing to caring as a way to improve the state of education for Puerto Rican students, and, by extension, all students.

This section would not be complete without the voice of one who is directly affected by the *Brown* decision — the student. In 1988, then fifteen-year-old Imani Perry, a high school student at a private school in Massachusetts, examined the differences between her private and public school experiences, adding new insight into the question, Which are more effective, private or public schools? Perry argues that, in her experience, public schools deny students their identity as intellectual beings and particularly repress the intellectual development of students of color. Private schools, on the other hand, can potentially be culturally isolating for students of color, although many presume that these institutions provide a higher level of intellectual support. While Perry does not advocate the abandonment of public schools for private schools, she offers a clear analysis of those aspects of public schooling that must be changed if these institutions are to serve the needs of minority students. Perry's examination of her own schooling experience speaks of a school system that is physically desegregated but not intellectually integrated. Due to teachers' low expectations and lack of cultural understanding, it is evident that there is considerable distance to travel until the promise of integration can be realized.

What makes the book's final essay so compelling is that Imani Perry — now a professor of law at Rutgers University — reflects on her 1988 *HER* article and her more recent experiences as an educator to examine the considerable progress made and gaps that remain in achieving equal access to educational opportunities for all students. Sixteen years later, Perry sets forth a theory of holistic integration, which she defines as an integration model where all students have equal and full access to the cultural and social skills necessary for full civic participation in American society. Perry leaves us with the goal of aspiring to Dr. Martin Luther King Jr.'s notion of the "beloved community," in which educational opportunity is accessible to all citizens.

Care and compassion are the prevailing notions in the beloved community, components that are supported by all of the authors in this section of the book.

We, the Editors of this volume, assert that regardless of one's political leaning, this fiftieth anniversary of *Brown* is an opportune time to reflect on both the incredible progress achieved in American education for people of color, women, people with disabilities, sexual minorities, and all citizens who have experienced discrimination in schools, and a time to rededicate our efforts to achieve true equality for all. These essays are intended to bring forth such reflections.

Notes

1. See, for example, Anderson, J. D., *The Education of Blacks in the South, 1860–1935* (Chapel Hill: University of North Carolina Press, 1998).
2. See Ancheta, A. N., *Race, Rights, and the Asian American Experience* (New Brunswick, NJ: Rutgers University Press, 1998); Gong Lum v. Rice, 275 US 78, 80 (1927). In this case, the Supreme Court upheld the segregation of Asian American students in Mississippi schools.
3. See Montejano, D., *Anglos and Mexicans in the Making of Texas, 1836–1986* (Austin: University of Texas Press, 1987). In 1963 and 1969, Mexican Americans in Crystal City organized and successfully wrested power from the overrepresented White population on the school board and city council. The latter movement prompted involvement from the U.S. Department of Justice, whose officials brokered a settlement that met student demands for bilingual education and cultural celebrations.
4. See Collier, J., Jr., "Survival at Rough Rock: A Historical Overview of Rough Rock Demonstration School," *Anthropology & Education Quarterly* 19.3 (1988): 253–269. The Rough Rock Demonstration School (now Rough Rock Community School) was founded in 1965 in Rough Rock (Tse chi'zhi), Arizona, by Navajo leaders with the assistance of the federal government and the Bureau of Indian Affairs. The school was designed to help Navajo people maintain their cultural heritage and receive a quality education, and its mission continues today.
5. See Lopez, I. H., "Hernandez v. Brown," *New York Times*, 22 May 2004, 17.

Communities of Difference:
A Critical Look at Desegregated Spaces
Created for and by Youth

MICHELLE FINE
LOIS WEIS
LINDA C. POWELL

The problem of the 20th century is the problem of the color line.
— *W. E. B. DuBois*

The problem of the 20th century is the problem of civilizing White people.
— *Nikki Giovanni*

It appears that W. E. B. DuBois, with Giovanni's friendly amendment, might have been a two-century prophet. The color line remains, stubbornly, the defining feature of social and economic relations in twentieth-century America, confounded with class and eclipsing ethnicities. Given the persistence of racial tensions, conflicts, and, most recently, the uninhibited and vile racist rhetoric embedded in the media and national politics, it seems absurd, indeed desperate, that we as adults look to youth to accomplish what we haven't been able to accomplish — to establish rich, vibrant, and cooperative interracial relationships, contexts, communities, and projects. Yet it is with youth that our hope for the future lies.

Among us (Michelle, Lois, Linda), we have spent years consulting with teachers, studying student behavior, and even testifying for racial and gender equity within schools that have achieved what Thomas Pettigrew would call "desegregation," that is, the coexistence of students from different racial and ethnic groups within the same institution. But rarely have we had the pleasure of working with, studying, or even testifying for a truly "integrated" school (Metz, 1994), a school that self-consciously creates intellectual and social engagement across racial and ethnic groups. In this article, we distinguish between desegregated and integrated spaces, and we note that even settings of minimal desegregation are disappearing rapidly as we close the twentieth century. Today, neighborhoods are further segregating as school

Harvard Educational Review   Vol. 67 No. 2 Summer 1997, 247–284

districts withdraw from desegregation decrees (Dreier & Moberg, 1996; Orfield & Eaton, 1996).

Our youth have had to manage the challenges of a rapidly changing racial and ethnic demography, and in some small corners of the earth they have done so, beautifully. Our objective here is to document three public school sites along a continuum from desegregated-but-racially-separate to integrated communities of differences in order to unravel systematically what it is that makes the latter work, so that these communities do not remain idiosyncratic, charisma-driven, precious, and, soon, extinct.

Having just finished editing *Off-White* (Fine, Weis, Powell, & Wong, 1997), in which we theoretically decentered Whiteness, the stance from which we launch this work takes seriously the past fifty years of extensive research on equal status and contact theory. It is our sense that the extensive, and at this moment dominant, frame on integration — equal status contact theory — must be repositioned within the broad theoretical context of community difference and democracy if we are to fully understand, document, and enable the creation and sustenance of more spaces designed for and by multiracial communities of youth.

Equal Status Contact Theory: What We've Been Told

The theory of equal status contact posits four necessary conditions:

1. *Equal status.* The contact should occur in circumstances that place the two groups in an equal status.
2. *Personal interaction.* The contact should involve one-on-one interactions among individual members of the two groups.
3. *Cooperative activities.* Members of the two groups should join together in an effort to achieve superordinate goals.
4. *Social norms.* The social norms, defined in part by relevant authorities, should favor intergroup contact. (Brehm & Kassin, 1996, p. 157)

Under these conditions, children from different backgrounds — even historically unequal backgrounds — are presumed to interact in ways that produce positive task and interpersonal outcomes. As Janet Schofield (1982, 1995) reminds us, however, it is the truly exceptional school or community-based context in which we can find all of these conditions. From Gordon Allport's (1954) original work on prejudice through Muzifer and Carolyn Sherif's Robber Cave Experiments (1958), in which competitive groups of boys joined together when faced with a common enemy, to more contemporary, school-based work by David and Roger Johnson (1995), Robert Slavin (1995), and Janet Schofield (1995), we have been shown that when the conditions of equal status contact are created, interracial relations, attitudes, and networks do indeed improve. However, researchers typically find that over time these contexts develop and ultimately suffer from what Jomills

Braddock, Marvin Dawkins, and George Wilson (1995) call inclusion and interaction barriers: for example, differential expectations, subtle forms of social exclusion, diminished verbal and nonverbal communication with and/or harassment of the now-included "other." All three of us have spent years in public schools and community settings as consultants, teachers, researchers, and organizers, bumping up against the stubborn persistence with which the formal structures, ideologies, informal practices of schooling, and often community life, resist inclusion. Thus we feel the need to surround equal status contact theory with a framework that draws on three traditionally independent literatures — those on community, difference, and democracy. We take as our premise that, in order for multiracial youth relations to flourish, three political and social conditions — none natural or automatic — must be intentionally set in place: a sense of community; a commitment to creative analysis of difference, power, and privilege; and an enduring investment in democratic practice with youth. In the absence of these three conditions, settings that are technically desegregated will corrode into sites of oppositional identities, racial tensions, and fractured group relations, which simply mirror the larger society. To create these conditions requires deliberate counter-hegemonic struggle by educators, activists, and youth, to invent and sustain multiracial intellectual and social sites for everyone — what integration means after all.

In our work, we are interested in understanding how to nurture these multiracial communities to be sustainable, in ways that engage groups of youth and adults who are not merely co-located but deliberately invested in a diverse group larger than self, rich in racially and ethnically diverse connections and differences. There is much evidence that designed cooperation has produced positive outcomes for such groups of youth in camps (Sherif, 1958), schools (Johnson & Johnson, 1995; Slavin, 1995), and laboratories (Gaertner, Dovidio, Anastasio, Bachman, & Rust, 1993; Gaertner et al., 1997). The beauty of these studies is that they enable us to know which micro-structures of cooperation foster positive consequences for sense of self, a more empathic view of other, and a reduction of stereotypical attitudes. But what we don't know is how a structured community of such relationships can be initiated, much less supported over time, for and by adolescents in actual communities that are porous and vulnerable to surrounding politics. Nor do we know much about how adults — enthused, hostile, ignorant, frightened, or merely unsupported — can create and sustain such communities.

Tony Bryk, Valerie Lee, and P. B. Holland (1993) have demonstrated the extent to which a communitarian ideology sits at the core of successful and diverse schools by instilling in community members a shared ideology, identity, and vision. Susan Opotow (1995) has written on the interior dynamics of such moral communities (groups of individuals who share a sense of identity and extend a common set of principles of justice across the group) with an eye on what happens both within and beyond them to maintain their borders. She raises important theoretical questions about the nature of cooperative bonds, the sense of shared purpose and trust, the agreed-upon boundaries, and the demarcated out-groups inherent in community life. In studying the conditions under which separate, sometimes competing, groups of youth can be motivated to see themselves no longer as "us" and "them," but as "we," Samuel Gaertner and colleagues (1997) focused on a shared out-group, a common enemy. But we are haunted by the recurrent assumption, traced to Henri Tajfel and John Turner (1979), that in-group identities are formed inherently at the borders in opposition to out-groups. Through our research, we seek to understand the emergence of multiracial community life and to challenge Tajfel's assumption of the necessity of out-groups. That is, we hope to deepen what is known by Bryk, Opotow, Gaertner, and colleagues by discerning the conditions under which youths are willing to aspire toward an in-group identity that is sufficiently compelling, while rejecting the need to derogate out-groups (Tajfel & Turner, 1979).

Thus we complicate community with "difference." The ever-hovering questions of community — multiculturalism, inclusion, identity — of the late twentieth century inspire our second theoretical interest (see Banks, 1995; Hare-Mustin & Marecek, 1990; Minow, 1990; Rhode, 1990; Steele, 1988). Reflecting back on equal status contact theory, we worry that, by intent, the theory and its implementations have failed to analyze or deal with the rich cultural differences in biographies, passions, expectations, stereotypes, troubles, and hopes that young people bring to their cross-racial and cross-ethnic relationships (Phillips, Penn, & Gaines, 1993; Plummer, 1995; Semons, 1991; Spencer, Swanson, & Cunningham, 1991; Stevenson, 1995). Equality doubles for sameness. Differences are whited out. In theory and practice, cross-group interactions are supposed to proceed as if differences in style, history, personal and social expectations, and power could be bracketed. But like political theorist Nancy Fraser (1990), who writes on the difficulties of creating democratically accessible public spheres that bridge pre-existing inequalities, we worry that the existing asymmetries in life experiences, sense of entitlement, and faculty/peer expectations can't and shouldn't simply be put aside for a moment by youth or adults. We worry that when educators ask students to bracket these differences as if we were all the same, a privileged center remains untroubled, questions of difference are suspended or suffocated, and the particular costs of bracketing differences are absorbed by students of color. Thus we seek to understand how differences disrupt or facilitate communities that are diverse in race and ethnicity. Our concern, of course, is that the bracketing assumption — leave your differences at the door — reproduces privilege, oppression, and opposition in the guise of neutrality or "color-blindness."

Following the lead of scholars such as Henry Louis Gates Jr. (1985), Stuart Hall (1991), and Martha Minow (1990), we believe that differences in race, ethnicity, class, and gender are, at this moment in history, constructed by politics, power, and biography, and are fluid and mutable. But, they are also, of course, intimately lived (Plummer, 1995; Stevenson, 1995). Differences are at once real and fictional, material and invented, enduring and mutable, rejected and embodied (Marcia, 1980; Semons, 1991). Drawing on the writings of Lani Guinier (1994), William Cross Jr. (1995), and Kimberlé Crenshaw (1992), we see race as a critical and defining feature of lived experience that young and old and people of all colors reflect upon, embody, challenge, and negotiate (see Marcia, 1980; Thorne, 1993). While race, class, ethnicity, and gender certainly influence the standpoint from which each of us views the world (Collins, 1990; Hartsock, 1984; Weis & Fine, 1993, 1996), it is as true that no one demographic box can fully contain one's point of view (Cross, 1995; Hurtado & Stewart, 1997). There is too much wonderful variety, too much moving around, and, indeed, too much playing with race for these categories to sit still. William Cross Jr. (1995), Stuart Hall (1991), and Howard Winant (1997) have taught us all that we cannot assume race to be a fixed entity. But we wonder about what conditions are in place that fix race, and what conditions must be in place in schools for such play with differences to flourish. What structures and practices, by adults and youth, enable young people to work with — not around or in spite of — race, ethnicity, and power-based differences? Within multiracial settings, when are young people invited to discuss, voice, critique, and re-view the very notions of race that feel so fixed, so hierarchical, so damaging, and so accepted in the broader culture? This invitation to re-view, we believe, marks a critical cleavage in the distinction between sites of desegregation and those of integration (Lawrence & Tatum, 1997). Merely including youth or teachers of different races and ethnicities in the same school clearly does not produce an integrated school.

The research and writings of social scientists (Clark & Saegert, 1995; Putnam, 1993; Vanderslice, 1995) have convinced us that the practice of participation and democracy must be at the heart of creating, and, even more so, of sustaining multiracial communities of difference invested in and by youths and adults. Social psychologist Virginia Vanderslice (1995) writes on the power, sustainability, and vulnerabilities of worker-owned cooperatives. Without intentional structures for and (re)education in democratic practice, Vanderslice finds these cooperatives often cave in to the powerful forces of competitive capitalism in their surround. The fissures of race, class, gender, management/labor will reemerge unless deliberate democratic process is practiced. Likewise, environmental psychologists Heléne Clark and Susan Saegert (1995) have conducted participatory action research in tenant-owned versus city-managed public housing, and documented substantially better outcomes for quality of life, safety, and civic engagement in the tenant-owned housing. These researchers provide substantial evidence of the enduring positive consequence of cooperative participation and, inversely, that diverse communities are too fragile to endure if they are simply the creation of a few charismatic, visionary, or even autocratic — if well-meaning — adults.

Thus, we now seek to extend these findings to reveal how contexts of diversity and democracy in schools can generate youth leadership, voice, and participation. We are not so naive as to think that any of the positive outcomes of democratic participation would evolve spontaneously within multiracial groups of youth or without enormous coordination and collaboration by adults and youth. But we are also not sanguine that hypercontrol of the multiracial contexts by adults produces the sense of ownership or community building among youth that needs to take place to sustain long-term, profoundly integrated education.

In this country we have few models for creating, much less sustaining, communities of difference. We may have harmonious, even successful, communities of homogeneity (although their fractures, too, are growing more public). In response to this paucity of examples and exemplars, we seek to understand public spaces — indeed schools — where differences are self-consciously drawn upon to enrich and texture the community; where negotiations of difference lie at the heart of the community; and where democratic participation is a defining aspect of decisionmaking and daily life within the community. If schools are to produce engaged, critical citizens who are willing to imagine and build multiracial and multiethnic communities, then we presume schools must take as their task the fostering of group life that ensures equal status, but within a context that takes community-building as its task. The process of sustaining a community must include a critical interrogation of difference as the rich substance of community life and an invitation for engagement that is relentlessly democratic, diverse, participatory, and always attentive to equity and parity.

Safe Spaces

Having a sense of place and space empowers. People achieve their place through interpersonal relations, initially through family linkages and then through friendships and conjugal ties as well as work-related associations. Belonging within a space ensures safety, a zone for being and acting according to rules known and shared by others familiar with this space. Young people in inner cities, subject to the transience of frequent moves and the rapid unpredictabilities of life . . . rarely feel that they have a secure or safe place. . . .

It is curious that, as the twentieth century nears its close, social and economic conditions within some urban areas of the United States are such that the working together across racial and ethnic lines celebrated in theory since the 1960s is in place *in practice*. . . . Here the young as full participants have the "right to emerge from the routine of life," so as to test and challenge official and habituated hierarchical differences. (Heath, 1995, pp. 52, 65)

As Heath so eloquently articulates, there are spaces now being created by and for youth that begin to meet our criteria of community, difference, and democracy, that invite young people to work within and across traditional fault lines of identity. These may be safe spaces in which old and new identities are tried on, played with, and tossed off. We ask, can such spaces be located in schools, or is that oxymoronic?

Heath and colleagues play off of Harry Boyte and Sara Evan's (1992) notion of what they call free spaces — spaces in which people, in spite of poverty and the associated features of late-twentieth-century oppression, are able to imagine life differently, joining together to nurture hopes and dreams, often producing real changes in their individual and collective lives. Recognizing that no space is free from larger social inequities, these are sites in which young men and women have created and/or found communities in which they can challenge some of the hegemonic assumptions that surround and consume them, in which they can imagine a world that *could be* but hasn't yet been, and in which they can learn with others while teaching about policies, experiences, and lessons of young adult life. In these spaces, whispers of hope and possibility tenaciously flourish in the midst of despair located in a collapsing private economy and public sector. While there is an abundance of cool cynicism in popular youth rhetoric, there are also pockets of sweet longing — bright lights shining through cracks of demoralization.

We place the nurturing of multiracial youth communities of difference within this free space conceptualization. These spaces, in which groups of youth cross racial and ethnic boundaries, are rare and cry out for documentation. We need to understand both the interior and the borders of these spaces, find out how and why they arise, what nurtures, sustains, and threatens them, and how they can be grown in the diaspora in order to begin the slow process of transforming (de)segregated urban and suburban landscapes into integrated safe spaces.

Our research spans three schools in three different communities. Lois researched one de facto desegregated school with no sanctioned, critical, or authorized address of race or ethnicity — a site in which oppositional racism flourishes, looking quite inevitable and natural, all the while institutionally fed. Linda researched a second desegregated school while working as a professional development consultant on re-forming teacher-teacher and teacher-student relationships. Michelle researched a third, desegregated but internally tracked school in which English teachers boldly, courageously, and even under surveillance by some local politicians, chose to detrack and integrate the ninth-grade English course, and in so doing, threatened the larger, more entrenched patterns of segregation that define tracking in this school.

On this continuum of race-work in public spaces, we journey through the three sites asking what must be put in place to build a community of differences — rich in academic rigor and replete with the windows and mirrors of race, ethnicity, culture, and gender. What needs to be in place for students, faculty, staff, and administrators? How much will the State, in the body of school boards, and how much will families, especially economically elite and educationally privileged families, tolerate the decentering of their privilege to create an education for all? Is the public sphere up to the challenge? In the following sections we describe three school scenes, asking in each what sustains oppositional racism or what allows truly integrated communities of difference to emerge.

Scene One: Supporting Racially Oppositional Co-Constructions (Lois Weis)

"Freeway" High School is the site of the first of these school scenes. Freeway, a small town located outside a medium-sized metropolitan area, was hit hard by the deindustrialization of the 1970s and 1980s. Freeway was particularly hurt by the downsizing and ultimate closing of Freeway Steel, a plant with a record high payroll of $168 million in 1969. In the first seven months of 1971, layoffs at the Freeway Plant numbered 4,000, and the decline continued into the 1980s. From 18,500 jobs in 1979, there were only 3,700 production and 600 supervisory workers left in 1983, and 3,600 on layoff. At the end of 1983, the plant closed, leaving in its wake unvisited "gin mills" and numerous other small businesses associated with the plant. Freeway is a true traditional working-class area, and Freeway families have been involved in the plant for generations, assuring that White male workers had jobs through which they could support their families. African Americans[1] moved up from the South after World War II to obtain jobs at Freeway Steel, and many were employed, although at far dirtier and lower-paying jobs than Whites. A small but noticeable population of Yemenites also moved to Freeway after World War II, along with an even smaller number of Puerto Ricans. Freeway remains a segregated town in terms of housing patterns, with many White former steelworkers living on one side of town, and African Americans, Puerto Ricans, and Yemenites, some of whom are also former steel workers, living on the other, although less successful White workers live among people of color. Like many U.S. cities, the side of town populated by people of color used to be inhabited by White ethnics who moved across town as they accumulated the capital necessary to buy a home. With the close of Freeway Steel and other industries located in the nearby metropolitan area, families now survive by piecing together the wages of several family members, exhibiting a sense of bitterness and loss as they try to raise the next generation. Mostly White, these workers consistently believe that affirmative action is largely responsible for their economic plight; they do not focus their criticism on the actions and policies of the elite who moved industries south of the border in search of greater profits (Weis & Fine, 1996).

The scene that follows from Freeway High describes what typically happens in a desegregated educational setting without the benefit of any meaningful interruption of racial antagonisms. This school did nothing to intervene in the production and dominance of White male culture. In fact, in many important ways it affirmed it, although not always in any conscious or intended sense (Weis, 1990). It is the institutional production and acceleration of Whiteness as center, with its associated racial tensions, that we seek to problematize. There is nothing "natural" about this story, even if it is fairly typical of American communities.

At Freeway racial tensions are high, and the school does nothing to reduce them. In fact, it does much to nourish the racially oppositional co-constructions I describe below. Data presented here were gathered as part of a large ethnographic study of Freeway High. I, Lois Weis, spent three days a week in the high school during the academic year 1986–1987 as a participant observer. I gathered data in classrooms, study halls, the cafeteria, during extracurricular activities, and conducted in-depth interviews with over sixty White juniors, and with teachers, the vice principals, social workers, guidance counselors, and others. The overall purpose of the study was to examine the identity formation processes among White working-class youth in the context of the deindustrialization of the U.S. economy. Although I certainly talked with many students of color, formal interviews were conducted only with White students, since they were the focus of this project. I was specifically concerned with the ways in which young men and women elaborated their identities and the ways in which the high school connected to these processes. Specifically, gendered identity forms were at the heart of the study. Data, therefore, were gathered from White working-class male and female students in Freeway High. Eighty individuals teach at the high school and approximately forty teach juniors; all of the teachers of juniors were interviewed. Two counselors, one social worker, two vice principals, and one principal comprise the non-teaching staff. Both counselors, the social worker, one of the vice principals, and the principal were interviewed as part of this study.

The faculty is overwhelmingly White. Three African American faculty members comprise 4 percent of the teaching population in a community that is approximately 20 percent people of color. There are no male teachers of color at Freeway High; the three African American females teach in non-academic areas. Two are in special education, where nationally a disproportionate number of African American youth is concentrated, and one is in the relatively low-paid female vocational area of secretarial studies. In terms of a broader gender breakdown, fifty-two teachers, or 65 percent, are male, with some tendency toward female ghettoization in secretarial studies, home economics, and cosmetology. All the "hard" vocational areas (which have increasingly little presence in the schools) such as automotive technology, woodworking, construction technology, machine shop, and the like, are taught by males. Females tend to spread rather evenly through the remaining subject areas, unlike the case nationally where there has been greater tendency toward academic subject matter ghettoization by gender (Kelly &

Nihlen, 1982). The administrative staff is entirely White male; there is one female counselor and one male; and all the secretarial staff in the school is White female. With the exception of the three African American female teachers, then, the entire counseling, administrative, and teaching staff at Freeway High is White.

All interviews were audiotaped and transcribed with the permission of the interviewees. Data collection centered on the junior class, since this is where, in several ways, students' futures are locked in. The juniors are given a set of state-mandated tests and, during this same year, they sit for the pre-liminary college entrance examination, the PSAT, both of which sort students into post-secondary options.

One of the most chilling things going on at Freeway High is that the school offers a space wherein working-class White males co-construct their own identities in relation to those of African American males and females and White females. The term "co-construct" is chosen carefully here. As demonstrated below, White male students in this school construct their own identity as White at the same time they construct the identity of the other. While Whites do not author the race script in its entirety (certainly African American students have their own race script that is not examined here), they do in this context author themselves as White. This construction of self as White is, as will be shown here, absolutely dependent on the co-construction of African American students as the opposite other, and on White female students as subordinate to White male students.

Although Puerto Ricans and Yemenites attend this school, White identities are not specifically elaborated in relation to these students. These students, particularly Yemenites, are largely ignored in the racial construction process outlined below, although they are seen as non-White, and, therefore, less valued. Rather, White male students, in particular, forge their raced and gendered identities in relation to what they construct as the Black other and the White female. While co-construction may suggest collaboration and shared commitment, indicating that this process is not necessarily negative, the particular content of these co-constructions, in a site perched within a racist U.S. society, is, in fact, exceptionally negative. It is a process that needs but does not receive interruption at the school level. What became clear to me over the course of the study is that the identities of young working-class White males are absolutely contingent upon the elaborated identities of the others against and with whom their own identities are woven. The discursive construction of Black males and females and White females became a means by which White males could assert themselves — a vehicle for the formation of their own positively felt identities in contrast with the constructed negative others. Heterosexuality, masculinity, and Whiteness are assertions of fierce and adversarial essentialisms sustained in the face of what these young White males construct as others — White females and African American males and females. The school provided a specific site in which these identities were encouraged to unfold. Thus Freeway High offered a space for the formation of Whiteness and enabled this Whiteness to define itself in relation to the constructed negative in the other. Curriculum could have been developed to expose and deconstruct assumptions of Whiteness. Teachers, administrations, and counselors could have intervened and attempted to derail these co-constructions. The point is that they didn't, leaving intact a set of processes that served to center White males, marginalize others, and contribute to a set of good and bad representations that undermined the building of a multiethnic and multiracial community. In this scene, "communities of difference" means the co-construction of ugly difference, difference that lays the basis for future vicious attack.

Among the White adolescent males at Freeway, Blacks are used reliably as a foil against which acceptable moral, and particularly sexual, standards are established. The goodness of White is always contrasted with the badness of Black — Blacks are involved with drugs; Blacks are unacceptable sexually; Black men attempt to invade White sexual space by talking to White women; Black women are simply filthy. This binary translated in ways that complemented White boys, as there is a virtual denial of anything at all good being associated with Blackness, and of anything bad being identified with Whiteness. Let us eavesdrop on interviews conducted at Freeway High, where much expressed racism centers on White males' perceived entitlement to White females, thus fixing Black males and females and White females as beneath them in the constructed social hierarchy. My graduate assistant, Craig Centrie, and I conducted individual interviews with White male and female students at Freeway. Held in a small nook with a closed door off the library, the interviews were private and confidential, although students understood that their interviews would be incorporated into later writing. All names used here are pseudonyms, including those of the teachers. Excerpts below illustrate points made by an overwhelming number of White males at Freeway High, whether interviewed by Craig or me.

> *Jim:* The minorities are really bad into drugs. You're talking everything. Anything you want, you get from them. A prime example, the ___ ward of Freeway; about twenty years ago the ward was predominately White, my grandfather used to live there. Then Italians, Polish, the Irish people, everything was fine. The houses were maintained; there was a good standard of living. . . . The Blacks brought drugs. I'm not saying White people didn't have drugs, they had drugs, but to a certain extent. But drugs were like a social thing. But now you go down to the ward; it's amazing, it's a ghetto. Some of the houses are OK. They try to keep them up. Most of the homes are really terrible. They throw garbage on the front lawn. It's sickening. You talk to people from [surrounding suburbs]. Anywhere you talk to people, they tend to think the majority of our school is Black. They think you hang with Black people, listen to Black music. . . . A few of them [Blacks] are starting to go into the ___ ward now [the White side], so they're moving around. My parents will be around there when that happens, but I'd like to be out of there.

. . .

Lois Weis: There's no fighting and stuff here [at Freeway], is there?

Clint: Yeah, a lot between Blacks and Whites.

Lois Weis: Who starts them?

Clint: Blacks.

Lois Weis: Do Blacks and Whites hang out in the same places?

Clint: Some do. [The Blacks] live on the other side of town. . . . A lot of it [fights] starts with Blacks messing [with] White girls. That's how a lot of them start. Even if they [White guys] don't know the White girl, they don't like to see [a Black guy with a White girl].

Lois Weis: How do you feel about that yourself?

Clint: I don't like it. If I catch them [Blacks] near my sister, they'll get it. I don't like to see it like that. Most of them [his friends] see it that way [the same way he does].

Lois Weis: How about the other way around? White guys and Black girls?

Clint: There's a few that do. There's people that I know of, but no one I hang around with. I don't know many White kids that date Black girls.

. . .

Bill: Like my brother, he's in ninth grade. He's in trouble all the time. Last year he got jumped in school . . . about his girlfriend. He doesn't like Blacks. They come up to her and go, "Nice ass," and all that shit. My brother don't like that when they call her "nice ass" and stuff like that. He got suspended for saying "fucking nigger," but it's all right for a Black guy to go up to Whites and say stuff like that ["nice ass"]. . . . Sometimes the principals aren't doing their jobs. Like when my brother told [the assistant principal] that something is going to happen. Mr. ___ just said, "Leave it alone, just turn your head." . . . Like they [the administrators] don't know when fights start in this school. Like there's this one guy's kid sister, a nigger — [correction] — a Black guy — grabbed her ass. He hit him a couple of times. Did the principal know about it? No!

Lois Weis: What if a White guy did that [grabbed a girl's ass]?

Bill: He'd probably have punched him. But a lot of it's 'cause they're Black.

In the above interview segments it is important to note the ways in which several discursive separations are occurring. To begin with, these White male students are constructing female students as people who need the protection of males. The young men are willing to fight for their young women, so that if anyone says, "nice ass," it is a legitimate reason to start a fight. It must be pointed out that young women did not request or require this — this protective stance is under the terrain of the males themselves, the young women never having expressed a desire for such protection during the year Lois was there, either in interviews or in any observed interactions. Black males in turn are being constructed as oversexualized: They "welcome themselves in," as Clint says more than once in the interview; they behave in ways that are inappropriate vis-à-vis White females. The complaint is communicated through the language of property rights — Black males intruding onto White property. What is at issue here is that Black males are invading White females, the property of White males, not a broader statement about the treatment of females. In addition, the discursive constructions of Black males as oversexualized enables White males to elaborate to themselves and others their own appropriate and civilized heterosexuality. At a time of heightened concern with homosexuality, by virtue of their age, the collective nature of their lives, the fear of being labeled homosexual, and the violence that often accompanies such labeling in high school, these boys are able to assert virulently their own heterosexuality and their ability to take care of their women by virtue of the co-constructions they engaged in (Messner & Sabo, 1994). This intersection of race, racism, and acting straight has not been explored, to our knowledge, but it is in serious need of analysis, as high schools such as Freeway offer a site for the simultaneous playing out of these discourses. It cannot be missed that the social construction of Black and White, good and bad, male and female, is intertwined with the construction of straight and gay (Messner & Sabo, 1994). Students elaborate identities in school, and, as we have shown, such identities are linked up with those of constructed others. We need to understand the consequences when educators choose to allow negative co-constructions to continue uninterrupted. In the worst case, educators participate in the proliferation of these co-constructions, as the following observations from my field notes illustrate:

March 5

I went to see Johnnie Aaron (the White football coach) to see if the Nautilus room could be used for my interviewing. He said, "It's always in use; there's always someone in there." William, an African American male student, was in Johnnie's room, as [was] John, a White male.

Johnnie: What happened to your hair, boy?

William: It fell out. I was nervous before the game. (He had shaved his head.)

Johnnie has on other occasions referred to Black males but never White males, as "boy."

. . .

Study Hall

Anthony (an African American male): Hi girls (to two White girls).

Mr. Antonucci (a White teacher): Stop talking to White girls.

Anthony: Got any colored ones?

Mr. Antonucci: You don't seem to understand why I moved you up here to (to the front). (He kicks Anthony out of the classroom.)

Although directly racist comments by the faculty, such as those above, were relatively infrequent, comments such as those below were not, suggesting that a deep racism lies within the teacher and school culture generally:

February 26, Lunchroom

Jean, a White business teacher, had left her lunch on top of the fridge. She threw it away, with the comment, "We all know what's in there."

Lois Weis: What?

Susan: Cockroaches.

Lois Weis: I never saw a cockroach here.

Susan: You're lucky.

Marsha (White teacher): You know, I have a friend that just got a job teaching in (the nearby city), on ___ and ___, or something like that (right in the middle of the African American part of town). She's straight from suburbia and is teaching middle-class values. She was using a big chart, she's teaching kindergarten to teach the "M" sound. The kids were saying "M," and all of a sudden a cockroach walked across the paper. She stiffened; the kids did not seem to even notice; they're used to it. She just took off her shoe and killed it. Then she had the kids say, "Mommy" to practice words with a "M" sound. One little boy burst out crying and said, "Mommy got drunk and left." She said to herself, "What am I doing here?"

Barbara: Oh yeah, and they [Black kids] love to come up and feel your hair. (She makes a face as if this is extremely distasteful to her.)

. . .

September 5, Talk with Mr. Weaver, the assistant principal

I ran into Mr. Weaver in the hall. He was telling me what a "good system" this is here. The kids are good. "This is a realistic situation here, about fifteen percent Black or minority." He thinks that if a school gets "too Black," it is no longer "serious." "Too many of their homes are giddy places, not serious enough. If you get too many Blacks in the school, it is not serious. Fifteen percent is fine. They can't act that way [giddy] in school if they are only fifteen percent."

There is a grotesqueness about the particular set of meaning-makings in the school, meaning-makings that are not interrupted by school personnel, and at times are actively and generally encouraged by teachers; this enables White male students to write themselves as pure, straight, and superior, while authoring African American males as dirty and oversexualized. It is most interesting that not one female in this study ever discussed African American males as a "problem" in this regard. This is not to say that White females are not racist, but this particular discursive rendering of African American males is quite noticeably the terrain of White males. Not insignificantly, it is always fathers, according to young White women, who oppose interracial dating. As Suzanne, a White female student, stated, "My father would kill me if I brought home a Black guy." This is, of course, tied to the history of racism and race relations in a White working-class community, where African Americans were used to break strikes and, therefore, were pitted against White men economically. Alongside economics, however, lies the discursive realm, wherein some are authored as always being better than others. The continuation of the authoring of the [White] race script is what we see here in Freeway High.

Surely these constructions are linked dialectically to discursive and material constructions in the wider society, both historically and currently. As these young White males weave their own form of cultural superiority vis-à-vis African American males and females and White females, they are encouraged by a larger society and societal institutions. The construction of African Americans in the media, for example, as Cameron McCarthy and colleagues (1997) point out, encourages viewers to perceive this group as dangerous and drug-crazed. Historically, African Americans have been depicted less than admirably in American culture. The discursive constructions detailed here are linked to such constructions in the broader society. However, as the next scene demonstrates, we do not have to accept the Freeway set of co-constructions as an inevitable outcome in desegregated schools. The co-constructions evident at Freeway High are a specific outcome located in an institution that did nothing to undermine these constructions and even, as suggested above in the case of the teachers and staff, did some things to promote them (Weis, 1991). It is our guess that Freeway is not unique. Rather, we suspect that it exemplifies what goes on in many desegregated high schools across the nation. Freeway is a site in which bodies of historic differentiation, privilege, and oppression are huddled together with little or no adult commitment to creating common ground. The fact that the teaching, administrative, and counseling staff is almost entirely White serves to both reflect and sustain this. The battle lines are drawn. We adults either affirm them or, more typically, stand by helpless, shaking our heads in disbelief. We now turn to Scene Two, where we argue that teachers in desegregated schools can begin to challenge negative constructions of difference rather than passively accept them.

Scene Two: Working the Authority Boundary — Supporting Young People in a Community of Difference (Linda Powell)

The "Arlingdale" neighborhood, once a thriving community populated by working-class factory workers of European descent who lived and worked in the hub of the textile mill industry, has been in decline and turmoil for thirty years. Today this community is racially mixed; Whites, African Americans, and Latinos live in physical proximity, but at a psychological distance. Arlingdale High School is located in an urban area where brutal poverty is the norm, racial tensions are explosive, and crime, due principally to drug trafficking, is the worst in the city. Well over half of the complaints to the Municipal Human Rights Commissions for racially based violence and other forms of racial discrimination originate in the greater Arlingdale community. The city in which Arlingdale is located continues to be in conflict over the twenty-plus-year desegregation suit, which recently confirmed that after twenty years of effort, most of the public schools continue to be "racially isolated."

Unlike many of the 134 schools in this northeastern city, Arlingdale High School has a richly diverse student population consisting principally of Latino students (45%), White working-class students (25%), African American students (20%), and Southeast Asian students (10%). Latino students are primarily Puerto Rican, with a small number from other Caribbean countries, and from Central and South American nations. The Southeast Asian students are primarily Vietnamese, although many of their families are ethnic Chinese who resettled in Vietnam prior to coming to the United States. There are also a small number of international students who have recently immigrated from the Middle East and Eastern Europe (primarily Poland). Over half of the student body does not speak English as its first language, and approximately 15 percent of the student body is placed in support classes for limited English language proficiency.

Over time, the greatest changes have been in the Latino population, which is increasing as the African American population is decreasing. The White ethnic community had effectively boycotted Arlingdale High School for many years, sending their children to local Catholic schools. Over the past fifteen years, however, rising tuition costs and the closing of nearby Catholic schools has resulted in the reluctant return of White students.

The faculty and school staff is also multiracial — White, African American, Latino, and Asian — though not as diverse as the student body. The predominant faculty group (55%) is White, approximately 40 percent are African American, with the remaining 5 percent Latino and Asian American.

Since 1990, teachers and staff at Arlingdale have been committed to developing Family Group as a school climate intervention and a student support mechanism. Family Group creates in-school groupings of students who meet weekly with a trained facilitator. The task of the group is to talk about whatever the students need to help them be successful in school. Relationships among students are cultivated as carefully as those between the students and the facilitator. A prepared curriculum is available, based on the common topics that arise.

Joining adults from eight other public high schools, Arlingdale staff have taken the lead in attempting to implement Family Group, which requires both structural changes in the way the school day is scheduled, as well as demanding preparation and support for the adults leading the groups. Family Group has been an intergroup experience from the outset, involving groups of students with groups of adults, groups of teachers with groups of staff, and groups from various schools. The boundaries between these groupings provide opportunities for learning in a variety of ways. For example, attending to the intergroup aspect of the city-wide component has been a form of community support, giving Family Group leaders a forum to air criticism of their individual schools, gain perspective on their common and unique problems, and draw support from like-minded colleagues.

Unlike other special programs or curriculum approaches that deal with specific students, Family Group is conceived as an organizational intervention. Ideally, every student in the school has a Family Group membership. Family Group is an enhanced advisory approach that builds on the substantial dropout prevention literature, which persuasively demonstrates that a caring adult can have a profound effect on a student's achievement. Family Group is a first step toward assuring that each child has regular and continuous contact with a single adult. Elsewhere I, Linda Powell (1994), have explored the ways in which anonymity operates as a social defense (Menzies, 1960) in urban schools. This notion draws on both systems and psychoanalytic ideas about organizations, and suggests that many behaviors that appear dysfunctional may actually serve crucial organizational purposes. In urban schools, for example, "not knowing anyone well" may be an effective way of managing the anxiety associated with the immense diversity in the school, the demands of learning, the complexity of the school climate, and the many forms of violence — some interpersonal, but most often institutional. And so, any intervention that increases the opportunity for adolescents and adults to be fully present at school — whether it is Family Group, a student-centered curriculum, a peer mediation program, or a multicultural study group for teachers — is likely to meet organizational resistance as it interrupts the social defense.

Considering that it is embedded in a community immersed in racial strife, Arlingdale High School appears to be surprisingly free of racial turmoil and to be a decidedly safe environment compared to other neighborhood high schools of comparable size and location across the United States. Students and staff manage to avoid overt or violent conflict related to racial difference; few racially motivated incidents are reported, and students and adults publicly assert in Family Group, professional development sessions, and informal settings that they "love their school." Race most typically emerges as an issue in Family Group when students talk about what is important to them. In one group, a young African American man reported having a difficult experience: while he was tutoring a young White child as part of community service, the younger child called him "a nigger." As he tried to sort out his reactions, he said that he couldn't really blame the child, who was simply replaying what adults had taught him. However, the young tutor said that he "heard the teacher say nothing." He was most stung by the failure of the teacher to intervene on his behalf.

Students at Arlingdale often "hear adults say nothing." This is likely due to the fact that race is a hidden and complex issue among the staff, making it far more complicated for them to support the students. This complexity can be observed in the various adult coalitions that form in the school according to race. The most visible example is staff lunchtime seating, which is strictly by racial groups; should a new adult interrupt this pattern, they are routinely rejected and quickly reeducated about "how things are done here." This identity group strategy among teachers may be their way of managing differences and intergroup conflict. This strategy, while sufficient to keep the peace, may mask profound opportunities for learning that could be leveraged by the skilled intervention of adults. This strategy may also be teaching inadvertent lessons about power and authority that are less apparent. Adults must commit to and be trained to confront and explore rather than to shut down the clash of differences that occur when questions about race emerge through conflict.

In earlier work in this community, I report (Powell, 1994) an incident in a city-wide professional development session. A White Family Group leader was approached by a White student who reported that an African American male student had overturned her chair; the young woman described it as a racial incident, saying that he did it because she was White. The adult replied unhesitatingly, "No, it wasn't." The Family Group leader reported this incident, almost casually, as part of her description of the behavior of young men in Family Group. When the group facilitator interrupted to ask how she determined that it wasn't a racial incident, the Family Group leader was stunned by the question, as were her Family Group leader colleagues. This question drew out an extended exploration of the role of Family Group with regard to race and racial identity, which had previously been inchoate and inarticulate. The Family Group leaders' theory-in-practice had been to treat all conversations with a racial component as dangerous, and by definition to be suppressed, cut off, and treated as "not to be learned from." My belief, in contrast, is that Family Group offers a sanctioned and protected forum to treat these experiences as opportunities to build a group capacity to explore conflict and to strengthen the racial identity of every student (Carter & Helms, 1990; Helms, 1990). In the words of *How Schools Shortchange Girls* (AAUW, 1992), Family Groups and the relationships developed within them provide the environment to explore rather than avoid the "evaded curriculum" (p. 95) of power.

Another example of a missed learning opportunity occurred at Arlingdale High School following a rich and compelling multicultural assembly that celebrated the contributions of Latinos to American culture. A group of White students approached the new Puerto Rican principal and asked, "Why are Black people getting all this attention?" The principal used this as an opportunity to convince and persuade his students that not all people of color are Black, and multiculturalism was a good thing, the glue that held this school together, a democratic value they should hold. What was also there — and would have been far more incendiary — was the additional opportunity to uncover Whiteness. What different factors would have allowed the principal to gently interrogate the arrogance and entitlement the White students exhibited in raising this question?

Arlingdale students and adults have found ways to minimize and suppress conflict by avoiding negative interactions, but how could they instead learn from difference? How could their conflicts be a source of information and growth? Paraphrasing William Ayers's (1996) recent question in the *Journal of Caring and Concern,* "What is it that makes a large number of poor, immigrant children of color in this school *wonderful?*" (p. 86). One answer to that question is the profound opportunity they present to explore and transform the historic American racial categorization in a live and authentic laboratory.

This "laboratory" is shaped by internal, structural factors. In his recent course "The Health Crisis in Poor and Disenfranchised Communities," Ronald David (1996, personal communication) has reminded us that relationship is primary and everything else is derivative. This fact is well known to physicians and psychotherapists. The quality and content of information shared is a measure of the relationship existent between the participants; the greater the trust and reliability, the more authentic and risky the data shared. For example, in a recent intervention in another Family Group school, students interviewed by strangers reported that they had little or no reaction to allegations of abuse of students by a popular school administrator. Students said that they were "fine about it" and "not upset." Students interviewed by adults they knew in more intimate settings like Family Group expressed more powerful reactions to the entire situation: They were worried about what gossip this would expose them to in the neighborhood. Seniors felt that their senior year had been ruined. Several noted pointedly that violent, abusive experiences were a common part of student life in school, but "psychologists only got airlifted in" when the administrator, an adult, was at risk.

The parallel to schools seems clear; the conversation about race and ethnicity will vary greatly by time, task, and the opportunity to connect in meaningful ways. Whether young people frame their personal and group-level identities in a complex and constructive manner is related in large part to three factors: one, the values, skills, and attitudes of the adults in their environment; two, the perceived learning task at the given moment; and three, the reliability of structures in place to support them in exploring complex ideas.

For the entering ninth-grade class at Arlingdale and their advisors, those three factors are consciously manipulated by the existence of their weekly Family Group sessions. Family Group also builds on research (MEE Foundation, 1993) and commentary (Bly, 1996) that suggest that adult authority with young people is decreasing in effectiveness, and that adults are surrendering to the increasing influence of the peer culture. This powerful peer culture tends to oversimplify complex issues and demand simplistic allegiances. At its best, the very existence of and process within Family Group provides young people the opportunity to stretch and explore that culture without surrendering it. The process of discussion mitigates a certain rigidity of the peer culture, learning to express and respect differences as part of a community, not simply as a threat to cohesiveness. This succeeds in moderating "in" and "out" as givens. The impact of this intervention is to encourage positive group-based interactions among adolescents, and to build greater trust between adolescents and adults while moderating the conformist values of the peer culture.

What difference can Family Group make in the construction of the narratives about race and ethnicity? First, the task is for students to talk about whatever they need to in order to be successful in school. Encouraged and facilitated by specially trained adults, each week's topic is student directed. Often the topic is power, race, and ethnicity, although it is coded in stories about their daily interactions with their environment. In response to a direct question about race, such as, "Is race an issue here at Arlingdale?" most students of all colors will say, "It's not important. I don't see color. Not a big deal." However, students of color will spontaneously reflect on their experiences in racial terms. For example, after a sports event with a suburban school, an African American young man stated: "They wouldn't let suburban kids in a building like ours." Decoding this response yields a highly raced and classed analysis: White kids who have money would be protected from a physical plant that is cold, graffiti-covered, and asbestos-filled. This comment is about race and power, but comes at an interesting tangent to the adult-framed question about race.

Second, preparing Family Group Leaders to facilitate rather than shut down raced conversation is absolutely crucial. In my work, I use the four-factor professional development for change model (Powell, 1997; Powell & Barry, 1995; Powell, Barry, & Davis, in press), which focuses on experiential learning, creation of safe spaces, development of complex analytic skills through the exploration of parallel processes, and the strategic use of theory. This kind of training is required to give adults access to the subtleties of their own racial identities, as well as information about group life and conflict management. For example, leaders explore their own racial and ethnic identities through activities such as constructing personal narratives of their racial identity and engaging in complex conversations about race.

The focused use of Family Group for the investigation of race in students' lives is in a new and fragile phase. Previously, Family Group was seen as a dropout prevention mechanism, and students focused on their day-to-day school life. During the next phase we pay closer attention to the impact of stability, regularity, and trained adults who facilitate the expression of narratives about race.

One of the most compelling paradoxes about Family Group is that despite an almost universal anecdotal sense that it works for students, it is almost impossible to maintain in urban schools. Schools report that Family Group improves student attendance, invigorates classroom work, and provides a structural forum to reshape school culture. It gives students a different opportunity to bring their most complex selves to schools and provides adults with sophisticated and practical professional development. This year, the commitment at Arlingdale was that every incoming ninth grader would have Family Group. Adults were trained, materials prepared, and students grouped. However, for a variety of rational and perhaps irrational reasons, sustaining the groups has been very difficult. There is often "something else" in the roster that bumps the small meetings (like a huge assembly), or there is not quite enough money for training (although other efforts with less connection to teaching/learning go forward), or there are insufficient opportunities for professional development and ongoing support (the intractability of the school day). We understand this as a form of organizational resistance and the strengthening of the social defense: Family Group does not neatly fit in an urban school because it is initially anxiety producing. If anonymity has functioned as a defense, and if we don't want to know about difference, then we certainly can't tolerate a more authentic conversation exploring race. As one reluctant Family Group Leader summed it up, "There's no doubt that it is good for the kids, but I can't stand the chaos it creates among the adults." There may be a connection between race and organizational resistance. A two-year process of investigating race relations among youth was announced at Arlingdale in the fall. Family Group leaders were invited to join a process where they, along with students, would explore multiculturalism and difference as it blossomed at Arlingdale. Since that announcement, difficulties have ensued and gotten worse. One hypothesis is that the school could not tolerate such knowledge about race, in either adult or student experience. Further, it is likely that adults are ambivalent about learning from/with young people about building community around racial difference due to the changes it might necessitate for us.

Arlingdale is at a point of cautious hope. The ingredients for a delicious experiment of knowing, being known, and making change are in place. A primary question is whether adults will use their authority to create and sustain the structures needed for students to develop and explore these questions. Will we create the relationships required for honesty and directness? Will we model approaches to difference and change that students can trust? Will we shut down conversations that make us uncomfortable with unresolved political and personal issues about race, or will we use our resources — both internal and external — to assure that these developmental conversations for adolescents will have a place? This scene is the center of a continuum — kids are struggling to create a new form of community, but adults must use their resources to support, provoke, and encourage their efforts. The kids are on track — we need to join them.

Scene Three: Bold Pedagogies — Moving Toward a Community of Differences (Michelle Fine)

In 1991, the "Clear Mount" High School English faculty voted unanimously to detrack its ninth-grade literature course. In Clear Mount, a commuter suburb well known for ambitious racial and class integration of its preK through 12 system, the high school is nevertheless more tracked than many in the high school would like to admit, producing more racial segregation than most in the town would say is desirable.[2] English faculty at the high school took it upon themselves to invent an intellectually ambitious, multicultural World Literature course — heterogeneous by gender, race, ethnicity, social class, and academic history — in which all ninth graders would enroll. Committed to its public image as a progressive and intentionally integrated town in a deeply segregated state, with families ranging from quite poor to very wealthy with a substantial Black elite, Clear Mount wrestles with the lived contradictions of race, ethnicity, and class amidst dreams of integration. The World Literature course reflects and makes public those contradictions. The course, as such, is fiercely contested both within and beyond the school walls (Fields, 1996).

The course has been the site of local controversy, given the community's intense ambivalence about retaining tracking at the secondary school (see Wells & Serna, 1996, for coverage of similar dynamics nationally). This course has sustained both high academic standards and serious community scrutiny. It has been supplemented by a nationally recognized Writers Center and was recently evaluated by Dennie Palmer Wolf and Willa Spicer (1994). At a meeting of the town's board of education on the merits of the course, scores of teachers, students, and parents across racial and ethnic groups and academic histories testified to its value, with few exceptions. Quantitative and qualitative data were presented by the evaluators to demonstrate that the course represents a space in which students can critically examine literature and produce intellectual, political, and emotional work within and across groups. Students and teachers testified their support of the course:

> *A White female junior:* It is valuable to have it not tracked. First it gives all of us a common background experience. And if we all learn the same things, we become a group, a class, not just separate little groups of our own.

> *A White male sophomore:* I think it was actually better than if it had been ranked. It made you see how diverse the school really is. That is better than hiding out in your honors classes and always being with the same people. It is very fulfilling to see what other people are thinking. You see that there are more cultures in the course. We have someone with Igbo ancestry, and that was very important when we were doing Africa.

A biracial female sophomore: Students, I believe as a result of heterogeneous grouping, attribute success to effort. This is critical. I also think that students realize they can contribute to the success of a class and/or small group in a variety of ways.[3]

One African American male sophomore, who had previously been tracked in low-level courses, put it boldly, "You live in the basement, you die in the basement. You know what I mean?" The combination of strong multiracial and multiethnic relationships among faculty and students, a rich multicultural curriculum, lots of support from writing coaches and the Writing Center, and high standards were presented as being sufficient factors to instill a sense of competence in substantial numbers of students, including those considered high risk.[4]

Following the external evaluation, the principal, a set of faculty, and a set of current and former students agreed to collaborate with me, Michelle Fine, on an ethnography of the course. My intent was (and is) to be a participant observer in four classes, one to two mornings a week, to meet with the faculty every other week, and to work with a group of students who will also be writing over the course of two years.[5] From this pedagogical window, I expect to learn much about the power of young adolescents' writing, the opportunities to explore their own perspectives as essential to empathic understandings of others, the consequences of differential academic histories on secondary school performance, and how to make heterogeneity real, not just in access but also in outcomes. The more time I spend with these students and teachers, the more I realize that this course is truly a window into the educational dilemmas and rich possibilities that sparkle across the school district, across public education. It is also a privileged opportunity to witness the brilliance of teaching for intellectual excellence and social justice.

As the following field notes and analyses distributed over four months suggest, we can see the critical pedagogical turns that occur as these classes shift from a discomforting desegregation to a slightly less awkward, growing, nudging integration. The critical moments include faculty trying to create community, decentering Whiteness, and youths exploring questions of "differences."

September 13: Faculty Trying to Create Community

It has only been two weeks, but I have already heard from parents and educators outside the high school that this course is "on the chopping block." The mayor "ran on a platform to get rid of it." A few vocal White parents have in the past called the superintendent, complaining, "My kid doesn't have other White students in her class," or "The class is too political, not literary enough." Many White and African American parents are stronger supporters. Rumor has it, there is a small silent but distressed group of African American middle-class parents deeply conflicted about the detracking.

In the midst, students are discussing George and Lennie's relationship at the end of *Of Mice and Men*. Carlton Jordan [one of the teachers] asks his students to form what he calls a value line: "Stand on my right if you think it was right for George to kill Lennie. Stand on my left if you don't. Stand in the middle if you are of both minds."

Much to my surprise (and dismay?), the room tips to the right. The crowd moves in those loud clumsy teenage feet over towards the "it's OK to kill" side. I look for patterns by gender, race. Nothing. To the left wander three boys, a bit surprised and embarrassed, two White and one Black, feeling like they are going to lose. "But it is never OK to kill a friend," insists Joshua.

Carlton, momentarily stunned but never stumped by his "pedagogical failure" to get equally distributed groups, undermining his "plan" to set up pairs to discuss their positions, invites them to sit in common position groups and discuss whether or not George should appeal.

The "it's OK to kill a friend" group get loud, committed, animated, vile. "Lennie stupid." "He's the biggest retard in the world. He likes to pet dead rabbits. He don't need to live," shouts Kizzy — Muslim, brassy, busty, wonderful, noisy, always the voice that provokes Darren, an African American boy, to respond with emotion. This group, however, is forming across their differences in opposition to Lennie. Here comes the Tajfel prediction about out-groups and enemies. Sofia, another young African American woman, "I study ballet 8 hours a day and they tell me I won't be able to be a famous dancer because I am Black." Kizzy puts on a "Vote for Eli Ginsburg-McCoy" sticker, with Eli, a White boy sitting next to her as Devon says, "No. Vote for Marcus Jordan." Border crossing dots the room. Kizzy declares herself a "free thinker," as she moves the sticker to her right arm where a tattoo would go, slipping it under her shirt sleeve. Sofia continues, "That Lennie could be Jeffrey Dahmer. He should have killed Lennie long ago; he's a burden." Kizzy continues: "He's stupid. He murdered cold-blooded. We got to make him bad if we're gonna get George off." Eli joins, "By killing him, it was like saving a life."

Carlton and I exchange glances. I'm thrown by the raw but vicious analyses of these young adolescents and their endless creativity. The screams of "stupid, useless, dumb" are rusting my soul.

Carlton is as visibly shaken as I am. A strong, bold African American educator, he begins to teach, to preach, to speak with his heart, his eyes, his arms, and his mouth. "Let me say something about Lennie, because as I walk around, I am disturbed. . . . What are the characteristics of Lennie?"

The class volunteers: "Stupid, slow, dumb!"

Carlton continues, "Dumb. Retarded. When you use language like that I have to speak. . . . You may say it was right for George to kill Lennie because Lennie killed someone else or Lennie would have been killed. There are many reasons. But because [he] is stupid, slow, no. Some of you have Learning Disabilities. Some of you have persons with autism or retardation in your family. And none of us know what's coming next. It is important to see Lennie as a man, as a human being, not as something that should be destroyed."

Kizzy: "But he stupid. You are coming down on our group."

My mind wanders. Remembering the calls [from some parents] to the superintendent about "Them," remembering talk at the School Board about how "those students" will hold back "the motivated ones," I am brought back to the room by Carlton's voice. "Some of you have been called stupid by others. You have to think about what it's like to be in a world where everyone seems to be getting it right, and you don't even know what you don't know. Some of you sit in lunchroom and won't eat tuna sandwiches because you are gonna save the baby whale, but you'd laugh at Lennie in our school. Some of you will send money to Rwanda and Bosnia to save children over there. But you would make fun of Lennie, throw stones or shun Lennie over here." The students have reproduced the discourse being narrated about them. "George should not be burdened by Lennie." That is just what some at the School Board meeting were trying to imply.

Carlton: "Let me say, I take this personally. If you can't walk with Lennie, if you can't see Lennie as a human, as a brother, what future is there for our community? What possibilities are there for us as a whole?"

Class is over. I'm feeling exhausted and depleted . . . and amazed at the strength of a teacher willing to speak, interrupt, listen, and educate. After a weekend of worries and exchanged phone messages with Carlton, I returned to class on Monday to find the pedagogical genius of "community," orchestrated by Carlton, already at play.

The lecture opens with a discussion of first person and third person narratives. Carlton asks students to "turn to a page of *Of Mice and Men* where George and Lennie are interacting. I want you to rewrite the passage as Lennie. In first person narrative. To see how Lennie's wheels turn."

"What wheels?" snipes Paul.

The students clip through the text, muttering, but writing eagerly. Carlton waits patiently for volunteers. Hands shoot up. "I am just a happy man, likin' my rabbits." "Why George callin' me a stupid so and so . . ." Hands of all hues fill the air. The room is alive with Lennies.

"How do you feel?" asks Carlton. "Stupid?" The point was made. Carlton was crafting a community not yet owned by students, but the students were growing extensions with which to connect in the room and beyond.

I am profoundly moved by how much work is involved in creating community amid such an enormous range of academic biographies and social standpoints. This is a course in which students with third-grade "official reading level" sit and converse, challenge and create with students who read at far more sophisticated levels. It is a course in which questions of race and ethnicity surface and then get complicated. Students for the first eight weeks focus on "perspectives," producing "name pieces" that unravel the textured fragments of culture that braid in their genealogies. Discoveries of mixtures such as "oops, I almost forgot I'm part Native American" from one student, and "Puerto Rican Jew actually" from another student, punctuate student talk. In reading *Of Mice and Men, Twelve Angry Men, Nectar in the Sieve, The Epic of Gilgemesh, Two Old Women,* writings of Sandra Cisneros and Homer, the poetry of Walt Whitman and June Jordan, and short stories by Rudolfo Anaya, young men and women crawl back in their personal histories to discover the many selves sitting inside their skins. They practice voices sanctioned and those long smothered. And they listen to others, not always easily, not always gracefully, but always with support from faculty. While most are engaged in the talk, they are still learning to hear, to listen, and to imagine the value of another's point of view. This is the slow, not always progressive, move toward community, toward authentic education.

Dana Sherman, another World Literature teacher, is passionate about creating writers among her ninth graders. Adolescents who otherwise walk around nailed shut or performing an essentialist caricature of their demographic box come alive in her course. They stretch across borders of self and others, and in so doing, they begin to knit a community, to trust each other enough to "come out" as "Latino," "mulatto," "part Native," "not really a writer," "left back." Tanika, an African American student with a "bad" — her word — academic history, is learning to hear her own voice as she gets an audience. And Max, White Jewish, of progressive parents, who has long been reading Whitman, Morrison, and Baldwin, is learning to listen to Tanika, to shift his optics, to see through window and mirrors to re-view himself and others, to position himself and others in a community. Carlton and Dana earn their keep as they try to create a community, a world not yet.

These teachers work hard to identify both talents and needs in all, to display the treasures of each, and to remove from the closet the weaknesses in every one of us. My own elitism, racism, and anxiety surface every time one of the faculty asks students to read aloud, or poses the question, "Who has finished *Gilgemesh? Bhagavad-Gita? Nectar in the Sieve?*" And when I dare to re-open my eyes, the hands are often attached to bodies I had suspected were reading, but as often to bodies for whom I was less sure. Students read *Twelve Angry Men.* Everyone has a role to read aloud. After I exhale, I can hear clearly that, of course, everyone stumbles when reading aloud.[6]

After a few weeks of bumping through attempts to create connections and commonalities, it is clear that the unspoken center — Whiteness — needs to be complicated and shifted. At the moment it is still defended territory not yet contested. Over the course of a few weeks, questions of difference within community erupt at times in pleasure, but more often in pain.

September 25: Decentering Whiteness

Having finished *Of Mice and Men,* the class has moved on to *Two Old Women,* by Velma Wallis, a Native woman from Alaska who retells a story told by her mother. The story spins around two old women left to die, abandoned by their community.

In two classes, a small set of White boys — some of the very ones who defended Lennie's right to live — are "pissed."

The conversation from one class exemplifies the tensions:

"She's trash," shouts Jeremy. "This woman is a terrible writer. The book has no pulse. It's not gripping."

"It has the heartbeat of a dead person," adds Ethan. These young men carry on about the book. Four White boys uncharacteristically huddle together, sit and spout as critics sitting on high.

"A good book," notes one of these fourteen-year-old critics, "has action, climax, movement. It's gripping."

Carlton draws a phallus on the board. "Like this?"

Jeremy reveals, "This book has stolen my soul."

While one might have a good discussion about whether or not this is a "good" book, the energy of disgust and critique explodes. It takes me by surprise. Jeremy, we later hear, ran off to the library for some Whitman.

While Carlton is trying to create a sense of entitlement, wonder, a critical voice, if you will, in Tasha, an African American girl who says little, and Pam, a White girl who says less, whose academic biographies have over-prescribed their silence, he is also trying to invite Jeremy and his friends to "get out of your box. Taste something different — even if you don't like it. Your box will be expanded."

They shut down. I worry the retreat of White male energy could sabotage the class. Their silence is loud. . . . My worries are embarrassingly elitist, racist, sexist . . .

With another brilliant pedagogic move, Dana (to help Carlton) searches that evening to find a Whitman poem, "On Silence." Imported to the class, students read it aloud. The boys are soothed. Something comforting, a blanket, has been returned to the center of the room. Velma has been exiled.

But then Carlton announces the homework assignment. "Please find pages 9–11 in Wallis — where the grandson sits mute, daring not to challenge the elders as he witnesses the abandonment of his grandmother. Compare that passage to Whitman's poem 'On Silence.' Answer the question: 'Where's Whitman in Wallis? Where has she gone further?'" Jeremy reminds Carlton — with an ironic smile — "It's an insult to put Wallis and Whitman in the same sentence."

Obsessively searching for threads of connection amid difference, multiple forms of knowledge, inviting explorations and stretches, creating conversations about readers and writers who might never have known each other — Kizzy and Jeremy or Wallis and Whitman — these teachers are deliberately, carefully, and with smarts creating "safe spaces" without denying — indeed revealing and interrogating — differences.

Always working with and for talent in its many hues and registers, eager to display the cultural biographies and strengths students import, these two faculty members also demonstrate the fractures within each, the "Black boy," the "White girl," the "athlete," the "resistor," and always the "intellectual" hiding inside of us all. Questions of difference are lifted up as quickly as they are problematized and pluralized. Interested in neither diversity nor difference per se, the work these educators are performing is the work of decentering — assuring that no race, no ethnicity, no position, no gender, no stance has hegemonic authority, silencing power, or monopoly on truth. They invite writers, speakers, and readers to emerge.

So youth in these courses, over time and unevenly, recognize that they can speak and that they deserve an audience. More slowly, some learn they must listen. Those who have been sitting in advanced and gifted classes sometimes sound arrogant. Those who have been frying in special education sometimes sound jaded. By November, each knows that someone will hear, someone is waiting. So they write. Once buried, silent, pumped up with too much Ritalin, surviving under too much weight, wearing too much make-up. Student bodies swimming in pants that don't fit. Crawling out of the basement of special ed and remediation. Listening under coats and hoods. Now they are speaking and writing.

In Dana's class, a rich conversation swirls around *Two Old Women.* Dana tosses out Wallis's sentence: "'The body needs food but the mind needs people.' What does that mean?" to which Rashin, an African American boy, offers: "Talking is another way of eating. You need it to live." Paul, an Irish American boy, joins Rashin: "If you don't have people you get lonely." April, a Jewish American girl, makes a connection to *Of Mice and Men:* "This is the perfect quote for Curly's wife." Randy, an African American girl, lays it out: "A person can go crazy if she can't let her story out. Bottled up. Doesn't matter. It gives you the challenge every day. You gonna let it out? [If not] that's how people go crazy. You need the bond."

These students couldn't have described more eloquently the community they are in the midst of creating — the one that is being created for them and with them.

As I learn in my too-hard chair on my Monday and Friday mornings, these courses have their flaws, their moments in which the magic doesn't prevail, in which the noise of the lecture drones, when looking out the window is more enticing than another round of *Nectar in the Sieve.* But these classrooms, teachers, and students are mostly magic — the magic of imagining and creating a world that does not yet exist, a world in which difference is lifted and complicated. Cultures get to speak and then fracture into beautiful, diverse, contradictory slices. Young adults narrate their still unformed selves and listen to their own brilliance and disappointments. Kizzy and Max have a conversation and learn from each other.

In the corner of this otherwise too stratified school sits this safe space for authentic integration. But even notions of integration get complicated. So, for instance, sometimes the finely balanced groups don't work academically. In some groups, African American males don't speak much. Heads fall to desks. When reading *The Odyssey* and allowed to choose "three classmates to work with," African American males in two classes chose to form their own group. They invented a (mini) historically Black school (for men), and they grew animated. This moment was a reminder to me that a flight into sameness by a marginalized group may be essential for and not a distraction from integration. This example raises questions about who benefits from presumed "balance" in integration (Cohen, 1972).

These spaces that Dana, a White woman, and Carlton, an African American man, create are sprawling, challenging, safe, and threatening; they open as a site for critical work, analysis, and sewing together fragments of self, marginalization, and questioning. Most profoundly, perhaps, this space poses a threat to the larger systems within which young people's lives sit. Tremors can be heard in the diaspora: the rest of their school, in some families, from some board members and the mayor. Safe spaces, for those of color, class, and/or of age groups that others want silenced, threaten by intent or not.

This course is chronically contested — from outside and from within. School and community members are wrestling right here, in this course, with unresolved issues of the school, the town, and the nation — issues of race, ethnicity, class, and gender. Seepage into the classroom creates an undertow. Perhaps this is too much of a burden for a small set of teachers. Or perhaps it is exactly the obligation, the responsibility, and the power of public education. How is it that a small course, one that barely creases the rigid racial and ethnic hierarchy of the school, has so traumatized a district?

We fast-forward now to November as youth in the class begin to assert the mantle of democracy themselves, redistributing power and interrogating differences within — without degenerating into difference as deficit.

November 22: Youths Doing "Differences"

Until this point, Dana and Carlton have been meticulous about creating groups of "balance," so that students who would never have spoken, do; so they hear each others' voices; so they learn to be audience for others. Usually these groups work with grace. Sometimes with incredible passion. At moments, they falter, dissembling along predictable race and class lines. On their own, among the students, there is some, and increasing, "border crossing." Often these are pairs of students who have found a common interest, in Antigone, the World Series, a poem by June Jordan. Often middle-class Black and White; some surprises too. In each class, there is consistently a group of students who coagulate like a cold, frozen white glacier, holding onto their space, their voices, their ownership of air time, defending against talk about "race all the time." As predictably, floating across these rooms, usually alone, often silent, is a very small fraction of African American boys who are not yet engaged as students in the class. Most have been doing all the reading (despite my wrong-headed misconceptions). I know because many mumble fascinating interpretations. But only for me, or a friend, or themselves to hear. In the back. Not ready for public exposure. Meanwhile, Dana and Carlton keep dancing up front, engaging, exploring, inviting, sweating, being very smart. I now see how hard this is; how much America needs it.

We read widely, internationally, globally, critically and have now wandered into India, late 1950s, with *Nectar in the Sieve*. I haven't finished the book yet and so find myself eavesdropping on class conversations about Rukmani, the Indian mother who lives by dharma, fate, asks few questions about why or what could be and Kenny, the White, Western trained physician, who prods Rukmani about the "ignorance and patience of you people" who don't ask questions, who don't demand a better life.

Students start today's conversation in Dana's class. Rallying for Kenny as a symbol of progress, the savior, Chelsea (White) affirms, "Kenny is trying to help them see what a better life could be. You have to admit Western medicine is scientifically better." Josh, an African American boy hovering in the back with me, fully clothed in jacket and hat, looking "baaad" mumbles, "I think Kenny's a racist. Rukmani ain't sad about her life." I invite him to speak up . . . his facial response suggests it may be too early in the year (or too late in his educational life).

The conversation heats up. I have been noticing, across classes, that these glaciers are now starting to melt. Some individual students have separated themselves, moving into solitary positions. Silent, but visibly withdrawn from the iceberg, moving towards some unformed "colored" polyglot. A few actively join in a inter-racial and inter-ethnic conversation, "Like she [pointing to an African American student] said . . ." There is, today, certainly more cross talk than was the case in September. Whites will now follow the comments of African American students, and will disagree with each other. Likewise, African American students will comment with and on White students' words, and even challenge what has been the heretofore unchallenged White dominance in some classes.

Amidst intense discussion about Rukmani and Kenny, Sondra — a young woman who calls herself African American but then explains, "really part Puerto Rican, Black, and part Native American" — pipes up, crawling out of her often silent mode, and says, "Sometimes I think I would like to be White. I mean to have your" — she points to Steven — "your house and cars and stuff." Steven, the implied White boy, turns and assures her, "If you try, you can have what I have." Kito, a first-generation Dominican American, emerging with barely audible insights sneaking out of a tiny mouth that has been under-exercised in all his years in special education, takes the floor: "But I do try hard. I try hard all the time. And I don't have what you have." Many African Americans in the class chime in to turn on Sondra, "You should be proud of who you are." "You don't really want to be White." "That's ignorant to want to be what you ain't." Sondra tries to explain, "It ain't about bein' White. It's about having what he has. Like if I was sittin' in a soft chair and you're in a hard, uncomfortable one, you'd want to be switchin' seats. That's it." She degenerates into apology, "I'm not being clear." Dana assures her of her clarity and turns to a small square of White students — maybe four, no more, but loud — giggling in the middle of the room. She asks them for silence and respect. Tony responds to Sondra, "It's not really ignorant to want something, but it is ignorant to sit around and expect it to come. It's not just comin' to you, you got to get it, like Rukmani's sons." Lots of nods and "uh-huhs" around the room. Now we get a multi-voiced mini-lecture on Black empowerment, and how "we" have to do it on our own — as the world abandons them. The room, however, is now alive with commentary. Jackets start to come off. Interruptions within and across "race." The old fault lines evaporate. A community is forming.

Kito is back, not letting this rest, but is cut off by Chelsea, who hitch-hikes on Tony's comment, "You think it's easy being a White girl? Getting called White bitch in the hallway?" She speaks for a long time, over seven minutes, responding in part to Sondra's muffled, "It's not easy being Black and female." Kito waits to respond, "Yeah, I know, but I just want to switch places with any one of you, for a week, live a week in my shoes and see how it feels. I just think you should be educated to all parts of the rainbow." This unexpected eloquence, vigor, and the length of his statement produces smiles and support from around the room. I note how much work some of the African American students and a few White students are exerting to create and sustain this conversation, and how hard it is for some of the White students to engage. The glacier seems to constrict, growing more defended.

Then Robert speaks. Robert, like others I had coded, correctly or not, as middle class and Black, has been one of the border crossers, hanging out with White and African American students. Engaged, interesting, and interested. "This conversation is really hard for me because I am both White and Black. And I understand both sides of what you're saying. I just don't know where I belong." He's near tears and the room is fixed in silence. "I usually just talk in here, but this is really hard." He stops short. His buddy, Caleb, a serious White boy sitting next to him, moves [toward] Robert, a quiet embodiment of support visible even through peripheral, teary vision. Robert finishes. Silence. And then suddenly from across the room, Elijah applauds, thanking Robert. Then Max. Soon most of the class. Robert has both informed and muted the conversation, but created an occasion in which "difference" could be lifted, power argued, and a sense of community — possible, liberal, too soft — nevertheless, could be imagined. And it's only Thanksgiving.

For the first three months of the class, these students who import vastly different biographies carved through families, schools, passions, curiosities, racism, poverty, privilege, entitlement, and special education, wandered around but rarely into difference. Except when Dana took them there. And even then, despite invitations from faculty, students would rarely engage the unspeakable elephant sitting in the middle of the room. Until this point, when it was finally clear that "differences" in privilege are not the same as "differences" in smarts. Suddenly the responsibility for engagement swept the room. Indeed, students of color needed to talk about race in order to be intellectually "free," unburdened by structured silences. In contrast, some White students stifle in the face of such talk, claiming to be silenced.

In the beginning of the course, a shared fantasy seemed to fill the room. Differences were fixed, immutable, maybe (painfully) organized in a hierarchy of ability. But by November, students were starting to notice the many ways to be smart, engaged, critical, a writer, a social and literary analyst. Asserting their insights through writing, conversing, challenging, and building coalitions, these students — White, African American, biracial, Latino, Indian, and those whose identities are too wonderfully complicated to be captured in a simple label — are willing to play, assert, listen, and work in conversation toward community. But for most, it's tough going.

For African American students and all students read as Black, relying upon the skills of doubled consciousness that W. E. B. DuBois (1903/1990) described almost a century ago, the hard part is to voice and trust that they will be heard; to bring to bear critical analyses that probably haven't gotten warm receptions in schooling to date. But even within-group differences flourish. Some, often those most impoverished economically, need to acquire academic skills that have not yet been acquired in school. Others, often those more middle class and/or biracial, describe a sense of "loyalty tests" that litter the room like mines in an academic terrain (Fordham, 1996).

For White students, especially those reared in relative economic privilege, surrounded by educated parents, books, and an ideology of entitlement and equality that refuses to question the perverse distributions of social resources, the hard part of the task — for some, not all, maybe just a vocal few — is to listen, to enjoy others, and not to worry that their smarts (more aptly their "A"s) will disappear or be stolen if merit is multiplied. For Latinos, Asians, the one young woman who calls herself "mulatto," the virulent categorization offends. John, a Colombian-born young man, expresses outrage at this Black-White-Other categorization, explaining, "I hate this. I resent it." Over time, the categories ebb and flow, as their borders grow more and less permeable, rigid, rejecting, and, at wonderful moments, stretchy and inclusive.

This course, then, signifies possibilities for a racial democracy, social challenge, and intellectual stretch from which public education has long walked away. It may present itself as a safe place, but indeed it represents a radically transgressive site in which the work of teachers and students continually reshapes, transforms, and challenges; in which the borders on learning keep moving out. The doubled representation of this space, as a sanctuary and as a site for social change, is part of the confusion. The sweet and benign course is, actually, on the ground enormously threatening while apologies reign — "it's only ninth grade"; "it's only English"; "it's academically rigorous" — in the diaspora, in homes, at school board meetings, and in other classrooms, the power of the course bleeds, seeps, leaks, explodes, and enables. Kizzy asks, "Whose history am I learning in Social Studies class?" John, who longs to return to the name Carlos, writes poetry about his Colombian roots, closeted in other arenas. Ra, steeped in and resistant to a fixed identity as African American and female, longs to escape from the narrow boxes that have tried to contain her. Kito, whose whispers of hesitant brilliance are released from his lips, asks, "Why am I in special education?" There is a slow and quiet yearning being expressed by students to stretch, to speak, write, listen, and challenge texts and each other beyond forty minutes each day. Now it gets subversive. They are demanding education. Are we — adults — prepared to deliver our end of the bargain (see Oakes, Wells, Yonezawa, & Ray, 1997)?

Reflections on Desegregation

The act of institution is an act of social magic that can create difference *ex nihilo*, or else (as is more often the case) by exploiting as it were pre-existing differences, like the biological differences between the sexes or, as in the case of the institution of an heir on the basis of primogeniture, the difference in age. In this sense, as with religion according to Durkheim, it is a "well-founded delusion," a symbolic imposition but *cum fundamento in re*. The distinctions that are the most efficacious socially are those which give the appearance of being based on objective differences (I think, for example, of the notion of "natural boundary" in geography). None the less, as is clear in the case of social classes, we are always dealing with continua, with continuous distributions, due to the fact that different principles of differentiation produce different divisions that are never completely congruent. However, social magic always manages to produce discontinuity out of continuity. (Bourdieu, 1991, pp. 119–120)

We conclude by borrowing from Pierre Bourdieu, who argues that "institutions" must be rethought as "verbs," not nouns, which produce "magic." For our purposes these institutions are schools, and the magic takes the form of identities: constructed, embodied, and resisted. In desegregated schools such as Freeway, student identities are often carved through race, typically in sharp opposition to each other. On rare occasions, as at Clear Mount, identities multiply instead, within communities of fluctuating differences, where self and other are mobile and intertwined, where faculty create a context for community, for decentering, and for democracy.

Usually, increasingly, almost everywhere in the United States today, desegregation, diversity, and heterogeneity are floating signifiers: legal, political, and social strategies that sadly, if typically, manufacture relentlessness and strident differences, as Bourdieu would predict. Race, ethnicity, class, gender, sexuality, and disability, layered one upon the other, fossilize the lines of demarcation. With this analysis, we see that the Freeway White boys are all too predictable and are institutionally produced; they embody and enact oppositional identities. We see that every time we as educators refuse to interrupt such institutional productions, we help make another Freeway boy and his "colored" counterpart. They are, of course, twins.

Thus it is only through deliberate commitment, as Dana Sherman and Carlton Jordan brilliantly exercise, to decenter privilege and to refuse the fixing of differences and oppositions, that educators can sever the parasitic hierarchies of race and enable differences to be at once engaged and exploded. In such spaces multiplicities are invited; borders are crossed; retreats to home spaces are understood; voices are heard; skills are sharpened; authority is exercised. In such spaces, everyone can see why we all need to get "out of the ditch" that Fannie Lou Hammer once described:

> I'd tell the White powers that I ain't trying to take nothing from them. I'm trying to make Mississippi a better place for all of us. And I'd say "What you don't understand is that as long as you stand with your feet on my neck, you got to stand in a ditch, too. But if you move, I'm coming out. I want to get us both out of the ditch." (quoted in Beilenson & Jackson, 1992, p. 15)

Given the stakes, it seems tragically predictable that institutional leaders like those at Freeway will continue to stand in the ditch, remaining "neutral" about race and ethnicity. As we see it now, however, declarations of institutional neutrality actually produce educational hierarchy, racial and ethnic opposition, and intergroup tensions, while peer culture more than adequately patrols these racialized, classed, and gendered hierarchies (see Fine, 1991, 1997). Meanwhile, we educators can believe that we are innocent. Wringing our hands as halls fill with chants of "bitch" and "faggot," as racial slurs echo, as sexual harassment complaints go unheeded (until they hit the papers), as White boys "protect" White girls from (always colored) others, as racial tensions percolate and boil over, we lament, "What do you expect? Look at the nation." Adult responsibility flees. Institutional collusion is erased. Desegregation might seem barely worth it: "They sit separately in the cafeteria anyway."

Meanwhile, those faculty and students who dare to imbalance privilege — to incite community, to both value and pluralize difference, to make hierarchy stutter, force "smart" to listen, invite "slow" to speak, circumscribe and circumcise privilege — will likely confront backlash from the State, some families, colleagues, and students dutifully patrolling the borders. Dana and Carlton, the teachers in Arlingdale, and millions of others are throwing their bodies in front of this racialized educational avalanche. The choice to watch or interrupt is ours.

Notes

1. In this section, Lois uses the term "African American" when she writes in her voice, and "Black" when she gives what she interprets as the Freeway point of view.
2. The student body is coded as roughly 45 percent African American, 45 percent White, and the remainder coded as "Other." Most faculty are White.
3. The faculty, a team of five (two of whom were observed by Michelle) that has diverse racial and ethnic backgrounds, has been intensively involved in the study of cooperative learning, heterogenous groupings, and multicultural literature. They, too, offered their comments on the evaluation. One teacher described the aspects of heterogeneous groupings most important to her: "1) The opportunity for all their voices to be heard, 2) The opportunity for all different perspectives to be presented, 3) No prior judgements — the notions that all 'good things can happen' for all students, 4) Lively discussion and interaction because of the unique gifts each student brings, 5) Atmosphere of mutual respect!" Wolf and Spicer (1994) reported that "All the students coming from school with lower expectations for them feel the course has been a real opportunity for them. A number now see themselves as able to choose between high honors, honors, and 'regular' instead of automatically destined for the lowest track" (p. 6).
4. After their exposure to "World Lit," ninth graders return to the real world of a tracked high school, in which they have to select at what level they will study tenth-grade English. After involvement in the World Literature course, the percentage who opted for tenth-grade High Honors English swelled from 33 percent in 1992–1993 to 50 percent in 1995–1996. Indeed, even a substantial proportion of "Three Level" ability students (considered the lowest achievement group) opted for High Honors or Honors.
5. At the time of this writing, I am only into the first four months of participant observation.
6. In this class, the gap in educational opportunities, the spaces between what would typically be seen as the "top" and the "bottom," could be seen as sprawling and not easily

bridged, except that these two educators, Dana and Carlton, are firmly committed to educating all and to hearing and producing the genius in all. They both, independently, recite a mantra. "I don't grade papers, that is, drafts, until I think they deserve the grade."

To redress the differences, indeed those deficits produced by very distinct academic biographies, these educators and colleagues designed a summer course for incoming freshmen who had failed English in eighth grade. In that summer experience, students were given a leg up to read and write, engage with peers and faculty about the texts they were about to encounter in the fall. The faculty, too, hang out after school. They review drafts. They narrate with exquisite explicitness what is expected, and how to get from here to there. They mine talent wherever they see it and invite students into the library club or to submit their papers for national competition. They read student papers out loud in class, making sure that students see the varied hues from which talent derives. These teachers have long abandoned pedagogical traditions designed and guaranteed to privilege only a singular best, designed to stratify, those strategies that insure fixedness, coherence, individualism, and hierarchy. Single definitions of merit have been revealed as amateur. Timed exams are distractions.

References

Allport, G. (1954). *The nature of prejudice.* Cambridge, MA: Addison-Wesley.

Ayers, W. (1996). Democracy and urban schooling for justice and care. *Journal for a Just and Caring Education, 2*(1), 85–92.

Banks, J. A. (1995). Multicultural education and the modification of students' racial attitudes. In W. D. Hawley & A. W. Jackson (Eds.), *Toward a common destiny: Improving race and ethnic relations in America* (pp. 315–339). San Francisco: Jossey-Bass.

Beilenson, J., & Jackson, H. (Eds.). (1992). *Voices of struggle, voices of pride.* White Plains, NY: Peter Pauper Press.

Bly, R. (1996). *The sibling society.* Reading, MA: Addison-Wesley.

Bourdieu, P. (1991). *Symbolic power.* Cambridge, MA: Harvard University Press.

Boyte, H. C., & Evans, S. M. (1992). *Free spaces: The sources of democratic change in America.* Chicago: University of Chicago Press.

Braddock, J. H., Dawkins, M. P., & Wilson, G. (1995). Intercultural contact and race relations among American youth. In W. D. Hawley & A. W. Jackson (Eds.), *Toward a common destiny: Improving race and ethnic relations in America* (pp. 237–256). San Francisco: Jossey-Bass.

Brehm, S. S., & Kassin, S. M. (1996). *Social psychology* (3rd ed.). Boston: Houghton Mifflin.

Bryk, A. S., Lee, V. E., & Holland, P. B. (1993). *Catholic schools and the common good.* Cambridge, MA: Harvard University Press.

Carter, R. T., & Helms, J. E. (1990). White racial identity attitudes and cultural values. In J. E. Helms (Ed.), *Black and White racial identity: Theory, research, and practice* (pp. 105–118). Westport, CT: Greenwood Press.

Clark, H., & Saegert, S. (1995). Cooperatives as places of social change. In A. Heskin & J. Leavitt (Eds.), *The hidden history of housing cooperatives.* Davis, CA: Center for Cooperative Change.

Cohen, E. G. (1972). Interracial interaction disability. *Human Relations, 25*(1), 9–24.

Collins, P. H. (1990). *Black feminist thought: Knowledge, consciousness, and the politics of empowerment.* Boston: Unwin Hyman.

Crenshaw, K. (1992). Whose story is it anyway? Feminist and antiracist appropriations of Anita Hill. In T. Morrison (Ed.), *Race-ing justice, en-gendering power: Essays on Anita*

Hall, Clarence Thomas, and the construction of social reality (pp. 402–440). New York: Pantheon Books.

Cross, W. E., Jr. (1995). Oppositional identity and African American youth: Issues and prospects. In W. D. Hawley & A. W. Jackson (Eds.), *Toward a common destiny: Improving race and ethnic relations in America* (pp. 185–204). San Francisco: Jossey-Bass.

Dreier, P., & Moberg, D. (1996). Moving from the 'hood. The mixed success of integrating suburbia. *American Prospect, 24,* 75–79.

DuBois, W. E. B. (1990). *The souls of Black folk.* New York: Vintage Books. (Original work published 1903)

Fields, W. (1996, November/December). The myth of Montclair. *New Jersey Reporter,* pp. 17–21.

Fine, M. (1991). *Framing dropouts: Notes on the politics of an urban public high school.* Albany: State University of New York Press.

Fine, M. (1997). Witnessing Whiteness. In M. Fine, L. Weis, L. Powell, & L. M. Wong (Eds.), *Off-White: Readings on race, power, and society* (pp. 57–65). New York: Routledge.

Fine, M., Weis, L., Powell, L. C., & Wong, L. M. (1997). *Off-White: Readings on race, power, and society.* New York: Routledge.

Fordham, S. (1996). *Blacked out: Dilemmas of race, identity, and success at Capital High.* Chicago: University of Chicago Press.

Fraser, N. (1990). Rethinking the public sphere: A contribution to the critique of actually existing democracy. *Social Text: Theory/Culture/Ideology, 25/26,* 56–80.

Gaertner, S., Dovidio, J., Anastasio, P., Bachman, B., & Rust, M. (1993). The common ingroup identity model: Recategorization and reduction of intergroup bias. *European Review of Social Psychology, 4,* 1–26.

Gaertner, S., Dovidio, J., Banker, B., Rust, M., Nier, J., Mottola, G., & Ward, C. (1997). Does White racism necessarily mean anti-Blackness? Aversive racism and pro Whiteness. In M. Fine, L. Weis, L. Powell, & L. M. Wong (Eds.), *Off-White: Readings on race, power, and society* (pp. 167–178). New York: Routledge.

Gates, H. L., Jr. (Ed.). (1985). *"Race," writing, and difference.* Chicago: University of Chicago Press.

Giovanni, N. (1993). Black is the noun. In G. Early (Ed.), *Lure and loathing: Essays on race, identity, and the ambivalence of assimilation* (pp. 113–126). New York: Penguin.

Guinier, L. (1994). *The tyranny of the majority: Fundamental fairness and representative democracy.* New York: Free Press.

Hall, S. (1989). Identity and difference. *Radical America, 23*(4), 9–20.

Hare-Mustin, R. T., & Marecek, J. (1990). *Making a difference: Psychology and the construction of gender.* New Haven, CT: Yale University Press.

Hartsock, N. (1984). *Money, sex, and power.* Boston: Northeastern University Press.

Heath, S. B. (1995). Race, ethnicity, and the defiance of categories. In W. D. Hawley & A. W. Jackson (Eds.), *Toward a common destiny: Improving race and ethnic relations in America* (pp. 39–70). San Francisco: Jossey-Bass.

Helms, J. E. (Ed.). (1990). *Black and White racial identity: Theory, research, and practice.* Westport, CT: Greenwood Press.

Hurtado, A., & Stewart, A. (1997). Through the looking glass: Implications of studying Whiteness for feminist methods. In M. Fine, L. Powell, L. Weis, & L. M. Wong (Eds.), *Off-White: Readings on race, power, and society* (pp. 297–311). New York: Routledge.

Johnson, D. W., & Johnson, R. T. (1995). Social interdependence: Cooperative learning in education. In B. B. Bunker, J. Z. Rubin, & Associates (Eds.), *Conflict, cooperation, and justice: Essays inspired by the work of Morton Deutsch* (pp. 205–251). San Francisco: Jossey-Bass.

Kelly, G., & Nihlen, A. (1982). Schooling and the reproduction of patriarchy: Unequal workloads, unequal rewards. In M. Apple (Ed.), *Cultural and economic reproduction in education* (pp. 162–180). London: Routledge and Kegan Paul.

Lawrence, S., & Tatum, B. (1997). White educators as allies: Moving from awareness to action. In M. Fine, L. Weis, L. Powell, & L. M. Wong (Eds.), *Off-White: Readings on race, power, and society* (pp. 333–342). New York: Routledge.

Marcia, J. (1980). Identity in adolescents. In J. Adelson (Ed.), *Handbook of adolescent psychology* (pp. 159–187). New York: Wiley.

McCarty, C., Rodriguez, A., Meecham, S., David, S., Wilson-Brown, C., Godina, H., Supryia, K., & Buerdia, E. (1997). Race, suburban resentment, and the representation of the inner city in contemporary film and television. In M. Fine, L. Weis, L. Powell, & L. M. Wong (Eds.), *Off-White: Readings on race, power, and society* (pp. 229–241). New York: Routledge.

MEE Foundation. (1993). Teaching the hip hop generation. In the MEE Symposium, *Final Report*. Philadelphia: MEE, Inc.

Menzies, I. E. P. (1960). A case study in the functioning of social systems as a defense against anxiety. *Human Relations, 13*, 95–121.

Messner, M., & Sabo, D. (1994). *Sex, violence, and power in sports: Rethinking masculinity.* Freedom, CA: Crossing Press.

Metz, M. H. (1994). Desegregation as necessity and challenge. *Journal of Negro Education, 63*, 64–77.

Minow, M. (1990). *Making all the difference: Inclusion, exclusion, and American law.* Ithaca, NY: Cornell University Press.

Oakes, J., Wells, A. S., Yonezawa, S., & Ray, K. (1997). Equity lessons from detracking schools. In A. Hargreaves (Ed.), *Rethinking educational change with heart and mind* (pp. 43–72). Alexandria, VA: Association for Supervision and Curriculum Development.

Opotow, S. (1995). Drawing the line: Social categorization, moral exclusion, and the scope of justice. In B. B. Bunker, J. Z. Rubin, & Associates (Eds.) *Conflict, cooperation, and justice:* Essays inspired by the work of Morton Deutsch (pp. 347–369). San Francisco: Jossey-Bass.

Orfield, G., Eaton, S. E., & the Harvard Project on School Desegregation. (1996). *Dismantling desegregation: The quiet reversal of Brown v. Board of Education.* New York: New Press.

Phillips, L., Penn, M. L., & Gaines, S. O. (1993). A hermeneutic rejoinder to ourselves and our critics. *Journal of Black Psychology, 19*, 350–357.

Plummer, D. L. (1995). Patterns of racial identity development of African American adolescent males and females. *Journal of Black Psychology, 21*, 168–180.

Powell, L. (1994). Interpreting social defenses: Family groups in an urban setting. In M. Fine (Ed.), *Chartering urban school reform: Reflections on public high schools in the midst of change* (pp. 112–121). New York: Teachers College Press.

Powell, L. (1997). The achievement (k)not: Whiteness and Black underachievement. In M. Fine, L. Weis, L. Powell, & L. M. Wong (Eds.), *Off-White: Readings on race, power, and society* (pp. 3–12). New York: Routledge.

Powell, L., & Barry, M. (1995). *Professional development for change: A working paper.* Philadelphia: Resources for Change.

Powell, L., Barry, M., & Davis, G. (in press). Facing reality in urban public schools: Using racial identity theory in family group. In L. Powell, M. Barry, & G. Davis (Eds.), *Racial identity theory: Applications for individual, group, and organizational interventions* (pp. 147–158). Mahwah, NJ: Lawrence Erlbaum.

Putnam, R. (1993). *Making democracy work: Civic traditions in modern Italy.* Princeton, NJ: Princeton University Press.

Rhode, D. L. (Ed.). (1990). *Theoretical perspectives on sexual difference.* New Haven, CT: Yale University Press.

Schofield, J. W. (1982). *Black and White in school: Trust, tension, or tolerance.* New York: Praeger.

Schofield, J. W. (1995). Promoting positive intergroup relations in school settings. In W. D. Hawley & A. W. Jackson (Eds.), *Toward a common destiny: Improving race and ethnic relations in America* (pp. 291–314). San Francisco: Jossey-Bass.

Semons, M. (1991). Ethnicity in the urban high school: A naturalistic study of student experiences. *Urban Review, 23,* 137–158.

Sherif, M. (1958). Superordinate goals in the reduction of intergroup conflict. *American Journal of Sociology, 43,* 349–356.

Slavin, R. E. (1995). Enhancing intergroup relations in schools: Cooperative learning and other strategies. In W. D. Hawley & A. W. Jackson (Eds.), *Toward a common destiny: Improving race and ethnic relations in America* (pp. 291–314). San Francisco: Jossey-Bass.

Spencer, M. B., Swanson, D. P., & Cunningham, M. (1991). Ethnicity, ethnic identity, and competence formation: Adolescent transition and cultural transformation. *Journal of Negro Education, 60,* 366–387.

Steele, C. (1988). The psychology of self-affirmation: Sustaining the integrity of the self. *Advances in Experimental Social Psychology, 21,* 261–302.

Stevenson, H. C., Jr. (1995). Relationship of adolescent perceptions of racial socialization to racial identity. *Journal of Black Psychology, 21,* 49–70.

Tajfel, H., & Turner, J. (1979). An integrative theory of intergroup conflict. In W. G. Austin & S. Worchel (Eds.), *The social psychology of intergroup relations* (pp. 33–47). Monterey, CA: Brooks/Cole.

Thorne, B. (1993). *Gender play: Girls and boys in school.* New Brunswick, NJ: Rutgers University Press.

Vanderslice, V. J. (1995). Cooperation within a competitive context: Lessons from worker cooperatives. In B. B. Bunker, J. Z. Rubin, & Associates (Eds.), *Conflict, cooperation, and justice: Essays inspired by the work of Morton Deutsch* (pp. 175–204). San Francisco: Jossey-Bass.

Weis, L. (1990). *Working class without work: High school students in a deindustrializing economy.* New York: Routledge.

Weis, L. (1991). Disempowering White working class females: The role of the high school. In C. Sleeter (Ed.), *Empowerment through multicultural education* (pp. 95–120). Albany: State University of New York Press.

Weis, L., & Fine, M. (Eds.). (1993). *Beyond silenced voices: Class, race, and gender in United States schools.* Albany: State University of New York Press.

Weis, L., & Fine, M. (1996). Narrating the 1980s and 1990s: Voices of the poor and working-class White and African American men. *Anthropology and Education Quarterly, 27,* 493–516.

Wells, A. S., & Serna, I. (1996). The politics of culture: Understanding local political resistance to detracking in racially mixed schools. *Harvard Educational Review, 66,* 93–118.

Winant, H. (1997). Behind blue eyes: Whiteness and contemporary U.S. radical politics. In M. Fine, L. Weis, L. Powell, and L. M. Wong (Eds.), *Off-White: Readings on race, power, and society* (pp. 40–53). New York: Routledge.

Wolf, D. P., & Spicer, W. (1994). *Evaluation of world literatures course.* Unpublished manuscript.

Serving the Purpose of Education

LEONA OKAKOK

Alaska! To many who have never been here, the mere mention of the word brings visions of a vast and barren land, a landscape shaped by the endlessly drifting snow, where the human quest for survival is thwarted at every turn by the malevolent forces of nature. Vast, yes. And though I would not dismiss perceptions of barrenness, cold, and a constant quest for survival, I want to put them in perspective.

When people read about northern Alaska — even excellent material — or come here for a short period of time, they form a perception of our land and people based on experiences having nothing to do with us. For instance, if you come from an area that is rich in varieties of landscape, the flat tundra of the high arctic — no matter how full of life — may seem barren to you. You will not see all the various signs of life that are obvious to longtime residents of the area. The same applies to the perception of cold. If your mind is focused on the seventy-degree temperatures back home, the spring here will seem cold to you — although it may be even warmer than usual to a seasoned resident.

Many non-Alaskans assume that everyone prefers warm weather. But, though warmth is certainly welcomed and appreciated during appropriate times of the year, for a hunting society in the North it is not the weather of choice during critical overland travel time into hunting areas. Our preference, then, depends more on necessity than sensation. Unusual warmth would concern an Alaskan hunter. An early thaw could severely jeopardize travel to his spring hunting sites, threatening his ability to provide food for his family for the coming year. Travel to hunting sites has to coincide with the migration of certain animals through these areas. If the rivers break up early, travel is hampered, at best, and life-threatening, at worst.

But Native people as well are not immune to applying old perceptions to new experience. My mother-in-law visited my husband and me in California while we were attending school there some years ago. Looking through the backyard window of our apartment, she remarked that someone "ought to cut down this tree back here. It just blocks an otherwise beautiful view." To her, a good view allowed one to see far away without obstruction. She did not realize that, in that part of the world, the tree was *a valued part of the view.*

Harvard Educational Review   Vol. 59 No. 4 November 1989, 405–422

We all know that we can go through life convinced that our view of the world is the only valid one. If we are interested in new perceptions, however, we need to catch a glimpse of the world through other eyes. We need to be aware of our own thoughts, as well as the way life is viewed by other people. It is my hope that this article will show you a different way of looking at northern Alaska and at us, the Inupiat Eskimos who live here.[1]

Northern Alaska Inupiat Eskimos

The Arctic has been home to the Northern Alaska Inupiat Eskimos for thousands of years. Our history as a people is rich in tradition, passed on through the centuries, generation to generation, by storytellers widely known for their skillful art. These stories and legends both entertain and help us to better understand who we are.[2] Because of the high value we place on the ability to retell these stories and legends accurately, we can better ensure that Inupiat strengths and values are passed on to each succeeding generation.

Oral history and the art of storytelling, highly developed in a society which used it to pass on subsistence techniques and cultural values, is still practiced today, but the critical element in the process — the audience — has changed. Audiences which used to be composed of young and old listeners now usually include only the elders. Our accelerated entry into the twentieth century has brought much confusion. Besides the daily chores critical to life in the Arctic, new and varied concerns, including Western education and religion, vie for the time and interest of the child. Even if children are interested, rarely do they have time to sit quietly, to listen and learn from their elders. The purpose of these long storytelling sessions — that of passing down values and other important elements of our culture — is severely restricted. The elders' role as *the* teachers and resource regarding contemporary life is no longer a given. Now, excellence in the subsistence way of life does not ensure survival in our modern world. The cash economy, Western civilization, and Christianity — concepts which the elders could not teach when they were introduced — emerged as standards against which others judged our life.

Parents, recognizing the inevitable encroachment of the Western way of life upon Inupiat land and culture, reluctantly released their young into the hands of schoolteachers, who assured them that this was best for their child. We respected the judgment of these newcomers to the area — teachers and ministers — because they were authorities on the new way of life. They represented the efforts of the United States Bureau of Education, which, through a contractual arrangement with churches, was committed to providing an education to children within what was then the District of Alaska. We did not realize that their objective was to educate our children enough to reject their own culture and to embrace the "more civilized" Western way of life. With this purpose firmly in mind, Western education began for our young.

The Early Years

In order to show the disruption caused by the displacement of our own educational system, I will briefly sketch the early development of Western education in our area of Alaska, which began in 1889 when the first school was established in Barrow (it was administered by the Presbyterian Church through a contract with the Federal Bureau of Education). This early phase continued until the 1920s, causing changes that affected the whole community: Children were no longer learning the ways of our people at home, and families were severely restricted from taking their children along on extended hunting trips — the children's prime learning experience. Families often had to depend on relatives willing to allow children to remain with them in the village while their parents were on extended hunting leave. Although many elders now gratefully acknowledge their relatives' hospitality back then and recall being treated as children of the household, there was much left to be desired. Certainly there were exceptions, but frequently those who were given the chance to attend school had to continue their basic education — achieving the ability to survive in their world — long after others their age had achieved success as subsistence hunters. The effort to mainstream the Inupiat children into Western society failed.

The focus of education in the North shifted only after local control was initiated in the mid-1970s. No longer were we, as a people, to be forced to assimilate into Western society. Western education *would* serve its purpose, but it would be a purpose determined by our own people.

The District

Eben Hopson, the power behind the formation of the North Slope Borough, our Home Rule Government, said in a speech before the local School Board in December, 1975:

> Possibly the greatest significance of Home Rule is that it has enabled us to regain control of the education of our children. . . .We must now begin to assess whether or not our school system is truly becoming an Inupiat School system reflecting Inupiat educational philosophies, or are we, in fact, only theoretically exercising political control over the educational system that continues to transmit White urban culture. Political control over our schools must include professional control as well in our academic institutions if our academic institutions are to become an Inupiat School System able to transmit our Inupiat traditions, values and ideas.[3]

In his speech, Mr. Hopson also reiterated the basic purpose behind the formation of the North Slope Borough School District: stopping the assimilation process which had long been advocated by Bureau of Indian Affairs schools as the only way to "civilize" our people.

In assuming control over our educational system, which began after the establishment of the North Slope Borough School District in the mid-1970s,

Steven Patkotok (r) teaches ivory carving to Vernon Rexford.

we, the people of the northern countries, have struggled with the problem of Western content and approaches to education in our schools. While seeking to produce students with scholastic achievements comparable to those of other areas of the United States, the board has also sought ways to bring into our schools certain elements of historical and contemporary Inupiat Eskimo culture and knowledge of our natural environment. We have found that the attainment of academic skills in our students is directly related to our ability to successfully introduce Inupiat Eskimo concepts and educational practices into our schools. This paper describes some of our actions in this area. After discussing some important differences between the Inupiat and Western concepts of education, I will describe some of the modifications to our school system and innovations that we have implemented with some success.

The North Slope Borough School District, established in 1972, is the northern-most school district in the United States and encompasses the northern third of Alaska, an area of approximately 88,000 square miles. The district serves nine schools in eight villages with over 1,500 students, a majority of whom are Inupiat Eskimo (Northern Alaska Eskimo). The largest of these villages is Barrow, the northernmost community in the United States. Ipalook Elementary School, the largest of the nine schools, is located here, with a school population of 580 children from ECE (Early Childhood Education) through grade six. (Barrow has a separate junior/senior high school.) The smallest of our schools is Cully School in Point Lay, Alaska, with a total pupil population of forty-six, ECE through twelfth grade. Most of the other schools fall somewhere in between Ipalook and Cully.

What draws these nine schools together is a common heritage, language, and the municipal government under which they were established. We decided that local control was the only way to ensure that our values as Inupiat people were reflected within the school system. Great strides have been made with the formation of the school district and the subsequent redefining of the purpose of education. We had to take a "foreign" system — the Western educational system — and strive to make it work for us. This has not happened without its share of problems, however. The differences between cultures and lifestyles were ignored for far too many years in the hope that what worked for the White population could be made to work for our Native people by mere persistence.

The Role of Local Culture in the Learning Process

We, the indigenous people of the United States, have had to overcome many obstacles in order to acquire basic education. One of the main obstacles was language. Not only were we required to learn to read, at the same time we also had to learn the language we were learning to read in. In the late 1930s and early 1940s, in order to help children learn English, teachers visited Inupiaq parents and instructed them to speak only English to their children. Most parents knew very little, if any, English, so they were effectively being told to sever communication with their children. Parents were willing to comply with this instruction, except that their great love for their children and the necessity to interact with them sustained Inupiaq in the household, thus keeping alive the foundation of our culture. But severe retardation of our native language did take place in time. Besides ordering that English be spoken at home, teachers punished children for speaking their mother tongue in the classroom. I remember clearly catching myself many times speaking in Inupiaq during my first few years in school and feeling guilty for doing so. I was rarely caught and, therefore, rarely punished, but others were not so lucky. Many times we'd hear the whack of the ruler either on the head or the palm of the hand of any student caught being "naughty" and speaking in our language.

But we spoke in our own language in order to survive. Imagine learning to say a word in a language you did not know, and having no earthly idea what that word represented. As hard as learning a foreign language was, however, it was easier than absorbing the content of Western education. The world view of the West, the perspective from which our schoolbooks were written, was totally different from ours. Therefore, understanding what we were learning to read in the English language came very hard. For example, as I was learning to read, one of my earliest realizations was that, in the Western world, grandparents and other relatives are not people you see or visit every day, even when they live nearby in the same town or city. A visit from them is an occasion, a cause for special preparations. This behavior was so foreign to my experience that it took me a long time to understand what I was reading and to realize that extended families are not the norm in the Western world.

In our communities, visiting relatives is a frequent, everyday occurrence, learned in early childhood. Unplanned, spontaneous visits (as opposed to purposeful visits) bond our relationships with relatives and friends. When visiting is unplanned, it does not require a formal invitation; tea or a soft drink is usually served unless it is near mealtime, when visitors will be expected to join in the meal. Other cultural practices, such as the special relationships between grandparents and grandchildren, reinforce these visiting patterns. A high degree of social interaction is the norm in our communities.[4]

During the years my husband and I attended the University of Alaska in Fairbanks, my father's first cousin, an elderly lady, lived right in town, an area where I frequently shopped. When I took my father there for a visit I was soundly scolded for visiting only when I had a purpose — in this instance, taking my father to see her. Although I was living in the same town, I had not nurtured my relationship with my aunt with intermittent, spontaneous visits.

In the western world privacy is considered such a basic right that I am afraid many find it hard to understand the value of spontaneous visits. It is equally hard for us to understand why anyone would want to have so much privacy that developing nurturing relationships becomes very difficult, if not impossible. This is an example of one area where two very diverse cultures have different but equally valid values; members of both cultures have to strive to acknowledge and to understand each other's differences.

Another example of the proliferation of Western concepts and Western "realities" contained within textbooks is the "fact" that the sun rises in the East and sets in the West. This is included in tests that evaluate the child's understanding of the world around him or her. In the Arctic, however, the sun behaves differently. Depending on the time of year, it can do almost anything, six examples of which are: 1) it doesn't rise at all; 2) it peeks through the horizon for a few minutes; 3) it rises in the South and sets in the South a few minutes later; 4) it rises in the East and sets in the West; 5) it rises in the North and sets in the North almost twenty-four hours later; *or* 6) it doesn't set at all. During the whole process of moving from the first instance to the last, so gradual is the sun's movement along the continuum that it is almost imperceptible. You will note that the Western world's "fact" about the sun rising in the East and setting in the West is only one of various northern Alaskan realities. Saying that the sun rises in the East and sets in the West up here would be like saying that a yo-yo with a two-foot string reaches twelve inches. Certainly it does, at some instant, reach the twelve-inch point, but there are infinite points along the string that it also reaches, including being fully wound and fully extended.

Because the rising and setting of the sun rarely changes in the rest of the United States, it does seem a useful gauge in determining a child's learning. But for children in the far North, there are too many variables for "the" fact of where the sun rises and sets for it to be useful. For Western students, the

---

My Life

Baxter Adams, Grade 8

When I was small I went to go camping with my family. When I was
one years old I walked. When I was two I learned to talk. When I was
three I had lots of fun. When I was four I went to Anchorage. When I
was five I went to Seattle. When I was six I went to school. When I was
seven I went to a circus. When I was eight I went to Fairbanks. When I
was nine I got a first shotgun. When I was ten I got a bike. When I was
eleven I got a duck. When I was twelve I got a goose. When I was thirteen my uncle caught a whale. When I was fourteen the crews went
down to go whaling. That is my life.

---

direction of shadows or looking in the direction of the rising or setting sun
are obvious clues to the time of day. But when these clues were presented in
schoolbooks, I was always looking also for clues as to the time of year, which, I
later realized, even if they were given, would not have helped at all. Although
I am a puzzle fan, I was often understandably stumped by what I later learned
was no puzzle at all to Western students.

Those of us who experienced these problems during our schooling realized that we had to find a better way to teach our children. We who work at
the grassroots level of education — the locals PTAs, advisory committees,
and school boards — are in a unique position to observe schooling in action.
We are often the first to know when something works and when it doesn't.

Contrasting Definitions of Education

To me, educating a child means equipping him or her with the capability to
succeed in the world he or she will live in. In our Inupiat communities, this
means learning not only academics, but also to travel, camp, and harvest
wildlife resources in the surrounding land and sea environments. Students
must learn about responsibilities to the extended family and elders, as well
as about our community and regional governments, institutions, and corporations, and significant issues in the economic and social system.

"Education" and "schooling" have become quite interchangeable in everyday speech. When we talk of a person being educated we usually mean he or
she has gone though a series of progressively higher formal systems of learning. Although a person may be an authority on a subject, we don't usually
think of him or her as "educated" if he or she is self-taught. Since all of our
traditional knowledge and expertise is of this latter type, the concept of "an
educated person" has worked against us as a people, creating conflicting atti-

tudes, and weakening older and proven instructional methods and objects of knowledge. Therefore, we, the North Slope Borough School District School Board, have defined "education" as a life-long process, and "schooling" as our specific responsibility. This is expressed in our Educational Philosophy statement:

> Education, a lifelong process, is the sum of learning acquired through interaction with one's environment, family, community members, schools and other institutions and agencies. Within the Home Rule Municipality of the North Slope Borough, "schooling" is the specific, mandated responsibility of the North Slope Borough School District Board of Education.
>
> The Board of Education is committed to providing academic excellence in the "schooling" environment. This commitment to academic excellence shall focus on the learner, recognizing that each student brings to the "schooling" environment his own interests, learning styles, cultural background and abilities.[5]

We decided that our role is to control the environment of the schooling process: the building, the equipment and materials, the quality of teaching and counseling services — everything about our schools — to ensure that education can take place in the classroom.

Remember that education is also the passing down of a society's values to children. Although I suppose there are people who would disagree, I think teachers pass down values by what they do in certain situations. Showing approval to a child for quickly attempting to answer a question — even wrongly — is valuing a quick answer to questions. At home, this same child may have been taught not to say anything until he or she has observed and observed and observed, and feels certain that his or her answer is correct. At home, the parents value accuracy more highly than a quick answer. They know that accuracy may mean the difference between life and death in the Arctic. In grade school, however, many of us learned that the teacher would "reward" us when we spoke up, whether we were right or wrong. Only by hearing our responses could she determine whether or not learning was taking place. If the answer was correct, she would have the opportunity to praise us. If a wrong answer was given, this gave her the opportunity to correct us.

Education is more than book learning, it is also value-learning. To address this issue, we, as a board, have incorporated a cultural component into our new-hire orientation. The bilingual department is an integral part of the orientation, highlighting differences in how our children learn. We hope that awareness lessens the frustration of teaching children who do not respond in ways teachers usually expect.

It is interesting that the root of the English word "educate" is very similar to our Inupiaq concept of education. According to Webster:

> It has often been said that *educate* means 'to draw out' a person's talents as opposed to putting in knowledge or instructions. This is an interesting idea, but it

is not quite true in terms of the etymology of the word. 'Educate' comes from Latin *educare*, 'to educate', which is derived from a specialized use of Latin *educere* (from *e-*, 'out,' and *ducere*, 'to lead') meaning 'to assist at the birth of a child.'[6]

This old meaning of the English word "educate" is similar to our own Inupiat Eskimo word "iñuguq-"[7] — which literally means "to cause to become a person." It refers to someone who attends to the child in the formative years and helps him or her to become a person. In our Inupiat Eskimo society, the first few years of a child's life are a time when they are "becoming a person." Anyone who attends to the child during that time of his or her life is said to cause him or her to become a person, "iñugugaa."

We Inupiat believe that a child starts becoming a person at a young age, even while he or she is still a baby. When a baby displays characteristics of individual behavior, such as a calm demeanor or a tendency to temper tantrums, we say "he or she is becoming a person." In our culture, such characteristics are recognized and accommodated from early childhood. As each child shows a proclivity toward a certain activity, it is quickly acknowledged and nurtured. As these children and adults in the community interact, bonds are established that help determine the teacher and the activities which will be made available to that particular child. As education progresses, excellence is pursued naturally.

Parents often stand back and let a child explore and experience things, observing the child's inclinations. If a child shows an aptitude for skills that the parents don't possess, they might arrange for their child to spend time

Poem

Timothy Oomituk, Grade 8

Me
Excited, Active
Visiting, Talking, Playing
Teachers, Friend, School, Barrow
Working, Learning, Walking
Laughing, Big

Timothy

Larry Chrestman (l) and Timothy Oomituk (author of poem above) during individual work.

with an expert, or an adult may ask to participate in the education of the child. Thus, many adults in the community have a role in the education of our children.

When you hear the word "educate," you may think more often of the primary Webster definition, which is "to provide with training or knowledge, especially via formal education." In the Western tradition, educating children depends heavily on a system of formal schooling with required attendance until a certain age.

Our concept of education has much in common with the Western concept of "child-rearing." It is interesting to us that Eskimo practices of child-rearing are commonly regarded as "permissive," in contrast to Western methods. Our perception is that Western child-rearing practices are overly directive and controlling, essentially interfering and intruding in the development of the child. The development of individuality is constrained and childhood is prolonged in Western society.

Though most of the education in our traditional society was not formal, it was serious business. For us, education meant equipping the child with the wherewithal to survive in our world. Because social interaction is a part of survival in the Arctic, this included education in proper social behavior, as well as in equipping the child with the means with which to make a living. As Robert F. Spencer wrote in his description of traditional North Alaskan Eskimo society: "The educative process . . . succeeded in a remarkable way [to produce] an individual capable of living in the cooperative situation demanded by the social and natural environment."[8]

In the traditional Inupiat Eskimo culture, education was everybody's business. It was okay to admonish, scold, or otherwise correct the behavior of any child, whether or not one was a relative. The success of the child's education depended in large part on how well his or her parents accepted admonishment of their child by other members of their own community. We as a people valued this acceptance highly because we knew that every member of our village was involved in some way with equipping our child for success.

Educating for Success

We need to equip our children for all the choices to be made upon graduation. In the North Slope Borough a majority of our students choose to remain in their villages after graduation. To provide an adequate education for each child, therefore, we need to teach Arctic survival skills, as well as the academic skills needed for success in the Western world.

As stated above, there were problems inherent in the displacement of our traditional educational system with the Western model, which have to be addressed if we hope to make schooling a success for our children. I will now discuss our innovations in several key areas.

Teacher-Student Ratio

Most survival education took the form of one-to-one learning. A "student" had many teachers, each teaching the child during different parts of the day or year. Young boys were taught hunting skills by their father, uncle, grandfather, or another skilled hunter. Young girls learned from their mother, grandmother, or sister all the various skills needed to run a household, feed the family, and keep them warm.

In the Western education model, on the other hand, groups of students are put in a classroom and taught many skills throughout the year by a single teacher. The one-to-one student-teacher relationship is absent, and the assumption is that a single teacher is proficient in *all* the skills to be taught to the whole group.

We have addressed this difference in two ways. First, a low student-teacher ratio helps us to better address the needs of individual students. Second, teacher aides hired from within the community provide critical role models for students, since an overwhelming majority of our classroom teachers still have to be brought in from outside our school district.

Although we can never hope to reach the traditional one-to-one ratio through Western classroom teaching, we can recognize the role of other

Reading Hour in Barrow, Alaska. Martha Hopson (r) reads to (counterclockwise) Salomi Ahgeak, Mandy Olemaun, and Asisaun Panigeo.

"teachers" — parents, grandparents, community and church members — in the child's life and work with them toward the child's successful learning. We also need to recognize that the hours children spend away from the classroom are as much a part of their education as classroom time. This means teaching them how to use any situation as a learning experience. Excellent teachers recognize and teach this already. These are points we need to keep in mind, as a school board, when planning our educational program.

Skills Taught

The traditional education of the Inupiat people focused not merely on survival but on excellence. Although all children were expected to master the basics of subsistence living, the inclinations exhibited by each child were noted and nurtured. All specialties were needed in order for the culture to survive. A storyteller and philosopher was as integral to the community as a good provider or an excellent seamstress. Once an Inupiat Eskimo child shows an inclination, such as an interest in archery, storytelling, or sewing, that interest is nurtured by all concerned with his "education." He or she may be apprenticed to a relative or another member of the community who is an expert in that field. Certain other areas of education may be deemphasized so that the child may develop his or her talent.

Some years ago, at a gathering of elders for a regional Elders' Conference, Otis Ahkivgak recalled how he developed his hunting skills to the exclusion of learning other things considered equally important:

> You see, when they would have the "nalukataq' [blanket toss] festival I would never pay much attention. I would push along a sled by its stanchions and go hunting down there. That is the reason I don't know the great songs of the 'nalukataq' feasts. . . . Although I listened from where the airport is now, when they were singing long and loud I was occupying myself delightfully with the snipes. Although I can try singing them by following my recollection of their singing, I do not know them very well.[9]

Once Western education models were introduced into our culture, the nurturing of individual interests virtually stopped. No matter what the unique interests of the child, all were taught the same subjects, at the same pace, in the classroom.

Although we can no longer deemphasize other subjects a child needs to learn, we can recognize the talent within and use that interest to help the child succeed in other areas. This requires talent and creativity on the part of the teacher. We have excellent, creative teachers, but in order to fully utilize this talent we need to identify policies or regulations that restrict the exercise of their creativity and search for alternatives that fully support teachers.

Another way of attending to the quality of skills taught to the children is through building partnerships within the community. For many years now, departments with the North Slope Borough, such as the Planning, Public Safety, and Health and Social Services departments, have willingly sent employees to classrooms to give talks to students on subjects ranging from secretarial work, to surveying, to management. The children need to see how their studies are applicable to real life: how the command of English is important in secretarial work; the use of calculus in surveying; the role of logic, mathematics, and social skills in management decisions.

Parent Involvement

Another challenge is parent involvement. In our traditional society, once a "teacher" is identified, parents do not interfere. Although they, themselves, may not be experts in whatever is being taught, they have complete faith that the "teacher" will do whatever needs to be done to equip the child with the skills to succeed in our world.

Since Western education was introduced in the Arctic, Western teachers were given the same courtesy previously extended to Native "teachers": they were left to do with the child what they needed to do to educate him or her. After all, the teachers were the experts in the areas being taught, something that they, the parents, knew nothing about. Then, as today, this was often misinterpreted by educators to mean that parents did not care about their child's education, when, in fact, they were doing what they felt was in the best interest of the child.

Parent involvement, or rather the lack of it, is often touted as the problem of educating Native youngsters. What we, as people interested in Native education, need to do, now that we are fully immersed in Western education, is to assure parents that this particular type of education needs parent involvement in order for the child to succeed. Parents will become more involved only when they learn that their knowledge, regardless of the extent of their schooling, is valued and plays an important part in their child's education. Teachers need to reach out to individual parents and to the community. Because school was not a positive experience for some of those who are now parents, going to the school, even for parent-teacher conferences, is often intimidating. We hope that through positive interactions these parents can eventually become not only involved but keenly interested in other aspects of education.

Parent involvement is an important element in another specific area of education in the North: that of passing down the language of our people. As is the case with indigenous languages anywhere in the world, our children are our only hope for the survival of our language. Our cultures, as peoples indigenous to the United States, are unique and to be found nowhere else in the world. Once our languages disappear, we have nowhere else in the world to turn to revive them. Yet there has not been much support for the language preservation programs which Native Americans have been trying to administer. We must make certain that indigenous languages within North America are not allowed to die, and we must employ every humanitarian effort it takes to do so.[10]

Cultural Identity

Some of our greatest successes in the schooling process can be attributed to the fact that we take advantage of both the historical and contemporary culture of an area. For example, we invite elders into the classroom to tell stories and teach cultural activities (songs, dances, sewing), because in our society respect for elders is a value taught very early in life, and the classroom has become the place where so much of the child's education transpires. Every year, in the North Slope Borough School District schools, elders go to the schools to teach Eskimo dancing. This is one of the most positive and well-attended programs of the whole year. Eskimo dancing is incorporated into the annual Christmas programs at the schools, along with the usual Christmas songs. The children are very enthusiastic about learning and performing these Native dances.

Inupiat people have a long tradition of competitive athletic events, which are integral components of gatherings, celebrations, and trade fairs involving many groups from different parts of the Arctic. These unique sports events, which involve skills of agility, strength, and endurance, are fundamental to work and survival in the Arctic environment. In addition to developing skills, sporting events are used to provide lessons about discipline, patience, good humor, cooperation, and sharing: "A different kind of kid gets involved in the Native games than gets involved in basketball or wrestling.

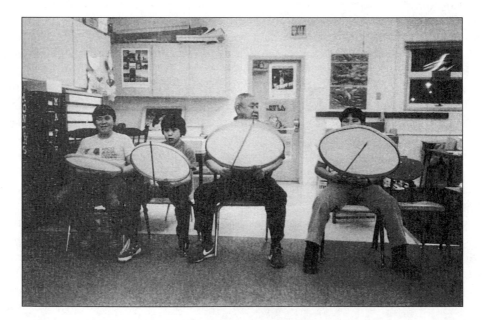

(L to r) Bradford Nageak, Kunneak Nageak, Larry Kaleak (teacher),
and Timothy Akpik practice Eskimo drums.

It's something Native kids can excel in, receive self-esteem from, that they get in no other way."[11] In the spring, Native high school children from throughout the state compete in Native Youth Olympics. Top finishers receive invitations to compete in the World Eskimo Indian Olympics in Fairbanks later in the summer, and the Arctic Winter Games, an international competition involving Canadian athletes, held every two years.[12]

In 1984, the North Slope Borough School District Board, recognizing that contemporary Inupiat culture now includes formal institutions, established Student Corporations. This is in response to the rapid growth of public and private institutions and organizations in the last fifteen years.[13] Among these institutions are specialized Native corporations that were mandated in the settlement of Native land claims by an act of Congress (Alaska Native Claims Settlement Act of 1971). Corporations are as much a part of everyday life in Arctic communities as subsistence hunting and fishing. Every child, in order to become capable of making life choices, needs to learn the basics of both realms. We, as a board, recognized that Native village and regional corporations needed employees and board members who are knowledgeable in all areas of corporate management. Thus, Student Corporations, established under the Laws of the State of Alaska, were incorporated into our schools. Children learn about how corporations are established, how proxies operate, and how elections and meetings are held. They also learn to evaluate moneymaking projects and, in the process, hone their decisionmaking skills.

These types of activities within the educational arena serve another, more basic, purpose. After decades of assimilation programs within the educational system that treated local cultures as detriments to the child's education, programs now teach that the culture of the area is *not* a detriment, but is indeed a valuable tool in the schooling of our children.

Bilingual Education

When bilingual education became a reality in the North, many parents and grandparents were very puzzled — and rightly so — by the about-face in the attitude of school staff in regard to speaking Inupiat. Suddenly children were not only allowed to speak Inupiaq in school but actively encouraged to do so. For many, however, this came too late. Parents who had been punished for speaking their native language in schools were raising their children using only the English language to communicate with them. Inupiaq in the home was being replaced by a broken Inupiaq, the English language interspersed with bits and pieces of Inupiaq. During this time, even bilingual education seemed a contradiction in terms to parents who had been persuaded that Native languages inhibit education.

It has sometimes been painfully hard work on the part of the local bilingual department and others interested in the survival of our language and culture to convince parents and the whole community about the need for language revival. But the efforts are paying off. Our district uses a very effective method, the Total Physical Response (TPR) method, of teaching our language to the children. The TPR method involves the whole learner, not just his or her mind. For instance, the teacher walks as he or she is teaching the world "walk," or portrays the emotions when teaching the words for these emotions. Each new word or sentence we hear a child use tugs at the heart, right in there where we hold memories of the times when we had almost . . . almost . . . lost one of the very abilities that make us uniquely who we are.

Addressing Issues

When we talk about educating our children for success we need to examine every facet of schooling to see if it is serving its purpose. Sometimes this requires making some hard decisions. A few years ago we, as a board, reevaluated our philosophy, goals, and policies to make them compatible. After careful research and deliberation we took a bold step. We changed from an individualized learning system to competency-based education. As hard as this decision was, we needed to address the issue of graduates who could not read or write, much less make life choices. We saw that our students were advanced to higher grades not on the basis of skills achieved, but through a process of "social advancement": students were advanced to the next grade even if their skills were not adequate. As a school board, we identified this practice with the way individualized instruction was interpreted and carried out within our district.

Individualized instruction, though very successful in other areas, was never satisfactorily demonstrated within the North Slope. For instance, in some high school classes students were given a book at the beginning of the semester and expected to go as far as possible with it at their own pace. There were no objectives given. The students were only told to read and to do what the text requested they do, with the teacher there as a resource if needed. This was explained to one parent as being individualized instruction. It is instances such as this which alerted us, the Board, to problems within our system which needed to be addressed, such as teacher accountability. Recently we instituted a competency-based approach to student advancement because we felt that it was more congruent with our traditional educational practices. In the competency-based approach, skills expected to be mastered by students in a certain grade are identified. The students, then, must demonstrate mastery of competencies before they are promoted to the next grade. This approach is similar to our traditional practices in which elders expected children to master certain competencies before they went on to more difficult tasks.

When the Western economic system became a viable way of life in the North, right along with subsistence, we, as Native people, should have felt an ownership of the educational system that taught our children how to survive in our contemporary world, a world which needs people with academic capabilities. But because it is a western educational system, we, as parents and local populace, have found it hard to identify with. We tend to view it still as a foreign system that was thrust on us. The move to mastery learning, a type of education which we identify with, has helped us attain ownership of the educational system in our schools. Since we, as a board, have determined that our children cannot survive in our world without also learning the basics of the Western way of life, we have chosen to teach them that way of life, but in the way that has proven to work in educating generation after generation of our children — through mastery learning.

Although competency-based education was widely supported by the parents because of identification with their own teaching style, others had to be convinced that it was in the best interest of our children. The school district, in order to ensure the success of the program, conducted many in-service programs with teachers and parent groups across our district on the elements of competency-based education, including how content is taught, how learning is assessed, long-range plans for curriculum and instruction, identification of competencies in texts and other instructional material, and lesson design. Now in its third year, it has already proven to be a success. We find that our youngest children are ready for advancement because competencies are identified at the beginning of the year, and the teachers know what the child needs to master in order to advance to the next grade.

With changes in our school system in past years happening so often, we also have had to deal with the fact that our educational system was a mishmash of new ideas which, although these were excellent concepts, were never quite synthesized into a coherent unit or system. What happened was

---

The Dollar Bill

Naomi Ann Itta, Grade 7

Last year, in 6th grade, Mrs. Albert gave all the graduating seniors a dollar bill along with a card.

The dollar bill that I received is very special to me because I liked Mrs. Albert like she was an aunt.

The same day we received the dollar bill, I thanked her by giving her a picture of myself.

At the end of the year I knew that Mrs. Albert was proud of us, not because of the dollar bill, but because of the smile that shined on us like the sun over the ocean.

---

that a group of students were taught using one system for a few years, and then were taught using another system. Because of this lack of continuity we have students in the upper grades who need extra help.

We are currently focusing on providing the very best atmosphere for learning for all children, and doing all we can to remedy the problems some of the older children have because of the deficiencies of earlier systems and the lack of continuity. One of the best ways we have found to address this problem is through enhanced guidance and counseling services. Besides providing counselors in each school site, we also provide a district-wide counselor who travels routinely to all schools, providing individual as well as group counseling. She is also available to travel to villages to help in crisis situations as needed. This coming year we are expanding services to give children better access to guidance and counseling, which may help them deal with difficulties for which they may not be well enough equipped.

Conclusion

In order to provide the best possible education for our children, we need first to identify the desired "product" of our schooling system and then to provide a system through which to acquire that product.

We, as a board, already know that we want young adults capable of becoming productive, happy citizens in whatever world they choose. We then need to make certain that all aspects of the schooling system, especially the environment, are conducive to the achievement of that goal. Above all, we must make certain that cultural differences in the way we view the goals and objectives of programs are addressed. The way different cultures choose to achieve the same goals and objectives varies greatly. We need to take as much care in choosing the system as we do in defining our goals.

We now have an excellent and effective school system in place, based on research that calls for specifying the school mission, educational expectations, curriculum and instruction, and monitoring time on task, student progress, and home-school relations. Profiles of these characteristics have been done on all of our schools in the District. Therefore, we are not as quick to turn to every current trend in education. We are not, however, hesitant to research new ideas. But we take extra effort to make certain the new ideas are compatible with our philosophy. In this way we assure our children the best education we can give them, as well as provide needed stability in programs and goals. Thus, we can ensure that we are, indeed, serving the purpose of education.

Notes

1. "Inupiat" is the plural form of the name we call ourselves, the singular being "Inupiaq." "Inuk," the stem, means "a person." The ending "-piaq" means "real,"

"most common," or "the most prevalent type." Although the plural form is commonly translated as "the real people," a more accurate translation would be "the most common type of people," or "the people we are most familiar with."

Although either the singular or plural form can stand alone, sometimes — for more clarity — additional nouns are used:

> If you are talking about one person, you use "Inupiaq" ("An Inupiaq [person] came to see me.")

> If you are talking about a people, you use "Inupiat" ("The Inupiat [people] love to sing.")

When the word is coupled with "Eskimo," which is an easily understood (though non-Inupiaq) word, convention has it take the plural form. Thus we have such sentences as: "She is a fluent Inupiat Eskimo speaker," or "She is a fluent Inupiaq speaker." Both are correct.

The word "Eskimo" is a common term for the circumpolar peoples, who include the Inupiat as well as other groups. We prefer "Inuit" to "Eskimo," but it is less easily recognized by non-Inuit. If we tried to uncomplicate this for the sake of non-Inupiaq speakers, the sentence would begin to lose meaning for Inupiaq-speaking readers. We ask English readers to bear with what seems to be inconsistencies. We are trying, as with everything else, to use a foreign system (English) to get across some Inupiaq concepts and have it make sense to both groups.

2. For more information on passing down values through traditional stories and legends, see Edna MacLean's keynote speech given at the Alaska Bilingual/Bicultural Conference in 1987, available through the State of Alaska Department of Education and Early Development, 801 West 10th Street, Juneau, AK 99801-1878.

3. Eben Hopson speech, December 1975. On file at the Inupiat History, Language and Culture Division of the Planning Department, North Slope Borough, P.O. Box 69, Barrow, AK 99723.

4. For more information on Inupiat extended family relationships, see Rosita Worl and Charles W. Smythe, *Barrow: A Decade of Modernization* (Anchorage: U.S. Department of the Interior, Minerals Management Service, Alaska OCS Region, Socioeconomic Studies Program Technical Report No. 125, 1986); Robert F. Spencer, *The Northern Alaskan Eskimo*, Smithsonian Institution, Bureau of American Ethnology Bulletin 171 (Washington, DC: U.S. Government Printing Office, 1959); or Ernest S. Burch Jr., *Eskimo Kinsmen: Changing Family Relationships in Northwest Alaska*, American Ethnological Society Monograph No. 59 (St. Paul: West, 1875).

5. North Slope Borough School District Policy Manual, Policy AD (Educational Philosophy), Adopted 10/13/76, Revised 8/11/87.

6. *Webster's II New Riverside University Dictionary* (Boston: Houghton Mifflin, 1984), p. 418.

7. Inupiaq words followed by a hyphen are stems that need at least an ending to make sense. For those interested in more information about the structure of the language, please see the introduction to *Iñupiallu Taŋŋillu Uqaluŋisa Ilaŋich, Abridged Iñupiaq and English Dictionary*, compiled by Adna Ahgeak MacLean (Fairbanks: University of Alaska, 1980).

8. *The Northern Alaskan Eskimo*, p. 239.

9. Kisautaq (Leona Okakok's Eskimo name), *Puiguikaat (Things You Should Never Forget), Proceedings of the 1978 Elders Conference*, North Slope Borough, 1981, p. 367.

10. For more information on efforts to preserve Alaska Native Languages, contact the Alaska Native Language Center, University of Alaska Fairbanks, Box 757680, Fairbanks, AK 99775.

11. Statement by Reggie Joule, in *Heartbeat: World Eskimo Indian Olympics*, Annabel Lund, writer; Howard Simons, editor; Mark Kelly, photographer, and Clark Mischler, photo editor (Juneau: Fairweather Press, 1986).

12. For more information on these sports, see *Heartbeat*; F. H. Eger, *Eskimo Inuit Games* (Vancouver: X-Press, n.d.).
13. For a description of the recent formation of a profusion of governmental institutions, corporations, boards, and commissions, in our areas, see Worl and Smythe, *Barrow: A Decade of Modernization.*

Fact and Fiction:
Stories of Puerto Ricans in U.S. Schools

SONIA NIETO

Puerto Rican youths have been attending U.S. schools for nearly a century. As a result of the takeover of Puerto Rico after the Spanish-American War, in the early 1900s Puerto Ricans began arriving in New York and other northeastern cities in increasing numbers. Sociologist Clara Rodríguez has suggested that all Puerto Ricans, regardless of actual birthplace, have been "born in the U.S.A." because all are subject to federal laws and to an imposed U.S. citizenship that was neither sought nor particularly desired (1991). One result of this citizenship, however, has been that Puerto Ricans have been free of the travel restrictions and similar limitations faced by other immigrants to the United States.[1] At first Puerto Ricans came in small numbers, but after the 1917 Jones Act was passed, which made Puerto Ricans U.S. citizens, the numbers grew steadily (Sánchez Korrol, 1983/ 1994). By the 1940s, a massive out-migration from the island was in progress, and at present, approximately two-fifths of all Puerto Ricans, or 2.75 million people, reside in the United States, a dramatic example of a modern-day diaspora (Institute for Puerto Rican Policy, 1992).

The Puerto Rican community is constantly changing, as families seeking a better economic future regularly arrive in the United States and return often to the island. This circulatory migration, called *vaivén* ("coming and going"), has helped to redefine immigration from the life-transforming experience that it was for most European immigrants at the turn of the century to "a way of life" for a great many Puerto Ricans in the latter part of the century (National Puerto Rican Task Force, 1982). The nature of the migration has also profoundly influenced such issues as language use, identity , and cultural fusion and retention.

Schools and classrooms have been among the sites most seriously impacted by the Puerto Rican presence in the United States, especially during the past two decades, during which Latino children have become the fastest growing ethnic group in public schools. A small number of Puerto Rican students have fared very well academically, and some have expressed gratitude for opportunities offered in U.S. schools that might have never been avail-

Harvard Educational Review Vol. 68 No. 2 Summer 1998, 133–163

able to poor, working-class children in Puerto Rico (see, for example, the comments of many of the writers interviewed in Hernandéz, 1997). The majority, however, have had difficult and unsatisfactory experiences, including low levels of academic achievement, severe ethnic isolation, and one of the highest dropout rates of all groups of students in the United States (National Center for Educational Statistics [NCES], 1995). The troubled history of the education of Puerto Ricans in U.S. schools is almost a century old, and although it has been chronicled for at least seventy years, it is, in the words of Catherine Walsh, "a disconcerting history of which most U.S. educators are totally unaware" (1991, p. 2). Thus, in spite of Puerto Ricans' growing visibility, much of their history in U.S. schools has yet to be heard.

More careful thought is now being given to that "disconcerting history," especially to the human face of the experiences of Puerto Rican students in U.S. schools, and such consideration is evident in the research literature, especially in more recent ethnographic research studies. It is also evident in a growing body of fiction as, over the past two decades, Puerto Ricans and their experiences in U.S. schools have become more visible as either a primary or an incidental topic in children's, young adult, and adult literature. As an educational researcher, I have concentrated much of my professional and personal attention and energy on the education of Puerto Rican youths, and I have learned a great deal about the promises and pitfalls of education in the United States. As a student of literature, I have also been fascinated by the growing number of fictional stories of Puerto Rican youngsters in U.S. schools, represented by such writers as Piri Thomas, Nicholasa Mohr, Judith Ortiz Cofer, Martín Espada, and others.

Yet fiction is not generally regarded as a legitimate source of data in the educational research community because it is thought to be overly subjective, emotional, and idiosyncratic. Precisely because of the emotional charge of fiction, however, it can be a rich source of knowledge about people's lives and experiences. As Anne Haas Dyson and Celia Genishi have asserted, "Stories are an important tool for proclaiming ourselves as cultural beings" (1994, p. 4). Santa Arias (1996) has suggested that Latino writers serve an important function in that they redefine "the border" as a place of multiple realities and of rebellion. The literature they write, she says, can be understood as a bridge between cultures: "They not only write in order to present a testimonial of survival, but to intervene at various levels in a definition of these borderlands, of what it is like to live in between geographical, linguistic, and cultural worlds" (p. 238).

Fiction can be used in schools to make the lives and experiences of Puerto Ricans more visible than they have been. Stories can also serve as liberating pedagogy in the classroom because they challenge the one-dimensional and largely negative image of Puerto Ricans pervasive in U.S. society. These negative depictions can motivate Puerto Rican writers to present another facet of their community through their writing. One such writer, Jack Agüeros, notes that he feels an obligation "to present our people as we know them, from the inside, from the heart, with all the details" (Hernandéz, 1997, p. 24). Such work can provide evidence of the debilitating experiences that some children have had, in addition to suggesting alternative and more positive possibilities for their future. Puerto Rican authors have written about schooling in the United States in numerous ways, from reports of confrontations with uncaring teachers and unthinking bureaucracies, to stories about teachers who have made a positive difference in the lives of children, to explorations of issues such as colonization, race, ethnicity, social class, and identity — all issues that are central to the lives of Puerto Rican youngsters. Jay Blanchard and Ursula Casanova (1996) suggest that fiction can be a convincing source of information for teachers, as well as a catalyst for thinking about teaching and learning, as demonstrated in their recent text of short stories geared to preservice and practicing teachers. In their book, Blanchard and Casanova use stories to help illustrate significant themes in teaching, such as the role of families, the need to develop meaningful relationships with students, and the world of imagination.

In summary, the growing body of fiction about Puerto Ricans in U.S. schools is a fertile avenue for exploring and analyzing issues that have heretofore been largely invisible in educational research. By using the title "Fact and Fiction" in this article, I do not mean to suggest that educational research always represents facts, or "the truth," and that fiction is make-believe. Quite the contrary: because the fiction I have used in my analysis includes the voices and experiences of students themselves (or authors' recollections of their experiences as students), stories can frequently teach lessons about life and reality more dramatically and candidly than educational research. A merging of these two arenas of literature — fact and fiction — can be both engaging and illuminating. Before considering the common themes in the literature, I first provide an overview of the education of Puerto Ricans in U.S. schools.

Puerto Rican Students in U.S. Schools

Puerto Ricans have achieved the questionable distinction of being one of the most undereducated ethnic groups in the United States. The story of this miseducation is infused with controversy concerning Puerto Rico's political status, conflicts over the role of culture and language in U.S. schools and society, harsh experiences with discrimination based on race, ethnicity, language, and social class, and the Puerto Rican community's determination to define and defend itself.

Almost from the time Puerto Rican students started attending schools in the United States, they have experienced problems such as high dropout rates, virtual absence from top ability groups, massive levels of retention, and low academic achievement (Association of Assistant Superintendents, 1948; ASPIRA, 1968; Margolis, 1968; Morrison, 1958; NCES, 1995; Walsh, 1991). The high dropout rate, for instance, is an issue that was discussed as early as 1958 in *The Puerto Rican Study,* a massive three-year investigation into the educational problems of Puerto Rican youngsters in New York City schools, who by then numbered almost 54,000. In the intervening forty years, when the U.S. Puerto Rican school-age population grew to nearly a million (Institute for Puerto Rican Policy, 1996), dropout rates as high as 70 to 90 percent have been consistently reported in cities throughout the Northeast (ASPIRA, 1993; Cafferty & Rivera-Martínez, 1981; Frau-Ramos & Nieto, 1993; U.S. Commission on Civil Rights, 1976).

As we shall see below, the standard explanations for the failure of Puerto Rican youths in U.S. schools have been rooted in the students themselves: that is, their culture (or lack of it), poverty, limited English proficiency, and poor parenting, among other issues, have been blamed for students' poor achievement (Nieto, 1995). On the other hand, schools' low expectations of these students, the poor preparation of their teachers, the victimization and racism they have faced, and the extremely limited resources of the schools themselves have rarely been mentioned as contributing to the lack of success of Puerto Rican students. Some of these problems are graphically documented in the poem "Public School 190, Brooklyn 1963" by Martín Espada:

> The inkwells had no ink.
> The flag had 48 stars, four years
> after Alaska and Hawaii.
> There were vandalized blackboards
> and chairs with three legs,
> taped windows, retarded boys penned
> in the basement.
> Some of us stared in Spanish.
> We windmilled punches
> or hid in the closet to steal from coats
> as the teacher drowsed, head bobbing.
> We had the Dick and Jane books,
> but someone filled in their faces
> with a brown crayon.
>
> When Kennedy was shot,
> they hurried us onto buses,
> not saying why,
> saying only that
> something bad had happened.
> But we knew
> something bad had happened,
> knew that before
> November 22, 1963. (1996, p. 25)

Another significant problem that has confounded the study of Puerto Ricans in U.S. schools is that historically much of the data have not been disaggregated according to ethnicity. Thus, Puerto Ricans are often lost in educational statistics labeled "Hispanic" or "Latino," as are Mexican Americans, Cubans, and Central and South Americans. There are valid reasons for using the overarching terms of Latino/a and Hispanic at times, including the fact that Latinos increasingly share physical space. This is the case, for example, with Puerto Ricans and Dominicans in the Northeast and Mexican Americans and Central Americans in California. Collectively, these groups have also tended to experience similar problems in education, housing, health care, and employment. However, the overarching terms do not recognize or take into consideration historic, regional, linguistic, racial, social class, and other important differences. Although many of the educational issues faced by Puerto Ricans are similar to those of Latinos in general, others are not. The tendency in research literature to lump all Latino groups together has resulted in muddling what might be sharp differences that could help explain how such issues as poverty, language dominance, political orientation, and school success or failure are manifested in different Latino ethnic groups.

As a subgroup within the Latino population, for instance, Puerto Ricans fare among the worst of all Latino groups in educational outcomes (Carrasquillo, 1991; Latino Commission, 1992; Meier & Stewart, 1991; Nieto, 1995), yet data to substantiate this situation are hard to find. For example, a national report by the National Council of La Raza found that more than one-third of all Latino children lived below the poverty line, compared with just one-eighth of White children (National Council of La Raza [NCLR], 1993). The even more distressing situation of Puerto Rican children is lost in these statistics, however, because the data were not disaggregated. Other research that centered specifically on Puerto Rican children found that they are at the *greatest* risk of being poor among other Latino ethnic groups, with a dramatic 58 percent living in poverty (ASPIRA, 1993; NCLR, 1993). Differences such as these may remain invisible unless the data are disaggregated. In this article, I use disaggregated data whenever possible, but I also use statistics on Latinos in general because they are more readily available.

Recurring Themes in Research and Fiction

Based on my reading of the literature in both educational research and fiction, I suggest that four interrelated and contrasting themes have emerged from the long history of stories told about Puerto Ricans in U.S. schools. They are: colonialism/resistance; cultural deficit/cultural acceptance; assimilation/identity; and marginalization/belonging. I explore here how each theme is illustrated in both research and fictional literature. To do this, I highlight significant literature in the educational arena, including historical analyses, commission findings and reports, and ethnographic studies. I also review and analyze works of fiction — short stories, novels, and poetry — that focus on the education of Puerto Rican students in U.S. schools. For every example of victimization or devaluation of Puerto Ricans there is a corresponding example of resistance or affirmation, and these examples can serve as important lessons for teachers and schools committed to helping Puerto Rican students succeed in school.

Ultimately, these four themes lead to the broader discussion concerning care as a significant motif missing from the research literature on the education of Puerto Rican children. I further argue that it is only through care that we can ensure that Puerto Rican students receive the affirmation they so urgently need in U.S. schools.

Colonialism/Resistance

The role that colonialism has played in the education of Puerto Ricans needs to be understood precisely because Puerto Rico and the United States are connected through colonial ties. Although officially called a "territory" by the United States, Puerto Rico has virtually no control over its own destiny. For the past five hundred years, it has been little more than a colony, first of Spain and later of the United States. The fact that Puerto Rico and the United States were joined as a result of conquest (Rodríguez, 1991) is overlooked by historians, educators, and researchers, or minimized in much of the research literature. As a result, Puerto Ricans are generally perceived as simply one of the latest "newcomers" in the traditional European-style model of the immigration experience (Rodríguez, 1991). In fact, early writers such as the sociologist/priest Joseph Fitzpatrick focused on overpopulation as the overriding reason for the migration of Puerto Ricans to the United States (Fitzpatrick, 1971/1987a). Conveniently sidestepped is the contribution of U.S. imperialism to creating the structural changes that adversely affected the Puerto Rican economy and that eventually led to the massive migration. These included the wholesale purchase of Puerto Rican farmlands by absentee U.S. landlords to grow and harvest sugar, in the process displacing an enormous number of local farmers. Many of these migrated to the United States (Melendez, 1991; Sánchez Korrol, 1983/1997). Later research, including Fitzpatrick's later work (1987b), challenged this initial analysis as overly simplistic (Bonilla & Campos, 1981; History Task Force, 1979; Melendez, 1991; Rodríguez, 1991; Sánchez Korrol, 1983/1994).

Recent critical research has focused more carefully on the impact that Puerto Rico's colonial status has had on education, both on the Island and in the United States (*Centro,* 1997; Nieto, 1995, 2000; Walsh, 1991). When people are stripped of their language and culture, they are also largely stripped of their identity as a people. However, dispossessing people of language and culture does not need to take place with the gun; it is frequently done more effectively through educational policies and practices, the effects of which can can be even more brutal than those of the gun. The violence that takes place within schools and classrooms is more symbolic than real. According to Pierre Bourdieu (1977), symbolic violence refers to the maintenance of power relations of the dominant society through the manipulation of symbols.

Given Puerto Rico's long-standing colonial relationship with the United States, it is not surprising that the schools in Puerto Rico have been and continue to be sites of symbolic violence. In a groundbreaking study of the Americanization of schools in Puerto Rico, Aida Negrón de Montilla documented how the United States began to change educational policies and practices almost as soon as it took possession of the island in 1898. Some of these changes were blatant, such as language policies that attempted to wipe out the Spanish language. Within the first several decades, however, it became apparent that total obliteration of the language was impossible, both because the policy was not working and because many Puerto Ricans perceived it as a crude example of cultural imperialism. By the late 1940s, the United States had settled for enforced ESL instruction in all island schools. Other colonizing policies in the schools included the wholesale adoption of U.S. textbooks, curriculum, methods, and materials in island schools; the imposition of the Pledge of Allegiance and other patriotic rituals; and the preparation and expectations of teachers as agents of English and U.S. culture (Negrón de Montilla, 1971).

The symbolic violence represented in these policies is translated into stories that are usually told in sardonic but amusing ways. For instance, the stories of Abelardo Díaz Alfaro are hilarious examples of colonialism gone awry. In "Santa Cló va a La Cuchilla" (1962), Santa Claus, with all the trappings of his Yankee identity, including a sweltering red suit, shows up in La Cuchilla, a rural community with no understanding of this cultural icon. The story is a humorous example of how colonies are saturated with culturally meaningless symbols, while culturally meaningful ones — in this case Los Reyes Magos, or the Three Wise Men — are displaced or disparaged.

In another story, "Peyo Mercé Enseña Inglés" ("Peyo Mercé Teaches English"), Díaz Alfaro (1978) relates the panic experienced by a rural teacher who speaks only Spanish when he receives the mandate from the central office to teach his students English: Peyo Mercé is horrified when he realizes that he has to teach "inglés en inglés!" ("English in English!") (p. 98). The mandate, a historically accurate event, makes for a comical story told with great humanity and insight. Like all good teachers, Peyo Mercé tries to find something in the U.S.-imposed textbook to which his students can relate, and he comes upon a picture of a rooster. Using the picture, he instructs the children to say "cockle-doodle-doo," the sound that roosters make in English. As the story concludes, one of the young students can no longer accept the lie that he and his classmates are learning: he rejects both the English of the rooster and, presumably, the cultural imposition that it represents by stating emphatically that perhaps this is *another* kind of rooster, but that the roosters in *his* house clearly say "¡cocoroco!" — the sound made by roosters in Spanish.

Other examples of the link between politics and education in the early colonization of Puerto Rico by the United States were the establishment of para-educational organizations and activities — for example, the Boy Scouts, the Girl Scouts, and the Future Homemakers of America — and the substitution of Puerto Rican holidays with U.S. holidays, such as Washington's Birthday and Thanksgiving (Negrón de Montilla, 1971). Ironically, even the U.S. celebration of independence became an official holiday in the colony. In fact, the colonial presence can be felt through the manipulation of the tastes, values, and dispositions of the Puerto Rican people. In another scene from *When I Was Puerto Rican*, Esmeralda Santiago (1993) recounts how the mothers of the children in Miss Jiménez's class were asked to attend a meeting with experts from the United States who would teach them "all about proper nutrition and hygiene, so that we would grow up as tall and strong as Dick, Jane, and Sally, the *Americanitos* in our primers" (p. 64). At the meeting, the experts brought charts with unrecognizable food staples:

> There were carrots and broccoli, iceberg lettuce, apples, pears, and peaches. . . . There was no rice on the chart, no beans, no salted codfish. There were big White eggs, not at all like the small round ones our hens gave us. There was a tall glass of milk, but no coffee. . . . There were bananas but no plantains, potatoes but no *batatas* [sweet potatoes], cereal flakes but no oatmeal, bacon but no sausages. (p. 66)

At the end of the meeting, the mothers received peanut butter, cornflakes, fruit cocktail, peaches in heavy syrup, beets, tuna fish, grape jelly, and pickles, none of which formed part of the Puerto Rican diet, and the mother of the protagonist, Negi, concluded, "I don't understand why they didn't just give us a sack of rice and a bag of beans. It would keep this family fed for a month" (p. 68). Such educational policies thus imposed U.S. mainstream cultural values, tastes, and attitudes on Puerto Rican children and their families.

Along with their luggage and other prized possessions, Puerto Rican families also bring with them to the United States this legacy of colonialism. Officially U.S. citizens, Puerto Ricans are not national immigrants, and therefore it is their language, culture, and ethnicity, rather than their nationality, that separate them from their U.S. peers (Cafferty & Rivera-Martínez, 1981). Because the colonial relationship has made Puerto Rican migration a constant experience, in the process it has created "the students in between," those who spend time on both Island and mainland (Quality Education for Minorities Project, 1990). One consequence of colonialism is that issues of identity, belonging, and loyalty are at the very core of the psychological dilemmas faced by Puerto Rican youngsters, and even adults, who know only too well what it means to be a "cultural schizophrenic." In fact, the image of an air bus connecting Puerto Rico to New York has made its way into popular Puerto Rican fiction through Luis Rafael Sánchez's story, "The Flying Bus," in which Sánchez describes one of the passengers as "a well-poised woman . . . [who] informs us that she flies over *the pond* every month and that she has forgotten on which bank of it she really lives" (1987, p. 19; emphasis in original). Joy De Jesús has described the resulting identity crisis in this way:

> What makes growing up Puerto Rican unique is trying to define yourself within the unsettling condition of being neither here nor there: "Am I Black or White?" "Is my primary language Spanish or English?" "Am I Puerto Rican or American?" For the Puerto Rican child, the answers to these questions tend to be somewhere in between, and never simple. (1997, p. xviii)

Sandra María Estevez poetically expresses the same sentiment of being "in-between," in "Here":

> I am two parts / a person
> boricua/spic
> past and present
> alive and oppressed
> given a cultural beauty
> . . . and robbed of a cultural identity (1991, p. 186)

Stories about divided identities and loyalties, even among children, are common in the work of Puerto Rican writers. Abraham Rodríguez's "The Boy Without a Flag" is a classic example of this idea. After listening to his father denounce U.S. imperialism in Puerto Rico and throughout the world, the eleven-year-old protagonist decides that he will no longer salute the U.S. flag. When his teacher asks him to explain this decision, he announces, using the very same words he had heard his father use, "Because I'm Puerto Rican. I ain't no American. And I'm not no Yankee flag-waver" (1992, p. 18). The principal, who tries to convince him that this posture may in the long run jeopardize his future, asks: "You don't want to end up losing a good job opportunity in government or in the armed forces because as a child you indulged your imagination and refused to salute the flag?" (p. 26). The young boy is crestfallen when he realizes that his father is not only embarrassed by his behavior but has, in fact, sided with the principal, a position he has no doubt taken to protect his son. Martín Espada tells a similar story through the poem "The Year I Was Diagnosed with a Sacrilegious Heart":

> At twelve, I quit reciting
> the Pledge of Allegiance,
> could not salute the flag
> in 1969, and I,
> undecorated for grades or sports,
> was never again anonymous in school. (1993, pp. 72–74)

José Angel Figueroa echoes this theme in "Boricua," a poem that speaks of cultural and political conflict. Referring to education, he writes

> s c h o o l s
> always wanted
> to cave in your
> PuertoRican Accent
> & because you
> wanted to make it
> you had to pledge
> allegiance lefthanded
> because you
> had lost your soul
> during some english exam. (1991, p. 222)

These flag stories allegorically describe resistance to colonialism even among young children.

Colonial status cannot explain all of the educational problems experienced by Puerto Rican students in U.S. schools. Although it is true that the educational instability that results from moving back and forth can lead to low academic achievement, poor language skills, and high dropout rates, there are many Puerto Rican youngsters who do not move back and forth between Puerto Rico and the United States and therefore do not experience this kind of educational disruption. By and large, however, they also experience educational failure. Some theorists have even speculated that colonial status per se may have an impact on students' actual academic achievement (Gibson & Ogbu, 1991; Ogbu, 1987). John Ogbu's (1987) theory concerning voluntary and involuntary immigrants is helpful in understanding this phenomenon. According to Ogbu, it is important to look not simply at a group's cultural background, but also at its political situation in the host society and the perceptions it has of opportunities available in that society. Thus, the major problem in the academic performance of U.S. Puerto Ricans is not that they possess a different language, culture, or cognitive or communication style than students in the cultural mainstream. Rather, the nature of their history, subjugation, and exploitation, together with their own responses to their treatment, are at the heart of their poor academic achievement (Ogbu, 1987).

Because the problem of the poor academic achievement of Puerto Rican youngsters cannot be blamed simply on the legacy of colonialism, I now turn to an exploration of a related concept, the pressure to assimilate, and its effect on the education of Puerto Rican students.

Assimilation/Identity

In the United States, public schools have always had a pivotal role in assimilating immigrant and other non-mainstream students because they have historically stripped them of their native cultural identity in order to impose the majority culture on them. The creation of the common school during the nineteenth century was based in part on the perceived need to assimilate immigrant and other students of widely diverse backgrounds (Katz, 1975). Hence, although the "melting pot" has been heralded as the chief metaphor for pluralism in the United States, a rigid Anglo-conformity has been in place for much of U.S. history. According to Joel Spring (1997), schools in the United States have assimilated students with practices that include flag ceremonies and other patriotic celebrations, the replacement in school curricula of local heroes with national ones, a focus on the history and traditions of the dominant White culture, and the prohibition of native language use in the school. The educational establishment repeated this process, at least in part, in schools in Puerto Rico, and it has been part of the educational landscape since the U.S. takeover of the island in 1898.

These socializing and assimilating agents, then, are no strangers to Puerto Rican students when they enter U.S. schools. Assimilation for Puerto Rican children continues in U.S.-based schools, usually in the urban centers of the Northeast. The image of decaying urban schools, graphically portrayed by a number of Puerto Rican writers, serves as a metaphor for the assimilation of newcomers. Historically, most newcomers to the United States have been poor, uneducated, and relegated to the urban ghettos from which earlier immigrants had fled. Schools in these urban ghettos often were old, worn, and dilapidated. Judith Ortiz Cofer, for instance, describes her first encounter with a school in Paterson, New Jersey, as follows:

> The school building was not a welcoming sight for someone used to the bright colors and airiness of tropical architecture. The building looked functional. It could have been a prison, an asylum, or just what it was: an urban school for the children of immigrants, built to withstand waves of change, generation by generation. (1990, p. 61)

In a powerful novel about a young girl's abuse-filled childhood, Alba Ambert compares the physical presence of her school in New York City with the apparent indifference of the staff who work there:

> Public School 9 was a red-brick structure built at the turn of the century. It loomed on 138th Street across from the Puerto Rico Theater like a huge armory vigilantly surveilling students, teachers, and staff who scuttled in and out of its wide staircase. . . . Teachers and principal lingered at the shore, their backs turned to the island of isolation in which the children lived. From the periphery, they looked away and refused to learn the language of the dispossessed. (1995, p. 113)

For El Cortes (2000), assimilation is portrayed through the rancid smells that are a result of the humiliation faced by children who throw up when they are prohibited from speaking Spanish, forced to eat strange foods, or ridiculed by their teachers for their customs and values:

School smells is a mess of bad smells and altogether they make one great big bad stink. Vegetable soup with smelly onions in it and rotten orange peel smells get mixed up with the King Pine old mop bleach smell and all of that gets mixed up with . . . throw up. School smells.

Assimilation takes place in numerous ways, and examples of this process, as well as its detrimental effects, abound in fact and in fiction. For instance, the extensive 1976 report by the U.S. Commission on Civil Rights concerning Puerto Ricans in the United States found that young people identified the schools' unresponsiveness to their cultural backgrounds as a primary reason for dropping out of school. Underpinning the pressure to assimilate newcomers is the ideology of "colorblindness"; that is, the view that failing to see differences epitomizes fairness and equality. *The Losers,* one of the early comprehensive reports on the education of Puerto Rican students in the United States, was commissioned by ASPIRA, an educational and leadership advocacy organization focusing on Puerto Rican youths. The report, among the first to challenge the prevalent melting pot ideology, persuasively described the ideology of colorblindness by focusing on the Puerto Rican children's teachers — mostly White, middle-class women with little or no personal or professional experiences with the Puerto Rican community:

> Denying her prejudices, the teacher also denies genuine differences among her students. . . . There is, of course, something to be said for the egalitarian belief that all people are basically similar; but teachers who deny authentic cultural differences among their pupils are practicing a subtle form of tyranny. . . . That is how the majority culture imposes its standards upon a minority, a cruel sort of assimilation forced onto children in the name of equality. (Margolis, 1968, p. 7)

In some cases, the situation has changed very little in the intervening three decades. A recent ethnographic study by Ellen Bigler (1997) in a classroom with a sizable proportion of Puerto Rican students in a small upstate New York town documented that almost all the teachers, most of whom were White, were uncomfortable acknowledging cultural, racial, and ethnic differences among their students; they insisted that they wanted to treat all their students "the same."

Schools also promote assimilation by mythologizing what Bigler calls "ethnic success stories" (1997, p. 9). The model for these Horatio Alger-type success stories is the struggling European immigrant who makes good by learning English and adapting to the cultural mainstream. The teachers and other residents of the town who perpetuated these stories were unaware of how Puerto Rican migrants differed from earlier European immigrants, due to their experiences with colonization, racism, and a different economic situation. One middle-school teacher remarked: "Why are these kids doing this? Why are they not speaking English when they can? Why aren't they trying to fit into the mainstream? . . . They're no different than earlier waves.

They worked, they learned the language, and that was your key to success" (p. 9).

One of the earliest and most exhaustively documented ethnographies concerning Puerto Rican children was carried out in 1965 in an East Harlem school (Bucchioni, 1982). Published years later, the study chronicled one case after another in which pressures toward assimilation took place in classrooms every day. In this particular study, the teacher recounted "the ethnic success story" when the children began to question why they lived in tiny, cramped apartments and shared a bathroom with other families, rather than in the kinds of spacious houses in middle-class neighborhoods that they were learning about in school. Juan, one of the children, mused aloud that only very rich people could live in those houses, to which his teacher Miss Dwight responded, "Not exactly rich, Juan. But they do work hard, and every day" (p. 210). When Juan answered that his father *also* worked hard, even on Sundays, Miss Dwight replied:

> It is difficult, sometimes, to earn enough money to do everything we want. It's important for you to remember that your work in school will some day help you to get a better job, earn more money, and live in a good home. . . . But let us remember that while we work toward something better, we must accept what we have now and try to appreciate the good things we have. (p. 210)

In the young-adult novel *Nilda*, Nicholasa Mohr articulates a cruder version of this myth through her character Miss Langhorn, who precedes the daily Pledge of Allegiance with "more or less the same speech": "Brave people they were, our forefathers, going into the unknown when man had never ventured. They were not going to permit the Indians to stop them. This nation was developed from a wild primitive forest into a civilized nation" (1986, p. 52).

The pressure to assimilate is also evident when schools identify the Spanish language as a problem. The first large-scale study of Puerto Rican children in the New York City schools, *The Puerto Rican Study* (Morrison, 1958), attempted to define and propose positive solutions to the problem of academic failure. It also identified the continuation of spoken Spanish in the home as "the chief deterrent" to Puerto Ricans' lack of academic progress. Several years later, the ASPIRA study roundly criticized this position and found the same message of "Spanish as a problem" still evident in many schools:

> In their eagerness to erase Spanish from the child's mind and substitute English, the schools are placing Puerto Rican children in an extremely ambiguous role. They are saying, "Forget where you came from, remember only where you are and where you are going." That is hardly the kind of message that inspires happy adjustments. (Margolis, 1968, p. 9)

Not only has the Spanish language been prohibited in the schools, but Puerto Rican students' accents and dialects have been disparaged as well. In

Nicholasa Mohr's *Nilda*, she describes in comic detail how Miss Reilly, the Spanish teacher in the all-female school attended by Nilda, speaks with a thick American accent while insisting that Castilian Spanish is the "real Spanish." She continues, ". . . and I am determined, girls, that that is what we shall learn and speak in my class; nothing but the best!" (1986, p. 214). Castilian Spanish raises issues of power and privilege because the general public, as well as many non-Latino Spanish teachers, consider it to be the variety of Spanish of the highest prestige. Nilda's experience has been shared by many Puerto Ricans and other Latinos, who end up either failing Spanish or dropping it.

Over the years, both fiction and research have chronicled the practice of Anglicizing students' names. In *The Losers,* Margolis documents a typical example: "José González, a kindergartner, has given up trying to tell his teacher his name is not Joe. It makes her angry" (1968, p. 3). Thirty years later, Ellen Bigler found a remarkably similar situation in her ethnography of an upstate New York school. There, a teacher anglicized Javier to Xavier, saying that "it would be better in the long run for him to have a more American-sounding name" (1997, p. 13). The same scenario forms the basis for the story in Alma Flor Ada's novel for young children, *My Name is María Isabel* (1993). María Isabel Salazar López, a new third-grader, is given the name "Mary" by her teacher to distinguish her from the other two Marías in the classroom. María Isabel has a hard time remembering her new name and she is repeatedly scolded by her teacher for not responding when called on. María Isabel loves her name because it includes the names of both her grandmothers. When the teacher assigns her students a composition entitled "My Greatest Wish," María Isabel tells the teacher in her essay why her name is so important to her and why her greatest wish is to be called by her real name. In this case, there is a happy ending: the teacher, basically a sensitive and caring person, calls her María Isabel the very next day. Unfortunately, in real life, it is not always this way.

Puerto Rican resistance to assimilation has been visible in the educational literature, as well as in fiction. Educational literature has rationalized assimilation on many grounds: the very creation of the common school was based on the need to homogenize millions of European immigrants into U.S. mainstream culture (Appleton, 1983; Katz, 1975). The schools' reaction to the cultural and linguistic differences of Puerto Ricans and other students of color have been even more negative, and for many years they resulted, for example, in prohibitions on using Spanish in the schools (Crawford, 1992). Recent research on cultural and linguistic identity has challenged the long-standing conventional wisdom that in order to get ahead one must sacrifice one's identity. In the case of Spanish, for instance, Ana Celia Zentella's study (1997) of language practices among Puerto Rican children growing up in a low-income community in New York City found that the most academically successful students in the study were also the most fluent bilinguals. They also happened to be in bilingual rather than monolingual classes. The reluctance to drop Spanish has been found in reports as long ago as the ASPIRA study, *The Losers* (Margolis, 1968). A more recent study cited by Kenneth Meier and Joseph Stewart (1991) found that Puerto Rican parents, more than any other Latino parents, wanted their childeren to retain their Spanish while they also wanted their children to become fluent in English. Resisting the push for assimilation, Puerto Rican students and their communities have always attempted to claim and maintain their identities, even within the school setting. In the Puerto Rican community, there has been an insistence that one can be *both* Puerto Rican *and* a good student, *both* English- *and* Spanish-speaking; in a word, that one can be bilingual and bicultural.

Linguistic and cultural maintenance have implications for academic success. For instance, a study by Jean Phinney (1993) of high school and college students of diverse racial and ethnic minority backgrounds found a significant correlation between ethnic identity and positive self-esteem. This link has important implications for student achievement. For example, in case studies of Puerto Rican and Vietnamese adolescents in a Boston bilingual program, Virginia Vogel Zanger (1987) found that the students' sense of stigmatization had a negative impact on their academic development. Another convincing counter-argument to the perceived need to assimilate is found in research on Cambodian refugee children by the Metropolitan Indochinese Children and Adolescent Service. In this study, researchers found that the more the children assimilated into U.S. mainstream culture, the worse was their emotional adjustment (*New voices*, 1988). Another study of Southeast Asian students found that higher grade point averages correlated with *maintaining*, rather than wiping out, traditional values, ethnic pride, and close social and cultural ties with members of the same ethnic group (Rumbaut & Ima, 1987).

In research with academically successful students of diverse backgrounds, I also found that there was a marked desire on the part of most to maintain their cultural and linguistic identification (Nieto, 1996). Further, in another study of high-achieving, college-bound Latino students in a comprehensive Boston high school, Zanger found similarly that these students voiced a tremendous resistance to assimilation. Referring to the pressure to assimilate that she felt from her teachers, one young woman stated, "They want to *monoculture* [you]" (1993, p. 172). These Latino students also demonstrated great pride in their cultural background and articulated a desire to be accepted for who they were. In the words of one student, "You don't need to change your culture to be American" (p. 175).

Cultural Deficit/Cultural Acceptance

In the search for explanations for the dismal educational failure of Puerto Rican students, a number of theories concerning cultural acceptance and "cultural deficit" have been used over the years. Numerous commissions, panels, and councils, as well as many individual researchers, who have studied the plight of Puerto Rican students in U.S. schools have used labels ranging from "problem" to "culturally deprived" to the more recent "at risk" to charcterize these students (Nieto, 1995). Such labels are at the very core of the deficit theories that began to define Puerto Rican students almost from the time they first entered U.S. schools. For example, a 1935 report by the New York City Chamber of Commerce described Puerto Rican students in general as "slow learners" (Sánchez Korrol, 1994). The previously cited *Puerto Rican Study* (Morrison, 1958) likewise indicated that teachers and schools were viewing Puerto Rican students' home language and culture as shortcomings and barriers to their education. Another early report stated that "some observers are of the opinion that the Puerto Rican, as well as members of the other Spanish-speaking groups, is less inclined to seek out educational advantages and follow them up by regular attendance than individuals of some of the other cultural groups" (Chenault, 1938/1970, p. 145). In another example, a teacher made the following comment about her Puerto Rican students: "The only way to teach them is to repeat things twenty-five times unless for some reason it means something to them" (Sexton, 1965, p. 58). Much of the early research literature similarly characterized Puerto Rican students as impulsive, undisciplined, and troublesome, all traits thought to be inherited from their families and which made them incapable of profiting from their education (Nieto, 1995).

That idea of cultural deficit has translated into lower teacher expectations for many Puerto Rican students. For instance, Virginia Vogel Zanger's (1993) research among high-achieving Latino students found that their perceptions of teachers' failure to push them was experienced emotionally as abandonment. Similar findings have been expressed over and over in the research literature (Darder & Upshur, 1993; Hidalgo, 1992; Margolis, 1968; National Commission, 1984). Fiction literature mimics this finding. *A Perfect Silence* (Ambert, 1995), for example, describes low expectations in depressing detail:

> Teachers never expected the children, who were mostly Puerto Rican and Black, with a smattering of Irish and Italians too poor to have fled the ghetto, to occupy the ivy-scented halls of distant universities or mark history with distinguished feats. Teachers felt grateful beyond their expectations when girls turned twelve without "getting themselves pregnant," and boys managed to elude reform school. (p. 113)

Clearly, teachers, schools, and society in general have assumed that the problem of Puerto Rican students' failure lies with the students themselves, be it in their culture, family, genes, or lack of English skills. Although such problems as poverty, racism, poor language skills, neglect, abuse, and crime cannot be dismissed as contributing to the academic failure that some Puerto Rican youngsters face, deficit explanations have rarely considered how schools and society have been complicitous in causing these failures. Instead, deficit explanations have often considered students and their families solely responsible for failure. These theories have influenced the framing of the problems, as well as proposed solutions to them.

The paradigm of cultural deficiency was nowhere more clearly and destructively articulated than in *La Vida,* an extensive anthropological investigation of one hundred Puerto Rican families living in poverty in New York City and San Juan, Puerto Rico (Lewis, 1965). *La Vida* personified "the culture of poverty" and its negative ramifications for future generations through an in-depth study of the Ríos family, whom author Oscar Lewis described as "closer to the expression of an unbridled id than any other people I have studied" (p. xxvi). A particularly insidious description of his subjects reads:

> The people in this book, like most of the other Puerto Rican slum dwellers I have studied, show a great zest for life, especially for sex, and a need for excitement, new experiences and adventures. . . . They value acting out more than thinking out, self-expression more than self-constraint, pleasure more than productivity, spending more than saving, personal loyalty more than impersonal justice. (Lewis, 1965, p. xxvi)

Characterizations such as these left a mark on how U.S. society in general, and schools and teachers in particular, were to view the Puerto Rican community for decades.

The schools' perceptions of Puerto Rican students have often echoed those of Lewis. For example, Eugene Bucchioni's ethnography of a school in Spanish Harlem documented the conversation of two teachers in the hall: "'The Puerto Ricans seem to learn absolutely nothing, either here or at home.' 'Yes,' said Miss Dwight, 'all they seem to care about is sleeping, eating, playing, and having parties'" (1982, p. 202). In Alba Ambert's novel *A Perfect Silence,* the narrator describes teachers' attitudes about their Puerto Rican students that speaks volumes about their teachers' lack of cultural knowledge:

> They expressed shock that little girls would have their ear lobes pierced, a savage tribal custom that, they thought, had to be some sort of child abuse. They criticized when children were absent from school to care for younger siblings if a mother had to run errands, or if they had to translate for a sick relative in the hospital. They accused children of cheating when they copied from each other's homework. (Ambert, 1995, p. 113)

The assumption that what needs changing are the students is still prevalent in many schools and is revealed in much of the research on Puerto Rican education. In their study of four public schools with large percentages of Latino children, Antonia Darder and Carol Upshur (1993) found that most teachers in the schools mentioned the problem of poor achievement as residing in the children's lack of conceptual understanding in English, lack of motivation, and lack of retention, while only occasionally mentioning the in-adequate curriculum, the negative views of staff towards bilingual education, or their lack of cross-cultural understanding. Puerto Rican children in the four schools had quite different ideas about improving their schooling. When asked what they would like school to be like, they mentioned, among other things, the need to feel safe, to have newer and more interesting books and computers, and to have humorous and friendly teachers who would not yell at them (Darder & Upshur, 1993).

In *The Losers,* Margolis documents the following scene demonstrating how teachers assume Puerto Rican students' culture to be a barrier to their aca-demic achievement: "An honor student asked her counselor for a chance to look at college catalogues. 'Is that Italian or Spanish?' asked the counselor, looking at the name on the girl's card. 'Spanish? Now this is just my opinion, but I think you'd be happier as a secretary'" (1968, p. 3). Another scene, striking in its similarity, was recounted several years later during the public hearings held by the U.S. Commission for Civil Rights in preparation for their report on Puerto Ricans in the United States. There, a high school stu-dent from Pennsylvania told the commission of her repeated attempts to gain admission to an academic course. Her counselor, she said, warned her that "I should not aim too high because I would probably be disappointed at the end result" (1976, p. 108).

For many years, another common practice in schools was to place students back at least a grade when they arrived from Puerto Rico, a practice based on the dubious assumption that this would help them learn English and catch up academically. The effect of retaining students was found to be "particu-larly acute" by the U.S. Commission on Civil Rights, and it was described by one witness from Massachusetts as a leading cause for the high dropout rate:

> They came from Puerto Rico, they're in the 10th, 11th, or senior year of high school. . . . They came to Boston and they placed them in the 6th and 7th grades. You're wondering why they dropped out. . . . Here's a kid trying to learn and he automatically gets an inferiority complex and quits. (1976, p. 101)

This experience is echoed in the novel *When I Was Puerto Rican,* when the author tells the story of Negi, unceremoniously put back a grade despite her excellent academic record simply because she does not speak English. Negi, however, fights back, convincing the principal that she is eighth-grade mate-rial: "I have A's in school Puerto Rico. I lern good. I no seven gray girl" (San-tiago, 1993, p. 226). Fortunately, he changes his mind and places her in an eighth-grade class (albeit 8-23, the class for the lowest achieving students and those labeled as learning disabled). By the following year, Negi is placed in one of the top ninth-grade classes, and from there she goes on to a top-rated public high school and then to Harvard. Needless to say, this story is pure fic-tion for all but a tiny minority of Puerto Rican students, most of whom have neither the wherewithal nor the resources to make the demands that Negi was able to make.

Although U.S. public schools have been the setting of most stories of Puerto Ricans, a small number have focused on Catholic and independent schools (Rivera, 1982; Vega, 1996). The cultural rejection faced by Puerto Ricans in these settings has been of a different kind than that faced in public schools. In *Family Installments,* Edward Rivera (1982) tells the story of Santos Malánguez and his family, who move to New York City from Puerto Rico and enroll Santos in second grade at Saint Misericordia Academy (affectionately dubbed Saint Miseria's) for Boys and Girls in East Harlem. Catholic school differed from public schools in many ways — notably in the strict rules, the heavy doses of homework, the high expectations of all students, and the corporal punishment — but Puerto Ricans were still generally assumed to be of inferior genetic stock. These seemingly contradictory attitudes were well described in Rivera's story: "There was something both cold-hearted and generous about our nuns that gave at least some of us reason to be grateful our parents had signed us up at Saint Miseria's" (p. 74). Specifically, there is the humorous scene in which Sister Felicia, without consulting with Santos's parents, decides that he and a number of other children are charity cases. Since they are preparing for their First Communion, she marches off with them to *La Marqueta,* the Puerto Rican market in Spanish Harlem, to buy their outfits for the big day. Rivera describes the patronizing attitude of the nuns: "First they hit you and make certain embarrassing hints about your family habits and your man-eating ancestors, and then they treat you to a free purchase of clothes" (p. 78).

Deficit explanations for students' academic failure were accepted fairly consistently and uncritically until the late 1960s and 1970s, when Puerto Rican educators and researchers themselves were more visible in the research studies, commissions, and panels studying the education of Puerto Rican youths (Nieto, 1995). In short, the research literature until quite recently tended to highlight what Puerto Rican youngsters *did not have, did not know,* and *could not do,* and, as a result, neglected also to consider what students *already had, knew,* and *could do.*

The development of cultural awareness represents a step away from the view that students' native languages and cultures hinder their learning. For instance, in research that was part of the report of the Latino Commission of the New York City Board of Education, Clara Rodríguez (1991) found substantial differences between two high schools with high dropout rates and two with low dropout rates. At the schools with low dropout rates, she found that cultural sensitivity was either present or neutral, that is, there was a feeling among the students that their culture would not work against them, and that they would be treated fairly in spite of their culture. Rodríguez notes that "in the absence of cultural sensitivity, an acceptable surrogate seemed to be neutrality toward cultural differences combined with good teaching" (1991, pp. 45–46).

Teachers and schools step closer to cultural acceptance when they acknowledge the Spanish language and the Puerto Rican culture as important resources and talents. For instance, Lourdes Díaz Soto, in research with parents of both low- and high-achieving Puerto Rican children, discovered that the parents of the high-achieving children preferred a native language environment at home to a far greater extent than did the families of lower-achieving children (1993). Similarly, the Massachusetts Advocacy Center found that bilingual programs can actually act as a "buffer" to prevent some students from dropping out of high school (Massachusetts Advocacy Center, 1990). In the short story "School Smells," El Cortes lovingly recalls Miss Powell, her favorite teacher, who used the students' language and culture in positive ways:

> In second grade when we spoke Spanish, we didn't get yelled at — SPEAK ENGLISH. NO SPANISH. YOU'RE IN AMERICA NOW — like it was a sin. . . . Miss Powell had us teach her and the kids who didn't know Spanish some words and we wrote invitations to the mothers to visit. They came and told stories about how it was when they were kids in Puerto Rico and we told it in English for the kids who didn't know Spanish. (2000)

In recent research among Puerto Rican families, Carmen Mercado and Luis Moll (1997) demonstrate an even closer step to cultural acceptance. Using a "funds of knowledge" perspective based on the assumption that all families have cultural resources that can be used in the service of their children's learning, the researchers asked their graduate students, all bilingual teachers in New York City, to investigate the knowledge and practices that their students' families possessed. As a result of the research, the teachers, some of whom felt that they already knew their students quite well, were surprised at the wealth of sociocultural knowledge and practices in the families, resources of which even the families themselves are not always aware. These included entrepreneurial skills, knowledge of health and medicine, and musical talent.

Jo-Anne Wilson Keenan, Jerri Willett, and Judith Solsken, a classroom teacher and two university faculty members who engaged in collaborative research in the teacher's second-grade classroom for two years, described a similar finding. Their research (1993) focused on schools' need to change in order to accommodate and serve the children in them, in contrast to the conventional wisdom that students and their families need to do all the changing. Through a series of inspiring anecdotes, the authors documented how the families of the students changed the culture of the classroom. There was, for instance, the story of Blanca Pérez's father, a cartoonist and martial artist, who visited the classroom. The authors concluded: "Jimmy Pérez does not typically spend his days in an elementary school classroom. Yet this gentle and immensely talented man is capable of teaching many things" (p. 59).

In addition, the authors explained how Jo-Anne, the teacher, attempted to learn Spanish, and how her attempts were appreciated by the parents: "As I risk speaking in another language, others feel free to take the same risk. As our struggle to appreciate each other's languages becomes public, language differences are no longer a barrier but common ground for generating conversations about language and cultural differences and similarities" (p. 63). When teachers and schools accept and, even better, when they affirm the language and culture of their Puerto Rican students, they also send students the message that their identity is not a barrier to their education. In the numerous examples above, we have seen that when teachers perceive only deficits in their students' backgrounds, the students' learning is not promoted. Conversely, when teachers see their students' individual and cultural talents, students are encouraged to continue their education.

Marginalization/Belonging

Marginalization has been a common theme in much of the research and fiction literature concerning Puerto Ricans in U.S. schools for many years, and it is no more poignantly expressed than in this segment of the poem "Broken English Dream" by Pedro Pietri:

> To the united states we came
> To learn how to misspell our name
> To lose the definition of pride
> To have misfortune on our side . . .
> To be trained to turn on television sets
> To dream about jobs you will never get
> To fill out welfare applications
> To graduate from school without an education . . . (1977, p. 22)

Puerto Rican youths have often felt that they simply did not belong in U.S. schools, and this feeling of alienation was well described by Piri Thomas in his 1967 novel, *Down These Mean Streets:* "School stunk. I hated school and all its teachers. I hated the crispy look of the teachers and the draggy-long hours they took out of my life from nine to three" (p. 64). In fact, for Thomas, sneaking out of school was like "escaping from some kind of prison" (p. 64). Research literature reflects these ideas. For example, ASPIRA conducted a survey in several schools to determine the adjustment of newly arrived students and found a good deal of alienation among Puerto Rican students:

> The conclusion of the survey, in short, was that despite the genuine good-will and effort of hundreds of teachers, many Puerto Rican children were being left out, were not participating in classroom activities, were not learning. Quietly and unobtrusively, they were "sitting out" months and years of their allotted school time. (Margolis, 1968, p. 125)

Almost two decades later, the National Commission on Secondary Education for Hispanics reached a similar conclusion:

The fundamental finding of the National Commission on Secondary Education for Hispanics is that a shocking proportion of this generation of Hispanic
young people is being wasted. Wasted because their education needs are neither understood nor met, their high aspirations unrecognized, their promising
potential stunted. (1984, n.p.)

Marginalization often begins when Spanish-speaking students enter
schools and find that their only means of communication is neither understood nor accepted. In the 1965 study, Eugene Bucchioni describes the role
of the Spanish language for Puerto Rican students: "Its use symbolizes the
cultural understanding and unity of Puerto Rican pupils, especially when
confronted by an outsider who . . . represents the imposed authority and
control of a superordinate group" (1982, p. 234). Using the Spanish language among themselves represents one of the few instances in which Puerto
Rican students can create a sense of belonging. Marisol, one of the students I
interviewed for a previous study, talked of her need to speak her native language in school even though she was fluent in English. She described a problem she had with a former teacher who had prohibited her from speaking
Spanish in class: "I thought it was like an insult to us, you know? Just telling
us not to talk Spanish, 'cause [we] were Puerto Ricans and, you know, we're
free to talk whatever we want. . . . I could never stay quiet and talk only English, 'cause, you know, words slip in Spanish" (Nieto, 1996, p. 157).

For Puerto Rican students, speaking Spanish generally represents nothing more than solidarity and belonging, but it is often interpreted as a lack
of respect.

In *Silent Dancing,* Judith Ortiz Cofer recounts her experience with a
teacher who struck her on the head when she thought she was being disres-
pected. Actually, Judith did not understand English. This was to be a painful
but quickly learned lesson: "I instinctively understood then that language is
the only weapon a child has against the absolute power of adults," she concluded (1990, p. 62).

Alba Ambert also powerfully describes the alienating experience of school
when her protagonist Blanca is placed in a class for the mentally retarded because she cannot speak English:

> During that year in a class for the mentally retarded, Blanca drew pumpkins in
> October, colored pine trees in December, and cut out White bunnies in April.
> She also picked up some English. When Blanca was able to communicate in
> English, school authorities no longer considered her retarded and placed her
> in a classroom for children without the deficiency of not knowing the English
> language. (Ambert, 1995, p. 79)

Marginalization, however, is not simply related to the lack of English-language skills. Many students have expressed feeling marginalized because
their culture, their social class, their traditions, and the values of their families are different from the culture found in mainstream schools. Virginia
Vogel Zanger's (1993) study of high-achieving, college-bound Latino stu-

dents in a Boston high school exemplifies this marginalization. Even the words that the students in her study employed to describe their perceived status within the school were striking examples of alienation: these included terms such as "not joined in" and "out to the edge," and prepositions such as "below," "under," "low," and "down." Further, Johanna Vega, in recounting her experiences of going from the South Bronx to becoming a scholarship student at Groton, a posh independent school in Massachusetts, writes of the terrible "psychic wounding" that she underwent for four years (1996).

When my colleague Manuel Frau-Ramos and I questioned young people in an exploratory study of dropouts in Holyoke, Massachusetts, we heard one student explain, "I was an outsider." When we asked Pedro, one of the students who was still in school, if the alienation he felt was due to his level of English proficiency, he said, "No, it is not the English . . . that's not the problem. . . . I don't know how to explain it, I don't know" (Frau-Ramos & Nieto, 1993, p. 160). Another student, José, explained that he "felt alone" at school, adding, "*Tu sabes, no son los míos*" ["You know, they are not my people"]. When we asked Pedro if he had any recommendations for teachers and schools to help solve the dropout problem among Puerto Rican students, he said, "*Hacer algo para que los boricuas no se sientan aparte*" ["Do something so that the Puerto Rican students would not feel separate"] (p. 161). That feeling of separateness is another word for marginalization.

Contrasting that feeling of separateness documented by Manuel Frau-Ramos and me is an immensely successful program for Latino students studied by Jeannette Abi-Nader (1993), which suggests that a sense of belonging can counter the cultural isolation that Puerto Rican students feel. One of the keys to the program's success was the teacher who directed the program by incorporating motivational strategies that built on the students' culture and their need for family-like affection and caring. In other words, the teacher created a world in the classroom in which the students felt they "belonged." The students in turn described him as "a father, brother, and friend to us."

Conclusion: Care as the Missing Ingredient in the Education of Puerto Ricans

I began this article by stating that the general public knows very little of the history of Puerto Ricans in U.S. schools, and this is indeed true, although a great deal has been written on the subject. For instance, the ASPIRA report on the education of Puerto Ricans, written thirty years ago (Margolis, 1968), pointed out that an impressive bibliography of 450 articles and studies focusing on the issue of Puerto Rican children in U.S. schools had already been compiled by 1968. More research might point to better solutions, but it may also only point to more solutions that are rejected, ignored, or overlooked. The major problem, however, seems to be not the lack of data, but rather the lack of will and resources to remedy the educational problems that Puerto Rican students face.

This is the point at which the use of fiction with fact can make a difference in the education of Puerto Rican students. The examples of fiction used in this article, almost all written by Puerto Ricans, represent the lived experiences of Puerto Rican students themselves. They are not clinical or sterile descriptions of faceless students in nameless schools; instead, these works of fiction serve to make the educational research come alive and make it harder to ignore or reject the facts described in educational research literature. Using fact and fiction together can be a powerful way of making the problems that Puerto Rican students face more visible to those who can make schools caring and affirming places, that is, the teachers, administrators, and policymakers.

The message that emerges from this study of fact and fiction is one that underlies all the others: *the care or rejection experienced by Puerto Rican students in U.S. schools can have a significant impact on their academic success or failure.* Research by Victor Battistich, Daniel Solomon, Dong-il Kim, Meredith Watson, and Eric Schaps (1995) indicates important connections among caring communities, the identification that students make with learning, and their academic achievement. These researchers examined relationships between students' sense of school community, poverty level, and their attitudes, motives, beliefs, and behavior in twenty-four elementary schools. Because Puerto Rican students live in greater poverty than those from most other groups, one of the major conclusions of the study has especially important implications for them: "Although the deleterious effects of poverty are well known, the most encouraging aspect of the present findings is the suggestive evidence that some of its negative effects can be mitigated if the school is successful in creating a caring community for its members" (1995, p. 649).

According to the National Commission on Secondary Education for Hispanics (NCSEH), "Hispanic students almost unanimously identified 'someone caring' as the most important factor in academic success" (1984, p. 13). Students attribute academic success to this quality of "caring" in their schools. As one young woman in the NCSEH report explained, "I got pregnant and I thought I'd never be anybody but I came here and the teachers and the kids gave me love and I know I'll make it . . ." (p. 29). In an ethnographic study of Puerto Rican adolescents who had dropped out of school and were now attending an alternative school (Saravia-Shore & Martinez, 1992), the researchers documented numerous similar examples of conflicting values of home, peers, and schools. Students were happy with the alternative schools because they felt that teachers there cared about them, whereas criticisms of their previous schools included teachers' lack of respect, care, and concern: "They would say things like, 'Do you want to be like the other Puerto Rican women who never got an education? Do you want to be like the rest of your family and never go to school?'" (p. 242).

Research and fiction often associate caring with Puerto Rican or other Latino teachers (Hornberger, 1990; Latino Commission, 1992; Mercado & Moll, 1997; Montero-Sieburth & Pérez, 1987; National Commission on Secondary Education for Hispanics, 1984). It is important, however, to mention that, in both fact and fiction, caring is not exclusive to Latino teachers. Non-Latino teachers, who represent the vast majority of teachers of Puerto Rican youngsters, also show care and concern for their Puerto Rican students (Abi-Nader, 1993; Ada, 1993; Ambert, 1995; Cofer, 1990; Mercado & Moll, 1997; Mohr, 1979; Santiago, 1993; Vega, 1996). Many commissions and reports have called for hiring more Latino teachers (Latino Commission, 1992; Meier & Stewart, 1991; Morrison, 1958; National Commission on Secondary Education for Hispanics, 1984; U.S. Commission on Civil Rights, 1976), a recommendation that makes eminent good sense. However, the literature is clear that while being Puerto Rican can be an advantage to teaching Puerto Rican youths, non-Puerto Rican teachers can also be extremely effective with them.

Latino youngsters explicitly mention "love" as the factor that can make or break their experiences in school. Voices recorded in the research literature from the 1950s until today suggest that the importance of caring and the price of rejection have always been significant, but no one chose to listen to them. This was true in research as early as *The Puerto Rican Study* (Morrison, 1958), when children and their parents were interviewed: "There were instances where, from the child's viewpoint, the present teacher, compared with previous teachers in Puerto Rico, seemed uninteresting, lacking in affection or in kindness" (p. 133).

Almost thirty years later, research on the strategies used by a bilingual teacher to relate to her Latino students also identified *cariño,* or endearment — especially as evident in hugging and other displays of affection — as a key element in the success of Latino youngsters. She identified herself as a "teacher, friend, mother, social worker, translator, counselor, advocate, prosecutor, group therapist, hygienist, and monitor" (Montero-Sieburth & Pérez, 1987, p. 183). A few years later, Nancy Hornberger's (1990) study of successful learning contexts draws a similar conclusion: in the Puerto Rican classroom that she studied, she found that the teacher openly displayed tenderness and affection, as well as a "motherly concern" for her students, expressions typical of the Puerto Rican community. Nitza Hidalgo explains the importance of this kind of interpersonal support: "Because of the propensity to place value on interpersonal relationships within the culture, the relationship between the teacher and Puerto Rican student becomes vital to the educational achievement of the student. Students have to feel liked by the teacher; they gain strength from their relationship to their teachers (1992, p. 36). A young woman in Zanger's research described the experiences of Latino students and the cost of rejection: "They just feel left out, they feel like if no one loves them, no one cares, so why should they care?"

(1993, p. 176). Still more recently, one of the Latina teachers in the research by Carmen Mercado and Luis Moll described how she viewed her profession: "It is not an 8:40 to 3:30 P.M. job but an extension of my life, as if it were part of my family" (1997, p. 31).

Fiction echoes the importance of caring that many have overlooked or ignored in the research literature. Alba Ambert's *A Perfect Silence* beautifully expresses this sentiment when she describes a number of exceptions to Blanca's generally uncaring and unfeeling teachers. Mrs. Wasserman, the teacher who first recognized the abuse Blanca had experienced, kept a collection of children's books in the classroom that Blanca transformed into "dreams of possible worlds" (1995, p. 114). Her second-grade teacher, Mrs. Kalfus, once kissed Blanca's swollen cheek when she had a toothache: "Years later, Blanca, who forgot much of her disrupted childhood, remembered that kiss" (p. 115).

Similarly, Mr. Barone, the guidance counselor in *When I Was Puerto Rican* (Santiago, 1993), sees promise in Negi and pushes her to go to an academic high school. The ensuing scene, in which Negi tries out for Performing Arts High School by reciting a monologue she memorized in a thick Puerto Rican accent using English that she does not understand, is a hilarious and touching example of care and concern in the fiction about Puerto Rican students in U.S. schools. By going out of his way to help Negi apply to a school with rigorous standards, Mr. Barone exemplifies how teachers and other educators can make caring and concern a vital part of the school community.

But what exactly does it mean to create such a caring community? The literature and research that we have seen describe "caring" as providing affection and support for students, building strong interpersonal relationships with them and their families, learning about and from them, respecting and affirming their language and culture and building on it, and having high expectations of them. Caring implies that schools' policies and practices also need to change because simply changing the nature of their relationships with teachers and schools will not by itself change the opportunities the children are given. Hence, changing both personal relationships among teachers and Puerto Rican students and the institutional conditions in their schools is essential if these students are to become successful learners.

These changes are, however, not enough. Care is demonstrated as well through the provision of adequate resources to ensure that learning can take place. The poignant plea of a student who addressed the National Commission on Secondary Education for Hispanics (1984) is even more explicit: "We work hard and we try and our teachers care, but we are not treated fairly. Our school is poor. If this commission cares, please make something happen" (n.p.). The commission's final word, that Latinos "are our children, a generation too precious to waste" (p. 45), is worth repeating if we are serious and truly care about creating the possibility of success for more Puerto Rican students.

Note

1. Puerto Ricans are not "immigrants" in the traditional sense of the word, since they arrive in the United States as citizens. They are also not strictly "migrants," since they have not simply moved from one geographic part of a culturally connected society to another. Some scholars refer to Puerto Ricans living in the United States as *[im]migrants*, highlighting the hybrid nature of their status. See, for example, Marquez (1995).

References

Abi-Nader, J. (1993). Meeting the needs of multicultural classrooms: Family values and the motivation of minority students. In M. J. O'Hair & S. J. Odell (Eds.), *Diversity and teaching: Teacher education yearbook 1* (pp. 212–236). Ft. Worth, TX: Harcourt Brace Jovanovich.

Ada, A. F. (1993). *My name is María Isabel.* New York: Atheneum.

Ambert, A. (1995). *A perfect silence.* Houston, TX: Arte Público Press.

Appleton, N. (1983). *Cultural pluralism in education: Theoretical foundations.* New York: Longman.

Arias, S. (1996). Inside the worlds of Latino traveling cultures: Martín Espada's poetry of rebellion. *Bilingual Review/Revista Bilingüe, 21,* 231–240.

ASPIRA of New York. (1968). *Hemos trabajado bien: Proceedings of the ASPIRA National Conference of Puerto Ricans, Mexican-Americans, and Educators.* New York: Author.

ASPIRA Institute for Policy Research. (1993). *Facing the facts: The state of Hispanic education, 1993.* Washington, DC: ASPIRA.

Association of Assistant Superintendents (1948). *A program of education for Puerto Ricans in New York City.* Brooklyn: New York City Board of Education.

Battistich, V., Solomon, D., Kim, D., Watson, M., & Schaps, E. (1995). Schools as communities, poverty levels of student populations, and students' attitudes, motives, and performance: A multilevel analysis. *American Educational Research Journal, 32,* 627–658.

Bigler, E. (1997). Dangerous discourses: Language politics and classroom practices in Upstate New York. *Centro, 9*(9), 8–25.

Blanchard, J. S., & Casanova, U. (1996). *Modern fiction about schoolteaching: An anthology.* Needham Heights, MA: Allyn & Bacon.

Bonilla, F., & Campos, R. (1981). A wealth of poor: Puerto Ricans in the new economic order. *Daedalus, 110,* 133–176.

Bourdieu, P. (1977). *Outline of theory and practice.* Cambridge, Eng.: Cambridge University Press.

Bucchioni, E. (1982). The daily round of life in the school. In F. Cordasco & E. Bucchioni (Eds.), *The Puerto Rican community and its children on the mainland* (3rd rev. ed., pp. 201–238). Metuchen, NJ: Scarecrow Press.

Cafferty, P. S. J., & Rivera-Martínez, C. (1981). *The politics of language: The dilemma of bilingual education for Puerto Ricans.* Boulder, CO: Westview Press.

Carrasquillo, A. L. (1991). *Hispanic children and youth in the United States: A resource guide.* New York: Garland.

Centro. (1997). Special issue on the education of Puerto Ricans, *9*(9).

Chenault, L. R. (1970). *The Puerto Rican migrant in New York City.* New York: Columbia University Press. (Original work published 1938)

Cofer, J. O. (1990). *Silent dancing: A partial remembrance of a Puerto Rican childhood.* Houston, TX: Arte Público Press.

Cortes, E. (2000). School smells. In S. Nieto (Ed.), *Puerto Rican students in U.S. schools.* Mahwah, NJ: Lawrence Erlbaum Associates.

Crawford, J. (1992). *Hold your tongue: Bilingualism and the politics of "English only."* Reading, MA: Addison-Wesley.

Darder, A., & Upshur, C. (1993). What do Latino children need to succeed in school? A study of four Boston public schools. In R. Rivera and S. Nieto (Eds.), *The education of Latino students in Massachusetts: Research and policy implications* (pp. 127–146). Boston: Gastón Institute for Latino Public Policy and Development.

De Jesús, J. L. (Ed.) (1997). *Growing up Puerto Rican.* New York: William Morrow.

Díaz Alfaro, A. (1962). Santa Cló va a La Cuchilla. In W. E. Colford (Ed. and Trans.), *Classic tales from Spanish America* (pp. 206–210). New York: Barrons Educational Series.

Díaz Alfaro, A. (1978). Peyo Mercé enseña inglés. In K. Wagenheim (Ed.), *Cuentos: An anthology of short stories from Puerto Rico* (pp. 98–107). New York : Schocken Books.

Díaz Soto, L. (1993). Native language for school success. *Bilingual Research Journal, 17* (1/2), 83–97.

Dyson, A. H., & Genishi, C. (1994). Introduction. In A. H. Dyson & C. Genishi (Eds.), *The need for story: Cultural diversity in classroom and community* (pp. 1–7). Urbana, IL: National Council of Teachers of English.

Espada, M. (1993). The year I was diagnosed with a sacrilegious heart. In M. Espada (Ed.), *City of coughing and dead radiators* (pp. 72–74). New York: W. W. Norton.

Espada, M. (1996). Public School 190, Brooklyn, 1963. In M. Espada, Ed.), *Imagine the angels of bread* (p. 25). New York: W. W. Norton.

Estevez, S. M. (1991). Here. In F. Turner (Ed.), *Puerto Rican writers at home in the U.S.A.: An anthology* (pp. 186–187). Seattle, WA: Open Hand.

Figueroa, J. A. (1991). Boricua. In F. Turner (Ed.), *Puerto Rican writers at home in the U.S.A.: An anthology* (pp. 221–224). Seattle, WA: Open Hand.

Fitzpatrick, J. P. (1987a). *Puerto Rican Americans: The meaning of migration to the mainland.* Englewood Cliffs, NJ: Prentice-Hall. (Original work published 1971)

Fitzpatrick, J. P. (1987b). *One church, many cultures: Challenge of diversity.* Kansas City, MO: Sheed & Ward.

Frau-Ramos, M., & Nieto, S. (1993). 'I was an outsider': Dropping out among Puerto Rican youths in Holyoke, Massachusetts. In R. Rivera and S. Nieto (Eds.), *The education of Latino students in Massachusetts: Research and policy implications* (pp. 147–169). Boston: Gastón Institute for Latino Public Policy and Development.

Gibson, M. A., & Ogbu, J. U. (Eds.). (1991). *Minority status and schooling: A comparative study of immigrant and involuntary minorities.* New York: Garland.

Hernández, C. D. (1997). *Puerto Rican voices in English: Interviews with writers.* Westport, CT: Praeger.

Hidalgo, N. M. (1992). *"i saw puerto rico once": A review of the literature on Puerto Rican families and school achievement in the United States* (Report No. 12). Boston: Center on Families, Communities, Schools and Children's Learning.

History Task Force, Centro de Estudios Puertorriqueños. (1979). *Labor migration under capitalism: The Puerto Rican experience.* New York: Monthly Review Press.

Hornberger, N. (1990). Creating successful learning contexts for biliteracy. *Teachers College Record, 92,* 212–229.

Institute for Puerto Rican Policy. (1992). The distribution of Puerto Ricans and other selected Latinos in the U.S.: 1990. *Datanote on the Puerto Rican community, 11.* New York: Author.

Institute for Puerto Rican Policy. (1996). The status of Puerto Rican children in the U.S. *IPR Datanote, 18.*

Katz, M. B. (1975). *Class, bureaucracy, and the schools: The illusion of educational change in America*. New York: Praeger.

Keenan, J. W., Willett, J., & Solsken, J. (1993). Constructing an urban village: School/home collaboration in a multicultural classroom. *Language Arts, 70*, 56–66.

Latino Commission on Educational Reform. (1992). *Toward a vision for the education of Latino students: Community voices, student voice* (Interim report of the Latino Commission on Educational Reform). Brooklyn: New York City Board of Education.

Lewis, O. (1965). *La vida: A Puerto Rican family in the culture of poverty, San Juan and New York*. New York: Vintage.

Margolis, R. J. (1968). *The losers: A report on Puerto Ricans and the public schools*. New York: ASPIRA.

Marquez, R. (1995). Sojourners, settlers, castaways, and creators: A recollection of Puerto Rico past and Puerto Ricans present. *Massachusetts Review, 36*(1), 94–118.

Massachusetts Advocacy Center. (1990). *Locked in/locked out: Tracking and placement practices in Boston public schools*. Boston: Author.

Meier, K. J., & Stewart, J., Jr. (1991). *The politics of Hispanic education: Un paso pa'lante y dos pa'tras*. Albany: State University of New York Press.

Melendez, E. (1991). *Los que se van, los que regresan: Puerto Rican migration to and from the United States, 1982–1988*. New York: Commonwealth of Puerto Rico, Department of Puerto Rican Community Affairs.

Mercado, C. I., & Moll, L. (1997). The study of funds of knowledge: Collaborative research in Latino homes. *Centro, 9*(9), 26–42.

Mohr, N. (1979). *Felita*. New York: Dial Press.

Mohr, N. (1986). *Nilda* (2nd ed). Houston, TX: Arte Público Press.

Montero-Sieburth, M., & Pérez, M. (1987). *Echar pa'lante*, moving onward: The dilemmas and strategies of a bilingual teacher. *Anthropology and Education Quarterly, 18*, 180–189.

Morrison, J. C. (1958). *The Puerto Rican study, 1953–1957*. Brooklyn: New York City Board of Education.

National Center for Educational Statistics. (1995). *The educational progress of Hispanic students*. Washington, DC: United States Department of Education, Office of Educational Research and Improvement.

National Commission on Secondary Education for Hispanics. (1984). *"Make something happen": Hispanics and urban school reform*. Washington, DC: Hispanic Policy Development Project.

National Council of La Raza. (1993). *Moving from the margins: Puerto Rican young men and family poverty*. Washington, DC: Author.

National Puerto Rican Task Force. (1982). *Toward a language policy for Puerto Ricans in the U.S.: An agenda for a community in movement*. New York: City University of New York Research Foundation.

Negrón de Montilla, A. (1971). *Americanization in Puerto Rico and the public school system, 1900–1930*. Río Piedras, PR: Editorial Edil.

New voices: Immigrant students in U.S. public schools. (1988). Boston: National Coalition of Advocates for Students.

Nieto, S. (1995). A history of the education of Puerto Rican students in U.S. mainland schools: "Losers," "outsiders," or "leaders"? In J. A. Banks & C. A. M. Banks (Eds.), *Handbook of research on multicultural education* (pp. 388–411). New York: Macmillan.

Nieto, S. (1996). *Affirming diversity: The sociopolitical context of multicultural education* (2nd ed.). White Plains, NY: Longman.

Nieto, S. (Ed.). (2000). *Puerto Rican students in U.S. schools*. Mahwah, NJ: Lawrence Erlbaum Associates.

Ogbu, J. U. (1987). Variability in minority school performance: A problem in search of an explanation. *Anthropology and Education Quarterly, 18,* 312–334.

Phinney, J. S. (1993). A three-stage model of ethnic identity development in adolescence. In M. E. Bernal & G. P. Knight (Eds.), *Ethnic identity: Formation and transmission among Hispanics and other minorities* (pp. 61–79). Albany: State University of New York Press.

Pietri, P. (1977). Broken English dream. In P. Pietri (Ed.), *Obituario puertorriqueño* (pp. 18–43). San Juan, PR: Instituto de Cultura Puertorriqueña.

Quality Education for Minorities Project. (1990). *Education that works: An action plan for the education of minorities.* Cambridge, MA: Author.

Rivera, E. (1982). *Family installments: Memories of growing up Hispanic.* New York: William Morrow.

Rodríguez, A., Jr. (1992). *The boy without a flag: Tales of the South Bronx.* Minneapolis, MN: Milkweed Editions.

Rodríguez, C. (1991). *Puerto Ricans: Born in the U.S.A.* Boulder, CO: Westview Press.

Rumbaut, R. G., & Ima, K. (1987). *The adaptation of Southeast Asian refugee youth: A comparative study* (Final Report.) San Diego, CA.: Office of Refugee Resettlement.

Sánchez, L. R. (1987). The flying bus. In A. Rodríguez de Laguna (Ed.), *Images and identities: The Puerto Rican in two world contexts* (pp. 17–25). New Brunswick, NJ: Transaction Books.

Sánchez Korrol, V. E. (1994). *From colonia to community: The history of Puerto Ricans in New York City.* Berkeley: University of California Press. (Original work published 1983)

Santiago, E. (1993). *When I was Puerto Rican.* Reading, MA: Addison-Wesley.

Saravia-Shore, M., & Martinez, H. (1992). An ethnographic study of home/school role conflicts of second generation Puerto Rican adolescents. In M. Saravia-Shore & S. F. Arvizu (Eds.), *Cross-cultural literacy: Ethnographies of communication in multiethnic classrooms* (pp. 227–251). New York: Garland.

Sexton, P. C. (1965). *Spanish Harlem.* New York: Harper & Row.

Spring, J. (1997). *Deculturalization and the struggle for equality: A brief history of the education of dominated cultures in the United States.* New York: McGraw-Hill.

Thomas, P. (1997). *Down these mean streets.* New York: Vintage Books.

U.S. Commission on Civil Rights. (1976). *Puerto Ricans in the continental United States: An uncertain future.* Washington, DC: Author.

Vega, J. (1996). From the South Bronx to Groton. In L. M. Carlson (Ed.), *Barrio streets, carnival dreams: Three generations of Latino artistry* (pp. 83–99). New York: Henry Holt.

Walsh, C. E. (1991). *Pedagogy and the struggle for voice: Issues of language, power, and schooling for Puerto Ricans.* New York: Bergin & Garvey.

Zanger, V. V. (1987). *The social context of second language learning; An examination of barriers to integration in five case studies.* Unpublished doctoral dissertation, Boston University.

Zanger, V. V. (1993). Academic costs of social marginalization: An analysis of the perceptions of Latino students at a Boston high school. In R. Rivera and S. Nieto (Eds.), *The education of Latino students in Massachusetts: Research and policy implications* (pp. 170–190). Boston: Gastón Institute for Latino Public Policy and Development.

Zentella, A. C. (1997). *Growing up bilingual: Puerto Rican children in New York.* Oxford, Eng.: Basil Blackwell.

A Black Student's Reflection on
Public and Private Schools

IMANI PERRY

My name is Imani Perry. I am a fifteen-year-old Black female who has experienced both private and public education. These experiences have led me to believe there are significant differences between the two types of education that deserve to be acknowledged and resolved by society as a whole.

After ten years in private schools I made the decision to attend a public school. I left because I felt isolated as a person of color. I yearned to have a large, strong Black community be a part of my development. I believed that I would find such a community in the public high school of my city, which is a fairly urban school with approximately 2,600 students, 20 percent of whom are Black.

Despite the fact that I had never been in a traditional public school environment, when I decided to go to one I had certain expectations about the teaching. I assumed that the teaching philosophy would be similar to that of the private schools I had attended. I expected that any teaching differences that did exist would be limited to less sophisticated reading, or a less intense workload. As I quickly learned, the differences were more substantial.

I believe the differences I found in the teaching between the private and public schools that I attended would best be illustrated by several examples of what I encountered. My initial realization of this difference began with an argument I had with a math teacher over a point value on a test. I felt that he should give partial credit for problems with computational errors rather than procedural errors, or conceptual misunderstanding. I presented this point to the math teacher, who responded by saying math is computation and the theories and concepts of math are only used to compute. I was astonished by this statement. Coming from a school whether the teachers' stated goal for freshman math was to begin to teach you how to become a "theoretical mathematician," my entire perception of math was different. Perhaps that emphasis on theoretical math was also extreme; nevertheless, I believe that a good math teacher believes that computation in math should be used to assist in the organization of theories. Computation is a necessary but not

Harvard Educational Review   Vol. 58 No. 3 August 1988, 332–336

sufficient step toward math knowledge. I felt this teacher was probably the product of schooling that did not emphasize the artistic qualities of math. While I could sympathize with his position, I felt that all I loved about math — new ideas, discussing unproved theorems, and developing personal procedures — was being ignored. I withdrew from this course only to find the ideological differences emerged again in my advanced English class at the public school, particularly in essay writing.

In this class, once we wrote a paper — mind you, with no assistance from the teacher — the process ended. We did not discuss papers, receive constructive criticism, or improve them through rewriting. Despite the fact that there was no proofreading assistance offered, 10 percent of the grade was taken off for sentence errors. It seemed as if the teacher assumed we no longer needed to continue developing our writing skills.

In my last school, which had an abundance of excellent essayists, my English teacher would give a detailed description of what he felt about each paper. At points where he felt one deserved praise or criticism, he would make comments in the margins. He would not neglect to correct punctuation errors — such as commas instead of semicolons — but these errors were not the sole criteria for our grades, especially if the writing was good. The emphasis was upon improving intellectual and organizational skills to raise the quality of the writing.

These examples illustrate my belief that my learning environment had changed from a place where thought and theory were emphasized to a place whether form and precision were emphasized. The teaching system at the public school appears to assume that at some point in our education, learning and thinking are no longer important. Schooling in this situation becomes devoted to making things look correct. This is in sharp contrast to my private schools, where proper form was something I learned was necessary, but secondary in importance to the content and organization of what is produced.

Because of this difference in the concept of teaching and learning, there is also a difference in what and who teachers consider intelligent. The teaching at the public school has less to do with thinking and processing ideas, and more to do with precision and detail in appearance. Therefore, students who are considered intelligent by the public school faculty possess different skills than those at the private schools I have attended. In the public school a student is considered intelligent if he or she is well-behaved and hard working. The ability to grasp a subject in its entirety — from theory to practice — is not valued.

For example, in the fall of 1987 there was an academic contest, where my school was competing against other public schools. All the teachers I encountered were very enthusiastic about it. The students who were selected to participate were raised on a pedestal. These students, most of whom were clean-cut and apparently straight-laced, were to serve as our models of very intelligent students. They were drilled in formulas, book plots, and other information for several days a week. It seemed as if the teachers were not concerned with whether the students digested the depth of these subjects and resources as long as the students completed all the reading, memorized the facts, and could repeat the information. The contest was more a demonstration of a memory function than anything else. In my opinion there is nothing wrong with such a contest, but it should be recognized for what it is and is not. One thing it is not is a true measure of knowledge and ability. This was never recognized by the school.

Another example of how a different view of intelligence is manifested in this public school is the school's view of two students whom I know. I will identify them as Student A and Student B. Student B is an intellectual. She reads, is analytical in her discussions and is knowledgeable. Student A is very precise with his homework, answers the patronizing questions the teachers ask ("What color was the horse?" "Black with a White spot!" "Correct!"), and is very "all-American" in behavior and appearance. Student A is considered more intelligent at this public school because he displays skills that are considered signs of intelligence at this school. The intelligence criteria at this school are more related to superficial qualities such as appearance, knowing facts, etc., rather than the intellectual qualities that student B possesses. Student B displays an ability to learn and write in creative and analytical formats. I left a school where the criterion for intelligence was the student's thought process resulting from the information, for a school where the information was the measure of intelligence.

In reflecting on schooling it is important to realize that all people, including teachers, have biases based on the physical appearances of other people. On the train most people are more likely to sit next to the clean-shaven Harvard freshman than next to the Mohawked, multiple-earringed punk-rocker. In teachers, however, these biases should diminish as they begin to know a student. Unfortunately, in the public school there is an absence of teacher-student contact. Because of this lack of contact there are no criteria by which intelligence can be determined, besides grades, appearance, and behavior. As I mentioned before, the grading system at this school often reflects one's ability to memorize and no one's thinking and analytical abilities. Moreover, since people are biased in their acceptance of different appearances, students who look different are judged differently. The only way they can make up for this difference is to be "well behaved," and, as I will mention later, the definition of well behaved is arbitrary.

All these issues I have discussed have very negative effects for students from minority groups, more specifically the Black and Hispanic youths who make up a large percentage of most urban schools. It is those Black and Hispanic students who retain strong cultural characteristics in their personalities who are most negatively affected by teachers' emphasis on behavior, appearance, and respect for authority.

Public schools' emphasis on the teaching of form merely trains students for low-powered or menial jobs that do not require analytical thought. It is evident when most students are discussing what they intend to be that their goals are most often focused toward areas and professions about which they have some idea or knowledge. If in class you've never spoken about how language and colloquialisms are reflections of the society you are studying, you definitely will not be thinking of being a linguist. And if you are only asked to type a paper summarizing the book, rather than writing an analysis of it, the primary skill shown is typing. This should not be the main skill that is emphasized.

The neglect of intellectual development also occurs in higher-level classes, but at least the resources, books, etc., available to students are not altogether lacking in intellectual value. Occasionally these resources will have depth and content, be philosophical, or insightful. But in lower-level classes, where minority students are most often found and where bad textbooks are used without outside resources, the reading has less content, and the point of reading is to perfect reading skills, not to broaden thinking skills or gain knowledge of how the subject is currently affecting us. It is often not possible to broaden your thinking skills or knowledge with the books used in lower-level classes, which are more often stripped of any content. In an upper-level class, if you have a parent who wants you to know the subject in depth, and to think about it, it is possible to do that detached from the school environment, because the subject matter may have content, or have some meaning beyond the words. My high-level sophomore English class read *Moby Dick* as an outside reading. We didn't discuss the symbolism or religious qualities of it, but I am aware of them because I read critical essays and discussed them with my mother. If one is reading a book that has been stripped of meaningful content, it is not helpful to do outside research, because it is lacking in meaning.

Many students from minority groups are being trained only in form and not in creative ways of thinking. This, I believe, causes disenchantment among students. Upper-class students are not as affected, because of their social class, and their "social responsibility" to be achievers. This is especially true of upper-class students in a public school whose social-class peers are in private schools. But instead of striving to be true learners, they quickly learn how to be good students by being well behaved. What well behaved means is always taking the teacher's word as absolute truth and never questioning the teacher's authority. This definition of well behaved is of course culturally based and can be in opposition to cultures of Black and Hispanic students.

In Black and Hispanic cultures, respect and obedience come and develop with the relationship. Rather than being automatic, respect must be earned. For example, one will occasionally hear a Black child say to a stranger, "You can't tell me what to do, you're not my mother." But at the same time, often one will see Black kids following the orders and rules of an adult friend of the family, whom they would under no circumstances disrespect. In addition, in Black and Hispanic cultures it appears that adult and child cultures are more integrated than those of other ethnic groups. For example, parties in the Hispanic community will often have an age range from toddler to elderly. Children are often present in the conversation and socializing of adults and are not treated as separate, as they may be in other cultures.

When this relationship is not made between teacher and student, it is not an acceptable educational situation, because the Black and Hispanic students are now expected to respect someone in a different manner than their culture has socialized them to. Often students are not aware of the fact that the demands being placed on them by the relationship conflict with those of their culture. They then show signs of what a teacher views as a lack of the respect that he/she deserves. The student might feel it is just a sign that they do not know the teacher and have no obligation to him or her. Many times I have seen a dumbstruck student of color sent to detention; when asked what he or she did, the student will seriously say that he or she has no idea; perhaps that he or she sucked his or her teeth in dismay, or something of that sort.

Black and Hispanic students have less of a chance at building strong relationships with any teachers because their appearance and behavior may be considered offensive to the middle-class White teachers. These students show signs of what White teachers, and some teachers of color, consider disrespect, and they do not get the nurturing relationships that develop respect and dedication. They are considered less intelligent, as can be seen in the proportion of Blacks and Hispanics in lower-level as opposed to upper-level classes. There is less of a teacher-student contact with "underachievers," because they are guided into peer tutoring programs. Perhaps this is understandable, because the teachers have less of a vested interest in the achievement of students that are not of their community, or have less of an idea of how to educate them. Public school teachers are no longer part of the same community as the majority of their students. The sad part of the situation is that many students believe that this type of teaching is what academic learning is all about. They have not had the opportunity to experience alternative ways of teaching and learning. From my experience in public school, it appears that many minority students will never be recognized as capable of analytical and critical thinking.

In the beginning of this article I spoke about my decision to leave my private school because of feeling isolated. After three months at a large urban public school I found myself equally isolated — intellectually as well as racially. My thinking process has gradually affected my opinions and character. I am in upper-level classes in which there are barely any kids of color, except Asians. Black and Hispanic students have been filtered down into lower-level classes. Most of the students I meet are kind, interesting people whom I like and respect. However, because the environment of the school is one in which ideas are not valued or fostered, I find it difficult to discuss issues with them, because my thoughtfulness has flourished, while others have been denied an opportunity to explore their intellectual development. I am now at a point of deciding which isolation is worse, cultural/racial or intellectual-opinion-based and slightly racial. This is a decision many Black students who have attended private schools at some time are wrestling to make, a decision that will affect their development, knowledge, and viewpoint of education, and their relationships to educators — those supposed possessors of greater knowledge than themselves.

Afterword: Since the writing of this article I have returned to a private school with the feeling that one's educational development is too much to sacrifice. I now attend a private high school with a strong unified Black community, as well as academic merit. Even though I did not remain at the urban public school, I valued my experience there, mostly because through it I learned one of the most blatant forms of oppression and inequity for lower-class students in American society, and I appreciate the opportunities with which I have been blessed.

Holistic Integration:
An Anniversary Reflection on the Goals
of *Brown v. Board of Education*

IMANI PERRY

In August 1988, the *Harvard Educational Review* published an article I wrote, entitled "A Black Student's Reflection on Public and Private Education."[1] I was fifteen years old then, and I was moved to write the piece because of two central observations I had made during my brief tenure at a public high school after many years of private education. My first observation was that there were gross disparities between the quality and sophistication of the education I experienced at elite private schools and that which was offered at this public school. The second observation was that even within an integrated public school setting, I witnessed dramatic racial inequalities and internal segregation, manifest primarily through academic tracking.

On this, the fiftieth anniversary of *Brown v. Board of Education*, and some sixteen years after the publication of my article, it is clear that the persistent educational inequality as experienced by Black children and other young people of color is in part a result of how class operates as a meta-narrative of race. Equal protection doctrine has not been understood as requiring class parity in U.S. Constitutional law. Because people of color are disproportionately impoverished, they disproportionately experience the social detriments of poverty — quite dramatically so in the educational context. Furthermore, they have limited direct legal recourse to address this class-based (and effectively race-based) unequal access to high-quality education. In addition, persistent educational inequity is evidence of the failure of legislatures, courts, school systems, and citizens to create meaningfully integrated academic settings that are universally excellent and equal.[2] In this article, I set forth a theory of integration to be applied in both legal and educational contexts. This theory is sensitive to our current legal system in which de jure segregation has been abolished, but de facto segregation persists. It is my hope that this theory of integration may be applied to articulate a vision of academic equity.

No thoughtful observer of the current system of public education would deny that integration, as articulated in *Brown*, has failed. However, when people assert that integration has failed, they can mean two very different things. For some, the failure of integration is a statement of demographic fact. Schools remain segregated, due to White flight and the prevalence of residential segregation, which is directly correlated to academic institutional segregation.[3] The prospect of addressing residential segregation is of course daunting, and the history of efforts to circumvent residential segregation for the sake of school integration or for more diverse neighborhoods is painful and violent. The pain and violence of these efforts have been so great that the prospect of attempting such desegregation is often repulsive to a wide range of citizens.[4] For others, the failure of integration is seen as the failure of its symbolic import: the equalization of educational opportunity. In this view, the struggle for desegregation was less about the actual physical integration of students and more about removing the legal barrier to integration that signified a belief in racial stratification. From this perspective, the ultimate goal of integration was equality of access.[5]

However, I want to posit a third notion of what the term *integration* should be understood to mean. The term I use to describe this is *holistic integration*. Holistic integration is a democratic principle defined as a model that suggests that, for a society to be truly integrated, all of its members must have equal and full access to the wealth of knowledge, skills, and political processes that are hallmarks of civic and cultural participation. This includes access to the arts, music, athletics, high-level academic preparation, civics education, and practical preparation for adulthood.

This theory of holistic integration considers the physical integration of individuals to be little more than a symbolic gesture made toward the goals of integration and social justice if it does not also entail concomitant meaningful participation in the body politic — of both the school and the state. As applied to education, this theory finds its roots in the union of three strands of philosophical inquiry: cultural capital, democratic education, and the beloved community. I will briefly discuss each strand and its significance for the theory and offer anecdotal evidence of how each strand of the theory relates to the practical realities of educational inequality.

French sociologist Pierre Bourdieu's observation that children are socialized into a culture that correlates to their social class, and that features of that culture operate as a form of currency upon which members of the elite are able to trade, is critical for understanding how inequality persists.[6] According to the theory of holistic integration, cultural capital, as defined by Bourdieu, should be accessible to all students. Bourdieu's assertion that the cultural experiences of elites translate into social resources is clearly instructive for understanding the deep nature of social inequality, but it also gives us clues to a means of providing equal access. It is useful for educators and policymakers seeking to address educational inequality to consider the elements of elite education that lead to greater social access — things as varied as language, the arts, and sophisticated understanding of economic markets — in order to make a concerted effort to provide "elite" education to all students regardless of social class. While this may appear to reify the cultural practices of the wealthy, it in fact acknowledges their power, makes the process of acculturation that leads to access less opaque and less exclusive, and enables people of color to trade the practice.

In a purportedly color-blind society, cultural capital is a dominant means by which inequality is replicated. At the same time, however, it is critical to nourish cultural capital with respect to a variety of cultural, racial, and ethnic communities. In fact, many elite educational institutions already have begun that process. If you look through the catalogs of elite New England prep schools, you frequently find the literature of Toni Morrison and courses in African American history alongside Shakespeare and Russian history.

In my work as a law professor, I see the operation of cultural capital directly. Admittedly, law school is a site of privilege for all its participants, but it is also a site of inequality. John, a working-class White ethnic student, came into my office last year and revealed to me how he was afraid to speak up in his classes. He said that so many of the other students spoke "eloquent" and that he was unable to speak in such a fashion. John referred to the professions of his classmates' parents, and said that his peers were raised to talk this talk. Intimidated by their cultural capital, he never spoke up. The silencing of this student had a negative impact in two ways. On a personal level, John's lack of linguistic cultural capital prevented him from speaking in class, which might have negatively impacted his grades. Additionally, if he had spoken up as a student without the linguistic cultural capital, it is quite possible that his fellow students and the professor would have assumed that he was less intelligent because he did not speak in the fashion that is customary for an "educated" and "intelligent" person, no matter how smart he was. Moreover, John's silencing prevented his full participation in the institution. He became a stakeholder without a voice, and those who felt free to speak up thus had "more votes," as it were. John was never holistically integrated into the school, even though he graduated and went into the world to practice law, and as such is a relatively privileged person.[7]

My response to John was three-fold. First I told him that his lack of familiarity with these codes of privilege said nothing about his intelligence or acumen — just his lack of privilege — and I warned him not to let it make him question his merit. Second, I told him that his experience as a working-class person would provide him with important insights for working with clients, and that the extra work it required to enter law school gave him important experience, thus acknowledging the benefits of his working-class background for his career. Finally, I told John that law school was in part a cultural education, and that he should work to learn the very codes that were silencing him as part of his preparation for the profession.

As a law professor, I also find cultural capital at work in student papers. While all students purportedly receive an equal education at law school, they do not create equal work product. This is not a result of some meritocratic curve; rather, in my admittedly anecdotal experience, students with elite educations at the high school and undergraduate levels generally produce papers that are composed and executed in superior fashion to their classmates with less elite educations. There is no difference between these groups in how compelling their arguments are or how thoughtful and intelligent their ideas. The difference lies in composition and execution. Nevertheless, those are critical elements to effective paper writing.

I have had students who have come from privileged backgrounds and graduated from elite institutions who produce papers that are so superior to those of other students that it is difficult to fairly measure them against others. However, I have also had students from working-class backgrounds who had access to superior undergraduate or high school educations also display excellent writing abilities. This is evident even if their language is not necessarily that of the dominant code; this hints at the possibilities present in an educational program that is intended to give all students cultural capital. For example, one of my brightest students (I will call him Angelo) who speaks African American Vernacular English (both comfortably and beautifully) the majority of the time, in class and out, wrote a superb paper on race and media representations in standard academic language. I wonder how many professors have been surprised by Angelo's writing after hearing his speech, and, moreover, how many have changed their assessment of him as a result.

Instruction in writing notwithstanding, it is my observation that law schools do little to compensate for the educational inequalities that the poor, the working class, and students of color experience before attending law school, and that affect them disproportionately. Within the academic institution, the impact of the cultural capital accrued by privileged students means that they will have enhanced opportunities for research assistantships, professorial contact, and letters of recommendation. Outside the institution, this means that less privileged students will be at a disadvantage in a profession that is highly dependent upon writing and will have a harder time finding employment.[8]

Bourdieu's concept of cultural capital is but one aspect of my theory of holistic integration. The cultural capital dimension seeks to address the practical significance of equalizing access to knowledge in order to achieve educational fairness. A necessary part of holistic integration would be a sort of "cultural capital education," which might echo W. E. B. DuBois' call for classical education in the early twentieth century. It would be an education that is at once superior and functional in that it would translate into greater access to social resources for people of color. But a cultural capital education alone would not lead to progressive social change with the goal of greater racial equality; this would also require an attached model of democratic education.

Philosopher John Dewey defined democratic education as an education that should enlarge and engage experience as well as prepare students for sharing in a common society. Dewey's model is also the sort of ideal that is critical to holistic integration.[9] Such a model of democratic education must consider the inclusion of the histories, literature, and cultures of people of color to be of paramount significance. That is to say, students of color must be allowed to participate not only by gaining the knowledge of the elites, but also by being part of the creation of institutions that respect their cultures and histories. University of Pennsylvania president Amy Gutmann has argued that, if schools are to be understood as incubators for a civil society, they must be institutions of inclusive multiculturalism and morally informed deliberation. This means that diversity is not simply a fact, but a basis for engagement and debate, which can only be encouraged by creating a culture of respect.[10]

When I taught a course on critical race theory to law students, they frequently mentioned how liberating it was to be in a classroom in which they could safely raise issues about race and class without fear of retribution or being shunned. This classroom culture was not effectuated by a blind policy of freedom of speech, but through the cultivation of an ideal of freedom of discourse with respect for personal experience. The class included students from a range of socioeconomic backgrounds, racial and religious groups, and undergraduate schools. The discussions were effective because students were willing to engage, argue, and listen. The intersection of democratic education and cultural capital were part of the course curriculum. My pedagogy emphasized the development of competency in understanding sophisticated academic articles on law and theories of race, a kind of education in cultural and social capital that enabled students to comprehend and converse in that elite discourse. Yet I also encouraged them to bring their own experiences, interpretations, and modes of communication to bear on the readings because they were the individuals, students, and lawyers for whom this work was intended to have social force. They were, and are, citizens of the law school, of the nation, and, prospectively, of the bar.

Students of color must have access to and be full participants in schools and society in order to experience holistic integration. What do we make of a society in which students in poor districts receive a substandard education and have inadequate access to museums, theaters, higher education, employment markets, public and university libraries, and multiple sites of intellectual engagement?[11] Clearly, such a society creates enhanced citizenship for some and depressed citizenship for others. The school, as a democratic institution, must provide a context for real equality and democracy. Otherwise, the diverse groups within our nation will persist in having neither a common life nor equal opportunities.

The backlash against multiculturalism and affirmative action exemplifies the deep hostilities that persist with regard to equality of citizenship for people of color, particularly within academic settings. In the wake of court challenges to affirmative action, anti-affirmative action students at campuses across the nation held "affirmative action" bake sales, which charged students of color lower prices for baked goods.[12] The symbolism of the act, suggesting that people of color hadn't "paid their fair share," was dramatic. Programs geared to increase the participation of people of color in various professions began to shut down.[13] Implicit in these actions is the notion of a meritocracy that efforts at integration have destroyed. The consequent assumption, and at times aggressive assertion, that students and faculty of color are undeserving of their positions, less talented, or less worthy than their White counterparts diminishes their value as stakeholders in academic institutions and in society. Even with compelling evidence of how class and race, through the operation of cultural capital and real capital (i.e., money, property, or wealth), often determine outcomes on measures of academic merit, deliberate efforts to create diverse institutions are often treated as though they are morally questionable.[14] The intersection of models of democratic education and cultural capital would at once advocate inclusiveness and attempt to obviate, or at least diminish, achievement gaps between Black and Latino students and their White counterparts — the gaps that purportedly justify hostility to diversity.

In my "Reflections" article, I noted the prevalence of academic tracking. The problem was not just that Black students had limited access to the best education in the public school I attended by being tracked in lower-level classes, the result being enduring inequities in achievement when compared to Whites. It was also that the Black students were not deemed worthy of receiving the best education offered by the institution. Hence, all students were educated to believe that there was merit-based justification for the devalued citizenship of people of color in the school. Though this was an integrated institution, it was not democratic.[15]

The third element of my theory of holistic integration brings it from the mechanics of pedagogy and policy toward an ideal to which its application aspires. This element is Dr. Martin Luther King Jr.'s ideal of the beloved community, which developed within the context of the social movement surrounding the *Brown* decision. Though *Brown v. Board of Education* did not result in widespread desegregation of the nation's schools, it signaled to the African American community for the first time in over half a century that federal law was open to appeals to racial justice.[16] This mandate for equal protection added legal authority to the moral authority of the civil rights struggle. Working from this foundation, Dr. King's model of the beloved community sought to extend the country's vision beyond the literal practice of desegregation to an integrated society in which all members are full participants — participants who understand their deep human interdependency. As Dr. King asserted,

Integration is the positive acceptance of desegregation and the welcomed participation of Negroes into the whole range of human activities. Integration is genuine intergroup, interpersonal doing. Desegregation then, rightly, is only a short-range goal. Integration is the ultimate goal of our national community. Thus, as America pursues the important task of respecting "the letter of the law," i.e., compliance with desegregation decisions, she must be equally concerned with the "spirit of the law," i.e., commitment to the democratic dream of integration.[17]

The ideal of the beloved community proposed that Black people, and indeed all people, would one day find full access to the range of human activities in our society. This model is consistent with the idea of cultural capital education, because it aims to expose all citizens to that which is often limited to a few, and it embraces all cultures. The ideal of the beloved community also suggests the usefulness of legal authority to support a vision of a more just society, as Dr. King said: "The habits, if not the hearts of people, have been and are being altered every day by legislative acts, judicial decisions, and executive orders."[18] Though hearts are not changed by law, the civil rights movement effectively created a dramatic change in the nation's consciousness, at the very least on a theoretical level, in that the majority of citizens disavow the ideology of racism. Today law, as a creator of habit, could be critical in facilitating the practical application of the citizenry's professed belief in racial justice.

Justice Sandra Day O'Connor, writing the U.S. Supreme Court opinion supporting the University of Michigan School of Law's affirmative action policy in *Grutter v. Bollinger*, understood the significance of law in support of racial justice. She wrote:

Effective participation by members of all racial and ethnic groups in the civic life of our Nation is essential if the dream of one Nation, indivisible, is to be realized. . . . It is necessary that the path of leadership be visibly open to talented and qualified individuals of every race and ethnicity.[19]

O'Connor went on to note that the benefits of affirmative action "are not theoretical but real, as major American businesses have made clear that the skills needed in today's increasingly global marketplace can only be developed through exposure to widely diverse people, cultures, ideas, and viewpoints."[20]

It was on the basis of models of democratic education that O'Connor interpreted the Constitution as allowing for a compelling state interest in race-conscious policies. She asserted that diversity is good for democracy and is imperative in order for democracy to actually occur. These words echo Dr. King's vision. Though King's message has been truncated and sanitized to such an extent that he is even cited now by members of the right wing, such as Ward Connerly (the former California Board of Regents member who was instrumental in ending the use of race in admissions to California public universities, and who frequently quotes one or two lines from King), it is irrefutable that he was an advocate of affirmative action. One example of this was his Operation Breadbasket program, which developed as a department of the Southern Christian Leadership Conference with the goal of securing more and better jobs for African Americans. It pursued this goal through several methods, one of which was to create a team to investigate businesses in a given community. This team would choose a particular business and find out the percentage of African American employees, their ranks, and their representation among the various ranks and salaries. They would then assess the data collected and develop a recommendation to the business as to how it should remediate the underrepresentation of African Americans in the employee pool. King writes about this practice:

> The decision on the number of jobs requested is usually based on population figures. For instance, if a city has a 30 percent Negro population, then it is logical to assume that Negroes should have at least 30 percent of the jobs in any particular company, and jobs in all categories rather than only in menial areas, as the case almost always happens to be.[21]

Such an argument today would be roundly disparaged as supporting racial quotas. Moreover, King's description in his "I Have a Dream" speech of the nation's unpaid promissory note indebted to African Americans implied a belief in reparations, as did the following words from his book, *Why We Can't Wait*:

> No amount of gold could provide an adequate compensation for the exploitation and humiliation of the Negro in America down through the centuries. . . . Yet a price can be placed on unpaid wages. The ancient common law has always provided a remedy for the appropriation of the labor of one human being by another. This law should be made to apply for American Negroes. The payment should be in the form of a massive program by the government of special, compensatory measures which could be regarded as a settlement in accordance with the accepted practice of common law.[22]

It is clear that, for King, remedial measures were an appropriate part of the goal of creating the beloved community.[23] It is no great step to extrapolate such a vision to the educational context from a man who described U.S. society as one that had "misus[ed] and abus[ed] Negro children," and where "Negro infants were born into ghettos, taking their first breath of life in a social atmosphere where the fresh air of freedom was crowded out by the stench of discrimination."[24] My theory of holistic integration embraces the serious contemplation of remedial measures as democratizing tools that might facilitate true integration.

Holistic Integration as applied to schools would bring together three elements: a practical structure for providing full access for all students to the forms of knowledge, socialization, and education usually limited to elites; a practice of democracy in action that would include enriched multicultural education, interaction, and participation of students, educators, and families; an ultimate goal of the beloved community that would be respectful of the individual, but protective of the community.

What does this model of holistic integration mean for professional practice? The road leading to *Grutter* is fantastically instructive. One simply has to take a sample of the amicus briefs in support of affirmative action to see interdisciplinary practice in support of educational equity. A range of voices — from the American Sociological Association and the American Psychological Association to Fortune 500 companies, to the American Educational Research Association and the Association of American Law Schools — each weighed in on the basis of their particular areas of expertise about the benefits of affirmative action. The theory of holistic integration requires such cooperative work across the disciplines that are relevant to education and education policy in order to develop knowledge, programmatic sophistication, and a diverse community of commitment.

A range of conferences and events will be held in 2004 to commemorate the fiftieth anniversary of *Brown v. Board of Education* at institutions such as the University of Washington, Georgetown University, the National Constitution Center, Howard Law School, Hofstra University, and Harvard University. These events are bringing together educators, lawyers, and social scientists. It is likely that, from these conversations and collaborations, new paradigms in the struggle for educational opportunity will emerge. The role of the law in this process is multi-tiered and complex. It might manifest in continued efforts at litigation to equalize school funding as a measure of equal opportunity, or it might be found in creative extensions of that principle to claims to equality of resources. Exempla of relevant resources might include the proportion of master teachers, facilities (labs, libraries, gymnasiums), and advanced course offerings.[25]

The role of law certainly manifests in the *Grutter* ruling that a compelling state interest may justify race-conscious practices. It manifests in ongoing efforts by critical race theorists and other scholars to impress upon judges, lawyers, legal academics, and law students the importance of developing an enriched notion of equal protection — one that is cognizant of the class dimension of racial inequality in areas as diverse as reproductive rights, health policy, housing, and education. As Martin Luther King Jr. so eloquently put it:

> We are simply seeking to bring into full realization the American dream — a dream yet unfulfilled. A dream of equality of opportunity, of privilege and property widely distributed; a dream of a land where men no longer argue that the color of a [person's] skin determines the content of his character; the dream of a land where every man will respect the dignity and worth of human personality — this is the dream.[26]

Notes

1. Perry, I., "A Black Student's Reflection on Public and Private Education," *Harvard Educational Review,* 58 (1988): 332–336.
2. See works such as Tatum, B. D., *Why Are All the Black Kids Sitting Together in the Cafeteria? and Other Conversations about Race* (New York: Basic Books, 1999); Kozol, J., *Savage Inequalities: Children in America's Schools* (New York: Perennial, 1991); Kozol, J., *Amazing Grace: The Lives of Children and the Conscience of a Nation* (New York: Perennial, 1996); Perry, T., Hilliard, A., & Steele, C., *Young, Gifted, and Black: Promoting High Achievement Among African American Students* (Boston: Beacon Press, 2003).
3. See Eaddy, W. R., Sawyer, C. A., Shimizu, K., McIlwain, R., Wood, W. S., & Segal, D., "Residential Segregation, Poverty and Racism: Obstacles to America's Great Society," unpublished report, Lawyer's Committee for Civil Rights Under Law, 1996; also see Orfield, G., Eaton, S. E., & The Harvard Project on School Desegregation, *Dismantling Desegregation: The Quiet Reversal of* Brown v. Board of Education (New York: New Press/Norton, 1996).
4. See Rubinowitz, L. S., & Perry, I., "Crimes Without Punishment: White Neighbors' Resistance to Black Entry," *Journal of Criminal Law and Criminology, Northwestern University School of Law,* 92 (2002): 335–425.
5. See Marable, M., *Race, Reform and Rebellion* (Jackson: University Press of Mississippi, 1991), for his discussion of liberal integrationism.
6. See Bourdieu, P., *Distinction: A Social Critique of the Judgment of Taste* (Cambridge, MA: Harvard University Press, 1987).
7. See Conley, D., "From Financial to Social to Human Capital," in *Being Black: Living in the Red* (Berkeley: University of California Press, 1999), for discussions of the role wealth plays in education attainment; see also Steele, C., "Thin Ice: Stereotype Threat and Black College Students," *Atlantic Monthly,* August 1999, 44–54, for discussion of identity, racism, and testing.
8. See Kelley, M., "Teaching Lessons," *Harvard Law Bulletin* (Summer 2002) for discussion of how Harvard Law School is the greatest supplier of law professors. Also see Mauro, T., "Court Faulted on Diversity," *USA Today,* 1998, June 5, A1, reporting the gross underrepresentation of women and people of color in the pool of Supreme Court clerks.
9. Dewey, J., *Democracy and Education: An Introduction to the Philosophy of Education* (New York: Free Press, 1996).
10. Gutmanm, A., "Challenges of Multiculturalism in Democratic Society," in *Philosophy of Education,* ed. A. Neiman (Urbana, IL: Philosophy of Education Society, 1995).
11. For support of this observation, see abundant sociological and educational literature on race and inequality by scholars such as Bobo, L., Delpit, L., Macedo, D., Perry, T., Omi, M., Winant, H., and Wilson, W. J. Also see philosophical and critical race theoretical writings on the social impact of residing in racially othered bodies in works such as Crenshaw, K., Gotanda, N., Peller, G., and Thomas, K., eds., *Critical Race Theory: The Key Writings That Shaped the Movement* (New York: New Press, 1996); Delgado, R., & Stefancic, J., *Critical Race Theory: The Cutting Edge* (Philadelphia: Temple University Press, 1999); Gordon, L. (Ed.), *Existence in Black: An Anthology of Black Existential Philosophy* (New York: Routledge, 1996).
12. "Bake Sales Used to Protest Affirmative Action" (2003, December 24), Associated Press.
13. See, for example, the dismantling of the Law and Society Pre-Dissertation Minority Fellowship program before the first fellows were admitted in the Spring of 2004.

14. See the discussion of relevant literature including the work of Steele and Fordham. In Berlak, H., "Race and the Achievement Gap," *Rethinking Schools*, 15 (2001). See also Conley, D., *Being Black, Living in the Red: Race, Wealth and Social Policy in America* (Berkeley: University of California Press, 1999), for his suggestion that wealth, rather than income, may play a significant role in the racial achievement gap, as evidenced by retention rates.

15. I should note here that while I generally agree with Gutmann's arguments about multiculturalism and democratic education, I differ with her characterization of Afrocentric schools as necessarily inconsistent with models of multicultural democratic education. Just as physical integration doesn't necessarily mean a holistically integrated experience, neither do single-race schools mean that students are necessarily uninformed or unengaged across racial lines. Structures of cross-racial interaction and multicultural education can be usefully created even in schools that are overwhelmingly single race, and an emphasis on African American history and culture need not be exclusive or based upon notions of superiority.

16. See *Plessy v. Ferguson*, 163 US 537 (1896), the case that affirmed the systematic state practice of de jure segregation.

17. King, M. L., Jr., "The Ethical Demands for Integration," in *A Testament of Hope: The Essential Writings and Speeches of Martin Luther King, Jr.*, ed. J. Washington (San Francisco: Harper, 1990), 118.

18. Ibid., p. 124.

19. *Grutter v. Bollinger*, 539 U.S. 306 (2003).

20. Ibid.

21. King, M. L., Jr., "Where Do We Go from Here: Chaos or Community?" in *A Testament of Hope: The Essential Writings and Speeches of Martin Luther King, Jr.*, ed. James Washington (San Francisco: Harper, 1990), 603.

22. King, M. L., Jr., *Why We Can't Wait* (New York: Penguin, 2000), 150.

23. For sophisticated discussions of Dr. King's vision with respect to remedial measures, see Dyson, M. E., *I May Not Get There with You: The True Martin Luther King, Jr.* (New York: Free Press, 2001); and Berry, M. F., "Vindicating Martin Luther King, Jr.: The Road to a Color Blind Society," *Journal of Negro History*, 81, No. 1 (1996): 137–144.

24. King, M. L., Jr., "Why We Can't Wait," in *A Testament of Hope: The Essential Writings and Speeches of Martin Luther King, Jr.*, ed. J. Washington (San Francisco: Harper, 1990), 603.

25. For an early history of school funding litigation, see Dayton, J., "An Anatomy of Public School Funding Litigation," *Education Law Reporter*, 77 (1992): 627–648. Also see Advocacy Center for Children's Success with Standards (ACCESS) online recording of ongoing school finance litigation, at www.accessednetwork.org/litigation.

26. King, M. L., Jr., "An Address Before The National Press Club, July 19, 1962," in *A Testament of Hope: The Essential Writings and Speeches of Martin Luther King, Jr.*, ed. J. Washington (San Francisco: Harper, 1990), 105.

Afterword

❖

In her opening essay, Martha Minow asks whether the civil rights battles of 2004 will seem the right battles to have fought fifty years from now. She illuminates the surprising and ever-evolving legacies of *Brown* as examples of struggles that will continue to emerge both expectedly and unexpectedly. In the closing essay of this volume, Imani Perry continues to push the promises of integration to areas beyond the classroom. Her theory of holistic integration incorporates the fundamental theories of a democratic and civil education that are required to desegregate and integrate beyond the presence of students of color in the classroom.

It is with these remaining and foreshadowed challenges that we assess the educational context of students in U.S. schools today. We are in the midst of a contested war in the Middle East in a post–September 11 reality. Students of this generation will understand civil rights not only as issues of educational access, voting, employment, and law, but also of national security and individual rights — issues not as prevalent for youth attending school in the 1990s.

Race-conscious policies in higher education admissions have been temporarily salvaged by the 2003 Supreme Court decision in *Grutter v. Bollinger*, but a mammoth challenge to transform schools into credible vessels of equal educational opportunity was also issued by the same Justice (Sandra Day O'Connor), who delivered the opinion in favor of affirmative action. Political action groups, unwilling to tolerate the life of affirmative action a day longer, are waging battles to eliminate race-conscious policies as soon as possible in Texas and Michigan. With such challenges issued to all those in favor of improving the educational plight of the disadvantaged, the complex No Child Left Behind Act (NCLB) has hit our schools in both negative and positive ways, with varying claims of effectiveness for different reasons depending on the student and educator interest group. The legacies of NCLB will be an interesting subject for the *Harvard Educational Review* to explore fifty years from now.

For now, though, race and ethnicity remain the primary indicators of the educational achievement gap. As the new generation of scholars enters the fields of academe, practice, and policymaking, will we study these indicators separately or in conjunction with other markers of difference that Minow documents? As editors, we ask the educational community, and ourselves,

How do we negotiate the attention given to other discriminatory factors, such as disability, gender, and sexual orientation, in the fight for equal opportunity in education without losing sight of the lasting and critical importance of race? Is it possible to do both equally?

Our concerns raise further questions regarding which legacies of *Brown* will garner the nation's attention. How do we execute this challenge without losing sight of the fact that race, more than other factors, remains a defining characteristic of access to opportunity in many areas of this country? As we enter a new phase of negotiations regarding continued war in the Middle East, when can we look forward to a day when the pathways to the highest forms of educational attainment and leadership are as diversified in terms of race, ethnicity, and class (acknowledging that gender is still an issue) as they are in the U.S. military?

The authors in this volume are soldiers for educational opportunity. Their commendable and lengthy record of research and advocacy in this area deserves acknowledgment. However, we also hope that, by presenting a chronology of these efforts, we highlight the changes in strategy, response, and recommendation that have occurred in the quest for equal and holistic educational opportunity. By presenting the history and vision of the legal, policy, and practice battles in education, we hope that the next generation of scholars, practitioners, and students will gain some insight into what legacies they wish to be a part of in their lifetimes.

About the Editors

Dorinda J. Carter is an advanced doctoral student and instructor of education at the Harvard Graduate School of Education (HGSE), where she teaches courses on race, identity, the urban context of schooling, and academic achievement in education. She is a former cochair of the *Harvard Educational Review* and has also worked as an advisor for interns in the teacher education program at HGSE. In addition to a former career as an industrial engineer, Carter has taught kindergarten in an independent school and high school math in an urban charter school in the Northeast, and in several suburban public schools in the South. Her current research examines the behaviors that high-achieving Black students employ to navigate a predominantly White high school.

Stella M. Flores is a doctoral candidate in Administration, Planning, and Social Policy at the Harvard Graduate School of Education, a research assistant at The Civil Rights Project at Harvard University, and a Spencer Research Training Grant recipient. Her work focuses on higher education policy and Latino educational attainment. Flores has worked as a program evaluator at the U.S. General Accounting Office, the U.S. Department of Commerce, and for the Texas State Legislature. She is coauthor of "Percent Plans in College Admissions: A Comparative Analysis of Three States' Experiences" (with C. L. Horn, 2003), and has been cited in the 2003 U.S. Supreme Court *Gratz v. Bollinger* decision and various amicus briefs in support of the University of Michigan affirmative action cases.

Richard J. Reddick is a doctoral candidate in Administration, Planning, and Social Policy at the Harvard Graduate School of Education, a research assistant for the National Campus Diversity Project at Harvard University, and a Spencer Research Training Grant recipient. His work focuses on the mentoring practices of African American faculty in relation to African American undergraduate students. Reddick has worked as an elementary and middle school teacher in Houston, a school director for Teach for America, and in student affairs at the Massachusetts Institute of Technology, Cal Poly–San Luis Obispo, and Emory University. He is the coauthor of *A New Look at Black Families* (5th ed., 2003, with C. Willie) and *The Case for Black Colleges in the Twenty-First Century* (forthcoming, with C. Willie and R. Brown).

About the Contributors

Michelle Fine is professor of psychology at the Graduate School and University Center of the City University of New York. Her research interests include urban education, social injustice, and integration and democracy. Her most recent books are *Construction Sites: Excavating Race, Class, Gender, and Sexuality in Spaces for and by Youth* (with L. Weis, 2000), *Speed Bumps: A Student Friendly Guide to Qualitative Research* (with L. Weis, 2000), and *Becoming Gentlemen: Women, Law School, and Institutional Change* (with L. Guinier and J. Balin, 1996).

Richard J. Hiller is a partner in the law firm of Silbert and Hiller, LLP, in New York City. Hiller's contribution to this volume was written during the mid-1970s when, as senior litigating attorney at the Puerto Rican Legal Defense and Education Fund and later as a partner at Teitelbaum and Hiller PC, he was involved in litigation and consulting related to bilingual education and other civil rights issues.

David L. Kirp is professor of public policy at the Goldman School of Public Policy at the University of California, Berkeley. Kirp writes on a wide variety of subjects, including education, race and gender discrimination, housing, public health, and civil liberties. He is the author of fourteen books, and his articles have appeared in law, public policy, political science, and education journals. His most recent book is *Shakespeare, Einstein, and the Bottom Line: The Marketing of Higher Education* (2004). He is a recipient of Berkeley's Distinguished Teaching Award and the Gustavus Meyers Human Rights Award. Kirp also was the founding director of the Harvard Center on Law and Education and was associate editor of the *Sacramento Bee*.

Martha Minow teaches at Harvard Law School, where she is the William Henry Bloomberg Professor of Law. She is the author of several books: *Breaking the Cycles of Hatred* (2003), *Between Vengeance and Forgiveness: Facing History after Genocide and Mass Violence* (1998), *Not Only for Myself: Identity, Politics, and the Law* (1997), and *Making All the Difference: Inclusion, Exclusion, and American Law* (1990). She was a law clerk for U.S. Supreme Court Justice Thurgood Marshall in 1980–1981.

Sonia Nieto is professor of language, literacy, and culture at the University of Massachusetts, Amherst. Her work focuses primarily on multicultural teacher education and the education of students of diverse backgrounds. Her books include *Affirming Diversity: The Sociopolitical Context of Multicultural Education* (4th ed., 2004), *What Keeps Teachers Going?* (2003), and *The Light in Their Eyes: Creating Multicultural Learning Communities* (1999), as well as an edited text, *Puerto Rican Students in U.S. Schools* (2000).

Leona Okakok is manager of the Arctic Education Foundation, a private foundation that provides financial assistance to eligible college and training students who have ties to the Arctic Slope region of Alaska. She served on the North Slope Borough School District's Board of Education from 1983 through 1989. She is author of "Why Publish Our Own Material?" in the *Native Press Journal* (1988), and the transcriber and translator of *Puiguitkaat (Things You Should Never Forget)* and Proceedings of the 1978 Elders Conference (1981), which was sponsored by the North Slope Borough Commission on History, Language, and Culture.

Imani Perry is assistant professor of law at Rutgers Law School in Camden, New Jersey. Perry's book *Prophets of the Hood: Politics and Poetics in Hip Hop* will be published in 2004. Perry is the author of numerous articles in the areas of race, cultural, legal, and literary studies. She is currently working on a book on metanarratives of race in U.S. law and culture.

Linda C. Powell Pruitt is currently senior fellow at the Research Center for Leadership in Action at the Wagner School of Public Service, New York University. She has been facilitating groups on power and social change since 1972, and for the past fifteen years has been involved with efforts by students, parents, and districts to improve urban education. She has worked with corporations and community organizations across the United States, in England, Ireland, and South Africa. Pruitt has served on the faculty of the Harvard Graduate School of Education and Teachers College, Columbia University, and has authored numerous articles on leadership and urban school reform. She is also coeditor of *Off White: Readings in Power, Privilege, and Resistance* (with M. Fine, L. Weis, and A. Burns, 2004).

Catherine Prendergast is associate professor of English at the University of Illinois at Urbana/Champaign. She is author of *Literacy and Racial Justice: The Politics of Learning after* Brown v. Board of Education (2003), and in 2003 was named winner of the W. Ross Winterowd for Best Book of the Year in Composition Theory award.

Guadalupe San Miguel Jr. is a professor in the history department of the University of Houston. His professional interests center around the history of Mexican Americans; of American, minority, and Latino education; and of Mexican music in the United States. He is the author of *Contested Policy: The Rise and Fall of Federal Bilingual Education in the U.S.* (2004), *Tejano Proud* (2003), *Brown, Not White* (2002), and *Let All of Them Take Heed* (1987).

Herbert Teitelbaum, who served as the first legal director of the Puerto Rican Legal Defense and Education Fund in the 1970s, is a litigation partner in the New York office of Bryan Cave LLP. His work in the area of civil rights has included education, employment, and housing discrimination cases, as well as voting rights cases that resulted in amendments to the Voting Rights Act that require bilingual voting materials and ballots throughout the United States. He has continued his interest in human rights by serving on the board of the New York Civil Liberties Union, as president of the Board of Directors of the New Israel Fund, and as a board member of the Berkshire Farm for Youth and Services.

Richard R. Valencia is professor of educational psychology and a faculty associate at the Center for Mexican American Studies at the University of Texas at Austin. His specialization is racial and ethnic minority education, with a particular focus on Mexican Americans. His areas of emphasis include educational history, social thought, school failure and success, factors in cognitive performance, testing and assessment issues, demographic trends, and educational policy. His most recent book is *Chicano School Failure and Success: Past, Present, and Future* (2nd ed., 2002).

Lois Weis is the author and coauthor of numerous books and articles pertaining to social class, race, gender, and schooling in the United States. Weis sits on a number of editorial boards and is the editor of the "Power, Social Identity, and Education" book series from SUNY Press. Her most recent books include *Silenced Voices and Extraordinary Conversations: Re-Imagining Schools* (with M. Fine, 2003), and *Speed Bumps: A Student Friendly Guide to Qualitative Research* (with M. Fine, 2000). Her new book, *Class Reunion: The Re-Making of the American White Working Class*, will appear in 2004.